ON SYMBOLS AND SOCIETY

THE HERITAGE OF SOCIOLOGY

A Series Edited by Donald N. Levine

Morris Janowitz, *Founding Editor*

KENNETH BURKE
ON SYMBOLS AND SOCIETY

Edited and with an Introduction by
JOSEPH R. GUSFIELD

THE UNIVERSITY OF CHICAGO PRESS
Chicago and London

The University of Chicago Press, Chicago 60637
The University of Chicago Press, Ltd., London
© 1989 by The University of Chicago
All rights reserved. Published 1989
Printed in the United States of America
04 03 02 01 00 99 98 97 96 95   3 4 5 6 7

Library of Congress Cataloging-in-Publication Data
Burke, Kenneth, 1897–
    On symbols and society / Kenneth Burke: edited and
with an introduction by Joseph R. Gusfield.
        p.   cm. —(The Heritage of Sociology)
    Bibliography: p. 317
    Includes index.
    ISBN 0–226–08078–1 (paper)
    1. Literature and society. 2. Symbols in literature
3. Rhetoric.   I. Gusfield, Joseph R., 1923–   . II. Title.
III. Series.
PN51.B86 1989
801'.95'092—dc20   89–32666
                                                        CIP

To the memory of Morris Janowitz,
whose vision and leadership made
this series possible.

Contents

Acknowledgments

I am grateful to a number of people who, over the years, have contributed to my understanding of Kenneth Burke. Among these are the late Michel de Certeau, Hugh Mehan, Barbara Herrnstein Smith, Bennett Berger, Helene Keysaar, Herbert Simons, Vito Signorelli, and Doug Mitchell. Dan Dickson, of the University of California Press, was helpful in arranging permissions to reprint various selections. I am especially indebted to Kenneth Burke, not only for his work, but for the valuable experience of meeting him when he was a Regent's Lecturer at the University of California, San Diego, several years ago. Part of this project was completed while I was a fellow at the Center for Advanced Study in the Behavioral Sciences, at Stanford, California, in 1985–86.

Doug Mitchell, of the University of Chicago Press, has been invaluable in seeing this project through. His initial enthusiasm when it was first broached never flagged. His support, goading, and friendship during a dilatory period of mine was essential. Without Morris Janowitz's effort in developing and shepherding the Heritage of Sociology series the entire work would have been impossible. This volume is dedicated to his memory. Donald Levine, now series editor, saw the volume through its final stages.

The University of California Press now holds the copyrights to all of Burke's books. All but two of the excerpts in the book are reprinted with their permission. The Macmillan Co. has given permission for the reprinting of Burke's article, "Interaction: Dramatism" from the *International Encyclopedia of the Social Sciences.* The final excerpt, "Ideology and Myth," is taken from *Accent,* a Quarterly Journal of Literature, which ceased publication in 1960, through the courtesy of Charles Shattuck.

INTRODUCTION

Joseph R. Gusfield

On Putting Things In Order
File this, throw out that.
Alert the Secretariat
In re each claim and caveat
To better serve the Cause of Alphabet.
Throw out this, file that

File this, throw that out,
We know beyond all doubt
how Perfect Order reconciles—

And now throw out the files.

(Kenneth Burke, *Collected Poems, 1915–1967,* 173)

Kenneth Burke has been an enigma for sociologists. Literary critic, philosopher, linguist, sociologist, social critic—he has been claimed by all of these fraternities and disclaimed by all as well. Sociologists who have casually "dipped into" this or that book of his have often come away puzzled and intrigued. They have been attracted by the force of original ideas and the provoking way in which he transgresses the property lines of academic fields, indiscreetly mixing concepts and subject matters usually thought to belong to the hunting preserves of discrete disciplines and divisions of intellectual thought and scholarly organization. At the same time they have been repelled by the seeming lack of clarity, the sudden leaps of frame, and the apparent absence of organized relationship between one part of a book or section and another. He has seemed, in the words of one literary scholar, "a critic for the adventurous" (Adams 1966). In this introduction and in the readings selected I hope to introduce a very orderly mind at work in understanding the complexity of human ordering of a complex world.

While Burke has exerted a persisting and for some a significant influence among sociologists, in the past decade his work has assumed a more vital attraction to social scientists. The confluence of the intel-

1

lectual movements of structuralism, symbolic anthropology, phenomenological sociology, critical theory, and the renaissance of symbolic
interaction have made Kenneth Burke's structuralism, dramatism, and
dialectical method suddenly contemporary. The work that he produced from the 1930s through the 1960s has come to be seen not only
as precursor but as immensely significant for the present. As the contemporary has caught up with the past the effort to gain access to his
thought has taken on a new importance for sociologists. Yet it has
been there since his earliest philosophical work, *Counter-Statement*,
was first published in 1931.

In this volume of selections from his work, and in this introductory
essay, I hope to help sociologists gain access to an immensely valuable
mode of thought and a perspective toward the study of behavior and
society that has for too long not received sufficient recognition. The
materials presented will, I hope, show that appearances, as Burke
would also say, are deceiving as well as conceiving. There is great
continuity and organization that, taken together, add up to a perspective which contains much reward for the sociologist. In his thinking,
Burke necessarily disdains the conventional fences that bound one discipline from another and the humanities from the social sciences. This
is not just the whim of an omniscient scholar. It arises from the very
content of his thought. Once you see literature as a form of human
behavior and human behavior as embedded in language, the place of
Burke in the sections of your bookstore becomes enigmatic indeed. As
one of his many appreciators put it, ". . . he has no field unless it be
Burkology" (Hyman 1969, 212).

There is a profound, original, and highly valuable approach to human action in the corpus of Kenneth Burke's writings. This introduction is an attempt to relate Burke's ideas to sociological thought and
practice. I want to describe his influence on sociologists and the potential of his thought for future sociological study. There are some
difficulties with Burkean ideas as guides for sociologists, and these too
will be analyzed.

Stages in Development

Kenneth Burke was born in Pittsburgh, Pennsylvania, in 1897. His
education was mostly that of an autodidact. He attended Ohio State
University for one semester and Columbia University for a year. He
left college to write, living in Greenwich Village with a group of avant-
garde writers, including Mathew Josephson, Hart Crane, and Burke's
close friend from high school, Malcolm Cowley, the literary critic. He
continued to write and hold editorial positions, including a position

on the editorial board of *The Dial,* a major critical review, from 1921 until it ceased publication in 1929. During this period he married (1919), purchased a farm in Andover, New Jersey, (where he still lives), and published his first book, *The White Oxen* (1924), a collection of short fictions. From 1927 to 1929 he was a music critic for *The Dial.*

Between 1929 and 1937 he worked at a variety of jobs, including researching drug addiction for the Rockefeller Foundation, editorial work for the Bureau of Social Hygiene, and writing music criticism for *The Nation* (from 1933 to 1936). He published a novel, *Towards a Better Life,* in 1932. In 1931 Burke published *Counter-Statement,* the first of his major nonfiction works, followed in 1935 by *Permanence and Change.*

In 1937 Burke began a teaching career marked by a form of nomadism. He was professor of literary criticism at Bennington College between 1943 and 1961, but he frequently interrupted that with visiting professorships and continued to teach in that fashion well after 1961. He has taught at many American colleges and universities, including the New School for Social Research, the University of Chicago, Harvard, the Universities of California at Santa Barbara and San Diego, and Emory University. Between 1937 and 1950 he published four of his major works: *Attitudes Toward History* (1937), *The Philosophy of Literary Forms* (1941), *A Grammar of Motives* (1945), and *A Rhetoric of Motives* (1950). In 1961 he published *The Rhetoric of Religion.*

He has continued to be a prolific contributor to many literary and philosophical journals. In 1966 a number of the more important contributions were collected and published under the title *Language as Symbolic Action.*

This recounting, or chronologizing, of Burke's vita is significant for understanding his work. Beginning as a fiction writer and a poet, he later gained a reputation as a literary critic, but not in the same sense as did Lionel Trilling, Edmund Wilson, or even Northrop Frye. That title has always seemed too specialized toward imaginative works of "literature" to describe his mix of interests. Even with the books where "literature" appears to be the primary subject, Burke has denied the special, privileged position of imaginative writing as a vehicle of study (Lentricchia 1983). With his later work, and especially after 1945, poetry, fiction, and drama are akin to other uses of language and other texts. Because the symbolic forms that humans use are similar in important ways, literature can be drawn on to instruct us in the uses of language in other, nonimaginative areas of life. The social sciences can, by the same considerations, illuminate what the poet and the artist are doing. While both arenas create cultural products which differ, they are also similar. It is in the similarities in what cultural products do that Burke finds his subject. It is in Burke's very eradication of the boundaries between the study of literature and the study of all human speech and writing that he becomes so significant for the sociological study of human action. As he became less the "literary critic" and more the generalist he assumed the great importance that so merits the attention of this volume. Recently I found the latest edition of his *Permanence and Change* classified in a major bookstore not in the section on literature but in a subsection called "general criticism" and perhaps we will let it go at that.

It is my contention that Burke's importance for the sociologist lies not so much in any particular content of any particular part of his writings but in the development of a method, a perspective about perspectives, which is a profound attempt to understand the implications for human behavior of the fact that humans are "symbol-using animals." It is primarily as a student of language and meaning that Burke's impact on the social sciences is greatest. He has himself coined a word to describe what he is up to: "logology"—words about words.

Much of this introductory chapter is built around central concepts in Burke: "symbolic action," "terministic screens," "dramatism," "rhetoric," and "dialectics and irony." In later sections I will examine Burke's past influence on sociology, his discussion of social order as ritual and hierarchy, and my own views of limitations in Burkean method. The essay will close with some reflections on what the study of human behavior can, and should, learn from Kenneth Burke.

Kenneth Burke and Sociological Theory: The Renaissance of Culture

One of the most influential sentences in the history of sociology has been Karl Marx's, "It is not the consciousness of men which determines their existence, but on the contrary it is their social existence which determine their consciousness" (Marx 1932, 11). In one form or another, sociological research and theory have been dominated by an emphasis on social structure and a relative exclusion of culture in the understanding of human behavior. Both interaction and institutions have typically been understood as consequences of structural factors such as social classes, power distributions, capitalist formations, urbanization, or the dynamics of formal organizations. Forms of thought, such as political ideologies or legal reasoning, and systems of knowledge or expression, such as science, religion or art, have been examined as consequences of the structure of social organization.

"Consciousness" has remained a dependent variable, a "superstructure" to the realities of social structure.

In recent years, roughly the past two decades, there has been a renaissance of interest in and examination of culture as an independent area of human life. This has been directed toward analysis of human action as it attains meaning, as it is interpreted. "It is not enough to say that one is conscious of something; one is also conscious of something being something" (W. E. Percy, quoted in Geertz 1964, 61). In one of the early challenges to social structural theories of ideas (which, incidentally, makes much use of Burke), Clifford Geertz pointed out that the dominant perspective toward ideas, the sociology of knowledge, ignored the meanings of the symbols and the processes of symbol formation necessary to understand how these forms operated to define the world of a social group. Ideas were seen only as weapons to support or defend interests locatable in the social structure. They were not seen as categories by which consciousness was itself organized. As Geertz put it, ". . . the question of how symbols symbolize, how they function to mediate meanings has simply been bypassed" (Geertz 1964, 57).

Although the concept of "interpretive sociology" has certainly existed at least since Max Weber, its current usage constitutes a renaissance of focus on the symbols and categories through which reality is defined and understood. The same larger movement appears in various forms with differences that sometimes mask an underlying commonality. Past sociological perspectives have ignored the cultural frameworks through which the world is given an understandable order. In such frameworks, culture has either been taken for granted or reduced to something else—a solution to social strains or the masking of economic or other interests. Both in European and American manifestations, "schools" such as symbolic interactionism, social constructivism, ethnomethodology, phenomenological sociology, semiotics, critical sociology, and structuralism share this focus on what phenomena mean to participants and observers and how such phenomena attain their meanings. They represent approaches that seek to understand how patterns of consciousness enable us to organize experience. Rather than taking experience as something given, the cultural sociologist seeks to understand how experience itself attains shape and content.

A newer sociology of knowledge has burst out of the boundaries of the old interest-focused perspectives of Mannheim and his followers. It recognizes the problem of meaning as being the core of sociological observation. The "social construction of reality," to use the title of a major and leading work in the movement (Berger and Luckmann 1966), signifies an area which studies how knowledge of reality is generated, including politics but also much more. But it is also an essential prelude to and part of any other study. Even the content of science, previously regarded as being in a privileged position beyond sociological analysis, has now come to be seen as amenable to the study of its cultural categories and methods of thought, what David Bloor has called "the strong case" in sociology of knowledge (Bloor 1976; Latour and Woolgar 1979). To have experience at all is to assume categories for understanding that exist prior to events. Those categories form the subject matter of much of the newer interpretive sociology.

Burke is well in the tradition represented by this movement toward the importance of interpretive procedures to the study of human behavior. A less cultural, more structural social science has acted to "reduce" ideas and interpretive schemes to aspects of institutional relationships; to find objects of concern as given and operative as "real" phenomena in contrast to the ideas that constitute superstructure. In this sense Burke has been ahead of his time, a precursor of Geertz, Habermas, Goffman, Garfinkel, Kuhn, Foucault, and even Lévi-Strauss.

But it is an error to see Burke only as a precursor of a perspective since developed by others and elsewhere. The corpus of his work constitutes a system of thought and analysis that is unique. It brings together several elements in the analysis of human actions that sees the focus of social study in communication. Burke is able to move easily from philosophy to literature to sociology because he sees all of these endeavors as displaying an underlying similarity. They all use language to achieve purposes and in doing so possess similar opportunities and face similar problems.

One way of expressing the elements to which Burke addresses his analysis of human communications is in terms frequently used by him: symbolic action, grammar, rhetoric, and dialectic. The first of these, symbolic action, refers to the multiple levels of meaning involved in human activity. Grammar refers to forms of language patterns through which the infinitude of events become selected, defined, and understood. Rhetoric refers to human behavior and communication seen as embodying strategies for affecting situations. Dialectic refers to the transformations of meaning involved in change. This set of categories will organize the selections included in this volume as well as the rest of the introduction.

STYLE AND RANGE IN KENNETH BURKE

The scope of Burke's writing is often staggering. Unable to classify Burke into the conventional departmental structure of current universities, one reviewer summed it up by calling him "the great know-it-all." He moves back and forth from Freud to Aristotle to Virginia Woolf to Cervantes to Marx to Keats with a deep knowledge and competence. That astonishing range is also paralleled by his ability to bring the perspectives of one discipline to bear on that of another. He does not respect academic "turf" because his work is about the erosion of boundaries. In this he gains the anger of the literary scholars by erasing the privileged position of certain matter as "literature." He may incur the animosity of sociologists because he sees sociological science as another form of literature. Both are strategies for affecting audiences. Both utilize dramatic frameworks to discuss human behavior. The lines of analyses, the methodological approaches, are not as different as each likes to assume.

It is this very lack of respect for the privileges of academic boundaries that often makes Burke enigmatic. A recent interpreter of Burke has stated it well:

> What may define him as an historical thinker, in fact, is a series of decisive engagements, spread over his entire intellectual development, with the idea of system itself. . . . the desire to be systematic is met at critical points by a resistance to system and in particular by a resistance to the essentializing consequences of systematic thought. (Lentricchia 1982, 121)

Systematic thinking about the limitations of systems is a clue to Burkean thought. This rejection of a world of essences, of a *Ding an sich,* is paramount in Burke and places him at odds with frames of thinking that search for the one true resolution of intellectual problems. Burke's dialectical quality is, for him, paralleled by his focus on behavior as drama—as conflict, resolution, and transformation. It further helps in understanding a style at once recondite and humorous.

In a phrase that Burke coined, his is a "perspective by incongruity" or, as he calls it elsewhere, it is the "comic corrective." If the world around us is at least partially a matter of how it is framed, how the situation is defined, then the reader, the observer, the audience can best understand how the procedure operates by getting outside the box of his own logics. In an example of Pitirim Sorokin's, the fish is best able to know water when it is outside of it, on land. Seeing the world from its opposite, from incongruity, is not a literary conceit. It is a serious method. Comedy is precisely that—holding the conventional up to its opposite, to irony and satire. It is a means for overcoming the limitations which any single system of thought and classification places on us. It is an unsettling process in which transformation is potentially possible.

Hence the intriguing, sometimes frustrating style of the comic in Burke. It is a way of revealing that things seem different from a different vantage point, when seen with different spectacles. Burke's frequent use of oxymorons (the union of two opposites, as in Veblen's "trained incapacity") is in keeping with a deeply dialectical mind. In a phrase which packs so much Burke in a short line, "every way of seeing is also a way of not seeing" *(Permanence and Change, 1965, 49).*

Symbolic Action

Several years ago Burke gave a lecture, subsequently published, entitled "Bodies That Learn Language" (Burke 1977). That title is a succinct presentation of his view of human beings. They are indeed biological organisms, but that by no means exhausts what is significant about them. The capacity for language, so central to Burke's system of analysis, provides for a reflective facility that imposes a symbolic interpretation of objects and events upon the raw world of sense data. The ability to use symbols enables human beings to imagine, to select, to create, and to define the situations to which they respond. Burke's social psychology is congruent with that of the pragmatic philosophers, especially John Dewey and George Herbert Mead. His thought, however, goes well beyond them. Burke builds from the existence of humans as symbol-using creatures. What is so emphatic in his thought is the primacy of language as itself a form of action rather than an opaque object through which events are perceived. How we talk, think, and conceive is a distinctive part of human action. It affects what we experience and what we do to others in communication.

The Forms of Social Action

The use of symbols to describe and define events is for Burke a source of the bridge between literature and sociology. He has used the term "dramatism" to describe his perspective toward both literature and human behavior. In using drama, which includes poetry and novels as well as stage plays, he is not simply indulging in a metaphorical conceit. What the dramatist must assume is also what the sociologist must assume if he or she is to be true to the human material which is being studied. Both novelist and sociologist must depict human activity as involved in conflict, in purpose, in change, insofar as they attempt to be convincing to readers. These elements of drama are inherent in how human acts are presented because they are inherent in human action.

At the base of Burke's use of drama as a model of human behavior is his distinction between motion and action. Motion is the animal side of human beings. Here human acts are determined. They are the summation of the forces and factors which impinge on people to produce behavior. The image of the human being is that of a passive reactor to external conditions. They move but they do not act.

Action implies assessments of situations and the people with whom the person interacts. It implies reflection upon one's interests, sentiments, purposes, and those of others. Human beings are animals and have biological natures, but they differ from other animals in the range and significance of their use of symbols, of language. They understand their world by depicting it in symbols and by placing meaning on events. Animals respond to stimuli directly; human beings interpret the events. In terms used by George Herbert Mead, this is the difference between a response to gestures and a response to significant symbols (Mead 1934, part two). As Burke wrote somewhere, human beings are the only animals who can see signs as signs. Both the dramatist and the sociologist must take cognizance of the difference between motion and action.

> Stimuli do not possess an absolute meaning. Even a set of signs indicating the likelihood of death by torture has another meaning in the orientation of a comfort-loving skeptic than it would for the ascetic whose worldview promised eternal reward for martyrdom. Any given situation derives its character from the entire framework by which we judge it. *(Permanence and Change*, 1965, 35)

It is from this position that Burke so frequently criticized behavioristic psychology. The behaviorist, he wrote, utilizes a view of human behavior as motion. His "representative anecdote" (a phrase of Burke's) is that of passive and predetermined response to stimuli. Laboratory experiments place subjects in atypical conditions and ignore the meanings which the subjects give to such experimental conditions, including the meaning of experimenting itself. The laboratory experiment has taken a complex action, involving a diversity of dimensions and levels, and "reduced" it to a simpler situation by excluding most of the diverse ways of seeing the original behavior. Having drawn conclusions from a simpler situation they then project it onto the nat-

ural situation as if the layers of possible meaning had been exhausted.
ments with children and adults. Differences in what children, as con-

The point is well illustrated in the study of psychological experiments with children and adults. Differences in what children, as contrasted to adults, do in similar experiments might be interpreted as
indicating differences in their behavior in other contexts as well. Jennings, in a study of children's conceptions of the experimental context,
found that unlike adults, children did not understand the nature of
experiments in the same fashion as did adults. The observed behavior
was not a sample generalizable beyond the experiment itself (Jennings
1972).

In his emphasis on the symbolic construction of situations, events,
and other people Burke has much in common with sociologists and
philosophers who have laid stress on the symbol-using and meaning-
construction aspects of human life. Talcott Parsons's voluntarism
(which Burke quotes appreciatively in his article "Dramatism"),
George Herbert Mead's "I" and "Me," and Alfred Schutz's "reflexiv-
ity" are all in the line of sociological theorists for whom the meanings
of acts and our assessments of them are central to a view of human
behavior (Parsons 1937; Mead 1934; Schutz 1967).

The point of dramatism is not that literature is a better depicter or
analyst of human action than are social scientists. The nature of action
is intrinsically dramatic and both sociology and literature should ac-
knowledge this. The concept of "drama" implies action rather than
motion. Action is dramatic because it includes conflict, purpose, reflection, and choice. Consequently, the possibility of transforming the
self and/or the society is omnipresent.

Language as Symbolic Action

Throughout his writings Burke represents language as a form of action. In a passage in "Terministic Screens" he quotes with approval
the *Webster's Dictionary* definition of "dramatism" as "a technique of
analysis of language and thought as basically modes of action rather
than as means of conveying information" *(Language as Symbolic Action,* 1966, 54).

Human beings are symbol-users. On the very first page of *The Philosophy of Literary Form,* Burke points out that if you know a man
has said "yes" you still do not know what was said unless you know
the preceding actions and to what his word was addressed *(The Philosophy of Literary Form,* 1957, 3). Objects and events are interpreted, are given meaning. The symbols that are used are ways of
naming and describing. In that process selections are made and mean-

ing is created. Language cannot be separated from action because what the action means and what it is addressed to is symbolic in its content. Action cannot be separated from language because the situation within which the actor acts is defined and understood by the actor through the concepts available to him.

In using language the actor is also accomplishing purposes of defining himself and the situation to others through the style and form in which the language is couched. Sociology and literature meet, for Burke, in that in both language must be understood by what it does, by how it affects the situation, the audience, to which it is addressed. Words are not empty folders, hanging in the air. They move audiences to responses and move the speakers to define and redefine their contexts.

In one of the earliest uses of Burkean thought among sociologists, C. Wright Mills refers to "vocabularies of motive" as terms used to understand actions (Mills 1940). For the psychologist, especially the clinical psychologists, the term "motive" is used to refer to springs that lie behind activity. For the sociologist, as for Burke, they cannot be separated from the situations to which they are responses. They are the terms that make action understandable. Burke makes much use of motive understood in this sense; not as a source of behavior but as a concept used by people to make actions understandable to them and to others.

Mills drew on a section in Burke's *Permanence and Change*, "Motives Are Shorthand Terms for Situations" (see pp. 126–33). In that essay Burke emphasizes that "motive" is a linguistic device, a concept by which the observer, including the self, explains and understands situations. They depend greatly on the symbols used in any particular social group. "These relationships are not *realities,* they are *interpretations* of reality—hence different frameworks of interpretations will lead to different conclusions as to what reality is" (*Permanence and Change*, 1965, 35).

There is much in common in this view of action with the concept of "definition of the situation" used by W. I. Thomas (Thomas 1923; McHugh 1968). Where Burke differs is in the emphasis he places on the cultural frameworks transmitted in language as part and parcel of the situation. How we think about the situations of life and how we use language to depict them to ourselves and to others is essential to the study of human life. When we talk, write, wear clothes, make love, make war, perform the many daily acts of our lives we are acting in a symbolic world. It is a world created in significant part by the language we use to portray it to ourselves and to others. Words and concepts are not neutral references. They have consequences that make experiences of particular kinds possible.

Burke's distinction between semantic and poetic meaning is a good place to see how symbolizing properties of language prevent the exclusive use of a scientific language after the fashion of physics, biology, or mathematics. Semantic meaning, which he equates with the uses of scientific language, is analytic. It distinguishes and defines, aiming at clarity through placing things in distinct and exclusive categories. As Burke so charmingly puts it, the aim of semantic meaning is "to give the name and address of every event in the universe" (*The Philosophy of Literary Form*, 1957, 123). Poetic meaning utilizes the multiplicity of meanings that a given act can have. In semantical meaning the expression "New York City is in Iowa" is nonsense. But when we contemplate the extension of cultural influence across the nation, the statement makes sense. "As a metaphor, it provides valid insight. To have ruled it out by strict semantic authority would have been vandalism" *(The Philosophy of Literary Form,* 1957, 126). It is the ambiguities and multiplicities inherent in human action that makes Burke's critique of conventional positivism in social science so powerful. Therein lies the rub!

The Prison-house of Language

If language is indispensable to human experience it also selects and narrows that experience. It acts as a filter and a screen. It limits the possibilities of experience in ways that present a crucial impediment to thought and action. Culture and language not only open doors to experiences, they also form a prison which constricts and narrows. Here Burke's view of words and concepts as terministic screens is crucial to his thought.

Typologies make a systematic ordering of experience possible but they also deceive, limit, and derail. Burke antedated Schutz in recognizing how the terms we use typify and prefigure situations. Burke, however, carries this thought a step further. Although he does not discuss Weber's notion of ideal types, he does indicate the problems it poses for the social analyst. The sociologist, like the layperson, uses typological concepts to create the order that enables understanding to take place. But terms become screens that are carried to their logical extremes. "Bureaucracy" and "capitalism," to name just two, become the phenomena they were coined to point at but not to represent. They become ultimate endings. So too do concepts and theories. The psychologists present a view of human beings that is "over-psychologized," the sociologists a view that is "over-socialized." Typologies become reified; they become concretized as descriptions of realities.

Even this account of Burke is overdrawn; it out-Burkes Burke by providing an even more consistent and systematic order than the totality of his writings give us. I am, in this essay, "reducing" Burke to a more abstracted form and "laundering" away the ambiguities, sideroads, and specific discussions that make up the corpus of any first-rate philosopher and critic.

It is with this sense of the imposition of singlistic and partial formulations of the range of the possible human experience that Burke coins a phrase to describe how humans push their screens to their terminal ends. In a definition of man (see p. 70) he wrote that human beings are "rotten with perfection." Their linguistic screens are terministic as well as deterministic. They carry their users to ultimate ends, to a *terminus ad quem*. They reduce the complexity of human acts to purer forms. "Men seek for vocabularies that will be faithful *reflections* of reality. To this end they must develop vocabularies that are *selections* of reality. And any selection of reality must, in certain circumstances, function as a *deflection* of reality" *(The Philosophy of Literary Form,* 1957, 4).

Always the enemy of specialization, in thinking as well as in university organization, Burke makes us aware of the limiting character of language forms. He makes us reflect on ways of escaping from the prison-house of language.

The Grammar of Social Action

Human behavior has both a cognitive side—the understanding of situations—and an active side—the operation of the person on the situation. For Burke both are embedded in language. The cognitive side of language is in its grammar—its system for defining the situation. The operative side is in its use of language to effect the situation—its rhetoric. "Grammar" and "rhetoric" are key terms in Burke's writings.

In the *Encyclopedia of the Social Sciences* article, "Dramatism" (see p. 135), Burke defines his method of dramatism as ". . . a method of analysis *and a corresponding critique* [my emphasis] of terminology designed to show that the most direct route to the study of human relations and human motives is via a methodological inquiry into cycles or clusters of terms and their functions"*(ESS,* 7).

The vocabularies or clusters of terms that a group utilizes in making sense out of events is Burke's subject matter. In a chapter title in his work *Attitudes Toward History,* he uses the phrase "acceptance frames." It is useful to think of Burke's orientation toward the importance of language with the imagery of the frame. Artists sometimes speak of frames as adding to the impact of a painting by providing a means to hold in and bring out the tensions in the composition. In recent years the term has again been used in the social sciences, following Bateson and Goffman, to point to how situations are defined by the systems or schemes drawn on (Bateson 1972, 177–92; Goffman 1974). Like Burke, and influenced by Burke, they demonstrate how raw sense data are selected and shaped into experienced reality by the symbolic forms through which data are organized. To use an example again from the world of art, the behavior of the model in a life drawing class illustrates the symbolic character of the behavioral frame. The model poses nude but cloaks himself/herself in the interludes between poses. "Nudity" is not a matter of raw sense data. It is symbolized, thought about, experienced, and interpreted in different ways. To be nude is not the same as being naked in the frame of art.

The language forms available for use in a culture are the stuff of the framing process. To understand them is to understand the structure of thought, the grammar of motives by which explanation and justification is arrived at. In *Attitudes Toward History* Burke compared the modes of explanation for the existence of social hierarchy in Aquinas and in Marx. Each draws on a different form of explanation. For Aquinas classes are punishment for the fall of man; for Marx they are a consequence of capitalism's exploitation. One was a program for passive acceptance; the other a program for revolution *(Attitudes Toward History,* 1984).

The Pentad

In the opening paragraph of *A Grammar of Motives,* probably his most influential work, Burke writes, "What is involved when we say what people are doing and why they are doing it?" *(A Grammar of Motives,* 1945, xv). His book, he writes, is about the "basic forms of thought" used in the attribution of motives. These forms of thought are to be found everywhere, from complex metaphysical systems to random gossip. The playwright, the poet, the sociologist, the physician, the postman—all human beings must make use of ways of framing or placing experience in order to make sense of it to themselves and to others.

How this is done is the subject of Burke's concern. He focuses his attention on the forms in which thought takes place. It is these forms which deeply affect the meanings of content. In the Pentad Burke describes five basic forms which are necessarily implicated in the process of defining situations. These are, he maintains, to be found everywhere language is in use.

Burke's development of the Pentad as an analytical device to analyze such "ways of placement" is indicative of the unity he forges between the diverse worlds of scholarly and lay thought and between science and literature. What the dramatist does in imaginative and creative work is no different from what we all do. Any complete answer to the question "What is happening?" offers answers to five questions.

1. Act: What took place?
2. Scene: What is the context in which it occurred?
3. Agent: Who performed the act?
4. Agency: How was it done?
5. Purpose: Why was it done?

Taken by themselves, the Pentad might seem commonplace, a little like a high school journalism instructor's admonition about what should go into the headline and lead paragraph of a news story. But for Burke, a culture, like a playwright, seizes on some parts of the Pentad and deemphasizes others. Sociologists, for example, are far more likely than psychologists to emphasize scene rather than agent. They utilize a paradigm that searches for explanations of action in institutional features, in the defined situation rather than the personality of the actor. So, too, a more "sociological" playwright like Arthur Miller will draw his audience toward understanding his characters as responsive to institutions, to the context, the scene.

Burke refers to this relationship between parts of the Pentad as a matter of "ratios," of the fit between parts. What is significant is the lack of balance between the parts. In a scene-agent ratio, for example, the scene may be portrayed as explainable through the agent or vice-versa. Different meanings are conveyed. In my research on auto deaths, I have pointed out that to describe the problem of *drinking-drivers* creates a different problem than to describe it as a problem of *drinking-driving* (Gusfield 1981). The first directs attention to the agent as the source of the act. The second frames the experience as an event, with the act as paramount. As Burke puts it, "The ratios are principles of determination" (*A Grammar of Motives*, 1945, 15). The first, *drinking-driver*, is a call to transform the motorist. The second, *drinking-driving*, directs attention to the auto, the road, the event.

In one of his classic essays, Erving Goffman has given a memorable illustration of how meaning is conveyed through the distortion of ratios of scene-act. On the merry-go-round the adult acts unlike the child. He or she stands, looks bored, feigns in obvious fashion a distorted fright and does whatever he or she can do to say, "I am not here to ride the merry-go-round as a passenger." In Burke's terms, act is out of proportion to the scene. That disproportion enables the pseudo-passenger to so define himself or herself. Goffman uses this example to discuss the concept of "role-distance" and the defining of a situation (Goffman 1961b, 105–15). The adult distances himself or herself from the scene so as not to be thought to be "childish."

What is significant for Burke is the ways systems of placement utilize the symbolic forms to select and deflect. In this sense his analysis is also a critique, as he states in the quotation in the first paragraph of this section. Cultures do not use the full range of all the possible terms in giving meaning to events. Characteristically, each set of terms is a reduction of reality, a way of seeing that is partial—". . . the tendency of the culture will be to see everything in terms of this particular recipe of emphases" *(A Grammar of Motives,* 1945, 113).

Schemes of Reduction

Seeing *"in terms of"* is the clue to Burke's continuous focus on the limits of specialized single terminologies. When we think and perceive we do so by reducing something to something else. It is in that process that the reduction occurs. Explanations are explanations "in terms of" something else on which the explainer draws, be it God, nature, capitalism, or the unconscious. Every explanation possesses a "circumference." We place the object of our concern within a setting of particular scope. It indicates where the explanation stops; where it satisfies the terminological cluster available. For the religious the circumference is vast, ending in God. For the psychologist it is restricted to the actor, the agent.

The importance of schemes of reduction has led Burke to a search for the terms at the center of explanations. His discussion of "money" as a basic term ("Money as Substitute for God," reprinted in this volume) is part of his analysis of how the institution of a market economy is conducted with a linguistic framework. The attribution of money as motive and the transformation of actions into money values constitute the experience of reality. We see life, and therefore experience it, "in terms of" monetary realities. Typification and abstraction are the barriers to seeing the world whole rather than in part. Our Western languages continue within that circumference. We *save, spend, waste, lose, budget, and put aside* time (Lakoff and Johnson 1980, 7–8).

The use of drama as a key is Burke's own "representative anecdote," using a term drawn from the stage to describe most varieties of human behavior, "in terms of" drama. But it is a fit use because human behavior shares with stage plays the occurrence of a grammar through which it conveys an orderly understanding of events. He states this clearly in the article on "Dramatism": ". . . Drama is employed, not as a metaphor but as a fixed term that helps us discover what the implications of the terms 'act' and 'person' really are" (*ESS* 448).

The grammar of motives is not merely a pattern for describing events. It constitutes the symbolic forms through which experience is constituted. Cultures are not reflections of material realities. They are the shapers of such realities.

This focus on the Pentad as a universal system for making sense of reality might lead one to consider Burke a precursor to Lévi-Strauss and the structuralists. There are two significant differences. First, structuralists present a monistic sense of how "deep structure" affects thought and behavior (Lévi-Strauss 1966; Leach 1976). Burke presents a deep-seated pluralism. There is much more than one meaning, one possible interpretation, one possible "structure." Second, Burke's position is dynamic and dialectical in contrast to the present-day structuralists. Precisely because there are multiple meanings the conflict and contrast of perspectives gives rise to transformations. Terminological sets carried to their logical conclusions give rise to new terminologies.

The Rhetoric of Social Action

Burke's remark in the introduction to *A Rhetoric of Motives* might be used to describe a great deal of his work, finding as he does, unexpected meanings and insights in strange, often exotic places: ". . . we seek to mark off the areas of rhetoric, by showing how a rhetorical motive is often present where it is not usually recognized, or thought to belong" (*A Rhetoric of Motives*, 1950, xiii).

Burke's importance for the sociologist is especially important in his conception of human action as rhetorical. The importation of rhetorical analysis into social research is enormously productive. Both the human action that the sociologist studies and the texts in which sociological analyses are reported are perceivable as interactive pursuits. We cannot avoid rhetoric. When we speak, act, dress, eat, and generally conduct our lives we communicate and, in doing so, persuade others, including ourselves. Seen, in Burke's frequently used phrase, "as strategies for situations" human events involve an actor and an audience. Action is seen as persuasional and therefore rhetorical. Goffman has used the idea, though not the direct language of rhetorical terminology, in describing human interaction as performance. It is this element of persuasional effect which makes Burke's mode of rhetorical analysis so pertinent to the sociologist.

Language is also performative as well as referential. Both literature and sociology end in a product—a work of art, a research report, a cultural product. That product is also capable of being construed as involving a strategy to affect situations in addition or in place of a report about referential objects and events. The way in which language is used, its form and style, affects the audiences to which it is addressed.

Again the unifier of the disparate, Burke shows us in *A Rhetoric of Motives* how rhetorical analysis can illuminate both literary texts and human relations in general. Identification is the key process through which poets and ordinary people further rhetorical purposes in attempts to persuade others. In the use of symbols there is a bid toward others, or to self, to be joined or to oppose the identities which are proffered. Thus the use of images of killing in Milton and in Matthew Arnold can become a paradigm for terms used in describing change and transformation, and thus illuminates the use of killing the father in Freud's *Totem and Taboo*. The identification of killing as transformation is the unifying element in the structure of thought created in these texts. The imagery of revolutionary violence may emerge in the clothing of death and destruction or in the vestments of the Utopian Eden to be attained through it. In all these examples violence is identified as passage, as transformation, and provided with justifications. Violence as transformation becomes a stage toward "higher" values and is more acceptable than violence described in terms of destruction. In each case the response of the reader is the sought-after goal of the author. Either identification of violence is a call—to action or inaction.

Identification is the key term in Burke's analysis of rhetoric. Here the analytical tools of the grammar are brought to bear in understanding how texts and performance are seen in relation to an audience. The reader, the listener, the observer is persuaded to something by the character ascribed to significant objects by the persuader. Slaying is a way of changing the identity of the object by its transformation to something else. Thus, for revolutionaries, changes described in terms of killing are also described as salutory; their aspirations are central to their identity. For the counterrevolutionaries the killing is identified as violence that is unnecessary. What is defined in terms of sacrifice by one is thought about in terms of senseless killing by another.

In his analysis of Hitler's 1920s book, "My Battle" (see pp. 211–

31), Burke brings many of these ideas to bear on an investigation of the rhetoric of that work. His discussion of the central ideas and images in Hitler's work are directed toward the persuasional aspects of the volume. Burke shows how the tensions and guilt of the postwar German world were used and directed by Hitler as strategies for achieving support. Written in the atmosphere of the 1930s, and first appearing in *The Southern Review,* Burke's paper may seem outdated. Yet it remains an illuminating example of rhetorical analysis.

There are three ways in which Burke's rhetorical perspective has been productive for sociologists. The first is found in the enormously insightful approach to human interaction as persuasional. The second is in the understanding of social science research as affected by rhetorical elements. Last, Burke demonstrates that the common framework which literature and literary analysis, as rhetoric, share with sociology provides basic categories for seeing and interpreting social action.

The first has been superbly realized in Goffman's analyses of human interaction as presentational and performative. To speak of "impression management" is to view interaction as audience-directed and persuasional. Goffman's work is filled with illuminating insights into the process by which human beings confer symbolic meanings on action otherwise interpreted as utilitarian or else as "meaningless." In studying institutions for those labeled "mentally disturbed" Goffman interprets behavior seen by psychiatrists as less than sane as better understood as attempts by the patients to persuade themselves and others that they are persons of autonomy and self-control (Goffman 1961a, 248–54). The "stashing" of small objects in special places is interpreted by Goffman as an action representing the extension and autonomy of the patient. This is a way of convincing themselves of their self-identity. In the asylum's institutional setting they have had to give up many other signs of their particularity. The patient acts in a context of protecting his or her sense of autonomy, persuading both himself and others that he still has some control over his life, even in this "total institution." The psychiatrist identifies the "stashing" behavior as foolish, irrational, and hence psychotic. The sociologist in describing the situation as the patient's rhetorical action also confers a different identity on the act than that in the psychiatrist's scheme. It is not the act of "crazy people" but strategy adapted to the situation of managing self-identity in an institution that threatens self-esteem and recognition. What is irrational is transformed into the rational. It is now logical, understandable, and what the reader would do were he or she in the same situation.

Rhetorical analysis has rich usage beyond the microlevel of interactions. It is also a way of seeing how public acts and artifacts serve to persuade audiences that legal, political, and social institutions have a particular character. Manning's analysis of the "police myth" (Manning 1977) is a clear example both of Burke's direct influence and of the rhetorical element in institutional procedure. The use of crime rates, the frequent depiction of the police as crime fighters, the emphasis on the gun—all present a performance in which police are the direct enemies of crime. They are identified as warriors against the enemy criminal. Closer study of police, as Manning maintains, indicates that police do much that is unrelated to crime. Nor can police do much to discover or prevent crimes. Neither can they do much to retrieve the losses caused by criminal acts (Black 1980). The "police myth" persuades audiences to view police as more powerful crime-fighters than close study warrants. It leads the public to see crime as more a matter of individuals than environments, as other terminologies might see it. A view of police as "servants of the people" leads to a less exciting, less dramatic sense of police and police work.

The Rhetoric of Research

Manning's study of police and Goffman's study of the asylum also utilize a rhetoric at another level. Not only do they describe the rhetorical action of their subjects—police and patients—they also write in ways which are persuasional. The audience is invited to change their view of police and patients. The police are not to be seen primarily as crime fighters. The behavior of the patient in the asylum is not to be seen as "crazy" but as an adaptation to life in a total institution. In the process of reporting their research, Manning transforms the image of the police from one of strength to one of weakness; Goffman transforms the psychiatrist from a figure of expert authority to a figure of misled obtuseness.

Consider also Burke's analysis of Marx and Mannheim in their treatments of ideology. Burke's discussion of positive, dialectical, and ultimate terminologies provides a tool with which to "uncover" the differences in the way each of these theorists has used the concepts dialectically. Both see ideas developing within historical contexts as dialectical opposites; feudal to capitalist to socialist; ideology to utopia; status quo to opposition. Marx places the dialectical conflicts in a developmental frame; he posits an ultimate—the socialist society— that transcends the dialectic. Mannheim, in not doing so, puts all ideologies on equal terms. As Burke suggests, Mannheim liberalizes Marx. All ideologies are described equally as systems of justification and persuasion. No one is ontologically superior.

Rhetorical concepts are also a way of describing and discussing the languages of social science, of finding rhetoric where it was previously unrecognized. In recent years, a number of social scientists have drawn heavily from Burke's conception of language to examine social science as a genre of writing. The language of social science is usually presented as if it had no literary or rhetorical functions. Social scientists have generally treated their language as scientific and not involving the arts of persuasion. Such perspectives ignore the ways in which scientific reporting of research is itself a style with persuasional qualities. Burke's influence has recently led to an analysis of the stuff of social science, its theories and its research reports as persuasional attempts (Brown 1977, 1987; McCloskey 1985; Gusfield 1976, 1981, 1986). As such, the linguistic style and the form of text become important parts of the research. Rhetoric is a key to their structure and thought.

Even the presentation of text as "scientific" requires attention to style and literary devices which persuade and instruct the audience in how it is to be taken. Science, including social science, has a particular style and often couches its language so as to convince an audience that it is "above" stylistic concern (Gusfield 1976). Such attempts to bring the analysis of rhetoric to what has been customarily viewed as outside the scope of such analyses, as privileged language, are part of the move toward the study of discourse and text as a major aspect of self-reflection in the social sciences.

Analysis of social science as literature pays attention to the language form of reporting research and formulating theory. It goes much further into the details of writing than is true of the conventional sociology of knowledge approach. Following Marx and Mannheim, that perspective emphasized the role of interests in directing attention to aspects of social structure. It did so both for the author and the audience. The perspective arising from Burke shifts attention to the language categories that frame and define the situations. The social construction of argument and analysis is the focus.

A concern for how the style and rhetoric of research operates to achieve belief highlights the affinity between social science writing and literary products. In my own work on law and alcohol I have pointed out how the focus on the "drinking-driver" rather than "drinking-driving" coerces thought to frame the problem as one of attributes of the motorist. The term "drinking-driving" focuses on an event and makes it more feasible to view environmental elements, including the nature of the automobile, as significant scenic elements (Gusfield 1981).

Burke's discovery of the ubiquitousness of rhetoric is echoed in Northrop Frye's remark that "anything which makes a functional use of words will always be involved in all the technical problems of words, including rhetorical problems. The only road from grammar to logic, then, runs through the intermediate territory of rhetoric" (Frye 1957).

Attention to the rhetoric of the social sciences is a growing and significant part of social science. It is not a debunking of social science but a method for understanding the cultural product social scientists create. From this perspective the social sciences produce a cultural artifact: the research report. That artifact is a text and, as such, is open to interpretation as are other texts, including *King Lear*, the Sunday supplement, a presidential speech and *Playboy* magazine.

Rhetoric in Goffman and Burke

The analyses of human interaction in Erving Goffman's studies have often been compared to Burke's. While Goffman was quite familiar with Burke's work and cites it at various places, there is a considerable difference between the dramatistic orientation of Burke and the dramaturgical one of Goffman. There are also some significant resemblances.

Goffman's interest was in the art and practice of deception. Through understanding how deception is carried out, he elucidates how it is that we understand "true" events and persons. The effective deceiver must know how to present himself so as to be convincing, to make the interaction "work." The stage actor is the professional deceiver. Dramaturgy is the art of stage-acting. It tells us how to present ourselves so as to be believable. A popular rendition of *The Presentation of the Self in Everyday Life* might have been "How to Convince Others That You Are Who You Claim to Be."

For Goffman the stage, the drama, is a metaphor. Like other metaphors it touches the subject only tangentially. In *Frame Analysis* he shows the reader the difference between "reality" and the stage. For example, on stage the actors know how it will all turn out. The audience does not. The actors recite lines without the stammers, pauses, ellipses, and errors that occur in natural speech (Goffman 1974, chapter 5).

Burke's use of drama is not its use as a metaphor. Both literature and sociology are dramatistic in two ways. First, they are formed by terminologies; they are linguistic enterprises. Second, both involve conflict. There is some opposition that provides the excitement and choice that is human action. What the dramatist does in imagining his characters is very much like what the human being does in reacting and responding. Both are imprisoned in language. Both use their actions, in behavior or in thought, as means for coping with situations. In those uses each has its own rhetorics. The playwright, the novelist, the poet, the sociologist are also rhetorical. Each frames writing in ways that persuade, cajole, and coax. An argument is constructed to convince an audience.

Dialectics: The Burkean Method

For what, then, is Burke's rhetoric a strategy? What is the situation to which his work is addressed? It might be possible to construct a political interpretation of Burke's writings, as Frank Lentricchia has attempted (Lentricchia 1983). This seems to me to be forced and to project Burke's more outspoken politics of the 1930s into later periods. A conventional sociology of knowledge, intent on placing him in a historical space and time, would miss the more useful understanding of what he has been about. More is to be gained by intellectual rather than sociological analysis here.

Burke is not shy about his targets for criticism. In his often-quoted phrase "perspective by incongruity," sometimes also expressed by "the comic corrective," he takes aim against a monistic thinking that fails to reveal the limits of a single form of thought to understand and experience reality. In the distinction between "action" and "motion" he holds up to a rigid stimulus-response social science the critique of determinist models of human beings. Throughout his dominating interest in language as a framer of experience there is the literary critic's insistence on the vital importance of words and thought for human life. Much of the study of human beings is "logology"—words about words (a term coined by Burke). The insistence that human beings carve out their experience through giving meaning to raw sense data is the humanist's criticism of the social scientist's "representative anecdote" of the experiment and the view that behavior is determined by environment and institution.

But if Burke is the humanist and pluralist addressing a deterministic social science he is also the social scientist talking to the humanistic coterie of historians, philosophers, and literature for whom literature and art are special categories and for whom a close textual analysis ignores any relation to an audience of readers. Art is also a form of behavior; it does something to and for the author and his audience. The title of one of Burke's best-known essays shows him at work: "Literature as Equipment for Living." To analyze poetry as a "thing in itself," with no sense of how the reader may be changed is to miss the moment of encounter. In the interaction between reader and writer—there is "where the action is."

Burke's pluralism calls into question the quest for the "right answer," the correct interpretation, the single perspective. It is in his version of dialectics that Burke offers a method to cope with the situation of life without certainty.

While Burke produced a volume on grammar, another on rhetoric, and completed an unpublished manuscript on the symbolic, he has not developed one specifically on the dialectic. Yet the method permeates all of his writing and he is often specific about it. "Dramatic" and "dialectic" are terms Burke characterizes as "equitable" (*A Grammar of Motives*, 1945, 511). Each perspective, each terminology, represents a partial view of reality. Dramatism refers to the actor while dialectic refers to the terms, the language which is, for Burke, so deeply a part of action. "Where the agents are in action we have drama; where the agents are in ideation we have dialectic"(*A Grammar of Motives*, 1945, 512). Yet, as he points out, the two are mutually influential. There are no ideas without persons; no persons without ideas. His analysis of language leads into a methodology in which no single perspective or single term can render a complete account of reality. The implications of terministic screens for social research lie in the plural possibilities of interpretation and the necessarily limited nature of any one schematic framework. The deliberate invitation to paradox, inconsistency, contradiction, and comedy are the mark of a method that, following Richard Brown, I refer to as dialectical irony—seeing something from the viewpoint of its opposite (Brown 1987).

In his insightful analysis of Burke, Wayne Booth (Booth 1979, chapter 3) refers to him as a "lumper" rather than a "splitter." Lumpers find similarities where others find only differences. Splitters are the opposite; they find differences where others find similarities (Parsons was a splitter; Goffman a lumper). Perhaps Burke is both; sometimes dividing what seems indivisible and sometimes merging what seems irreconcilable.

The Paradox of Substance

For the thorough-going dialectician nothing is as it seems to be. Burke's discussion of the paradox of substance prepares us for this. Description implies differentiation. The concepts we use require contrast. Nothing, except God, can exist without a context. To define, to "split," necessitates a negation; saying what the object is not in order to say what it is. To define we must distinguish; we must divide the object from its context, indicating what it is by what it is not.

The implications of adopting a dialectical method are quite profound for social science; far beyond and beside the Hegelian-Marxian usage. Unlike that well-worn shibboleth of contemporary coffeehouses, Burke's dialectic has no synthesis except as its method is its ultimate. It directs us toward the complexities that are lost when great concern for clarity in method leads us to overlook the essential ambiguities in human action and interpretation. The exclusive search for cause and effect, treating human action as animal motion, leads us again to the partiality and monism dialectical perspective overcomes.

Burke presents a good illustration of what this means for the social sciences in discussing what a dialectical history would look like:

> History, in this sense, would be a dialectic of characters in which, for instance, we should never expect to see "feudalism" overthrown by "capitalism" and "capitalism" succeeded by some manner of national or international or non-national socialism—but rather should note elements of all such positions (or "voices") existing always, but attaining greater clarity of expression or imperiousness of proportion of one period than other. (*A Grammar of Motives*, 1945, 513).

There is, in this, a warning against the use of typologies without a constant awareness of their deceptive qualities. Weber viewed his use of "ideal types" as an heuristic device to find one's way into historical analysis. He distinguished it from the reality of the situation (Weber 1949). In their classic article on sociological concepts, written three decades ago, Bendix and Berger examined the uses of "paired contrasts" frequently used in sociology. These are found in such dichotomies as "primary and secondary" or "community and society." A major difficulty in the use of such concepts, they argued, has stemmed from being treated as dichotomous, as "tradition or modernity," "folk or urban." Quoting Burke on "perspective by incongruity," they argue for a less oppositional, more interactive perspective toward the use of such concepts. "The paired concepts of sociological theory, then, must always be considered *together* when one is engaged in developing testable hypotheses" (Bendix and Berger, 1959, 101). Seeing types as revealing the spectrum of possibilities existing rather than an "either-or" situation is a positive step toward a more "realistic" sociology.

The Comedic Stance

Here then is the clue to the Burkean style of puns, jokes, and downright comedy, sometimes descending into buffoonery. Comedy is the art of criticism as irony is the trope of dialectics. The search for the opposite is the method of the dialectician. Burke's admonition to adopt a "perspective by incongruity" is a logical (or logo-logical) conclusion from his dialectical perspective. "In violating one order of classification ... [we are] stressing another" (*Permanence and Change*, 1965, 112).

Perspective by incongruity is more than style in Burke. It is an exhortation to see the limited nature of any one cognitive framework. The terminologies in use are terministic screens that shield us from the multiplicity of possibilities. The wise observer recognizes that opposites are not so different after all. Comedy points up the limits of intelligence and knowledge. As Burke says in *Attitudes Toward History* people are not vicious but they are often mistaken and necessarily mistaken; "*every* insight contains its own special kind of blindness" (*Attitudes Toward History*, 1984, 41).

A new taxonomy, a new vocabulary produces an additional angle from which to see reality. The comic enables us to increase the use of incongruity and in this a fashion to produce new ways of seeing, to overcome the particular blindness of our accustomed usages: "The universe would appear to be something like a cheese; it can be sliced in an infinite number of ways—and when one has chosen his own pattern of slicing, he finds that other men's cut fall at the wrong places" (*Permanence and Change*, 1965, 103).

A Dialogic Social Science

What this implies for the social sciences is implicit in the blurring and blunting of the sharply defined edges of typologies. The logic and method of the hard sciences as the model for conventional sociological research depend upon just that precise and rigid definition which a pluralistic method denies. It is an implicit assumption of such methods that there is a right answer to the questions posed in the social sciences. The belief that only one answer is the true answer and others are false is the ideal toward which, in their Enlightenment spirit, the social sciences have aspired.

A deeply held pluralism recognizes two barriers in the way of this ideal. The first is the limiting effects of language, of theory, in representing the multifold character of the real world. The second is the importance of the researcher to the total project. His or her theories, biases, attitudes, and dramatistic categories are essential to the process of selectivity. But, at the same time, they prevent social science from being even an approximation of the model of knowing in use in the natural sciences. As Anthony Giddens has put it, "But those who still wait for a Newton are not only waiting for a train that won't arrive, they're in the wrong station altogether" (Giddens 1976, 13).

What emerges is a more dialogic picture of the social sciences in place of the monistic model that is even today the accepted standard. No one perspective, no single study, can do justice or mercy to the complexity of human behavior. The sociologist is then the supreme ironist, the critic whose task is to point to the multiple understandings, the alternative possibilities inhering in situations, to bring new meanings and metaphors to bear on taken-for-granted assumptions. Our aim, as Burke suggests in his discussion of dialectic and irony, is to include all the relevant terms of development in a perspective of perspectives (*A Grammar of Motives,* 1945, 503–19). But even as we do so, we must recognize that no one designation, no one solution, no one answer is final, encompassing, or ultimate. The dialogue of all voices is itself the answer and not a road to a consensus of voices around a unified conclusion.

Armed with Burkean method, the sociologist's trope is that of irony. What sociology can achieve is a form of criticism that reveals the limits, the assumptions of what is taken for granted by culture. It does so by incongruity, by seeing the world from as many vantage points as possible. As Rueckert puts it: "Burke admonishes us that, if we want to see something accurately, we should at least try to see it whole" (Rueckert 1982).

What this implies is a reach for a kind of wisdom rather than the goal of certain knowledge. Knowledge is a scientific term and implies a certainty which is contradicted by the interpretive and reflexive character of human action. It is the wisdom stemming from a humility that recognizes, through comedy, the human limitations on knowledge. Being self-critical, the sociologist realizes that his own designations, his own metaphors, are also ways of constructing and creating a way of seeing. Burke puts this dialectical method and a possible view of sociological perspective in a passage from *Attitudes Toward History:* "The audience, from its vantage point, sees the operation of errors that the characters in the play cannot see; thus seeing from two angles at once, it is chastened by dramatic irony . . ." (1984, 41).

The sociologist is like the child watching the stage. Knowing more parts and having read the script he or she cries out to the players and tries to warn them to avoid the ending as it has been written. Alternatively the sociologist provides the playwright with several other possible ways to bring the play to its last curtain.

The Limits of Dialectic

Is Burke a sixty-six-percent Hegelian: thesis-antithesis but no synthesis? Burke leaves many of his readers unsure of where his dialectical pluralism leaves us. Although he many times protested that his is not a relativism, nevertheless the reader who looks for an umbrella under which to find the manifold perspectives huddled together against the cruel sun will be disappointed. Burke has not addressed himself to these questions in ways which resolve doubts and queries. He shakes hands with Mannheim, ending in the same Olympian equality of perspectives.

What can be meant by seeing it whole? Is it an additive method by which the real situation is revealed through a perspective of perspectives? Let a hundred viewpoints bloom? Even if we restrict the analysis to logology, would a matrix of all the possible ratios of the terms of the Pentad yield the sum total of perspectives? And does this mean that, in some sense (which?) they are all equally acceptable?

To be sure, a pragmatic approach might well insist that not all perspectives are equally adequate at any time and place, for all situations. But that thought suggests a form of the Serenity Prayer used by Christian Scientists and members of Alcoholics Anonymous: God, give us the serenity to accept what cannot be changed; give us the courage to change what should be changed; give us the wisdom to distinguish one from the other.

There is an analogy here to Foucault and Burke. In the historian's concept of the *episteme* there are reverberations of the Burkean notion of perspectives. Both are limiting and blinding. In an essay on Foucault, Hayden White suggests that the French historian's ideal is to get beyond language to a state of direct confrontation with empirical realities (White 1978). I am not sure that this would apply to Burke but my lack of assurance is itself indication of Burke's unwillingness to confront these questions at any length.

That Burke has not successfully addressed the problem does not diminish the virtue of the perspective. Burke is above all the analyst of language, the interminable student of terminology. His admonition regarding dialectical method is an admonition about language. Important as it is, it does not exhaust the issues of how we are to grapple with observation of events. It does, however, lead to the recognition of the blinders and constraints language (read culture) creates. In the prison-house of language it is important to search for the key even if we never find it. The process is itself transformative.

Symbol, Ritual, and Society

John Dewey wrote somewhere that society exists in and through communication. What a group of people share that distinguishes them from others is often labeled their "culture." A distinctive framework of language and attendant categories makes common experiences possible and shareable. It becomes a source of the tacit, understood but unstated assumptions about the world which, being collectively shared, makes one group distinct from another and one historical era distinct from its past and its future. Once immersed as a member of a society, we do not "see" our common culture.

For Burke, as well, society is best studied through the symbolic content of its culture. This includes examining not only language in the narrow sense of conveying information but the ceremonies and rituals through which that common culture is created and perpetuated. An analysis of society is thus an analysis of its linguistic frameworks, its vocabularies, and of the symbols with which it describes itself.

Burke's discussion of social institutions is scattered through the corpus of his work. Nowhere has he produced a definitive statement setting forth a general perspective about "society" as an object, in the manner of one of the Holy Trinity of Sociology—Marx, Durkheim, or Weber. Nor has he attempted a grand theory of *the* social system, in the manner of Talcott Parsons. His article, "Dramatism," in the *Encyclopedia of the Social Sciences,* is the closest we have. In *Rhetoric of Religion* he has further given much thought to what makes a social order possible.

In *The Philosophy of Literary Forms* his segment "Ritual Drama as 'Hub'" sets out his view of the significance of ritual and style in human life. Description of the scene, he tells his readers, is the province of the physical sciences. Drama is the province of the social sciences and ritual is the earliest, clearest, the Ur-form of drama (*The Philosophy of Literary Form,* 1957, 87–113). Here the human being as responder, as in conflict with self or other, engages in action, in unpredictable response not given by the scenic qualities to which he is exposed. Public rituals have much in common with other forms of social action. Both involve stylization of conduct. At one point in his writing Burke maintains that to perceive what is said or done we must know not only *what* but *how* it was said or done. In this sense human action is replete with action presented ceremoniously and ritualistically.

Social order is stated in rituals and social order is deeply hierarchical. Here Burke, as usual, finds a literary, verbal aspect to something general, conventionally, considered in other ways. In our language we distinguish between levels of being and appreciation. Some things are higher and some are lower. In Marx, while the bourgeoisie occupy better places in society, they are relegated to a lower status than the proletariat, who are the source and origin of the highest values and to whom the future is dedicated. In Burke's own framework, "dialectic" is superior to other tropes, such as metonymy or synecdoche.

Societies are engaged in drama through the linguistic device of the "thou shalt not." Some system of social control is made necessary by the fact of putative rebellion, of disobedience. The fact that humans are enjoined not to do something implies that they are capable of doing it. Without an order there is no disorder. Myths, legends, archetypes of all sorts act out and perpetuate the commands of the group. Language and ritual do more than reflect the experience of group life; they create it. To be a member of a community is to share in a name, a history, a mutual consciousness. These are conveyed through language and ritualization through style.

You can observe the process at work as new "communities" are formed and old ones disappear. The Hispanic and Asian communities are emerging in the United States where once there were Puerto Ricans, Spanish-Americans and Mexican-Americans; Japanese, Korean, and Chinese. The Creole has long since disappeared as a distinctive type as it has disappeared from our language (Gusfield 1975). Such communities are symbolic in that they are social constructions, formed by a new consciousness of identity and new naming devices (Gusfield 1975; Hunter 1974; Suttles 1972).

This is not to say that language and ritual alone are creating new communities. The symbolic process is, as Burke says again and again, a strategy for a situation. In that same discussion of ritual drama Burke wrote:

> In equating "dramatic" with "dialectic" we automatically have also our perspective for the analysis of history, which is a "dramatic" process, involving dialectical opposition. . . . we are reminded that every document bequeathed us by history must be treated as a strategy for encompassing a situation . . . as the answer or rejoinder to assertions current in the situation in which it arose. (*The Philosophy of Literary Form,* 1957, 93).

Such ritualization and stylization, through common language and common ceremony, provide the way in which the social order maintains and controls the hierarchies both of structure and of language. Those rejoinders are to be found in the symbolic attributes of action, both as verbal and visual forms, as art. There are practical acts, he writes, such as building a house and there are symbolic acts which present a representation, such as an artist might draw to characterize a subject through how he or she sits. "The symbolic act is the 'dancing of an attitude'" (*The Philosophy of Literary Form,* 1957, 9). It presents the stylized encompassing or telescoping of a more complex situation.

Burke, then, points us toward the multiple, polysemic meanings of actions. In seeing symbolic attributes, he prompts us to go beyond a single interpretation of actions. In adopting the utilitarian paradigm as the only source of orderly understanding, the observer will miss much of how events and objects are involved in the common experiences of a social group. Both the poetic and the semantic meanings are required if we are to see very far. We always see things in terms of something else, simplifying and analogizing.

> Our own proposal to cultivate so ambivalent a concept as trained incapacity clearly involves us in a clash with the vestigial congruities still upheld by language. For if one is interested in noting how a certain *insight* can be called a *bluntness* when approached from another point of view, one has necessarily vowed himself to conflicts with the classification of everyday speech, which is primarily designed for calling things *good or bad, intelligent or stupid, this or that,* and being done with it. (*Permanence and Change,* 1965, 109)

In recent years a good many anthropologists and sociologists have paid attention to the symbolic acts, or symbolic order, as a significant aspect of what has often been seen as "purely" practical or instrumental (Gusfield and Michalowicz 1984). Ceremony and ritual, in the form of religious ritual or national ceremony, have long been seen in such terms but the character of symbolic action, as Burke has used it, has either been denied or overlooked in other, especially institutional, areas. It is here that Burke's conception of society is capable of significant use.

The Social Drama

J. L. Austin has made us aware of the performative, as well as descriptive, character of language (Austin 1975). In speaking we are doing something as well, or in distinction from, reporting something. Speech is a performance as well as a reference. Goffman has made a somewhat similar point in referring to what we "give off" as well as what we "give to" in interaction (Goffman 1959, 4ff). How we ask a question conveys the character of the person and the relationship as well as being a search for information.

The account of an event in the life of a friend of mine is a vivid example of symbolism at an individual level. He reports that during his undergraduate days at the University of California, Los Angeles, there was a woman who, in attending a class once a week, had a walk so provocative that men on campus talked about it and would gather once a week, from many points on the campus, to see her walk. What makes this example so vivid is that the woman later became famous as the Hollywood actress Marilyn Monroe. Twenty-five years after her death she has retained that fame, emerging for many artists as a symbol of American culture, an "American icon" as several critics have called her. She has come to serve as a representation to the society of something about itself, perhaps the tragedy of success or the mixture of innocence and lust that many interpret as the American vision of sexuality.

Although Burke does not use the term very often, his image of social life is dominantly "cultural." Like Marshall Sahlins and others his attack has been against the view of material aspects of social activities, devoid of an understanding of meaning, as explanatory tools for modern life (Sahlins 1976). To use Suzanne Langer's term, the conception of symbolic action goes beyond the use of symbols as denotative and connotative. Symbols are what the person uses in *the formulation of experience* (Langer 1964, 59). They are essential to the framing of events. They create or construct the meaning of situations for which actions are strategies.

It would follow from Burke's perspective of symbolic action that societies are formed around collective symbols. What unites is common experience and that requires symbolic similarity, common meanings. Sociology, like other studies of human action, must necessarily grasp the meanings of events to those whom they study. Institutions, as well as interaction, cannot be understood apart from their symbolic and symbolizing attributes.

Authority and Acceptance

Burke's view of society is congruent with both his emphasis on symbolic acts and the implicit criticism of social determinism in his dialectics. One can picture much of his work as an attempt to rid us of the view of appearances as understandably ordered and to go beyond the disorder of appearances to perceive the forms which are constant. This form of structuralism is found in his characterization of *A Grammar of Motives* as a book concerned with basic forms of thought "in accordance with the nature of the world as all men necessarily experience it" (*A Grammar of Motives,* 1945, xv). These basic forms are entailed in his view of "social structure" in emphasizing the prefiguring with which a society is experienced.

The problem of order is central to Burkean sociology. Just as language frames provide us with order in interaction, so too the terminologies we develop create frames of acceptance and rejections of authority. It is the fact of authority (hierarchy) that is the source of order and rejection in society. Human beings, being talkers and writers, can think "Thou shalt" and also "Thou shalt not." The acceptance and rejection of morals, of authority, of division is ever present. We are capable of thinking the negative and are also "goaded by the spirit of hierarchy" as he writes in his definition of Man. Relations between groups, between classes, between the powerful and the powerless, between the priest and the parishioner are thought about and organized through our terms. Frames of acceptance are, as he puts it in the title of the book *Attitudes Toward History* (1959), not forms of passivity but the terms of relationship.

If there is hierarchy and social order, there is also the rejection of order and the consequent guilt. Here is the foundation of Burke's society: if drama, then conflict. If conflict, then hierarchy. If hierarchy, then guilt. If guilt, then redemption. If redemption, then victimage. Rejection means the need to expiate the resulting guilt. Rituals, dramatic enactments, provide us with visible symbols in which hierarchy is built up and in which rejection is atoned for. The scapegoat, the victim, is essential to the order of society, as recognized in Durkheim's presentation of crime as normal to societies (Durkheim 1958). The sacrificial principle is essential. The Christian drama is enacted again and again. Even Manning's "police myth" is a form for accepting policing as the drama of good against evil in which police represent the potential sacrificial lambs redeeming the citizenry from the guilt of criminality.

Consider the phenomenon of "deviance"—a word which itself carries with it a hierarchy of the normal and the deviant in the imagery of a standard deviation curve, stylizing a diversity of situations and persons. Foucault has carried the thought out in a striking manner in his conception of imprisonment. In the modern penitentiary movement, the aim of providing a rationalized organization and life-style for the prisoner is an act assuming the prisoner's defect of character and, through those acts, making it evident. Foucault contrasts this mode of punishment with the earlier, sometimes horrendous, punishment of the body in which the monarch "ritualized" his absolute authority (Foucault 1977).

Hierarchy is constant in Burke's perception of society because in every area of life there is an orderliness of principle, of higher and lower, nobler and baser. Diversity, conflict, division portend the disruption of order, the clash of frames. The fact of hierarchy itself dictates the need for unity as well. Later in this chapter I discuss how Burke uses the idea of courtship to examine the overcoming of hierarchy both in literature and in social rituals. There the modes of courtship are the stylized rituals through which social relations are pursued.

The theory of deviance sketched above is illuminated in this light. Punishment and redemption can be seen as acts that ritualistically offer the society a means of conviction that the social order is sustained, that adequate sacrifice has been obtained. The social order is crystallized in such symbolic resolutions of tensions and conflicts. I have used such considerations in interpreting the symbolic use of legal decisions and legislation about drinking-driving (Gusfield 1981). There is a considerable difference between the harsh condemnation of drinking-driving embodied in legal decisions or legislation and the daily routine of police and courts. The ritual of condemnation and the severe punishments expressed in words reinforces the social designation of the action. It crystallizes and symbolizes the concept of the moral social person. It explains death and the risk of auto use as the result of faulty, immoral people rather than random fate or the costs of traffic. At the same time, the leniency of the enforcement process is the recognition of diversity in styles of life, cultural assessments of risk, and the practical enforcement contingencies that grow out of it.

Burke's interest in theology is occasioned by this interest in how the social order is achieved through symbols of order, disorder, and the resolution of the attendant tensions. His is not, in *The Rhetoric of Religion* or elsewhere, an interest in religion *per se* but in the language through which theologians grappled with these fundamental problems.

The Theatrical Metaphor

The social sciences are filled with metaphors. The "market" is the image of a bazaar where merchants and customers bargain over price. "Social stratification" borrows from geology and imagines the society in the guise of layers of rock formation. That central concept of the sociologist, "social role," is a term taken directly from the theater. A language devoid of metaphorical allusions would be poverty-stricken or so abstract as to be uncommunicative.

Such metaphors are frequently also expressed as major images that unite a cluster of terms into a single image of the human being and the human society. "Root metaphor," "world hypothesis," "paradigmatic image" and a number of other concepts have been developed by philosophers and social scientists to state this idea. Images of "mechanism," "organism," "rational choice," "evolution," "system" dot the terminological landscape of the social sciences. Burke refers to these as "representative anecdotes." His own is human beings as "symbol users."

One way in which Burke has often been portrayed is as a major user of the stage as the metaphor for human behavior. In an anthology of materials using "the perspective of life as theatre" the editors, who give great homage to Burke as the seminal figure, describe the selections as all deriving from the idea that "many 'real-life' actions and events can most adequately be understood *in terms of* drama" (Combs and Mansfield 1976, xiv [my emphasis]). As I read Burke, all thought expressed through language is *in terms of* something else. To talk of some concepts as metaphorical and others as literal is to pretend to a privileged position for one terminology over another.

In using drama as a term to describe human action, Burke may appear to find the staged play a metaphorical form for expressing something about human social life. To describe Burke in this fashion is a significant mistake in understanding what he is about. He wrote, at one point, that drama is not a metaphor for human action. It is a term of description. As I have written above, life is as dramatic as is theater. Human language is poetic as well as semantic. Literature is not a metaphor for sociology. The two domains are similar in being dramatic, in using a grammar and a rhetoric of motives, in facing both utilitarian and symbolic representations.

Much of Burke can be read as an effort to unseat two privileged systems of language from their regal thrones. One is the position of literature as a distinctive form of human expression. The other is science, the language of motion rather than action, as the only form for describing and analyzing social acts.

In a book on organizations as theatre, Mangham and Overington express the sense in which social science theory is metaphorical in the same sense as theatre is metaphorical:

> Both dramatic performance and social theory are non-literal representations of some domain; they formally depict situations, persons, events and the like which are elsewhere. Theatre stages life in dramatic performances; theory represents life through interrelated sets of concepts. Both are metaphors of the domains they represent, seeking to interpret realities through the scrutiny of appearances. . . . Both theory and theatre are speculations on the meaning of human action that propose conventions through which we can grasp the appearances they feature as representations of realities that we *mistakenly* take for granted. (Mangham and Overington 1987, 53)

"Drama" is no more a metaphor for human action than any other term. It is, for Burke, inherent in human existence because human language enables us to imagine the negative, the "Thou shalt not." The drama of the playwright depends on conflict and contrast because human life contains conflict, contradiction, disobedience, negation as well as affirmation. Action takes its meaning from the context of situations and the interpretations in use. These make the act understandable to those within it. Action as strategy for a situation is the crux of human drama.

Erving Goffman and the Dramaturgical Perspective

Erving Goffman has frequently been described as the major exponent of Kenneth Burke in the social sciences. The relation between these perspectives toward human interaction is more complicated than that formulation would suggest. A further discussion of Goffman's work will bring out the differences and similarities and clarify Burke's potential impact on the social sciences.

Goffman was quite aware of Burke well before his (Goffman's) earliest work. As a graduate student he had read and discussed *A Grammar of Motives* and *A Rhetoric of Motives*. References to Burke's writing are found in several of Goffman's books. There are numerous citations to him and two quotations in *The Presentation of the Self in Everyday Life,* for example. He refers there to one chapter as being "heavily drawn" from Burke (Goffman 1959, 194). Nowhere, however, is there a considered and specific discussion of Burke. Burke's influence on Goffman is less important for this discussion than the nature of the thought and terminology which Goffman employed in his work.

In the description and analysis of interaction Goffman described his method not as "dramatistic" but as "dramaturgical":

> The perspective employed in this report is that of the theatrical performance; the principles employed are dramaturgical ones. I shall consider the way in which the individual in ordinary work situations *presents himself and his activities* [my emphasis] to others, the ways in which he guides and controls the impression they form of him, and the kinds of things he may or may not do while sustaining his *performance* [my emphasis] before them. (1959, xi)

Certainly Burke and Goffman both emphasize the importance of the audience to human action. For Burke the image, the metaphor, the "representative anecdote" is the drama, the play, the interaction between characters. Human life is dramatic. For Goffman the image is that of the actor. Dramaturgy is the art of acting; of making appearances seem to be realities. Through much of his analyses of interaction Goffman dealt with the art of deception. His earliest publication, "On Cooling the Mark Out," was a study of confidence men, people who manage to deceive others and how they "get away with it" (Goffman 1952).

His interest in deception was the obverse of his interest in conviction; how the impression created by the performer convinces the audience that he is as he pretends to be. Successful and especially unsuccessful deception teaches us how interaction proceeds; how the social self is a product of social interaction.

In one sense Goffman is the supreme rhetorician. Action is observed as strategies for persuading audiences. In this sense there is much affinity to Burke. But where Burke's central occupation is as the analyst of language, Goffman's preoccupation is with acting. For Burke, the play's the thing. For Goffman it is the actor. The differences between "dramatistic" and "dramaturgical" are considerable.

Not until *Frame Analysis* (1974) does Goffman begin to evince interest in language as a central concern and not until *Forms of Talk* (1983b) and in work undertaken with sociolinguists shortly before his death is language a major focus of his work. The center of his interest remained what he called "the interaction order" (Goffman 1983a). The theatre was clearly a metaphorical model because it is the clearest instance we know of in which performance is the crux of action; acting not action is his concern.

Nor does Goffman engage in a systematic fashion to study the limitations and opportunities which divergent perspectives offer in analyzing human behavior. In utilizing the metaphor of the theater, "dramaturgy," he is not suggesting that "life is a theater" while he is, indeed, maintaining that "theater is life."

Burke's concept of "drama" in its literary sense is not only that of the stage. It is a general term to encompass literature in its many manifestations, poetry and novels as well as plays. It is the dramatic quality of life that is represented in literature. The homology is not between sociology and drama but between the similar views of human action which each holds. Such views are embedded in the assumptions which the dramatic performance, as literature, makes about human behavior and about how it is described.

An Image of Society

In a part of *The Rhetoric of Motives* entitled "Order" Burke considers courtship as a form by which social distinctions, such as classes, are transcended. In examining literary depictions of courtship, as in Shakespeare and in Castiglione's work on courtiers, Burke finds in sexual courtship the form of transcendence being worked out in social terms as well. It is, for him, the form through which social and economic classes "court" each other in the process of addressing and interacting. Here, as in the discussion of dialectic, there is a focus on the dialectical transformation toward ultimate resolutions. In his discussion of Marx and Mannheim, Burke again stresses the difference between Mannheim's acceptance of ideological conflict and Marx's movement beyond to the ultimate terminology of utopian revolution.

Society is profoundly hierarchical, as is language. There are "higher and lower," "right and wrong," "better and worse," "upper and lower." We are beings who are, Burke reminds us in his definition of Man, "goaded by the spirit of hierarchy." But that very hierarchy sets up the characteristic social elements which, as symbol-users, humans cope with. The very conception of rules, of laws, implies the possibility of anarchy, of lawlessness. Most of the concepts used in human relationships are dialectical terms; we cannot imagine them without imagining their opposites. "Peace" and "war" are co-existent. "Society" and "community" gain their meaning from the contrast they generate.

Here is the foundation of Burke's image of society. In his often-used sequence: If drama then conflict; if conflict then hierarchy. If hierarchy then guilt; if guilt then redemption. If redemption, then victimage. The Christian drama is re-enacted again and again. Ritual, dramatic enactments provide us with tangible, visible symbols by which we can understand and transform the conflicts between groups and within selves. Manning's "police myth" is a form for accepting the authority of police as representing good against evil. They are the sacrificial lambs redeeming the citizenry from the guilt of criminality. In a similar fashion, the drinking-driver, as projected in the myth of the "killer-drunk" is, in my studies, the acceptable explanation for traffic fatalities. As such, it transforms the conflict over the use of the automobile into a ritual of crime and punishment.

Ritual and the Symbolic Order

In understanding Burke's image of society I find it necessary to realize the wider usage that he gives to terms such as ritual and symbol and rhetoric. As he says in discussing rhetoric, he aims to show how rhetorical motives are present where they are not usually so considered. Burke's own rhetoric, his both insightful and puzzling method, utilizes just such transporting of terms from one field, often literature, into another, sociology. If we utilize the concept of ritual less as a term to describe collective ceremonies, such as Fourth of July parades or religious acts, and as a more generic term to describe the stylization of language and behavior, we are closer to what I believe Burke is doing. In using courtship as a metaphor for social relationships, for example, he is discussing the stylized way in which groups approach each other. These become evident in the rituals of address, the public display of equality and the suggestions of deference.

Here the similarity to Goffman has much point. Both see human action as performative. Burke goes further in extending this image of action as performance, as a way of affecting a situation. He utilizes it as a general principle of social life, not confined to the interaction order. Others have so used Burkean ideas in studying institutions and even total societies. Murray Edelman has interpreted much governmental action and labor-management relations as performances to persuade their audiences of realities often belied by the "backstage" practices (Edelman 1964; 1971). Labor and management must always act to persuade their audiences that the outcomes are the result of intense negotiation. Geertz has presented a picture of government in Bali as a drama of ceremonies that both depict and form the culture of that island (Geertz 1980).

It is in symbols, rituals, and ceremonies that societies reflexively perceive themselves. Burke directs us to ways in which social order is understood by its members. One can describe and analyze society as a symbolic order. To do so is to depict the ways in which institutions operate to create consistent and recurrent images of their organization and processes. An example can be drawn from the study of law. The assertion of the use and significance of legal reasoning and a legal science was challenged in the 1930s by the work of the legal realists, such as Jerome Frank and Thurman Arnold (Frank 1949; Arnold 1935). They argued that the legal reasoning of the appellate courts was a poor map with which to understand the day-to-day events of police, lawyers, and courts. Law becomes a way of dramatizing, of symbolizing, ideals. As Arnold put it, "the function of law is not so much to guide society as to comfort it" (Arnold 1935, 34).

The sociologist examining the symbolic order of a social group is inquiring into the concepts and ideas used to produce understanding in that group. They are the visions and versions of reality through which the perception of physical and social life is expressed and experienced. An analysis of age levels, for example, would examine the terminologies of age differences and the depictions of age differences in a society. In his classic study, *Centuries of Childhood,* the French historian Phillipe Ariès has studied artistic renditions of children and, along with other documents, given us a picture of how childhood has been differently conceived in other historical periods. In earlier centuries children were seen as only smaller versions of adults, with the same propensities and characters. As Ariès remarks in the introduction to his book, ". . . it is not so much the family as a reality that is the subject here as the family as an idea" (Ariès 1962, 9).

Instrumentalism and the Symbolic Order

Some of the confusion implicit in the common use of symbolic action stems from the dual meanings so frequently attached to the term "symbol." In one usage symbols are units of language. Words, concepts, terms are ways of symbolizing tangible objects, like one's arm, or conceptual objects, such as capitalism. In another usage symbols are a contrast to something else, in the sense that a flag is a symbol of national sentiment or a tiger is a symbol of energy ("Put a tiger in your tank" is an advertising slogan for a brand of gasoline). In the first usage Burke is underlining the social construction of reality—the ways in which language and thought, by defining situations and framing events, are part of the act and not "neutral" to it.

The second usage suggests a separation of meanings or dimensions that may be misleading. Elsewhere, I have distinguished between instrumental and symbolic meanings (Gusfield 1963, chap.7). By the former, I have meant the manifest, explicit understandings conventionally expressed and understood. This can be contrasted with the symbolic meanings which exist in a context and which connote other meanings to those in that context. I used the distinction to suggest that legislation to prohibit or limit the use of alcohol had one meaning, its instrumental one as a method to control drinking. In another, its symbolic meaning, that action was a performance which served the function of maintaining and expressing the dominance of old American Protestant middle classes over the rising Catholic immigrant and urban populations. That distinction, however, shares much with problems occasioned by Burke's own work and which are at the core of cultural analysis.

Gramsci, Burke, and the Sociological Study of Culture

Antonio Gramsci is credited with directing Marxists toward the independence of culture in the study of modern societies (Gramsci 1972; Joll 1978). In attempting to understand the impediments to revolution he criticized the assumption that culture—in the form of ideas—was only a "superstructure" which changes with shifts in the social structure and the economic institutions. From a Gramscian standpoint, cultural forms can support social structure by patterning the perception of experience. Such forms cannot be dismissed as "false consciousness"; they are hegemonic: controlling because they are givens and unnoticed. They are the very terms and standards by which experience is interpreted and judged. As a political leader among Italian Communists he preached the necessity of establishing alternative forms of consciousness, alternative cultures.

Sigmund Baumann has expressed this in a criticism of the development of socialist societies:

> Contrary to many socialists' expectations, the development of capitalism, far from precipitating a naked and brutal confrontation between classes, has brought about a replacement of domination by hegemony (as Gramsci foresaw). The stability of capitalism acquired a cultural foundation. This means that the ideals of a good life, accepted ends of action, wants perceived as a reflection of needs, cognitive schemata which organize world perception, and above all the way in which the borderline between the "realistic" and the "utopian" has been drawn, sustain and perpetuate the totality of capitalist relations with little or no interference by the political state. It means also that whatever change may take place within the realm of the state, the capitalist type of human relations is unlikely to give way unless driven away by new culture. (Baumann 1976, 102–3).

There is much that is similar between Burke and Gramsci in this respect. Both see the significance of cultural forms—language, art, scientific reasoning, religious cosmology, and other modes of consciousness—in directing and constructing experience. But where Burke is vague and implicit about the relation of symbol systems to social structure, Gramsci is explicit. His is a search for how symbols affect structure—its continuance or change.

This remains the central problem in the study of culture. The simplicity and directness of the old sociology of knowledge, implicit in Marx and explicit in Mannheim, has given way to a greater sense of the complexity of knowledge. But must the baby be thrown away with the bath water? The issue of the relation between culture and social structure remains and is far from resolution at theoretical or empirical levels.

Of course Burke is cognizant of social structure. However, his perspective, rich and productive as it is, is weakest at the point where the context in which symbols emerge or exist is approached. The social context is taken for granted. At many points in his writings, Burke hints at another sociology, a return of the repressed and unrecognized structure. Here for example, is a statement from his article "Dramatism": ". . . dramatic analysis also contends that property in any form sets the *conditions* [my emphasis] for conflict (and hence culminates in some sort of victimage)." Strange word-conditions—in a context of action rather than motion. In what ways does property impinge on cooperation and conflict? The problem of how that institution is involved in language and thought is unexplored. Here I find Burke either mute or confusing and sometimes confusing in muteness. Having lifted the Pandora's box by bringing social structure in, I wish him to draw out some new wrapping.

Burke's emphasis on language places him in the same cage as the rest of us who challenge an excessive positivist intellectual domination with the perspective of social constructionism. If the frameworks of thought limit and constrain how experience is conceived, from where do we develop interpretations of objects and events? In the Burkean world, society becomes only a cognitive world without interests or sentiments, without group loyalties and without the emotive forces of love or greed or search for glory. The body is there but under the hood the motor is empty.

The Status of the Symbolic Order

For Burke, as for Mannheim, the critique of perspectives is an endless process. All perspectives are suspect, are limited. For the wise man wisdom consists in using all perspectives, treating each with slim respect and searching for their transformation in satire, comedy, and dialectic. Burke puts us on our guard; we are not to be taken in by this or that perspective, this or that theory, this or that academic indiscipline.

For some the study of the symbolic order is itself a form of guard-taking, a way of finding the reality through the miasma of the linguistic and ceremonial jungles through which it is hidden. Murray Edelman, in his studies of political symbolism, has placed the quiescent function of public institutional action at the center of his analyses (Edelman 1964). In this view the rituals of politics, including voting, the political language and the stylized forms of negotiation in management and labor are masks which hide the real and instrumental actions which shape events. There is an illusory world of symbols and symbolic acts and there is an instrumental, "real" world where actions have consequences. In some sense this is the theory of ideology re-represented. There are "true" and "false" accounts. Symbolic actions have the ring of irrelevance or "false" consciousness.

From another standpoint, closer I believe to Burke, all conceptualizations are distortive. They produce a static sense of social life that belies the reality of a constant flux. Thus in his classic study of Highland Burma, E. R. Leach maintained that cultural forms and ritual expression always treat social systems as if they were in equilibrium while they are, in fact, in considerable dynamic change (Leach 1954). But, for Leach, such inconsistencies are necessary though fictive. The social structure which informants portray to inquisitive anthropologists has more consistency, more order and rationality than the events contain. They are not reports; they are explanations. The investigator, Burke would remind us, must be attentive to the context in which the communication is given, must understand it as performance and ritual as well as, or instead of, a scholar's report on research.

Burkean Irony and Its Sociological Importance

Burke may not provide the sociologist with a full-blown theory of society. He does not add a fourth deity to the Holy Trinity of the sociological pantheon—Durkheim, Marx, and Weber. The considerable magnitude of his contribution is in the understanding and significance of the symbol-using, symbol-creating, and symbol-effective elements in social life. Three aspects of Burke's work have great import for sociology. They are summed up in the concepts of grammar, rhetoric, and dialectic.

GRAMMAR

The message underlying Burke's intensive analysis of language is one of constraint. Language constrains our experience. It creates frameworks and foci; defines situations and events in ways which give us a partial experience. The full spectrum is missing. What the sociologist sees is action oriented to objects and events whose meaning to the actors is encased in the symbolic mediations of culture. It presents to the sociologist the need for understanding the symbolic meaning of the subject's world if he or she is to understand the action. That subject is also the sociologist himself, whose own vocabularies, like those of his subjects, limits his versions of reality.

The symbolic order provides an important clue to the maintenance and change of institutions. Culture is not the simple epiphenomenon of institutions. It is the necessary box of consciousness within which the contents of social relationships "make sense." It is this *a priori* character of culture which becomes essential for sociological study. In a famous passage Lévi-Strauss once wrote, in criticism of functional theories of totemism, that totems are "chosen not because they are 'good to eat' but because they are 'good to think'" (Lévi-Strauss 1963, 89). Certainly it is in this fashion that the symbolic order is a vital part of social studies. It is this phenomenological form that makes the role of language so important for sociology. To study experience without studying what kind of experience is possible and operating is to fail to appreciate the historical and contextual aspect of social life. It leads us to take such aspects as childhood for granted as having the same meaning and characteristics in all societies as it has in the present.

RHETORIC

This search for the ways in which experience is possible leads the sociologist to a greater sense of the limited character of whatever human arrangements have evolved in contemporary society. The emphasis on rhetoric is a focus on human action as performative. Goffman has already demonstrated the enormous insight which can be achieved with a perspective which views interaction as presentational, as rhetorical in its persuasional features. Again the polysemic character of behavior is evident.

But in another dimension, Burke turns us toward social science as itself rhetorical; as a presentation within a context. As social science is itself embedded in language and culture, the sociologist requires a self-awareness of the framework of consciousness within which social research and theorizing is conducted. The limited nature of the paradigms we utilize in turn limit us to part of the spectrum. A great deal of innovation and creativity in social science is less a matter of cumulating new studies than of seeing new problems or couching old orientations in new forms.

The message is again clear. Social science is itself a performance and a cultural product. The text of the sociologist is also a part of his/her work. Here the literary theorist and the sociological analyst meet on common ground. Both need to examine texts as artful accomplishments whose style, form, and presentation affect audiences. In his essay "Literature as Equipment for Living" Burke sounds this theme of the unity of art and science as users of symbols to effect situations: "They would consider works of art . . . as strategies for selecting enemies and allies, for socializing losses, for warding off evil eye, for purification, propitiation and desanctification, consolation and vengeance, admonition and exhortation, implicit commands or instruction of one sort or another" (*The Philosophy of Literary Form,* 1957, 262).

All communication, whether Shakespeare, Dashiell Hammett, income-tax returns, deodorant ads, or *The American Sociological Review,* is both sociological and artistic. They are analyzable as documents in relation to a time, a place, an institution, an audience. They are analyzable as texts whose style and form are placed within a culture of writing and speaking, of a literary context. As performances they share with all documents a rhetorical function.

DIALECTIC

Burke's pluralism is not an abdication of intellect. It is instead a means of transforming situations and events through the knowledge and/or wisdom which awareness of the "prison-house of language" can produce. Positivist social science has fostered an engineering, Saint-Simonian ideal of an authority in social relationships akin to that of science in the physical world. Burke, as we have seen, disclaims the wisdom and infallibility of this deterministic and monist perspective. There is no "right" answer but some are better than others in being "fuller."

There runs through much of Kenneth Burke's writings the constant admonition to see from as many perspectives, with as many linguistic avenues, as is possible. Especially salient is his insistence, in his style as well as in his content, that we adopt the "comic corrective." Negation is the espoused method and irony is the message. In a section of *The Grammar of Motives* he advises his readers to merge what seems divided and divide what seems merged; to be both "lumpers" and "splitters." Where others, like C. Wright Mills, have trumpeted the value of "the sociological imagination," Burke has given it an address and a map with which to search for it.

Burke's dialectic, as he instructs us in the essay on the master tropes (see pp. 247–60), is the trope of irony—seeing something as its opposite. The thorough ironist is always the negator. He is conservative when the dominant mood is not and always on the outside, or as I put in the title of a paper, "on the side" (Gusfield 1984).

There is much in common here, I believe, between Burke and Mannheim's vision of the "free-floating" intellectual who is the commentator to the society but uncommitted to social structure, ideology, or any cultural system. As an ideal it may be unattainable, but as a working aspiration it has much merit.

What the sociologist, and the artist as well, can do is to self-consciously develop the perspectives from which alternatives become possible. The sociologist as critic without portfolio is both the utopian pathfinder and the Cassandra. In all guises he serves to warn, to expand, to cajole and to clarify. He acts to make us aware of the assumptions we take as unthinking constraints.

Burke has himself characterized his teaching as a neo-liberal ideal (*A Grammar of Motives*, 1945, 441–43). He encourages a "tolerance by speculation" (p. 442). "Linguistic skepticism," he writes, "in being quizzical, supplies the surest ground for the discernment and appreciation of linguistic resources" (p. 443).

In the scope of his thought, in the depth of his understanding and in the originality of his insight Burke has produced a corpus of work with a richness and significance that deserves a high priority for sociologists. He has challenged a major working assumption of social scientists: that the realm of art and the realm of social science are continents apart. He has shown us that intercontinental travel broadens, deepens, and leaves us not with a new way of seeing but with a new way of seeing how we see.

Bibliography to Introduction

Adams, Robert M. "Restoration." *New York Review of Books,* 20 October 1966, pp. 31–33

Aries, Phillipe. 1962. *Centuries of Childhood.* New York: Vintage Books.

Arnold, Thurman. 1935. *The Symbols of Government.* New Haven: Yale University Press.

Austin, J. L. 1975. *How to Do Things with Words.* Cambridge, MA: Harvard University Press.

Bateson, Gregory. 1972. *Steps to an Ecology of Mind.* New York: Ballantine Books.

Baumann, Zygmunt. 1976. *Socialism: The Active Utopia.* New York: Holmes and Meier.

Bendix, Reinhard, and Bennett Berger. 1959. "Images of Society and Problems of Concept Formation in Sociology." In *Symposium on Sociological Theory,* edited by L. Gross. Evanston, IL: Row, Peterson and Co.

Berger, Peter, and Thomas Luckmann. 1966. *The Social Construction of Reality.* Garden City, NY: Anchor Books, Doubleday and Sons.

Black, Donald. 1980. *The Manners and Customs of the Police.* San Diego, CA: Academic Press.

Bloor, David. 1976. *Knowledge and Social Imagery.* London: Routledge and Kegan Paul.

Booth, Wayne. 1979. *Critical Understanding: The Powers and Limits of Pluralism.* Chicago: University of Chicago Press.

Brown, Richard H. 1977. *A Poetic for Sociology.* Cambridge: Cambridge University Press.

_____. 1987. *Society as Text.* Chicago: University of Chicago Press.

Burke, Kenneth. 1945. *A Grammar of Motives.* New York: Prentice-Hall.

_____. 1950. *A Rhetoric of Motives.* New York: Prentice-Hall.

_____. [1941] 1957. *The Philosophy of Literary Form: Studies in Symbolic Action.* New York: Vintage Books.

_____. [1935] 1965. *Permanence and Change: An Anatomy of Purpose.* Indianapolis: Bobbs-Merrill.

_____. 1966. *Literature as Symbolic Action: Essays on Life, Literature and Method.* Berkeley and Los Angeles: University of California Press.

_____. [1931] 1968. *Counter-Statement.* Berkeley and Los Angeles: University of California Press.

_____. [1961] 1970. *The Rhetoric of Religion: Studies in Logology.* Berkeley and Los Angeles: University of California Press.

_____. 1977. "Bodies That Learn Language." Lecture at University of California, San Diego.

_____. [1937] 1984. *Attitudes Toward History.* Berkeley and Los Angeles: University of California Press.

Combs, James, and Michael Mansfield, eds. 1976. *Drama in Life.* New York: Hastings House.

Durkheim, Emile. [1895] 1958. *The Rules of Sociological Method.* Glencoe, IL: The Free Press. Original publication in French.

Edelman, Murray. 1964. *The Symbolic Uses of Politics.* Urbana, IL: University of Illinois Press.

_____. 1971. *Politics as Symbolic Action.* Chicago: Markham Publishing Co.

Foucault, Michel. 1977. *Discipline and Punish.* New York: Pantheon Books.

Frank, Jerome. 1949. *Courts on Trial.* Princeton, NJ: Princeton University Press.

Frye, Northrup. 1957. *Anatomy of Criticism.* Princeton, NJ: Princeton University Press.

Geertz, Clifford. 1964. "Ideology as a Cultural System." In *Ideology and Discontent,* edited by D. Apter. Glencoe, IL.: The Free Press.

_____. 1980. *Negara: The Theatre State in Nineteenth-Century Bali.* Princeton, NJ: Princeton University Press.

Giddens, Anthony. 1976. *New Rules of Sociological Method.* New York: Basic Books.

Goffman, Erving. 1952. "On Cooling the Mark Out: Some Aspects of Adaption to Failure." *Psychiatry* 15: 451–63.

_____. 1959. *The Presentation of the Self in Everyday Life.* New York: Anchor Books.

_____. 1961a. *Asylums.* Garden City, NY: Anchor Books.

_____. 1961b. *Encounters.* Indianapolis: Bobbs-Merrill.

_____. 1974. *Frame Analysis.* New York: Basic Books.

_____. 1983a. "The Interaction Order." *American Sociological Review* 48 (Feb.): 1–17.

_____. 1983b. *Forms of Talk.* Philadelphia: University of Pennsylvania Press.

Gramsci, Antonio. 1972. *The Prison Notebooks.* New York: International Publishers.

Gusfield, Joseph. 1963. *Symbolic Crusade: Status Politics and the American Temperance Movement.* Urbana: University of Illinois Press.

_____. 1975. *Communities.* New York and London: Basil Blackwell.

_____. 1976. "The Literary Rhetoric of Science." *American Sociological Review* 41 (Feb.): 16–34.

_____. 1981. *The Culture of Public Problems: Drinking-Driving and the Symbolic Order.* Chicago: University of Chicago Press.

_____. 1984. "On the Side: Practical Action and Social Constructivism in Social Problems Theory." In *Studies in the Sociology of Social Problems,* edited by J. Schneider and J. Kitsuse. Beverly Hills: Sage Publications.

———. 1986. "Science as a Form of Bureaucratic Discourse: Rhetoric and Style in Formal Organizations." In T. Bungarten, *Wissenschaftsprache und Gesellschaft*. Hamburg: Edition Akademion.

———. In press. "Two Genres of Sociology: A Literary Analysis of *The American Occupational Structure* and *Tally's Corner*." In *The Rhetoric of Social Research*, edited by A. Hunter. New Brunswick, NJ: Rutgers University Press.

Gusfield, Joseph, and Jerzy Michalowicz. 1984. "Secular Symbolism: Studies of Ritual, Ceremony and the Symbolic Order in Modern Life." *Review of Sociology* 10: 417–37. Palo Alto, CA: Annual Reviews Inc.

Hammond, Phillip, ed. 1967. *Sociologists at Work*. New York: Anchor Books, Hastings House.

Hunter, Albert. 1974. *Symbolic Communities: The Persistence and Change of Chicago's Local Communities*. Chicago: University of Chicago Press.

Hyman, Stanley. 1969. "Kenneth Burke and the Criticism of Symbolic Action." In *Critical Responses to Kenneth Burke, 1924–1966*, edited by W. Rueckert. Minneapolis: University of Minnesota Press.

Jennings, Kenneth H. 1972. "Language Acquisition: The Development and Assessment of Rational and Rationalizable Skills." Ph.D. dissertation, Department of Sociology, University of California, Santa Barbara.

Joll, James. 1978. *Antonio Gramsci*. New York: Penguin Books.

Lakoff, George, and Mark Johnson. 1980. *Metaphors We Live By*. Chicago: University of Chicago Press.

Langer, Suzanne. 1964. *Philosophical Sketches*. New York: Mentor Books.

Latour, Bruno, and Steven Woolgar. 1979. *Laboratory Life: The Social Construction of Scientific Fact*. Beverly Hills, CA: Sage Publishing.

Leach, Edmund. 1976. *Culture and Communication*. Cambridge: Cambridge University Press.

———. 1954. *The Political Systems of Highland Burma*. Boston: Beacon Press.

Lentricchia, Frank. 1982. "Reading History with Kenneth Burke." In H. White and M. Brose, *Representing Kenneth Burke*. Baltimore: Johns Hopkins Press.

———. 1983. *Criticism and Social Change*. Chicago: University of Chicago Press.

Lévi-Strauss, Claude. 1963. *Totemism*. Boston: Beacon Press.

———. 1966. *The Savage Mind*. Chicago: University of Chicago Press.

Mangham, Iain, and Michael Overington. 1987. *Organization as Theatre*. New York: John Wiley and Sons.

Manning, Peter. 1977. *Police Work*. Cambridge, MA: MIT Press.

Marx, Karl. 1932. *The German Ideology*. In *Capital, The Communist Manifesto*, and other writings. New York: The Modern Library.

McCloskey, Donald. 1985. *The Rhetoric of Economics*. Madison: University of Wisconsin Press.

McHugh, Peter. 1968. *Definition of the Situation*. Indianapolis, IN: Bobbs-Merrill.

Mead, George Herbert. 1934. *Mind, Self and Society.* Chicago: University of Chicago Press.

Mills, C. Wright. 1940. "Situated Action and Vocabularies of Motive." *American Sociological Review* 5 (Dec.): 904–13.

Parsons, Talcott. 1937. *The Structure of Social Action.* New York: The Free Press.

Perelman, Chaim, and L. Olbrechts-Tytecka. 1969. *The New Rhetoric.* Notre Dame, IN: University of Notre Dame Press.

Roeh, Itzhak. 1982. *The Rhetoric of News in the Israeli Radio.* Bochum: Studienverlag Dr. N. Brockmeyer.

Rueckert, William. 1982. "Some of the Many Kenneth Burkes." In *Representing Kenneth Burke,* edited by Hayden White and Margaret Brose. Baltimore: Johns Hopkins Press.

Sahlins, Marshall. 1976. *Culture and Practical Reason.* Chicago: University of Chicago Press.

Schutz, Alfred. 1967. *The Phenomenology of the Social World.* Evanston, IL: Northwestern University Press.

Suttles, Gerald. 1972. *1972: The Social Construction of Communities.* Chicago: University of Chicago Press.

Thomas, W. I.. 1923. *The Unadjusted Girl.* Boston: Little, Brown, & Co.

Weber, Max. 1949. *Max Weber on Methodology in the Social Sciences,* edited by Edward Shils and Henry Finch. Glencoe, IL: The Free Press.

White, Hayden. 1978. "Foucault Decoded: Notes from Underground." In *Tropics of Discourse.* Baltimore, MD: Johns Hopkins University Press.

White, James B. 1985. *The Legal Imagination.* Chicago: University of Chicago Press.

I

THE FORM OF SOCIAL ACTION

1

The Nature of Human Action

The Nature of Symbolic Action

Within the practically limitless range of scenes (or motivating situations) in terms of which human action can be defined and studied, there is one over-all dramatistic distinction as regards the widening or narrowing of circumference. This is the distinction between "action" and "sheer motion." "Action" is a term for the kind of behavior possible to a typically symbol-using animal (such as man) in contrast with the extrasymbolic or nonsymbolic operations of nature.

Whatever terministic paradoxes we may encounter en route (and the dramatistic view of terminology leads one to expect them on the grounds that language is primarily a species of action, or expression of attitudes, rather than an instrument of definition), there is the self-evident distinction between symbol and *symbolized* (in the sense that the *word* "tree" is categorically distinguishable from the *thing* tree). Whatever may be the ultimate confusions that result from man's intrinsic involvement with "symbolicity" as a necessary part of his nature, one can at least *begin* with this sufficiently clear distinction between a "thing" and its name.

The distinction is generalized in dramatism as one between "sheer motion" and "action." It involves an empirical shaft of circumference in the sense that although man's ability to speak depends upon the existence of speechless nature, the existence of speechless nature does not depend upon man's ability to speak. The relation between these two distinct terministic realms can be summed up in three propositions:

(1) There can be no action without motion—that is, even the "symbolic action" of pure thought requires corresponding motions of the brain.

From "Dramatism" by Kenneth Burke. Reprinted by permission of Macmillan Publishing Co. from the *International Encyclopedia of the Social Sciences,* edited by David L. Sills, vol. 7, pp. 447–48. © 1968 by Crowell Collier and Macmillan, Inc.

(2) There can be motion without action. (For instance, the motions of the tides, of sunlight, of growth and decay.)

(3) Action is not reducible to terms of motion. For instance, the "essence" or "meaning" of a sentence is not reducible to its sheer physical existence as sounds in the air or marks on the page, although material motions of some sort are necessary for the production, transmission, and reception of the sentence. As has been said by Talcott Parsons:

> Certainly the situation of action includes parts of what is called in common-sense terms the physical environment and the biological organism . . . these elements of the situation of action are capable of analysis in terms of the physical and biological sciences, and the phenomena in question are subject to analysis in terms of the units in use in those sciences. Thus a bridge may, with perfect truth, be said to consist of atoms of iron, a small amount of carbon, etc., and their constituent electrons, protons, neutrons and the like. Must the student of action, then, become a physicist, chemist, biologist in order to understand his subject? In a sense this is true, but for purposes of the theory of action it is not necessary or desirable to carry such analyses as far as science in general is capable of doing. A limit is set by the frame of reference with which the student of action is working. That is, he is interested in phenomena with an aspect not reducible to action terms only in so far as they impinge on the schema of action in a relevant way—in the role of conditions or means. . . . For the purposes of the theory of action the smallest conceivable concrete unit is the unit act, and while it is in turn analyzable into the elements to which reference has been made—end, means, conditions and guiding norms— further analysis of the phenomena of which these are in turn aspects is relevant to the theory of action only in so far as the units arrived at can be referred to as constituting such elements of a unit act or a system of them. (1937, 47–48)

Is Dramatism Merely Metaphorical?

Although such prototypically dramatistic usages as "all the world's a stage" are clearly metaphors, the situation looks quite otherwise when approached from another point of view. For instance, a physical scientist's relation to the materials involved in the study of motion differs in quality from his relation to his colleagues. He would never think of "petitioning" the objects of his experiment or "arguing with them," as he would with persons whom he asks to collaborate with him or to judge the results of his experiment. Implicit in these two relations is the distinction between the sheer motion of things and the actions of persons.

In this sense, man is defined literally as an animal characterized by his special aptitude for "symbolic action," which is itself a literal term. And from there on, drama is employed, not as a metaphor but as a fixed form that helps us discover what the implications of the terms "act" and "person" *really are*. Once we choose a generalized term for what people do, it is certainly as literal to say that "people act" as it is to say that they "but move like mere things."

2

The Human Actor: Definition of Man

I

First, a few words on definition in general. Let's admit it: I see in a definition the critic's equivalent of a lyric, or of an aria in opera. Also, we might note that, when used in an essay, as with Aristotle's definition of tragedy in his *Poetics,* a definition so sums things up that all the properties attributed to the thing defined can be as though "derived" from the definition. In actual development, the definition may be the last thing a writer hits upon. Or it may be formulated somewhere along the line. But logically it is prior to the observations that it summarizes. Thus, insofar as all the attributes of the thing defined fit the definition, the definition should be viewed as "prior" in this purely nontemporal sense of priority.

Definitions are also the critic's equivalent of the lyric (though a poet might not think so!) in that the writer usually "hits on them." They are "breakthroughs," and thus are somewhat hard to come by. We should always keep trying for them—but they don't always seem to "click."

A definition should have just enough clauses, and no more. However, each clause should be like a chapter head, under which appropriate observations might be assembled, as though derived from it.

I am offering my Definition of Man in the hope of either persuading the reader that it fills the bill, or of prompting him to decide what should be added, or subtracted, or in some way modified.

II

Man is the symbol-using animal.

Granted, it doesn't come as much of a surprise. But our definition is being offered not for any possible paradoxical value. The aim is to

From "Definition of Man," in *Language as Symbolic Action,* pp. 3–20. Reprinted by permission of The University of California Press. © 1966 by The Regents of the University of California.

get as essential a set of clauses as possible and to meditate on each of them.

I remember one day at college when, on entering my philosophy class, I found all blinds up and the windows open from the top, while a bird kept flying nervously about the ceiling. The windows were high, they extended almost to the ceiling; yet the bird kept trying to escape by batting against the ceiling rather than dipping down and flying out one of the open windows. While it kept circling thus helplessly over our heads, the instructor explained hat this was an example of a "tropism." This particular bird's instinct was to escape by flying *up,* he said; hence it ignored the easy exit through the windows.

But how different things would be if the bird could speak and we could speak his language. What a simple statement would have served to solve his problem. "Fly down just a foot or so and out one of those windows."

Later, I ran across another example that I cite because it has further implications with regard to a later clause in our definition. I witnessed the behavior of a wren that was unquestionably a genius within the terms of its species. The parents had succeeded in getting all of a brood off the nest except one particularly stubborn or backward fellow who still remained for a couple of days after the others had flown. Despite all kinds of threats and cajolery, he still lingered, demanding and getting the rations which all concerned seem to consider his rightful lot. Then came the moment of genius. One of the parent wrens came to the nest with a morsel of food. But instead of simply giving it to the noisy youngster, the parent bird held it at a distance. The fledgling in the nest kept stretching its neck out farther and farther with its beak gaping until, of a sudden, instead of merely putting the morsel of food into the bird's mouth, the parent wren clamped its beak shut on the young one's lower mandible, and with a slight jerk caused the youngster, with his outstretched neck, to lose balance and tumble out of the nest.

Surely this was an "act" of genius. This wren had discovered how to use the principle of leverage as a way of getting a young bird off the nest. Had that exceptionally brilliant wren been able to conceptualize this discovery in such terms as come easy to symbol systems, we can imagine him giving a dissertation on "The Use of the Principle of Leverage as an Improved Method for Unnesting Birds or Debirding a Nest." And within a few years the invention would spread throughout all birddom, with an incalculable saving in bird-hours as compared with the traditional turbulent and inefficient method still in general practice.

There are three things to note about this incident:

1. The ability to describe this method in words would have readily made it possible for all other birds to take over this same "act" of genius, though they themselves might never have hit upon it.

2. The likelihood is that even this one wren never used the method again. For the ability to conceptualize implies a kind of *attention* without which this innovation could probably not advance beyond the condition of a mere accident to the condition of an invention.

3. On the happier side, there is the thought that at least, through lack of such ability, birds are spared our many susceptibilities to the ways of demagogic spellbinders. They cannot be filled with fantastic hatreds for alien populations they know about mainly by mere hearsay, or with all sorts of unsettling new expectations, most of which could not possibly turn out as promised.

The "symbol-using animal," yes, obviously. But can we bring ourselves to realize just what that formula implies, just how overwhelmingly much of what we mean by "reality" has been built up for us through nothing but our symbol systems? Take away our books, and what little do we know about history, biography, even something so "down to earth" as the relative position of seas and continents? What is our "reality" for today (beyond the paper-thin line of our own particular lives) but all this clutter of symbols about the past combined with whatever things we know mainly through maps, magazines, newspapers, and the like about the present? In school, as they go from class to class, students turn from one idiom to another. The various courses in the curriculum are in effect but so many different terminologies. And however important to us is the tiny sliver of reality each of us has experienced firsthand, the whole overall "picture" is but a construct of our symbol systems. To meditate on this fact until one sees its full implications is much like peering over the edge of things into an ultimate abyss. And doubtless that's one reason why, though man is typically the symbol-using animal, he clings to a kind of naïve verbal realism that refuses to realize the full extent of the role played by symbolicity in his notions of reality.

In responding to words, with their overt and covert modes of persuasion ("progress" is a typical one that usually sets expectations to vibrating), we like to forget the kind of relation that really prevails between the verbal and the nonverbal. In being a link between us and the nonverbal, words are by the same token a screen separating us from the nonverbal—though the statement gets tangled in its own traces, since so much of the "we" that is separated from the nonverbal by the verbal would not even exist were it not for the verbal (or for our symbolicity in general, since the same applies to the symbol systems of dance, music, painting, and the like).

A road map that helps us easily find our way from one side of the continent to the other owes its great utility to its exceptional existential poverty. It tells us absurdly little about the trip that is to be experienced in a welter of detail. Indeed, its value for us is in the very fact that it is so essentially inane.

Language referring to the realm of the nonverbal is necessarily talk about things in terms of what they are not—and in this sense we start out beset by a paradox. Such language is but a set of labels, signs for helping us find our way about. Indeed, they can even be so useful that they help us to invent ingenious ways of threatening to destroy ourselves. But even accuracy of this powerful sort does not get around the fact that such terms are sheer emptiness, as compared with the substance of the things they name. Nor is such abstractness confined to the language of scientific prose. Despite the concrete richness of the imagery in Keats's poems, his letters repeatedly refer to his art as "abstract." And the same kind of considerations would apply to the symbol systems of all other arts. Even so bodily a form of expression as the dance is abstract in this sense. (Indeed, in this regard it is so abstract that, when asking students to sum up the gist of a plot, I usually got the best results from dance majors, with music students a close second. Students specializing in literature or the social sciences tended to get bogged down in details. They were less apt at "abstracting.")

When a bit of talking takes place, just what is doing the talking? Just where are the words coming from? Some of the motivation must derive from our animality and some from our symbolicity. We hear of "brainwashing," of schemes whereby an "ideology" is imposed upon people. But should we stop at that? Should we not also see the situation the other way around? For was not the "brainwasher" also similarly motivated? Do we simply use words, or do they not also use us? An "ideology" is like a god coming down to earth, where it will inhabit a place pervaded by its presence. An "ideology" is like a spirit taking up its abode in a body: it makes that body hop around in certain ways, and that same body would have hopped around in different ways had a different ideology happened to inhabit it.

I am saying in one way what Paul said in another when he told his listeners that "Faith comes from hearing." He had a doctrine which, if his hearers were persuaded to accept it, would direct a body somewhat differently from the way it would have moved and been moved in its daily rounds under the earlier pagan dispensation. Consider the kind of German boys and girls, for instance, who became burghers in the old days, who during the period of inflation and U.S.-financed reparation payments after World War I wanted but to be Wandering Birds and who, with the rise of the Third Reich, were got to functioning as Hitlerite fiends.

With regard to this first clause in our definition (man as the "symbol-using" animal) it has often been suggested that "symbol-making" would be a better term. I can go along with that emendation. But I'd want to add one further step. Then, for the whole formula we'd have: the "symbol-using, symbol-making, and symbol-misusing animal."

In referring to the misuse of symbols, I have in mind not only such demagogic tricks as I have already mentioned. I also think of "psychogenic illnesses," violent dislocations of bodily motion due to the improperly criticized action of symbolicity. A certain kind of food may be perfectly wholesome, so far as its sheer material nature is concerned. And people in some areas may particularly prize it. But our habits may be such that it seems to us loathsome; and under those conditions, the very thought of eating it may be nauseating to us. (The most drastic instance is, of course, provided by the ideal diets of cannibals.) When the body rebels at such thoughts, we have a clear instance of the ways whereby the realm of symbolicity may affect the sheerly biologic motions of animality. Instances of "hexing" are of the same sort (as when a tribesman, on entering his tent, finds there the sign that for some reason those in authority have decreed his death by magic, and he promptly begins to waste away and die under the burden of this sheer thought).

A merely funny example concerns an anecdote told by the anthropologist, Franz Boas. He had gone to a feast given by Esquimaux. As a good anthropologist, he would establish rapport by eating what they ate. But there was a pot full of what he took to be blubber. He dutifully took some and felt sick. He went outside the igloo to recover. There he met an Esquimau woman, who was scandalized when she heard that they were serving blubber. For they hadn't told her! She rushed in—but came out soon after in great disgust. It wasn't blubber at all, it was simply dumplings. Had the good savant only known, he could have taken dumpings in his stride. But it was a battle indeed for him to hold them down when he thought of them as blubber!

So, in defining man as the symbol-using animal, we thereby set the conditions for asking: Which motives derive from man's animality, which from his symbolicity, and which from the combination of the two? Physicality is, of course, subsumed in animality. And though the *principles* of symbolism are not reducible to sheerly physical terms (quite as the rules of football are not so reducible despite the physicality of the players' hulks and motions as such), the meanings cannot be conceived by empirical organisms except by the aid of a sheerly physical dimension.

One further point, and we shall have finished with our first clause. In his analysis of dream symbolism, Freud laid great stress upon the two processes of "condensation" and "displacement." His observations are well taken. But, since we are here using the term "symbolism" in a much wider sense, we might remind ourselves that the processes of "condensation" and "displacement" are not confined merely to the symbolism of dreams and neuroses, but are also an aspect of normal symbol-systems. A fundamental resource "natural" to symbolism is *substitution.* For instance, we can paraphrase a statement; if you don't get it one way, we can try another way. We translate English into French, Fahrenheit into Centigrade, or use the Greek letter *pi* to designate the ratio of the circumference of a circle to its diameter, otherwise stated as 3.14159. . . . In this sense, substitution is a quite rational resource of symbolism. Yet it is but a more general aspect of what Freud meant by "displacement" (which is a confused kind of substitution).

Or, as Horne Tooke pointed out a century and a half ago, a typical resource of language is abbreviation. And obviously, abbreviation is also a kind of substitution, hence a kind of "displacement," while it is also necessarily a kind of "condensation." And language is an abbreviation radically. If I refer to Mr. Jones by name, I have cut countless corners, as regards the particularities of that particular person. Of if I say, "Let's make a fire," think of what all I have left out, as regards the specific doing. Or if I give a book a title, I thereby refer to, while leaving unsaid, all that is subsumed under that title. Thus, condensation also can be viewed as a species of substitution. And a quite "rational" kind of "condensation" has taken place if, instead of referring to "tables," "chairs," and "rugs," I refer to "furniture," or if we put "parents" for "mother and father," and "siblings" for "brothers or sisters."

To say as much is to realize how many muddles such as Freud is concerned with may also be implicit in the symbols of "condensation" in his particular sense of the term. For my remarks are not intended as a "refutation" of Freud's terminology. By all means, my haggling about "condensation" and "displacement" as aspects of *all* symbolizing is not meant to question his line of investigation. All I am saying is that there still are some dividing lines to be drawn between the two realms (of symbolism in his sense and symbolism in general).

In any case, Freud (like Frazer) gives us ample grounds for trying never to forget that, once emotional involvement is added to symbolism's resources of substitution (which included the invitations to both condensation and displacement) the conditions are set for the symbol-using animal, with its ailments both physically and symbolically engendered, to tinker with such varying kinds of substitution as we encounter in men's modes of penance, expiation, compensation, paying of fines in lieu of bodily punishment, and cult of the scapegoat.

Obviously, to illustrate this point, there is an embarrassment of riches everywhere we choose to look, in the history of mankind. But, almost by accident, let us pick one, from a book, *Realm of the Incas,* by Victor W. Von Hagen. I refer to the picture of a

> propitiatory cairn, called *apacheta,* found in all of the high places of Peru on the ancient road. As heavily laden travelers passed along the road, they placed a stone on the *apacheta* as a symbol of the burden, "and so left their tiredness behind."

We are further told that "the Persians, the Chinese, and the Greeks adopted more or less the same custom."

Substitution sets the condition for "transcendence," since there is a technical sense in which the name for a thing can be said to "transcend" the thing named (by making for a kind of "ascent" from the realm of motion and matter to the realm of essence and spirit). The subterfuges of euphemism can carry this process still further, culminating in the resources of idealization that Plato perfected through his dialectic of the Upward Way and Downward Way.

The designation of man as the symbol-using animal parallels the traditional formulas, "rational animal" and *Homo sapiens*—but with one notable difference. These earlier versions are honorific, whereas the idea of symbolicity implies no such temptation to self-flattery and to this extent is more admonitory. Such definitions as "two-footed land-animal" (referred to in Aristotle's *Topics*) or "featherless biped" (referred to in Spinoza's *Ethics*) would be inadequate because they would confine the horizon to the realm of motion.

So much for our first clause.

III

The second clause is: *Inventor of the negative.* I am not wholly happy with the word, "inventor." For we could not properly say that man "invented" the negative unless we can also say that man is the "inventor" of language itself. So far as sheerly empirical development is concerned, it might be more accurate to say that language and the nega-

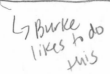
↳ Burke likes to do this

tive "invented" man. In any case, we are here concerned with the fact that there are no negatives in nature and that this ingenious addition to the universe is solely a product of human symbol systems. In an age when we are told, even in song, to "accentuate the positive," and when some experts in verbalization make big money writing inspirational works that praise "the power of positive thinking," the second clause of my definition must take on the difficult and thankless task of celebrating that peculiarly human marvel, the negative.

I have discussed elsewhere what an eye-opener the chapter, "The Idea of Nothing," was to me, in Bergson's *Creative Evolution.* It jolted me into realizing that there are no negatives in nature, where everything simply is what it is and as it is. To look for negatives in nature would be as absurd as though you were to go out hunting for the square root of minus-one. The negative is a function peculiar to symbol systems, quite as the square root of minus-one is an implication of a certain mathematical symbol system.

The quickest way to demonstrate the sheer symbolicity of the negative is to look at any object, say, a table, and to remind yourself that, though it is exactly what it is, you could go on for the rest of your life saying all the things that it is not. "It is not a book, it is not a house, it is not Times Square," etc., etc.

One of the negative's prime uses, as Bergson points out, involves its role with regard to unfulfilled expectations. If I am expecting a certain situation, and a different situation occurs, I can say that the expected situation did *not* occur. But so far as the actual state of affairs is concerned, some situation positively prevails, and that's that. If you are here but someone is expecting to meet you elsewhere, he will *not* meet you elsewhere because you positively *are* here. I can ask, "Does the thermometer read 54?" And if it registers anything in the world but 54, your proper answer can be "It is not 54." Yet there's no such thing as it's simply *not* being 54; it *is* 53, or 55, or whatever.

However, I would make one change of emphasis with regard to Bergson's fertile chapter. His stress is a bit too "Scientistic" for specifically "Dramatistic" purposes. Thus, in keeping with the stress upon matters of knowledge, he stresses the propositional negative, "It *is* not." Dramatistically, the stress should be upon the hortatory negative, "Thou *shalt* not." The negative begins not as a resource of definition or information, but as a command, as "Don't." Its more "Scientistic" potentialities develop later. And whereas Bergson is right in observing that we can't have an "idea of nothing" (that we must imagine a black spot, or something being annihilated, or an abyss, or some such), I submit that we *can* have an "idea of No," an "idea of don't."

The Existentialists may amuse themselves and bewilder us with paradoxes about *le Néant*, by the sheer linguistic trick of treating no-thing
as an abstruse kind of something. It's good showmanship. But there's
no paradox about the idea of "don't," and a child can learn its meaning early.

No, I must revise that statement somewhat. In one sense, there is a
paradox about "don't." For the negative is but a *principle*, an *idea*,
not a name for a *thing*. And thus, whereas an injunction such as "thou
shalt not kill" is understandable enough as a negative *idea*, it also has
about its edges the positive *image* of killing. But the main point is:
Though a child may not always obey the "thou shalt not," and though
there may inevitably be, in the offing, an image positively inviting disobedience, the child "gets the idea."

In this sense, though we can't have an "idea of nothing," we can
have an "idea of no." When first working on the negative, I thought
of looking through the documents on the training of Helen Keller and
Laura Bridgman, whose physical privations made it so difficult to
teach them language. And in both cases the records showed that the
hortatory negative was taught first, and it was later applied for use as
propositional negative, without explicit recognition of the change in
application.

There is a superbly relevant passage in Emerson's early long essay,
Nature, in the chapter "Discipline," a paragraph ending thus: All
things "shall hint or thunder to man the laws of right and wrong, and
echo the ten commandments." In our scheme, this could be presented
thus: "Reverse the statement, start with the principle of negation as in
the Mosaic Decalogue, and everything encountered along your way
will be negatively infused."

In other words, if our character is built of our responses (positive
or negative) to the thou-shalt-not's of morality, and if we necessarily
approach life from the standpoint of our personalities, will not all
experience reflect the genius of this negativity? Laws are essentially
negative; "mine" equals "not thine"; insofar as property is not protected by the thou-shalt-not's of either moral or civil law, it is not
protected at all.

The negative principle in morals is often hidden behind a realm of
quasi-positives. One can appreciate this situation most readily by
thinking of monastic discipline. The day may be filled with a constant
succession of positive acts. Yet they are ultimately guided or regulated
by proscriptive principles, involving acquiescence to vows consciously
and conscientiously taken, while such vows come to fulfillment formally in such admonitions as are embodied in the Decalogue. Next,

bearing in mind such clear evidence of the moralistic negativity that underlies the "quasi-positives" of the monastic rituals and routines, look at sheerly secular ambitions, with their countless ways of "justifying" oneself—and all such efforts too will be seen for what they are, not simply positives, but "quasi-positives," countless improvised ways of responding to the negativity so basic to man as moral agent.

Thus, all definitions stressing man as moral agent would tie in with this clause (if I may quote a relevant passage from a recent book of mine, *The Rhetoric of Religion*):

> *Action* involves *character*, which involves *choice—and the form* of choice attains its perfection in the distinction between Yes and No (shall and shall-not, will and will-not). Though the concept of sheer *motion* is non-ethical, *action* implies the ethical, the human personality. Hence the obvious close connection between the ethical and negativity, as indicated in the Decalogue.[1]

Is more needed on this point? We might say a few words about the role of antithesis in what are often called "polar" terms, not just Yes-No, but such similarly constructed pairs as true-false, order-disorder, cosmos-chaos, success-failure, peace-war, pleasure-pain, clean-unclean, life-death, love-hate. These are to be distinguished from sheerly positive terms. The word "table," for instance, involves no thought of counter-table, anti-table, non-table, or un-table (except perhaps in the inventions of our quite positively negative-minded poet, E. E. Cummings).

We need not now decide whether, in such paired opposites, the positive or the negative member of the pair is to be considered as essentially prior. We can settle for the indubitable fact that all *moral* terms are of this polar sort. And we can settle merely for the fact that such positives and negatives imply each other. However, in a hit-and-run sort of way, before hurrying on, I might avow that I personally would treat the negative as in principle prior, for this reason: (1) Yes and No imply each other; (2) in their role as opposites, they *limit* each other; (3) but limitation itself is the "negation of part of a divisible quantum." (I am quoting from the article on Fichte in the *Encyclopaedia Britannica*, eleventh edition.)

There is an implied sense of negativity in the ability to use words at all. For to use them properly, we must know that they are *not* the things they stand for. Next, since language is extended by metaphor which gradually becomes the kind of dead metaphor we call abstrac-

1. It suggests the thought that our second clause might be rephrased: "Moralized by the negative."

How can all this negative talk apply to empathy?

tion, we must know that metaphor is *not* literal. Further, we cannot use language maturely until we are spontaneously at home in irony. (That is, if the weather is bad, and someone says, "What a beautiful day!" we spontaneously know that he does *not* mean what the words say on their face. Children, before reaching "the age of reason," usually find this twist quite disturbing, and are likely to object that it is *not* a good day. Dramatic irony, of course, carries such a principle of negativity to its most complicated perfection.)

Our tendency to write works on such topics as "The Spirit of Christianity," or "The Soul of Islam," or "The Meaning of Judaism," or "Buddha and Eternity," or "Hinduism and Metempsychosis," leads us to overlook a strongly negativistic aspect of religions. I refer here not just to the principle of moral negativity already discussed, but also to the fact that religions are so often built *antithetically* to other persuasions. Negative motivation of this sort is attested by such steps as the formation of Christianity in opposition to paganism, the formation of Protestant offshoots in opposition to Catholicism, and the current reinvigoration of churchgoing, if not exactly of religion, in opposition to communism. So goes the dialectic!

Only one more consideration, and we are through with thoughts on this clause in our definition:

In an advertising world that is so strong on the glorification of the positive (as a way of selling either goods or bads), how make the negative enticing? At times the job has been done negatively, yet effectively, by the threat of hell. But what sanctions can we best build on now?

What a notable irony we here confront! For some of man's greatest acts of genius are in danger of transforming millions and millions of human agents into positive particles of sheer motion that go on somehow, but that are negative indeed as regards even the minimum expectations to which we might feel entitled.

And what is this new astounding irony? Precisely the fact that all these new positive powers developed by the new technology have introduced a vast new era of negativity. For they are deadly indeed, unless we make haste to develop the controls (the negatives, the thou-shalt-not's) that become necessary, if these great powers are to be kept from getting out of hand.

Somewhat ironically, even as the possibilities of ultimate man-made suicide beset us, we also face an opposite kind of positive technologic threat to the resources of our moral negativity. I refer to the current "population explosion." In earlier days, the problem was solved automatically by plagues, famines, a high rate of infant mortality, and such. But now the positive resources of technology have undone much of those natural "adjustments," so that new burdens are placed upon the Muscles of Negativity as the need arises for greater deliberate limitation of offspring.

However, ironically again, we should not end our discussion of this clause until we have reminded ourselves: There is a kind of aesthetic negativity whereby any moralistic thou-shalt-not provides material for our entertainment, as we pay to follow imaginary accounts of "deviants" who, in all sorts of ingenious ways, are represented as violating these very don'ts.

IV

Third clause: *Separated from his natural condition by instruments of his own making.* It concerns the fact that even the most primitive of tribes are led by inventions to depart somewhat from the needs of food, shelter, sex as defined by the survival standards of sheer animality. The implements of hunting and husbandry, with corresponding implements of war, make for a set of habits that become a kind of "second nature," as a special set of expectations, shaped by custom, comes to seem "natural." (I recall once when there was a breakdown of the lighting equipment in New York City. As the newspapers the next day told of the event, one got almost a sense of mystical terror from the description of the darkened streets. Yet but fifty miles away, that same evening, we had been walking on an unlit road by our house in the country, in a darkness wholly "natural." In the "second nature" of the city, something so natural as dark roadways at night was weirdly "unnatural.")

This clause is designed to take care of those who would define man as the "tool-using animal" (*homo faber, homo economicus*, and such). In adding this clause, we are immediately reminded of the close tie-up between tools and language. Imagine trying to run a modern factory, for instance, without the vast and often ungainly nomenclatures of the various technological specialties, without instructions, education, specifications, filing systems, accountancy (including mathematics and money or some similar counters). And I already referred to the likelihood that the development of tools requires a kind of attention not possible without symbolic means of conceptualization. The connection between tools and language is also observable in what we might call the "second level" aspect of both. I refer to the fact that, whereas one might think of other animals as using certain rudiments of symbolism and rudimentary tools (for instance, when an ape learns to use

tools
+
instructions

a stick as a means of raking in a banana that the experimenter has
purposely put beyond arm's length), in both cases the "reflexive" dimension is missing. Animals do not use words about words (as with
the definitions of a dictionary)—and though an ape may even learn to
put two sticks together as a way of extending his reach in case the
sticks are so made that one can be fitted into the other, he would not
take a knife and deliberately hollow out the end of one stick to make
possible the insertion of the other stick. This is what we mean by the
reflexive or second-level aspect of human symbolism. And it would
presumably apply also to such complex sign systems as bees apparently have, to spread information about the distance and direction of
a newly discovered food supply. Apparently investigators really have
"cracked" such a code in certain dancelike motions of bees—but we
should hardly expect ever to find that student bees are taught the language by teacher bees, or that there are apiaries where bees formulate
the grammar and syntax of such signaling. "Information" in the sense
of sheer motion is not thus "reflexive," but rather is like that of an
electric circuit where, if a car is on a certain stretch of track, it automatically turns off the current on the adjoining piece of track, so that
any car on that other piece of track would stop through lack of power.
The car could be said to behave in accordance with this "information."

However, in saying that the human powers of symbolicity are interwoven with the capacity for making tools (and particularly for
making tools that make tools), we still haven't answered one objection. If the two powers involve each other, if the same reflexive trait is
characteristic of both, why start with symbol-using rather than with
toolmaking? I'd propose an answer of this sort:

Formally, is not the choice implicit in the very act of definition itself? If we defined man first of all as the tool-using animal (or, old
style, as *homo faber* rather than as *homo sapiens*), our definition
would not be taking into account the "priority" of its very own nature
as a definition. Inasmuch as definition is a symbolic act, it must begin
by explicitly recognizing its formal grounding in the *principle* of definition as an act. In choosing *any definition at all*, one implicitly represents man as the kind of animal that is capable of definition (that is
to say, capable of symbolic action). Thus, even if one views the powers
of speech and mechanical invention as mutually involving each other,
in a technical or formal sense one should make the implications explicit by treating the gifts of symbolicity as the "prior" member of the
pair.

Also, we should note that one especially good result follows from this choice. Those who begin with the stress upon *tools* proceed to define language itself as a species of tool. But though instrumentality is an important aspect of language, we could not properly treat it as the *essence* of language. To define language simply as a species of tool would be like defining metals merely as species of tools. Or like defining sticks and stones simply as primitive weapons. Edward Sapir's view of language as "a collective means of expression" points in a more appropriate direction. The instrumental value of language certainly accounts for much of its development, and this instrumental value of language may even have been responsible for the survival of language itself (by helping the language-using animal to survive), quite as the instrumental value of language in developing atomic power now threatens the survival of the language-using animal; but to say as much is not by any means to say that language is in its essence a tool. Language is a species of action, symbolic action—and its nature is such that it can be used as a tool.

In any case, the toolmaking propensities envisioned in our third clause result in the complex network of material operations and properties, public or private, that arise through men's ways of livelihood, with the different *classes* of society that arise through the division of labor and the varying relationships to the property structure. And that brings us to our fourth clause.

V

Fourth clause: *Goaded by the spirit of hierarchy.* But if that sounds too weighted, we could settle for, "Moved by a sense of order." Under this clause, of course, would fall the incentives of organization and status. In my *Rhetoric of Motives,* I tried to trace the relation between social hierarchy and mystery, or guilt. And I carried such speculations further in my *Rhetoric of Religion.* Here we encounter secular analogues of "original sin." For, despite any cult of good manners and humility, to the extent that a social structure becomes differentiated, with privileges to some that are denied to others, there are the conditions for a kind of "built in" pride. King and peasant are "mysteries" to each other. Those "Up" are guilty of not being "Down," those "Down" are certainly guilty of not being "Up."

Here man's skill with symbols combines with his negativity and with the tendencies toward different modes of livelihood implicit in the inventions that make for division of labor, the result being definitions and differentiations and allocations of property protected by the negativities of the law. I particularly like E. M. Forster's novel, *A Pas-*

sage to India, for its ingenious ways of showing how social mystery can become interwoven with ideas of cosmic mystery. The grotesque fictions of Franz Kafka are marvelous in this regard. The use of the word "Lord," to designate sometimes the Deity and sometimes an aristocrat, in itself indicates the shift between the two kinds of "worship." In *Book of the Courtier* Castiglione brings out the relationship nicely when he writes of kneeling on one knee to the sovereign, on both knees to God. Or, in ancient Rome, the application of the term *pontifex maximus* to the Emperor specifically recognized his "bridging" relationship as both a god and the head of the social hierarchy. Milton's use of terms such as Cherubim, Seraphim, Thrones, Dominations, Powers, reflects the conceiving of supernatural relations after the analogy of a social ladder. The religious vision of the city on a hill is similarly infused—making in all a ziggurat-like structure without skyscrapers. (Recall a related image, El Greco's painting of Toledo.) And, of course, the principles of such hierarchical order are worked out with imaginative and intellectual fullness in Dante's *Divine Comedy.* The medieval pageant probably represents the perfection of this design. All the various "mysteries" were represented, each distinct from all the others, yet all parts of the same overarching order.

VI

By now we should also have taken care of such definitions as man the "political animal" or the "culture-bearing animal." And for a while, I felt that these clauses sufficiently covered the ground. However, for reasons yet to be explained, I decided that a final codicil was still needed, thus making in all:

> Man is
> the symbol-using (symbol-making, symbol-misusing) animal
> inventor of the negative (or moralized by the negative)
> separated from his natural condition by instruments of his own making
> goaded by the spirit of hierarchy (or moved by the sense of order)
> and rotten with perfection.

I must hurry to explain and justify this wry codicil.

The principle of perfection is central to the nature of language as motive. The mere desire to name something by its "proper" name, or to speak a language in its distinctive ways is intrinsically "perfectionist." What is more "perfectionist" in essence than the impulse, when one is in dire need of something, to so state this need that one in effect "defines" the situation? And even a poet who works out cunning ways of distorting language does so with perfectionist principles in mind, though his ideas of improvement involve recondite stylistic twists that may not disclose their true nature as judged by less perverse tests.

Thoughts on this subject induce us to attempt adapting, for sheerly logological purposes, the Aristotelian concept of the "entelechy," the notion that each being aims at the perfection natural to its kind (or, etymologically, is marked by a "possession of telos within"). The stone would be all that is needed to make it a stone; the tree would be all that is needed to make it a tree; and man would (or should!) be all that is needed to make him the perfectly "rational" being (presumably a harder entelechial job to accomplish than lower kinds of entities confront). Our point is: Whereas Aristotle seems to have thought of all beings in terms of the entelechy (in keeping with the ambiguities of his term, *kinesis,* which includes something of both "action" and "motion"), we are confining our use of the principle to the ream of symbolic action. And in keeping with this view, we would state merely: There is a principle of perfection implicit in the nature of symbol systems; and in keeping with his nature as symbol-using animal, man is moved by this principle.

At this point we must pause to answer an objection. In *Beyond the Pleasure Principle* (near the end of chapter five) Freud explicitly calls upon us "to abandon our belief that in man there dwells an impulse towards perfection, which has brought him to his present heights of intellectual prowess and sublimation." Yet a few sentences later in that same closing paragraph, we find him saying, "The repressive instinct never ceases to strive after its complete satisfaction." But are not these two sentences mutually contradictory? For what could more clearly represent an "impulse to perfection" than a "striving" after "complete satisfaction"?

The alternative that Freud proposes to the striving after perfection is what he calls a "repetition compulsion." And near the end of chapter three he has described it thus:

> One knows people with whom every human relationship ends in the same way: benefactors whose protégés, however different they may otherwise have been, invariably after a time desert them in ill-will, so that they are apparently condemned to drain to the dregs all the bitterness of ingratitude; men with whom every friendship ends in the friend's treachery; others who indefinitely often in their lives invest some other person with authority either in their own eyes or generally, and themselves overthrow such authority after a given time, only to replace it by a new one; lovers whose tender relationships with women each and all run through the same phases and come to the same end, and so on. We are less astonished at this

I get the sense that Burke has a pessimistic view of human nature.

"endless repetition of the same" if there is involved a question of active behavior on the part of the person concerned, and if we detect in his character an unalterable trait which must always manifest itself in the repetition of identical experiences. Far more striking are those cases where the person seems to be experiencing something passively, without exerting any influence of his own, and yet always meets with the same fate over and over again.

Freud next mentions in Tasso's *Gerusalemme Liberata* the story of the hero Tancred who, having unwittingly slain his beloved Clorinda, later in an enchanted wood hews down a tall tree with his sword, and when blood streams from the gash in the tree, he hears the voice of Clorinda whose soul was imprisoned in the tree, and who reproaches him for having again "wrought" the same "baleful deed."

Freud sees in all such instances the workings of what he calls the neurotic attempt to so shape one's later life that some earlier unresolved problem is lived over and over again. Freud also calls it a "destiny compulsion," to bring out the thought that the sufferer unconsciously strives to form his destiny in accordance with this earlier pattern.

My point is: Why should such a "destiny compulsion" or "repetition compulsion" be viewed as antithetical to the "principle of perfection"? Is not the sufferer exerting almost superhuman efforts in the attempt to give his life a certain *form*, so shaping his relations to people in later years that they will conform perfectly to an emotional or psychological pattern already established in some earlier formative situation? What more thorough illustrations could one want, of a drive to make one's life "perfect," despite the fact that such efforts at perfection might cause the unconscious striver great suffering?

To get the point we need simply widen the concept of perfection to the point where we can also use the term *ironically*, as when we speak of a "perfect fool" or a "perfect villain." And, of course, I had precisely such possibilities in mind when in my codicil I refer to man as being "rotten" with perfection.

The ironic aspect of the principle is itself revealed most perfectly in our tendency to conceive of a "perfect" enemy. (See " 'Perfection' as a Motive," in *Permanence and Change*, Hermes edition, 292–94.) The Nazi version of the Jew, as developed in Hitler's *Mein Kampf*, is the most thoroughgoing instance of such ironic "perfection" in recent times, though strongly similar trends keep manifesting themselves in current controversies between "East" and "West." I suppose the most "perfect" definition of man along these lines is the formula derived from Plautus: *homo homini lupus*, or one to suit the sort of imaginary herding animal that would fit Hobbes's notion of the *bellum omnium contra omnes.*

The principle of perfection in this dangerous sense derives sustenance from other primary aspects of symbolicity. Thus, the principle of drama is implicit in the idea of action, and the principle of victimage is implicit in the nature of drama. The negative helps radically to define the elements to be victimized. And inasmuch as substitution is a prime resource of symbol systems, the conditions are set for catharsis by scapegoat (including the "natural" invitation to "project" upon the enemy any troublesome traits of our own that we would negate). And the unresolved problems of "pride" that are intrinsic to privilege also bring the motive of hierarchy to bear here; for many kinds of guilt, resentment, and fear tend to cluster about the hierarchal psychosis, with its corresponding search for a sacrificial principle such as can become embodied in a political scapegoat.

Similar ominous invitations along these lines derive from the terministic fact that, as Aristotle observes in his *Rhetoric,* antithesis is an exceptionally effective rhetorical device. There is its sheerly *formal* lure, in giving dramatic saliency and at least apparent clarity to any issue. One may find himself hard put to define a policy purely in its own terms, but one can advocate it persuasively by an urgent assurance that it is decidedly *against* such-and-such other policy with which people may be disgruntled. For this reason also, the use of antithesis helps deflect embarrassing criticism (as when rulers silence domestic controversy by turning public attention to animosity against some foreign country's policies). And in this way, of course, antithesis helps reinforce unification by scapegoat.

The principle of perfection (the "entelechial" principle) figures in other notable ways as regards the genius of symbolism. A given terminology contains various *implications,* and there is a corresponding "perfectionist" tendency for men to attempt carrying out those implications. Thus, each of our scientific nomenclatures suggests its own special range of possible developments, with specialists vowed to carry out these terministic possibilities to the extent of their personal ability and technical resources. Each such specialty is like the situation of an author who has an idea for a novel, and who will never rest until he has completely embodied it in a book. Insofar as any of these terminologies happen also to contain the risks of destroying the world, that's just too bad; but the fact remains that, so far as the sheer principles of the investigation are concerned, they are no different from those of the writer who strives to complete his novel. There is a kind of "terministic compulsion" to carry out the implications of one's terminology, quite as, if an astronomer discovered by his observations and computations that a certain wandering body was likely to hit the earth and destroy us, he would nonetheless feel compelled to *argue for the correctness of his computations,* despite the ominousness of the outcome. Similarly, of course, men will so draw out the implications of their terminologies that new expectations are aroused (promises that are now largely interwoven with the state of Big Technology, and that may prove to be true or false, but that can have revolutionary effects upon persons who agree with such terministic "extrapolations").

Whereas there seems to be no principle of control intrinsic to the ideal of carrying out any such set of possibilities to its "perfect" conclusion, and whereas all sorts of people are variously goaded to track down their particular sets of terministically directed insights, there is at least the fact that the schemes get in one another's way, thus being to some extent checked by rivalry with one another. And such is especially the case where *allocation of funds* is concerned.

To round out the subject of "perfection," in both honorific and ironic senses, we might end by observing that, without regard for the ontological truth or falsity of the case, there are sheerly technical reasons, intrinsic to the nature of language, for belief in God and the Devil. Insofar as language is intrinsically hortatory (a medium by which men can obtain the cooperation of one another), God perfectly embodies the petition. Similarly, insofar as vituperation is a "natural" resource of speech, the Devil provides a perfect butt for invective. Heaven and Hell together provide the ultimate, or perfect, grounding for sanctions. God is also the perfect audience for praise and lamentation (two primary modes of symbolic action, with lamentation perhaps the "first" of all, as regards tests of biological priority). Such considerations would provide a strictly logological treatment of Martin Buber's "I-Thou Relation."

II

LANGUAGE AS SYMBOLIC ACTION

3

Symbolic Action

Situations and Strategies

Let us suppose that I ask you: "What did the man say?" And that you answer: "He said 'yes.'" You still do not know what the man said. You would not know unless you knew more about the situation and about the remarks that preceded his answer.

Critical and imaginative works are answers to questions posed by the situation in which they arose. They are not merely answers, they are *strategic* answers, *stylized* answers. For there is a difference in style or strategy, if one says "yes" in tonalities that imply "thank God" or in tonalities that imply "alas!" So I should propose an initial working distinction between "strategies" and "situations," whereby we think of poetry (I here use the term to include any work of critical or imaginative cast) as the adopting of various strategies for the encompassing of situations. These strategies size up the situations, name their structure and outstanding ingredients, and name them in a way that contains an attitude toward them.

This point of view does not, by any means, vow us to personal or historical subjectivism. The situations are real; the strategies for handling them have public content; and insofar as situations overlap from individual to individual, or from one historical period to another, the strategies possess universal relevance.

Situations do overlap, if only because men now have the same neural and muscular structure as men who have left their records from past ages. We and they are in much the same biological situation. Furthermore, even the concrete details of social texture have a great measure of overlap. And the nature of the human mind itself, with the function of abstraction rooted in the nature of language, also provides us with "levels of generalization" (to employ Korzybski's term) by which situations greatly different in their particularities may be felt to belong in the same class (to have a common substance or essence).

From *The Philosophy of Literary Form,* third revised edition, pp. 1–3, 8–18. Reprinted by permission of The University of California Press. ©1973 by The Regents of the University of California.

Consider a proverb, for instance. Think of the endless variety of situations, distinct in their particularities, which this proverb may "size up," or attitudinally name. To examine one of my favorites: "Whether the pitcher strikes the stone, or the stone the pitcher, it's bad for the pitcher." Think of some primitive society in which an incipient philosopher, in disfavor with the priests, attempted to criticize their lore. They are powerful, he is by comparison weak. And they control all the channels of power. Hence, whether they attack him or he attacks them, he is the loser. And he could quite adequately size up this situation by saying, "Whether the pitcher strikes the stone, or the stone the pitcher, it's bad for the pitcher." Or Aristophanes could well have used it, in describing his motivation when, under the threats of political dictatorship, he gave up the lampooning of political figures and used the harmless Socrates as his goat instead. Socrates was propounding new values—and Aristophanes, by aligning himself with conservative values, against the materially powerless dialectician, could himself take on the rôle of the stone in the stone-pitcher ratio. Or the proverb could be employed to name the predicament of a man in Hitler's Germany who might come forward with an argument, however well reasoned, against Hitler. Or a local clerk would find the proverb apt, if he would make public sport of his boss. These situations are all distinct in their particularities; each occurs in a totally different texture of history; yet all are classifiable together under the generalizing head of the same proverb.

Might we think of poetry as complex variants and recombinations of such material as we find in proverbs? There are situations typical and recurrent enough for men to feel the need of having a name for them. In sophisticated work, this naming is done with great complexity. Think of how much modern psychology, for instance, might be placed as a highly alembicated way of *seeing through to the end* the formulation now become proverbial: "The wish is father to the thought." Or think of how much in the Hegelian dialectic might be summed up, as an overall title, in the idealist Coleridge's favorite proverb, "Extremes meet." And in all work, as in proverbs, the naming is done "strategically" or "stylistically" in modes that embody attitudes of resignation, solace, vengeance, expectancy, etc.

Symbolic Action

We might sum all this up by saying that poetry, or any verbal act, is to be considered as "symbolic action." But though I must use this term, I object strenuously to having the general perspective labeled as "symbolism." I recognize that people like to label, that labeling *comforts* them by *getting things placed*. But I object to "symbolism" as a label, because it suggests too close a link with a particular school of poetry, the Symbolist Movement, and usually implies the unreality of the world in which we live, as though nothing could be what it is, but must always be something else (as though a house could never be a house, but must be, let us say, the concealed surrogate for a woman, or as though the woman one marries could never be the woman one marries, but must be a surrogate for one's mother, etc.).

Still, there is a difference, and a radical difference, between building a house and writing a poem about building a house—and a poem about having children by marriage is not the same thing as having children by marriage. There are *practical* acts, and there are symbolic acts (nor is the distinction, clear enough in its extremes, to be dropped simply because there is a borderline area wherein many practical acts take on a symbolic ingredient, as one may buy a certain commodity not merely to use it, but also because its possession testifies to his enrollment in a certain stratum of society).

The symbolic act is the *dancing of an attitude* (a point that Richards has brought out, though I should want to revise his position to the extent of noting that in Richards' doctrines the attitude is pictured as too sparse in realistic content). In this attitudinizing of the poem, the whole body may finally become involved, in ways suggested by the doctrines of behaviorism. The correlation between mind and body here is neatly conveyed in two remarks by Hazlitt, concerning Coleridge:

> I observed that he continually crossed me on the way by shifting from one side of the foot-path to the other. This struck me as an odd movement; but I did not at that time connect it with any instability of purpose or involuntary change of principle, as I have done since. . . .
>
> There is a *chaunt* in the recitation both of Coleridge and Wordsworth, which acts as a spell upon the hearer, and disarms the judgment. Perhaps they have deceived themselves by making habitual use of this ambiguous accompaniment. Coleridge's manner is more full, animated, and varied; Wordsworth's more equable, sustained, and internal. The one might be termed more *dramatic,* the other more *lyrical.* Coleridge has told me that he himself liked to compose in walking over uneven ground, or breaking through the straggling branches of a copse-wood; whereas Wordsworth always wrote (if he could) walking up and down a straight gravel-walk, or in some spot where the continuity of his verse met with no collateral interruption.[1]

1. The quotations are lifted from Lawrence Hanson's excellent study, *The Life of S. T. Coleridge.*

We might also cite from a letter of Hopkins, mentioned by R. P. Blackmur in *The Kenyon Review* (Winter, 1939):

> As there is something of the "old Adam" in all but the holiest men and in them at least enough to make them understand it in others, so there is an old Adam of barbarism, boyishness, wildness, rawness, rankness, the disreputable, the unrefined in the refined and educated. It is that that I meant by tykishness (a tyke is a stray sly unowned dog).

Do we not glimpse the labyrinthine mind of Coleridge, the *puzzle* in its pace, "danced" in the act of walking—and do we not glimpse behind the agitated rhythm of Hopkins' verse, the conflict between the priest and the "tyke," with the jerkiness of his lines "symbolically enacting" the mental conflict? So we today seem to immunize ourselves to the arrhythmic quality of both traffic and accountancy by a distrust of the lullaby and the rocking cradle as formative stylistic equipment for our children.

The accumulating lore on the nature of "psychogenic illnesses" has revealed that something so "practical" as a bodily ailment may be a "symbolic" act on the part of the body which, in this materialization, *dances* a corresponding state of mind, reordering the glandular and neural behavior of the organism in obedience to mind-body correspondences, quite as the formal dancer reorders his externally observable gesturing to match his attitudes. Thus, I know of a man who, going to a dentist, was proud of the calmness with which he took his punishment. But after the session was ended, the dentist said to him: "I observe that you are very much afraid of me. For I have noted that, when patients are frightened, their saliva becomes thicker, more sticky. And yours was exceptionally so." Which would indicate that, while the man in the dentist's chair was "dancing an attitude of calmness" on the public level, as a social façade, on the purely bodily or biological level his salivary glands were "dancing his true attitude." For he *was* apprehensive of pain, and his glandular secretions "said so." Similarly I have read that there is an especially high incidence of stomach ulcers among taxi drivers—an occupational illness that would not seem to be accounted for merely by poor and irregular meals, since these are equally the lot of workers at other kinds of jobs. Do we not see, rather, a bodily response to the intensely arrhythmic quality of the work itself, the irritation in the continual jagginess of traffic, all puzzle and no pace, and only the timing of the cylinders performing with regularity, as if all the *ritual* of the occupational act had been drained off, into the *routine* of the motor's explosions and revolutions?

In such ways, the whole body is involved in an enactment. And we might make up a hypothetical illustration of this sort: imagine a poet who, on perfectly rational grounds rejecting the political and social authority of the powers that be, wrote poems enacting this attitude of rejection. This position we might call his symbolic act on the abstract level. On the personal, or intimate level, he might embody the same attitude in a vindictive style (as so much of modern work, proud of its emancipation from prayer, has got this emancipation dubiously, by simply substituting prayer-in-reverse, the oath). And on the biological level, this same attitude might be enacted in the imagery of excretion, as with the scene of vomiting with which Farrell ends the second volume of his Studs Lonigan trilogy.

Sir Richard Paget's theory of gesture speech gives us inklings of the way in which such enactment might involve even the selection of words themselves on a basis of tonality. According to Paget's theory, language arose in this wise: If a man is firmly gripping something, the muscles of his tongue and throat adopt a position in conformity with the muscles with which he performs the act of gripping. He does not merely grip with his hands; he "grips all over." Thus, in conformity with the act of gripping, he would simultaneously grip with his mouth, by closing his lips firmly. If, now, he uttered a sound with his lips in this position, the only sound he could utter would be *m*. M therefore is the sound you get when you "give voice" to the posture of gripping. Hence, *m* would be the proper tonality corresponding to the act of gripping, as in contact words like "maul," "mix," "mammae," and "slam." The relation between sound and sense here would not be an onomatopoetic one, as with a word like "sizzle," but it would rather be like that between the visual designs on a sound track and the auditory vibrations that arise when the instrument has "given voice" to these designs (except that, in the case of human speech, the designs would be those of the tongue and throat, plastic rather than graphic).

The great resistance to Paget's theory doubtless arises in large part from the conservatism of philological specialists. They have an investment in other theories—and only the most pliant among them are likely to see around the corner of their received ideas (Paget cites remarks by Jespersen that hit about the edges of his theory). But some of the resistance, I think, also arises from an error in Paget's strategy of presentation. He offers his theory as a *philological* one, whereas it should be offered as a contribution to *poetics*. Philology, because of its involvement in historicism, really deals with *the ways in which, if*

*Paget's theory were 100 percent correct, such linguistic mimesis as he
is discussing would become obscured by historical accretions.*

Let us suppose, for instance, that *f* is an excellent linguistic gesture
for the *p* sound prolonged, and the lips take the posture of *p* in the act
of s*p*itting—hence, the *p* is preserved in the word itself, in "spittle"
and "puke," and in words of re*p*ulsion and re*p*ugnance. The close
phonetic relation between *p* and *f* is observed in the German exclamation of repugnance, "*pfui*." Mencken, in *The American Language,*
cites two synthetic words by Winchell that perfectly exemplify this
faugh-*f*: "phfft" and "foofff." These are "nonsense syllables" Winchell
has invented to convey, by tonality alone, the idea that is denoted in
our word "*pest*." Here, since the inventor has complete freedom, there
are no historical accidents of language to complicate his mimesis, so
he can symbolically spit long and hard.

Imagine, however, a new movement arising in history—and, as is
so often the case with new movements, imagine that it is named by
the enemy (as "liberalism" was named by the Jesuits, to convey connotations of "licentiousness," in contrast with "*servile*," to convey
connotations of "loyal"). If we hypothetically grant the existence of a
faugh-*f*, we should discover that the enemy danced the attitude toward
this new movement with perfect accuracy in naming the new movement "phfftism" or "fooffism." However, as so often happens in history, the advocates of "fooffism" accepted the term, and set out to
"live it down" (as with "liberalism"—and also "nihilism," which was
named by the enemy, but in the late nineteenth century recruited ni-
hilistic *heroes*). And let us finally imagine, as so often happens in history, that the new movement, beginning in great disrepute, finally
triumphs and becomes the norm. Though the attitude toward the
name is now changed, the name itself may be retained, and so we may
find earnest fellows saying, "I hereby solemnly swear allegiance to the
flag of fooffism."

Now, philology would deal with these historical developments
whereby the originally accurate mimesis became *obscured*—and it is
in this sense that, to my way of thinking, Paget's theory should be
presented as a contribution not to philology, but to poetics. The greatest attempt at a *poetics* of sound is Dante's *De Vulgari Eloquio,* which
is equally concerned with a *rational selection* of a poetic language, its
systematic isolation from a common speech that had developed by the
hazards of historical accretion. And Paget's theory should, I contend,
be viewed as a corresponding enterprise, except that now, given the
change of reference from Dante's day to ours, the theory is grounded
on a *biological* or *naturalistic* base.

A possible way whereby these theories might be empirically tested is this: We should begin by asking whether our system of phonetic recording might be inaccurate. Might there, for instance, be at least *two* sounds of *f,* whereas both were recorded in writing as the same sound (as in French three different sounds of *e* are explicitly indicated, whereas the English ways of recording *e* do not indicate such differences)? Why, in the light of such evidence, should we assume that there is but one *f* simply because our mode of recording this sound indicates but one? Might there, let us say, be a faugh-*f* and a flower-*f* (with the second trying to bring out the smoothness of *f,* as were one to recite sympathetically Coleridge's line, "Flowers are lovely, love is flower-like," and the other trying to stress its expulsive quality, as when I once heard a reactionary orator, spewing forth a spray of spittle, fulminate against "fiery, frenzied fanatics")? I do not know how accurate the electric recordings of a sound track are, or how close a microscopic analysis of them could be: but if these recordings are accurate enough, and if microscopic analysis can be refined to the point of discriminating very minute differences in the design of the sound track, one could select flower-passages and faugh-passages, have them recited by a skilled actor (without telling him of the theory), take an electric recording of his recitation, and then examine the sound track for *quantitative* evidence (in the design of the sound track) of a distinction in *f* not indicated by our present conventions of writing. We might perhaps more accurately use *two* symbols, thus: *f'* and *f''*. *It should be noted, however, that such a difference would not be absolute and constant.* That is, one might pronounce a word like "of" differently if it appeared expressively in a "flower" context than if it appeared in a "faugh" context. Which would again take us out of philology into poetics.

Similarly, inasmuch as *b* is midway between mammal *m* and the repulsion *p,* we might expect it to have an *m*-like sound on some occasions and a *p*-like sound on others. Thus, in the lines

O blasphemy! to mingle fiendish deeds
With blessedness!

we could expect "*b*lasphemy" to approximate "*p*lasphemy," and "*b*lessedness" to be more like "*m*lessedness," the explosive possibilities of *b* being purposely coached in the first case and tempered in the second. (Incidentally, no words are more like home to an idealist philosopher than "subject" and "object"—and we are told that when Coleridge had fallen into one of his famous monologues, he pronounced them "sumject" and "omject.")

Our gradual change of emphasis from the spoken to the documentary (with many symbols of mathematics and logic having no tonal associations whatsoever, being hardly other than designs) has made increasingly for a purely ocular style—so that children now are sometimes even trained to read wholly by eye. And there are indeed many essayistic styles that profit greatly if one can master the art of reading them without hearing them at all. For they are as arrhythmic as traffic itself, and can even give one a palpitation of the heart if he still reads with an encumbrance of auditory imagery, and so accommodates his bodily responses to their total tonal aimlessness. But whatever may be the value of such styles, for bookkeeping purposes, they have wandered far afield from the gesturing of heard poetic speech. Paradoxically, their greatest accuracy, from the standpoint of mimesis, is in their *very absence* of such, for by this absence they conform with our sedentary trend from the bodily to the abstract (our secular variant of the spiritual). It is the style of men and women whose occupations have become dissociated from the bodily level and whose expression accordingly does not arise from a physical act as the rhythms of a Negro work song arise from the rhythms of Negroes at work.

In any event, as regards the correlation between mind and body, we may note for future application in this essay, that the poet will naturally tend to write about that which most deeply engrosses him—and nothing more deeply engrosses a man than his *burdens,* including those of a physical nature, such as disease. We win by capitalizing on our debts, by turning our liabilities into assets, by using our burdens as a basis of insight. And so the poet may come to have a "vested interest" in his handicaps; these handicaps may become an integral part of his method; and insofar as his style grows out of a disease, his loyalty to it may reinforce the disease. It is a matter that Thomas Mann has often been concerned with. And it bears again upon the subject of "symbolic action," with the poet's burdens symbolic of his style, and his style symbolic of his burdens. I think we should not be far wrong if, seeking the area where states of mind are best available to empirical observation, we sought for correlations between styles and physical disease (particularly since there is no discomfiture, however mental in origin, that does not have its physiological correlates). So we might look for "dropsical" styles (Chesterton), "asthmatic" (Proust), "phthisic" (Mann), "apoplectic" (Flaubert), "blind" (Milton), etc. The one great objection to such a nosological mode of classification is that it leads to a Max Nordau mode of equating genius with degeneracy. This is not the case, however, if one properly dis-

counts his terminology, reminding himself that the true locus of assertion is not in the *disease,* but in the *structural powers* by which the
poet encompasses it. The disease, seen from this point of view, is
hardly more than the *caricature* of the man, the oversimplification of
his act—hence, most easily observable because it is an oversimplification. This oversimplifying indicator is deceptive unless its obvious-
ness as a caricature is discounted.

4

Types of Meaning: Semantic and Poetic Meaning

This eassy may be taken as a rhetorical defense of rhetoric. It is intended to give support, sometimes directly and sometimes indirectly, to the thesis that the ideal of a purely "neutral" vocabulary, free of emotional weightings, attempts to make a totality out of a fragment, "till that which suits a part infects the whole."

The historian Toynbee, I am told, has laid stress upon the period of "withdrawal" undergone by founders of religious structures. It is a period of hesitancy, brooding, or even rot, prior to the formation of the new certainties they will subsequently evangelize and organize. Stated in secular terms, it marks a transition from a system of social values grown unfit for the situation they would encompass, to a new order of values felt, correctly or not, to be a more scrupulous fit for the situation. "Circumstances alter occasions," and for the altered occasions they would round out a new strategy.

In the semantic ideal, we get an attenuated variant of this "withdrawal" process. It would build up a technical mode of analysis that gave us permanently and constantly a kind of mitigated withdrawal, thereby converting a transitional stage into an institution. Like the monastic orders, it would "bureaucratize" a purgatorial mood, turning a "state of evanescence" into a fixity by giving it an established routine. It would prolong a moment into a "way of life."

While attempting to uphold the thesis that there is no basic opposition between the ideals of semantic and poetic naming, that they are different rather than antithetical in their ultimate realistic aims, I do grant that there is a "dialectical process" whereby a difference becomes converted into an antithesis. You have, for example, noted that when two opponents have been arguing, though the initial difference in their position may have been slight, they tend under the "dialectical

From "Semantic and Poetic Meaning," in *The Philosophy of Literary Form*, third revised edition, pp. 138–67. Reprinted by permission of The University of California Press. ©1973 by The Regents of the University of California.

pressure" of their drama to become eventually at odds in everything. No matter what one of them happens to assert, the other (responding to the genius of the contest) takes violent exception to it—and vice versa. Thus similarly we find the *differences* between "bourgeois" and "proletarian" treated, under dialectical pressure, as an *absolute antithesis*, until critics, accustomed to thinking by this pat schematization, become almost demoralized at the suggestion that there may be a "margin of overlap" held in common between different classes. And if a man has at one time been engrossed in music, and at a later time becomes engrossed in painting, he will probably evolve an emotional economy whereby music and painting become for him the *opposite* of each other (as in Odets' *Golden Boy* violin and prizefight are filled out as antitheses, the violin signifying home and harmony, the prizefight leaving-home and competition). And likewise with the semantics-poetry issue, where semantic meaning, that may be considered as a partial aspect of poetic meaning, tends to become instead the *opposite* of poetic meaning, so that a mere graded series, comprising a more-than and a less-than, changes instead into a blunt battle between poetry and antipoetry, or "poetry vs. science." Only by a kind of "synecdochic fallacy," mistaking a part for the whole, can this opposition appear to exist.

The Semantic Ideal Illustrated

For our point of departure, let us take the address on an envelope:

M..........	(name)
....	(street and number)
....	(city or town)
....	(state)
....	(nation)

By filling out those few lines, you can effectively isolate one man among two billion, quite as though each individual were identified by an automobile license, with a record kept in some central bureau, like the Bertillon measurements of known criminals.

Perhaps we have exaggerated the case. The formula wouldn't work for getting an advertisement to a mid-African chieftain. Yet it can effectively isolate one of the two billion, if he happens to be among the hundreds of millions available through postal organization. The matter to be emphasized is this: In whatever areas the postal organization prevails, this brief formula generally serves to isolate the desired individual.

The formula has no orientative value in itself. It depends for its significance upon the establishment of a postal structure, as a going concern. It is like the coin in a slot machine. Given the machine, in good order, the coin will "work." The address, as a counter, works insofar as it indicates to the postal authorities what kind of operation should be undertaken. But it *assumes* an organization. Its *meaning*, then, involves the established procedures of the mails and is in the instructions it gives for the performance of desired operations within this going concern.

The man who writes the address on an envelope may know very little about the concreteness of these operations. Likewise, the sorter who first tosses the letter into the "state" or "nation" bin will not correctly envision the act of final delivery, after the letter has been sifted down through various subclassifications, until it reaches the pouch of the mailman on his route. Any single worker, handling the letter in its various stages of transit, interprets the address as instructions for a different kind of operation. Its "totality" is in the organized interlocking of these operations themselves, whereby each "specialist," performing a "partial" act, yet contributes to the performing of a "total" act, the entire arc of the letter's transit, from insertion in the mailbox at the corner to delivery at the door.

This kind of meaning I should call a *semantic* meaning. And extending from that I should state, as the semantic ideal, the aim *to evolve a vocabulary that gives the name and address of every event in the universe.*

Such naming would require the kind of "operational" test put forward in Bridgman's theory of meaning, which has recently been overzealously advocated by Stuart Chase in his *The Tyranny of Words.*[1] It is also, I think, the ideal of the logical positivists. Logical positivism would *point* to events. It would attempt to describe events after the analogy of the chart (as a map could be said to describe America). And the significance of its pointing lies in the instructions implicit in the name.

An ideal semantic definition of a chair would be such that, on the

---

1. However, Chase's book is so much closer to scissor-work than to composition that no characterization by a summarizing proposition is wholly adequate. We might, rather, classify the work by reference to its manner, thus: "A rhetorical farewell to rhetoric—or, the tyrannicide as tyrant." And we might attempt quickly to convey the quality of his "revolt" against words (done in the extreme debunking mode) by noting such chapter headings as "Promenade with the Philosophers," "Swing Your Partners with the Economists," and "Round and Round with the Judges."

basis of the definition, people knew what you wanted when you asked for one, a carpenter knew how to make it, a furniture dealer knew how to get it, etc. An ideal definition of an electron is such that the specialist knows what to do (within the limits of his technique and equipment) to bring about the kind of manifestation called an electron.

On the other hand, when you have isolated your individual by the proper utilizing of the postal process, you have not at all adequately encompassed his "meaning." He means one thing to his family, another to his boss, another to his underlings, another to his creditors, etc. All such meanings are *real* enough, since at every point people act toward him on the basis of these meanings. And at many points they impinge upon purely semantic meanings. His meaning for his creditors, for instance, may be involved in a credit report from Dun and Bradstreet's. His meaning to his underlings may lead them to adopt certain proportions of familiarity and aloofness. His wife may have found out that, as the case may be, she can get him to buy a new refrigerator either by saying that the Joneses already have one or that the Joneses do not have one. His boss may have decided that he is especially good at certain kinds of business, and especially poor at certain other kinds of business. And much of this can actually be "tested," though in a less organized way than would apply to the instructions for the filling of a medical prescription.

But though this kind of meaning *impinges* upon semantic meaning, it cannot be encompassed with perfect fidelity to the *semantic ideal*. You can't give the names and addresses of all these subtle significances. There is no organization like the postal service or the laboratory or the factory, with a set of patly interlocking functions. This kind of meaning I shall call *poetic* meaning.

Seen from this angle, poetic meaning and semantic meaning would not be absolute antitheses. Poetic meaning would not be the *opposite* of semantic meaning. It would be different from, or other than, or more than, or even, if you want, less than, but not antithetical to.

Poetic Meaning

Semantic meaning would be a way of pointing to a chair. It would say, "That thing is a chair." And to a carpenter it would imply, in keeping with his organized technique, "By doing such and such, I can produce this thing, a chair." Poetic pointing, on the other hand, might take many courses, roughly summed up in these three sentences:

"Faugh! a chair!"
"Ho, ho! a chair!"
"Might I call your attention to yon chair?"

Of these, the third style of pointing obviously comes nearest to the
semantic ideal. The first two, most strongly weighted with emotional
values, with *attitudes*, would be farther off. *Meaning* there would unquestionably be, since an attitude contains an implicit program of action. An attitude may be reasonable or unreasonable; it may contain
an adequate meaning or an inadequate meaning—but in either case,
it would contain a meaning.

   In aesthetics, you find the word "art" used indeterminately in two
ways. Sometimes the thinker appears to mean "art, any art, all art,"
and at other times, "good art." And similarly, in theories of meaning,
the concept sometimes seems to imply "any meaning, whether right
or wrong, sound or fallacious," and at other times "correct meaning."

   Meaning, when used in the sense of "correct meaning," leads to an
either-or approach. "New York City is in Iowa" could, by the either-
or principles, promptly be ruled out. The either-or test would represent the semantic ideal. But I am sorry to have to admit that, by the
poetic ideal, "New York City is in Iowa" could *not* be ruled out.

   Has one ever stood, for instance, in some little outlying town, on
the edge of the wilderness, and watched a train go by? Has one perhaps suddenly felt that the train, and its tracks, were a kind of arm of
the city, reaching out across the continent, quite as though it were
simply Broadway itself extended? It is in such a sense that New York
City can be found all over the country—and I submit that one would
miss very important meanings, meanings that have much to do with
the conduct of our inhabitants, were he to proceed here by the either-
or kind of test.

   "New York City is in Iowa" is "poetically" true. As a metaphor, it
provides valid insight. To have ruled it out, by strict semantic authority, would have been vandalism.

   "Poetic" meanings, then, cannot be disposed of on the true-or-false
basis. Rather, they are related to one another like a set of concentric
circles, of wider and wider scope. Those of wider diameter do not
categorically eliminate those of narrower diameter. There is, rather, a
progressive *encompassment*. To say that "man is a vegetable" contains
much soundness. There is a vegetative level of human response, and
one can find out much about it (much more, in fact, than we now
know, as more is to be learned, for instance, about the ways in which
the biologic organism responds to seasonal periodicity, changes in so-

lar radiation, and the like). Again: to say that "man is an ant" does not "refute" the vegetational metaphor. The ant may be "vegetation-plus," since it too vegetates. And to say that "man is a communicant" is more comprehensive still, including the other metaphors but not abolishing them. These are examples of progressive encompassment that does not admit of mutual exclusion—and they are examples of what we take poetic characterizations to do.

A Different Mode Proposed for the Test of Poetic Meaning

Hence, for the validity of "poetic" meanings, I should suggest that the "test" cannot be a formal one, as with the diagrams for testing a syllogism. Poetic characterizations do not categorically exclude each other in the either-true-or-false sense, any more than the characterizations "honest" or "tall" could categorically exclude the characterizations "learned," "unlearned," or "thin." The test of a metaphor's validity is of a much more arduous sort, requiring nothing less than the *filling-out, by concrete body, of the characterizations which one would test*. There is no formal procedure, for example, for choosing among the three metaphors:

> man a vegetable
> man an ant
> man a communicant.

One can simply ask that the contestants advocate their choice by *filling it out*. That is: *let each say all he can* by way of giving body to the perspective inherent in his choice. Let each show the scope, range, relevancy, accuracy, applicability of the perspective, or metaphor, he would advocate. And only after each has been so filled out, can we evaluate among them. Thus, though there be no *formal* basis for a choice among the three metaphors offered above, the test of filling-out, of embodiment in concrete application, would, I think, demonstrate the greater value of the third for interpretative purposes. One could *do more* with it. He could integrate wider areas of human relationship. Hence, as so tested, it would be assigned a higher place than the other two in a hierarchy of possible perspectives. No perspective could be formally ruled out, but one could be shown to include another.

Such testing would also involve more than merely expository meaning, of the "graph" sort. The third metaphor would likewise be richer in hortatory significance. It would not merely give the names and addresses of events, but would also suggest exhortations for the promotion of *better* names and addresses. The metaphor would thus serve not only a descriptive function, but also a normative function.

The Moral Aspect of Poetic Meaning

Much of the *partial* descriptive matter now developed, as in the behaviorists' experiments with conditioning, would still be usable. But instead of being taken as the description of man's *essence*, it would be considered simply for its value in revealing *certain important things to look out for* in any attempt to plead for a more satisfactory communicative or cooperative structure. Thus, if the data on conditioning were presented as *an admonishment* about people, rather than as *the* "low down" on them, the interpretative enterprise would be restored in its proper *moralistic* basis, in contrast with the "neutral" or "nonmoral" ideals of meaning implicit in the attempt to get merely descriptive labels (an attempt that, if it succeeded, would find its very success a mockery, for it would describe social events in a way that led to no moral exhortation and would then have simply to let moral purposes creep in as contraband, a kind of irrational weakness, or benign error).

In general, primitive magic tended to transfer an animistic perspective to the charting of physical events. And positivistic science, by antithesis, leads to an opposite ideal, the transferring of a physicalist perspective to human events. Each is the migration of a metaphor in ways that require correctives, though I am willing to admit that, of the two excesses, I consider the savages' tendency to consider natural forces as spirits less deceptive than the positivists' tendency to consider people after the analogy of physical behavior. Semantic ideals of meaning could not possibly provide a proper vocabulary in which to consider the complexities of moral growth, because there is here no pragmatic routine to be "learned by repetition," as with proficiency in a trade. There is nothing to be "practiced" in the sense that one may practice tennis or carpentry. Qualitative growth cannot be "practiced" any more than biological growth can be "practiced." Given the faculty of speech, one can by practice master a new language. But there is no way for a dumb animal to acquire this faculty itself by practice. There is no "operation" for seeing a joke—though there may be operations for removing obstructions to the seeing of the joke.

The difference between the semantic ideal and the poetic ideal of moralistic interpretation would, I think, get down to this:

The semantic ideal would attempt to *get a description* by the *elimination* of attitude. The poetic ideal would attempt to *attain a full moral act* by attaining a perspective *atop all the conflicts of attitude.*

The first would try to *cut away*, to *abstract*, all emotional factors that complicate the objective clarity of meaning. The second would try to derive its vision from the maximum *heaping up* of all these emotional factors, playing them off against one another, inviting them to reinforce and contradict one another, and seeking to make this active participation itself a major ingredient of the vision.

This "poetic" meaning would contain much more than pragmatic, positivistic, futuristic values. A fully moral act is basically an act *now.* It is not promissory, it is not "investment for future profit." It is not the learning of a technique in the hopes this technique, when learned, will enable one to make wheels go or to add a few more metallurgical alloys to the 500,000 or so that "business" and "industry" have not yet found "use" for. A fully moral act is a total assertion at the time of the assertion. Among other things, it has a *style*—and this style is an integral aspect of its meaning. If it points to the chair by saying "faugh," it pledges itself to one program—to quite another if it adopts the style of "ho, ho" or "might I?" The style selected will mold the character of the selector. Each brand of imagery contains in germ its own "logic." If he says "faugh" and deeply means it, he thereby *vows* himself to "faugh"; he must go *through* the faughness, until he has either persisted by the buttressing of his choice or has burnt it out.

But I seem to be contradicting myself, since I called a stylistic act an act *now,* whereas I have been talking about its future implications. For there is a sense in which every act involves a future—but within this generalization there is a distinction. The distinction may be suggested in this way: To name something in the style of "faugh" is symbolically to act out a present attitude toward it, in the naming. To label it "Q271-Vii" is to withhold my act as a total present expression. The value of such naming will not reside so much in the rewards at the time, but in the "uses" I may subsequently put my nomenclature to. The name "Q271-Vii," for instance, may be much more serviceable as tested by some actuarial requirement or some problem in traffic regulation. To call a man a son-of-a-bitch is symbolically to make a complete assertion of attitude toward him now; it is itself a culmination, a "total summing up." To call him "Q271-Vii," on the other hand, is to put the value of the name in its future alone. It depends solely upon what you do with it, "in our next." In this sense it is relying upon the "promissory," whether mistaken or real.

"Beyond Good and Evil"

The semantic ideal envisions a vocabulary that *avoids* drama. The poetic ideal envisions a vocabulary that *goes through* drama. In their ideal completion, they have a certain superficial resemblance, in that both are "beyond good and evil." But the first seeks to attain this end by the programmatic elimination of a weighted vocabulary at the start (the neutralization of names containing attitudes, emotional predisposition); and the second would attain the same end by exposure to the *maximum profusion* of weightings. The first would be aside from the battle, stressing the rôle of the observer, whose observations it is hoped will define situations with sufficient realistic accuracy to prepare an adequate *chart* for action; the second would contend, by implication, that true knowledge can only be attained through the battle, stressing the rôle of the participant, who in the course of his participation, it is hoped, will define situations with sufficient realistic accuracy to prepare an *image* for action.

The poetic ideal being obviously aesthetic, we could in contrast call the semantic ideal "anesthetic"; for though *aesthetic*, in its etymological origins, derives from a word meaning "to perceive," it has come to include the idea of emotionality in the perception, whereas the semantic ideal would aim at perception without feeling. Perhaps, in view of the etymological difficulties, we should sacrifice our pun on *aesthetic-anesthetic* and instead offer as the semantic counterpart of aesthetic, "analgesic."

We should also point out that, although the semantic ideal would eliminate the *attitudinal* ingredient from its vocabulary (seeking a vocabulary for events equally valid for use by friends, enemies, and the indifferent) the ideal is itself an attitude, hence never wholly attainable, since it could be complete only by the abolition of itself. To the logical positivist, logical positivism is a "good" term, otherwise he would not attempt to advocate it by filling it out in all its ramifications. This observation spoils the symmetry of our case, in suggesting that semantics itself may be considered as an attenuated form of poetry, that "Q271-Vii" may itself be a gesture, secretly saying in a very mild way what "fiend" or "darling" says eagerly.

It would seem fair to take the symbols of Russell and Whitehead's *Principia Mathematica,* or the formulae of Carnap, as the nearest approach we have to the vocabulary of the semantic ideal. Or one may feel that we are stacking the cards here. Perhaps the semantic ideal does not show up at its best in ultimate overall theories, but in the specific vocabularies of technological specializations. The vocabulary of chemistry, for instance, may be much the same for communist, fascist, and liberal. A theory of ballistics may be couched in one set of symbols, whether it is to be studied by progressives or reactionaries. A topographical survey may be as "neutral" as the situation it surveys; it needs only to be *accurate,* and the soundings that the Japanese are said to be taking of our Western coast line aim at precisely the same kind of description as would the soundings taken by strategists of the U.S. Navy.

So, for our purposes, you may, as you prefer, consider the semantic ideal most fully embodied in either the vocabulary of any specific technique, or in the coordinating theory designed to make a body of generalizations that would *mutatis mutandis* cover all the specific techniques. In any case, even if you do prefer to insist that the vocabularies of the physical sciences represent the semantic ideal at its best, you must concede that it is the hope of the semanticist to build a vocabulary for the discussion of human, or social, events after the same model. A vocabulary that does not *judge,* but *describes* or *places,* as the psychologists' terminology is designed simply to name *how things are,* regardless of what you *want* them to be.

The coyness of the semantic strategy might be conveyed like this: A theory of ballistics, as a physical science, merely tells you how to shoot ammunition. As such, it is "neutral," capable of being taken over by friends or enemies. If, however, you extended the same kind of vocabulary to describe the situation of friends and enemies also, their enmity likewise would be neutralized. Leave the process half completed, develop neutrality in the vocabulary of the physical sciences while leaving prejudice in the vocabulary of social relations, and technology as a power becomes an ominous power. But extend the technological ideal throughout the social sciences as well, and technological power becomes equated with good power. If this account of the semantic hope is fair, it would justify us in saying that the overall semantic theories, rather than the vocabularies of specific scientific disciplines, are to be taken as representative of the ultimate semantic ideal.[2]

---

2. Enough has been said, incidentally, to suggest that the overall semantic chart is itself the riding of a metaphor, quite as the poet may carry some underlying metaphor, as a theme with variations, throughout his sonnet or his play. In logical positivism, according to one expositor (Julius Rudolph Weinberg: *An Examination of Logical Positivism*), "propositions are pictures of possible empirical facts." Thus the controversy does not resolve itself into an opposition between poetry as metaphorical and semantics as nonmetaphorical. Every perspective requires a metaphor, implicit or explicit, for its organizational base (as I tried to make clear in the section on "Perspective by Incongruity" in *Permanence and Change*)—and semantics as a perspective cannot skirt this necessity. This point may well be borne in mind at those places where I would ask to have the semantic perspective encompassed within the poetic perspective (considering semantics as a kind of special "poetic school" that would seek to erect its *partial* truth into a *whole* truth).

Letting In and Keeping Out

Plays like Shakespeare's *Tempest* or Aeschylus' *Eumenides* would represent the ideal poetic vocabulary. Lucretius' *De Rerum Natura* is a mixture of both ideals. Wedded, as a materialist ("philosophical scientist") to the aim of analgesia, Lucretius nonetheless builds up extremely emotional moments. For example, in trying to make us feel the great relief that would come to us from the abolition of the gods, Lucretius exposes himself to the full rigors of religious awe. He must make us realize *awe,* in the contemplation of heavenly distances and storms, in order to make us realize the full measure of the *relief* that would follow from the dissolution of this awe (by dissolving the gods which have become the symbols, the "charismatic vessels," of it). So he becomes somewhat an advocate against his own thesis. For in trying to build up a full realization of the awe, in order to build up a full realization of the freedom that would come of banishing this awe, he leaves us with an unforgettable image of the awe itself. We are left with the suspicion that he has never really freed himself of awe, but that he has been fighting valiantly to repress it (thereby indirectly reinforcing our sense of its pressure). He has tried, by the magic of his incantations, to get analgesia (perception without emotion); but he builds up, aesthetically, the motivation behind his anesthetic incantatory enterprise, thereby making us tremble all over again at the lines in which he reconstructs the sublimity of natural vastnesses and power, a vision reinforced by the tonal suggestiveness of his sentences (that contribute in their musicality to violate the genius of "Q271-Vii").

The pure semantic ideal, on the other hand, would have avoided this strategic difficulty at the start. For one thing, it would never discuss awe in words that, by their incantatory power, themselves suggested awe. It would spare itself Lucretius' losing task of refutation by never once giving aesthetic embodiment to the sense of awe. By never letting awe in, it would skirt the embarrassing problem of trying to get it out again. From the very start, its mode of naming "simply wouldn't give awe a chance." This feeling might possibly be lying there, in the background, as a motive in the semanticist's enterprise, but only by highly dubious detective work, by modes of metaphorical analysis that the semanticist himself would question as science, could you disclose such a motive. What the semanticist would put out, he never lets in.

Aeschylus' *Eumenides* to Illustrate Full Poetic Meaning

In the *Eumenides,* I think, we see the poetic method in its complete-ness. Where the semanticist does not fight, and Lucretius fights while stacking the odds against himself, Aeschylus completely gives himself to aesthetic exposure and surmounts the risk. Here, to be sure, is the ideal of analgesia—but it appears at the *end* of a most painful trilogy, devoted to an aesthetic reconstruction of struggle, horror, and the tor-tures of remorse. And to comfort us, the dramatist undertakes nothing less than the *conversion of the gods themselves.*

In this respect the play parallels explicitly the change we get as we turn from the wrathful Jehovah of the Old Testament (a warrior god, like warrior gods partaking of the rage that is in the Grecian Furies and the Norse Valkyries) to the Living Logos of the New Testament. Here is a ritual for the conversion of the Furies from a malign identity (named the Erinyes, from *erinyo,* to be wrathful toward) to a benign identity (named the Eumenides, from *eumeneo,* to feel kindly toward). Henceforth, we are informed, the emphasis of their function will be radically altered. No longer will they devote their ingenuity and enter-prise to the *punishment of evil,* but the stress henceforth will be upon the *protection of good.* Logically, the two functions are certainly not at odds, but psychologically they are in far different realms. Fittingly, for our analysis, the Furies are characterized as *older* gods; and their conversion from malign to benign emphasis was done under the per-suasion of such *younger* gods as Apollo and Athena. (Incidentally, I am indebted, for the form of this thought, to John Crowe Ransom's *God Without Thunder,* a work that has not generally been given the recognition it deserves. Unfortunately, I also have a responsibility to bear in this matter, as I was assigned *God Without Thunder* for re-view, but became so tangled in various ramifications of the critic's thesis that my review was never finished. In particular, as I see it now, I was struggling between a desire to salute his basic observation and a muddled disagreement with the uses he made of it. In any case, the incident has been on my conscience, for works of such incision are too rare for us to afford their neglect, and I shall feel better insofar as I have here belatedly made amends.)

What went on, in this play? Recently I caught a glimpse, or at least thought I caught a glimpse, of the exhilaration that must have lifted up the Athenian audience when it first felt the medicinal action of this ritual. On the personal plane, we have the redemption of Orestes, with whose sufferings the audience had presumably been profoundly identified, so that they would also profoundly take part in his release. On the religious plane, this personal redemption is contrived by nothing less important than a reordering of divinity itself, as the persecutional gods of wrath relinquish their torture of Orestes only after they have been persuaded to change their very office, taking a new temple in Athens where, underground, they will zealously and jealously do well by Athenian virtue, if any. And to round out the pattern for this polis-minded people (one of the names for Zeus was Zeus Agoraios, Zeus the forensic) Orestes' restoration from division to unity is the occasion for the solemnizing of a pact between Athens and Argos. When all this had been put together (the personal, the religious, and the so-cial—while the quick convergence toward the close must have been breathtaking), there is one final stroke still to be delivered:

> ATTENDANTS: Then come, ye dread powers, kind and faithful to Athens, nor waken to wrath;
> Come hither, be cheered by the flame, pine-consuming, that lightens your path.
> HERALD: Shout, ye folk, a new age hath begun!
> ATTENDANTS: Torch-illumined libations henceforward the people of Pallas shall bring
> To your dwelling—so Fate hath made compact with Zeus the Olympian King.
> HERALD: Shout, ye people, the chanting is done!

"A new age!" Thus had the cornerstone been grandiloquently laid for an ancient structure of "modernity." May one not also discern even a certain playwright's cunning here? For is not the final exhortation of the Herald an invitation to let the stage flow over into the audience, making participation between actors and audience complete, as they are asked to weld their shout of approval *for* the play with a shout that has meaning *within* the play? Could they know quite what their applause would signify: whether it was applause for Aeschylus, or stage applause, or applause for the slogan that so deftly put the coming era of enlightenment under good auspices, thereby "filling a civic need"? Thomas Mann, in his letter to the official of Bonn University, who had notified him of the retraction of his honorary degree, begins by taking up this matter—but before he has finished, the issue has been subtly transformed into something of much broader implications. It is hard to remember, in retrospect, just when we shifted from a point of controversy between Mann and the subservient official to a discussion of cultural trends in their most sweeping aspects. Such are the persuasive ambiguities of identification. And might we note something similar, as we cannot tell whether the shout is within the play, for the play, for Athens or for Aeschylus, for the tactics of the ritualistic compliment whereby the "new age" is evangelically announced, or for the "new age" itself? Such complexity is what I glimpsed, or thought I glimpsed, when this firm architecture of action was first unveiled before the Athenian audience. The play itself had offered its audience ample grounds to shout—and in its closing line it gives them explicitly a cue to shout.

"Through" and "Around"

The particular "curve" of Aeschylus' development is to be caught perhaps as we contrast the Orestes trilogy with an earlier drama, *The Persae*, a "factional" drama where the crime is committed by "the enemy," the foreigner Xerxes, in contrast with the later work in the mode of "universal" tragedy, where the crime is committed by Everyman.

But, like or dislike this whole mode of assuagement, as you prefer: the important point to be stressed for our purposes is that it is accomplished by going *through* drama, not by going *around* drama, or perhaps more accurately, *forestalling* drama. Similarly in Socrates, both the man and the protagonist formalized by Plato, there is a "dialectical" approach (through the dramas of conflict) to the ultimate philosophic vision. With Aristotle, however, you move toward something different. Here there is somewhat the tendency "to take up where Plato left off," as though Plato were still living and were making a definitive revision of his own first draft. Aristotle's *Rhetoric* and *Poetics* are evidence that he still retained a strong appreciation of the dramatic experience. But the risk of attenuation, successfully weathered by him, becomes progressively greater as we move toward disciples who would, in turn, "take up where Aristotle left off." Such development operates to perfection in the quantitative realm, as in the successive improvements made atop a mechanical invention. But one may question whether it applies to the qualitative realm, as with some recent young composers who, impressed with the tonal inventions of Beethoven's last quartets, would attempt simply to "begin" where he had ended, as though there could be handed to them, on a platter, the imaginative grasp of this ultimate period, which Beethoven himself earned by all that had gone before it. They tend, of course, simply to "project" his last style with efficiency into a mannerism, quite as Western borrowers of Chinese or African art tend to get the shell without the egg, or as a child will "imitate" a workman by merely making the same kind of noise.

Now, there is a crucial difference between the peace of a warrior who lays down his arms (Aeschylus wanted to be remembered, not as a poet, but as a soldier), and the peace of those who are innocent of war (innocence untried being like snow fallen in the night; let us not praise it for not melting until the sun has been full upon it). And the semantic ideal, I submit, would attempt to give us the final rewards of *Versöhnung*, of atonement, before we had ever gone through the conflicts by which alone we could properly "earn" it.

No, we are here being too thorough. Let us revise the fable in this wise: Men, out of conflict, evolve projects for atonement, *Versöhnung*, assuagement. They hand these on to others. And the heirs must either make these structures of atonement the basis of a new conflict or be emptied. Much of the best in thought is evolved to teach us how to die well; whereupon it is studied and built upon by those who have never lived well. Either anesthesia is earned by aesthesia, or it is empty. When philosophy advances beyond the quality of Lucretius, who builds up the fear as well as the antidote, it approaches inanition.

The best thing to be said in favor of the semantic ideal is that it is a fraud: one may believe in it because it is impossible. Because poetry has been so arrantly misused, in the sophistries of the press and of political demagogues, there is apparent justification for the attempt to eliminate it. But one could with as much logic abolish printing itself, since printing has been misused. To paraphrase Mallarmé: semantics would make us Promethean inventors, minus the vulture (*"égaux de Prométhée à qui manque un vautour"*).

A comprehensive vocabulary, for social purposes, will persistently outrage the norms of the semantic ideal. It will not be unweighted; rather, it will have a maximum complexity of weighting. It will strike and retreat, compliment and insult, challenge and grovel, sing, curse, and whimper, subside and recover. Repeatedly, it will throw forth observations that are as accurate, in the realistic charting of human situations, as any ideal semantic formula. Many proverbs are brilliantly so. It will "neutralize" a meaning at any desired point. But such behavior must be merely taken in its stride. And its test of a "true" meaning will be its ability to fit into a piece with all other meanings, which is something radically different from the sheer expectancy that comes with conditioned salivation at the sound of a bell. (I sometimes wonder whether all of human "progress" is to be summed up as the insertion of an "i" in the word "salvation.")

Complaints

The semantic style is bad style, except in those who violate its tenets, as Newton violated them in the resonance of the language in which he gave account of his "celestial mechanics." Charts, graphs, crop reports, "intelligence," editorial comment, low-powered description— all such is justifiable only insofar as "we gotta live," justifiable in short by the real or hoped-for "return on the investment."

Perhaps it is unfair to attack all this in the name of semantics, yet it is more legitimate to characterize it as poor semantics than as poor poetry. Information is quite often "semantically" sound. But it is rarely resonant. The percentage of such stuff has become too high. Unawares, we have allowed ourselves to take it as the *norm*, thereby confusing a norm with an average.

Even in poetry itself, "the norm" has encroached. I wonder how long it has been since a poet has asked himself: "What would I say if I wanted to present Miss Q with a gift, accompanied by a deft verbal compliment?—or what would I say if I wanted to knife someone *neatly?*" Or since someone told himself: "Suppose I did not simply wish to load upon the broad shoulders of the public medium, my own ungainly appetites and ambitions? Suppose that, gnarled as I am, I did not consider it enough simply to seek payment for my gnarledness, the establishment of communion through evils held in common? Suppose I would also erect a structure of encouragement, for all of us? How should I go about it, in the sequence of imagery, not merely to bring us most poignantly *into* hell, but also *out* again? Should I leave the curse of a malign spell upon us, insofar as I am able, and insofar as my audience cannot shake it off of themselves by discounting and triviality? Must there not, for every flight, be also a return, before my work can be called complete as a moral act?"

The thought suggests what must have been going on when the symphonic form was vital. The opening allegro: calm before storm. The sorrows, risks, and the ingenious struggles of movements two and three. And the final celebration, as a "way out," the bright clapping of the hands that releases the hypnotic spell (or should we say, supplants it with a daylight spell?). Then, as we move from the symphony toward the tone poem, we turn from this *rounded* aesthetic to the aesthetic of the Poe story. The one corrosive spell, leaving it for the reader's own enterprise or superficiality to shake himself free of the burden it would shift from the writer's shoulders upon his, as sacrificial goat. Alpheus without Arethusa.

It is possible that writers are forgetting what to ask of their paragraphs? And should we think all the more on this subject, since we seem threatened with a period of political gloom ranging anywhere from a repellent aimlessness to an even more repellent aim (and if we get the latter, men will give blows with twice the fury of blows, striking the external enemy with vengeance and making him also the recipient of their rage against the past uncertainties within themselves, a double-duty form of assertion we may fear especially in our frustrated businessmen, whose businesses have got in each other's way, and who are looking earnestly for someone to serve as vessel of their rage). We must get sturdiness from somewhere—we must seek some kind of physical muscle and its mental counterparts.

If a dismal political season is in store for us, shall we not greatly need a campaign base for personal integrity, a kind of beneath-which-not? And I wonder whether we might find this beneath-which-not in a more strenuous cult of style. This effort has been made many times in the past—and as regularly has been despised at other times, when there was no longer any need for it. Style for its own sake? Decidedly, not at all. Style solely as the *beneath-which-not*, as the *admonitory and hortatory act*, as the *example* that would prod continually for its completion in all aspects of life, and so, in Eliot's phrase, "keep something alive," tiding us over a lean season. And there is all the more reason for us to attempt doing what we can by *present* imagery, since the promissory, the rewards of "postponed consumption," hold out so little of encouragement for the political future within our lifetime. So might we, rather than living wholly by a future that threatens so strongly to refute us, do rather what we can to live in a present that may in good time spread into the future?

Do not get me wrong. I am pleading for no "retreat" to anything. No literary Buchmanism, no off-by-itself, no back-to. Let our enlistments remain as they are. I am asking simply that the *temper* of our enlistment undergo a change of emphasis. That the *norm* of our tone cease to be the insulting tone that "talks down" to people. Nor would it be a presumptuous tone, that laid claim to uplift them. But rather a tone that would plead with us all, with the writer-to as well as the written-to. In it there must also be disdain, for those who have been giving the final insult to democracy, as they contrive to suggest that one almost has a moral obligation to write trivially and superficially, as though one could only show a proper love of mankind by plying the citizenry with flimsy items, "to be used once and thrown away."

The editor was late. The paper was ready for the printer, all but the columns reserved for him. Yet he knocked off his opinions on the state of the world in time to beat the deadline. Reading them, one recalled:

"Yours of the twelfth inst. to hand, and have noted same. In reply would beg to state that we . . . etc." This is "the norm." By it all else is tested. It has its place. And unquestionably, the opinions of a trained opinionator, situated at a strategic point with relation to the channels of information and advice, may even thus haphazardly make better comment than could a man deprived of his advantages. The question is: have they done anything? Can they, in this form, possibly do anything? I submit that they cannot. And further, I submit that, insofar as they become "the norm," they serve to prevent the doing of anything. On the other hand, out of attempts to key up the values of style, there could emerge writers whose muscularity was a fit with the requirements of the people. As things now stand, "the norm" prevents even an attempt at such selectivity.

In keeping with this norm, bright boys are imported from the provinces, put through the mill, stamped with a method, and used hard until they are used up—whereupon other bright boys are imported to take their places, the whole being kept on its toes despite disgust and boredom by muscling in and the fear of muscling in, with financial hashish as the positive incentive.

Or imagine this hypothetical case: Imagine an investigator who confided: "I've finished collating my material; I have my findings; but I haven't been able to write them up; I can't get the right sentence to start the whole thing going." The notion seems almost impertinent. The fact is that he would say his say, without a qualm, though his sentences rattled like dice in a box. When considering the welter of minor investigations that are now taken as the normal output of the academic bureaucracy, arising from the fact that everybody is expected to codify something or other for his degree, while the disproportionate flow of incomes act to support a vast quantity of such low-powered collations—when considering these stamp collections of an overly proliferating priesthood, I have wondered whether we might legitimately try to introduce some new kind of Occam's Razor, some new test for exclusion of the inessential. Suppose, for example, that a man were permitted only to say something that he could grow eloquent about. That is, suppose he were to place this requirement upon himself. I grant that there would be much persiflage released upon the world. But every once in a while it wouldn't be persiflage. And much that now gets "scientific immunity" by reason of its very pallor (a kind of "protection by unnoticeableness") would in its attempt keying-up expose itself the more readily to weeding-out. As things now stand, its pallor enjoys protective coloration by its close likeness to the journalistic pallor, that is "the norm."

Conclusion

It would be unfair to lay all these ills to the "semantic ideal." It might be more just to say that the semantic ideal is the *perfection* of trends which we find here in their aggravatedly *imperfect* state. At its best, it has an incisiveness, an accuracy of formulation, a nicety, that makes it itself a style. But anything short of it becomes the mere riding of a convenience. And even at its best, when isolated from the total texture of language, it is insufficient and promotes the upbuilding of a fallacious equipment.

Above all, it fosters, sometimes explicitly, sometimes by implication, the notion that one may comprehensively discuss human and social events in a nonmoral vocabulary, and that perception itself is a nonmoral act. It is the moral impulse that motivates perception, giving it both intensity and direction, suggesting *what to look for* and *what to look out for.* Only by wanting very profoundly to make improvement, can we get a glimpse into the devious personal and impersonal factors that operate to balk improvement. Or, stating this in reverse, we could say that the structural firmness in a character like Iago is in itself an evidence of Shakespeare's moral depth. For it was in knowing what to look for that Shakespeare also knew what to look out for. We might even say that Shakespeare constructed this archdemon by making him an ominous caricature of the playwright's own methods, so that he becomes an admonishment not only to us, but to his inventor. For that peculiarly subtle variant of the "confidence game" in which Iago was an adept, inciting Othello to participate by leading him always to complete the surmises for himself, never wholly saying them, but all-but-saying them, and saying them in such a way that there is only one course for Othello to follow in building "logically" upon them, and taking double precautions to keep him in this track by constant repetition of goatish imagery—are not these Shakespeare's own profoundest wiles, here made sinister? So let the poetic ideal be sloganized as *Iago-plus-Ariel*—and let the semantic ideal be sloganized as a *neutral realm eliminating both.*

By our choice here, we should seek for neutralization *at moments,* for given purposes, and not as a blanket program for vocabulary, since the loss in *action now* (that is, in full moral asseveration) would be too great were the semantic ideal to prevail. We can understand why adepts at any given specialization might want to erect these neutralizing moments into a whole trade, asking that the whole world be seen from the perspective of their "occupational psychosis." We can understand why, through living professionally with a neutral vocabulary, they should favor the thought of its ideal extension until it has encompassed all vocabulary. But merely because they have found a way of prolonging the insight of one moment through a life-work, giving it body in documentation and routine, even that is not argument enough to make us believe that the realm of the affections can or should be expressed *ordine geometrico* (an aim that Spinoza expressed explicitly, whereas the humane attractiveness of his Ethics owes much to the fact that he implicitly violated his own program repeatedly, beginning perhaps with his first proposition, *Substantia prior est natura suis affectionibus,* for "substance" has since been shown to be a very *resonant* word).

We have, as it happens, the "neutral" word *shoe,* capable of designating equally well the shoe worn by a communist and the shoe worn by a fascist. One can imagine that we had instead only two weighted words, *bims* and *bams,* so that the same object worn by a communist *had* to be called a bim that, if worn by a fascist, could only in the pieties of poetry be called a bam. A liberal shoe manufacturer, making footwear for export, might then label his consignments to Germany bams and his consignments to Russia bims. And he would be grateful for some "neutralizer" who helped him simplify the keeping of his ledgers by inventing a purely "scientific" word, *shoe,* that would include both classes. But I have purposely imagined inventing a neutral word that we already have, to replace two weighted words we don't have, as a way of suggesting that spontaneous speech can, and repeatedly does, neutralize, where the occasion requires.

So, the poetic vocabulary, when complete, will take us into-and-out-of (the complete play with its exhilaration at the close). When incomplete, it will take us into, and seek to leave us there (the "aesthetic of the Poe story"). While the semantic vocabulary would, I think, unintentionally cheat us, by keeping us without, providing a kind of quietus in advance, never even giving the dramatic opposition a chance, avoiding the error which Lucretius made, at the sacrifice of his work as "science" and to its great gain as "poetry."

Paradoxically, however, we may also judge the semantic vocabulary as "imagery," as "secular prayer," as itself exemplifying a form of consolational dance, all in the tone of perfect peacefulness. Judged as a refuge from something, that would not permit even the mere mention of that from which it was a refuge, it becomes itself an attenuated form of poetry, with its own modes of hypnosis. Or we may consider it valuable as a *stage,* a kind of purgatorial disembodiment helpful for transition from an old poetic vocabulary whose weightings are all askew to a new poetic vocabulary whose weightings will be better fitted to the situations it would encompass. As preparation, as discipline, as itself pointing out some important things "to look for and to look out for," it can be saluted. It is only when it is considered as an ideal in itself, rather than as a preparation for new and more accurate weighting, that one need turn against it.

The ideal word is in itself an act, its value contained in its use at the moment of utterance. Its worth does not reside in its "usefulness" and promise (though that is certainly a part of it) but in its *style* as morals, as petition, in the *quality* of the petition, not in the *success* of the petition. For preparations, anything may serve, everything does serve—but preparations must not usurp the guise of fulfillments.

5

The Symbol as Formative

Patterns of Experience

Universal Experiences

The various kinds of moods, feelings, emotions, perceptions, sensations, and attitudes discussed in the manuals of psychology and exemplified in works of art, we consider universal experiences. Mockery, despair, grimness, *sang-froid*, wonder, lamentation, melancholy, hatred, hopefulness, bashfulness, relief, boredom, dislike—for our present purposes it does not matter how these are grouped, which are "basic" and which derivative, how many or how few there are said to be: we call them universal because all men, under certain conditions, and when not in mental or physical collapse, are capable of experiencing them. Nor does it matter whether we choose to call them mental or somatic; it is sufficient that they arise. They could equally well be discussed as processes; for convenience' sake we discuss them as states.

Modes of Experience

The universal experiences are implicated in specific modes of experience: they arise out of a relationship between the organism and its environment. Frustration and gratification of bodily needs; ethical systems; customs; the whole ideology or code of values among which one is raised—these are involved in the modes of experience. A newborn child manifests fear at loss of physical support; but an adult may experience loss of support with pleasure, as in diving, while greatly fearing the loss of support which would be involved in his alienating the good opinion of his neighbors. At restriction of movement the infant manifests rage; and a man who might without rage endure the binding of his arms for hours would flare up in two minutes at an attempt to confine him in an argument. Grief at deprivation is universal—yet grief at deprivation may be exemplified in lovers' partings,

From "Lexicon Rhetoricae," in *Counter-Statement*, pp. 149–58. © 1931, 1953, 1968 by Kenneth Burke.

financial ruin, or subtle loss of self-esteem. The range of universal experiences may be lived on a mountain top, at sea, among a primitive tribe, in a salon—the modes of experience so differing in each instance that people in two different schemes of living can derive very different universal experiences from an identical event. The hypochondriac facing a soiled glove may experience a deep fear of death to which the trained soldier facing a cannon is insensitive.

The same universal experience could invariably accompany the same mode of experience only if all men's modes of experience were identical.

Patterns of Experience

Experience arising out of a relationship between an organism and its environment, the adjustments of the organism will depend upon the nature of the environment. By "adjustments of the organism" we refer to any kind of adaptation; thus: firm musculature as the concomitant of life under pioneer conditions; obesity as the concomitant of plenty and confinement; vindictiveness as the concomitant of oppression; timidity as the concomitant of protection; trustfulness as the concomitant of fair dealing—a distinction in the environment calling forth a distinction in the organism. An "adjustment" need not be a "good adjustment." It is as much an "adjustment," in our sense, for the organism to die of a bullet as for the organism to dodge one. It is equally an adjusutment to avoid a calamity, to remove the cause of a calamity, or to become so "closed" by philosophy or hysteria that the calamity is unfelt. We do not mean that a given distinction of the environment always calls forth the same distinction of the organism. A condition of plenty and confinement may lead, for instance, not to obesity but to a regime of diet and calisthenics. Protection may lead, not to timidity, but to the protected person's determination to put himself upon his own resources. We refer simply to the fact that the adjusting organism will take some particular environmental condition into account. A particular environmental condition may be: a cruel father, an indulgent mother, a long stretch of poverty, the death of a favorite aunt, rough treatment at the hands of other boys, gentle years in a garden, what you will. Any such specific environmental condition calls forth and stresses certain of the universal experiences as being more relevant to it, with a slighting of those less relevant. Such selections are "patterns of experience." They distinguish us as "characters." The protest of a Byron, the passive resistance of a Gandhi, the hopefulness of a Browning, the satirical torment of a Swift, the primness of a Jane Austen—these are all patterns of experience.

We do not imply that these patterns are wholly the result of environment. They result from the combination of organism and environment—and organisms presumably differ as much as environments. A more sensitive organism, for instance, might need a less emphatic environmental condition to cause it pain—indeed, too emphatic an environmental condition might cause it, not pain, but a compensatory blunting of pain. A direct and simple personality may arise when the environment reinforces the best aptitudes of the organism. A complex, hesitant personality may arise when the process of "learning," or adjustment to the environment, entailed the slighting of the organism's best aptitudes and the forcible development of lesser ones. However, the essential fact for our discussion is not the genesis of the patterns, but their existence.

Once they exist, though they may be in themselves results, they become in turn "creative." The method of adjustment (the particular selection of universal experiences) which the organism has developed to face specific environmental conditions is subsequently applied to other environmental conditions. A man who has been betrayed in a matter of vast importance to him may henceforth distrust people deserving of his full confidence. Such selectiveness may be a temporary pattern, or it may influence his judgments and social relationships for the remainder of his life. Whether the pattern is permanent (as a lasting state of distrust) or temporary (as a sudden state of grief following a loss), while it endures it tends to make over the world in its own image. Jealousy is a "creative" or "interpretive" principle, enabling the jealous man to find startling grounds for jealousy where less jealous persons would note nothing at all. Thus, arising presumably as a method of adjustment to one condition, the pattern may become a method of meeting other conditions—may become a typical manner of experiencing.

The Symbol

The symbol is the verbal parallel to a pattern of experience. The poet, for instance, may pity himself for his undeserved neglect, and this self-pity may color his day. It may be so forceful, and so frequently recurrent as to become selective, so that he finds ever new instances of his unappreciated worth. Self-pity assumes enough prominence in his case to become a pattern of experience. If he converts his pattern into a plot, "The King and the Peasant" (about a King who has but the trappings of kingliness and a Peasant who is, in the true sense, a King) he has produced a symbol. He might have chosen other symbols to verbalize the same pattern. In fact, if his pattern continues to obsess him, he undoubtedly will exemplify the same pattern in other symbols: he will next produce "The Man Against the Mob," or "A Saint Dying in Neglect." Or he may be still more devious, and finding his own problems writ large in the life of some historic figure, he may give us a vigorous biography of the Little Corporal.

The symbol is often quite obvious, as in *Childe Harold, Madame Bovary, Euphues, Don Quixote, Tom Sawyer, Wilhelm Meister, Hamlet*. In lyrics of mood it is not so readily summed up in a name. It is pervasive but not condensed. The symbol of *The Tempest?* Perhaps it is more nearly condensed in the songs and doings of Ariel than elsewhere in the play, but essentially it is a complex attitude which pervades the setting, plot, and characters. The symbol might be called a word invented by the artist to specify a particular grouping or pattern or emphasizing of experiences—and the work of art in which the symbol figures might be called a definition of this word. The novel, *Madam Bovary*, is an elaborate definition of a new word in our vocabulary. In the lyric, in *The Tempest*, the symbol is present as definition, though not as a word. The symbol is a formula.

Appeal of the Symbol

The symbol is perhaps most overwhelming in its effect when the artist's and the reader's patterns of experience closely coincide. *Childe Harold*, the symbol for Byron's patterns of experience, becomes thus the word or formula which mute Byrons, with the same patterns, were awaiting. The symbol may also serve to force patterns upon the audience, however, the universal experiences being capable of other groupings or patterns than those which characterize the particular reader; thus: As people in fright (artist's pattern) cry out (symbol), so an outcry (same symbol) will be most terrifying to those already tense with fright (audience's pattern same as artist's pattern)—but the outcry (same symbol) may also frighten those who were at rest (audience with different pattern, but susceptible to the authority of the symbol).

A symbol appeals:

As the interpretation of a situation. It can, by its function as name and definition, give simplicity and order to an otherwise unclarified complexity. It provides a terminology of thoughts, actions, emotions, attitudes, for codifying a pattern of experience. The artist, through experiencing intensively or extensively a certain pattern, becomes as it were an expert, a specialist, in this pattern. And his skill in articulation is expended upon the schematizing of his subject. The schematizing is done not by abstraction, as in science, but by idealization, by presenting in a "pure" or consistent manner some situation which, as it appears among the contingencies of real life, is less effectively co-ordinated; the idealization is the elimination of irrelevancies.

By favoring the acceptance of a situation. At times the situation revealed by the symbol may not be particularly complex, but our minds have been closed to the situation through the exigencies of practical life. The symbol can enable us to admit, for instance, the existence of a certain danger which we had emotionally denied. A humorous symbol enables us to admit the situation by belittling it; a satirical symbol enables us to admit the situation by permitting us to feel aloof from it; a tragic symbol enables us to admit the situation by making us feel the dignity of being in such a situation; the comic symbol enables us to admit the situation by making us feel our power to surmount it. A symbol may also force us to admit a situation by the sheer thoroughness of the symbol, but if the situation is one which we had strong motives for denying, and if the symbol is not presented by some such accompanying attitude as above noted, the admitting of the situation will probably be accompanied by a revulsion against the symbol.

As the corrective of a situation. Life in the city arouses a compensatory interest in life on a farm, with the result that symbols of farm life become appealing; or a dull life in the city arouses a compensatory interest in symbols depicting a brilliant life in the city; etc. In such cases the actual situation to which the symbol is adapted is left unformulated. Most stories of romantic love are probably in this class.

As the exerciser of "submerged" experience. A capacity to function in a certain way (as we have pointed out in the discussion of form) is not merely something which lies on a shelf until used—a capacity to function in a certain way is an obligation so to function. Even those "universal experiences" which the reader's particular patterns of experience happen to slight are in a sense "candidates"—they await with some aggression their chance of being brought into play. Thus though the artist's pattern may be different from the reader's, the symbol by touching on submerged patterns in the reader may "stir remote depths." Symbols of cruelty, horror, and incest may often owe their appeal to such causes.

As an "emancipator." (The explosive success of "scarlet-sister" literature, for instance, as *La Dame aux Camélias*.) The situation in which the reader happens to be placed requires of him an adjustment which certain of his moral values prohibit (in this case, sexual inclinations discountenanced by the Church). The symbol, by appealing to certain other of his moral values (in this case, the respect for heroines possessing "deep humanity," "fine womanly qualities") may make the attitude "morally" acceptable. Here certain moral assumptions are pitted against others, with the reader's "need" on the side of the attacking assumptions. (Assumptions of what is admirable, that is, are pitted against assumptions of what is contemnable, with the reader's desire for greater laxity serving to weight the assumptions of what is admirable. Accordingly, if some kind of conduct is, by our code of values, called wicked, absurd, low-caste, wasteful, etc., and if the situation in which we are placed requires this reprehensible kind of conduct, that symbol will be effective which, by manipulating other values in our code, makes such conduct seem virtuous, discerning, refined, accurate, etc. The appeal of the symbol as "emancipator" involves fundamentally a mere shifting of terms in this way: leisure for indolence, foolhardiness for bravery, thrift for miserliness, improvidence for generosity, et cetera or vice versa.

As a vehicle for "artistic" effects. A Malvolio, a Falstaff, a Coriolanus. To a degree their appeal is in their sheer value as inventions. They are a nimble running of scales; they display the poet's farthest reaches of virtuosity. The love of the impromptu—the feeling that brilliance is being given out with profusion and overwhelming spontaneity. Inasmuch as everybody yearns to say one brilliant thing, perhaps this appeal of the symbol is most poignant of all. At least, it claims a major rôle in the smart repartee of the American theatre.

This discussion of symbolic appeal is not offered as exhaustive, but as illustrative. Nor are the means of appeal mutually exclusive. Essentially, we might summarize the entire list by saying that the symbol appeals either as the orienting of a situation, or as the adjustment to a situation, or as both.

The Symbol as Generating Principle

When the poet has converted his pattern of experience into a symbolic equivalent, the symbol becomes a guiding principle in itself. Thus, once our poet suffering self-pity has hit upon the plot of "The King and the Peasant," he finds himself with many problems remote from his self-pity. Besides showing his King as a weakling, he must show him as a King—whereupon accounts of court life. Similarly the treatment of the Peasant will entail harvest scenes, dances, descriptions of the Peasant's hut. There will be the Peasant's Wife and the Queen and a host of subsidiary characters. As the symbol is ramified, symbols within symbols will arise, many of these secondary symbols with no direct bearing upon the pattern of experience behind the key symbol. These secondary or ramifying symbols can be said to bear upon the underlying pattern of experience only insofar as they contribute to the workings of the key symbol.

Again: Symbols will be subtilized in ways not contributory to the pattern. The weak King cannot be too weak, the manly Peasant cannot be too manly—thus we find the Poet "defending" to an extent the very character whom he would denigrate and detracting from the character who is to triumph. Such considerations arise with the adoption of the symbol, which is the conversion of an experiential pattern into a formula for affecting an audience.

The symbol, in other words, brings up problems extrinsic to the pattern of experience behind it. The underlying pattern, that is, remains the same whether the poet writes "The King and the Peasant," "The Man Against the Mob," or "A Saint Dying in Neglect." But in each case the symbol is a generating principle which entails a selection of different subtilizations and ramifications. Thus, the difference between the selectivity of a dream and the selectivity of art is that the dream obeys no principle of selection but the underlying pattern, whereas art, which expands by the ramifying of the symbol, has the symbol as a principle of selection.

6

Language as Action: Terministic Screens

Directing the Attention

We might begin by stressing the distinction between a "scientistic" and a "dramatistic" approach to the nature of language. A "scientistic" approach begins with questions of *naming, or definition.* Or the power of language to define and describe may be viewed as derivative; and its essential function may be treated as attitudinal or hortatory: attitudinal as with expressions of complaint, fear, gratitude, and such; hortatory as with commands or requests, or, in general, an instrument developed through its use in the social processes of cooperation and competition. I say "developed"; I do *not* say "originating." The ultimate *origins* of language seem to me as mysterious as the origins of the universe itself. One must view it, I feel, simply as the "given." But once an animal comes into being that does happen to have this particular aptitude, the various tribal idioms are unquestionably *developed* by their use as instruments in the tribe's way of living (the practical role of symbolism in what the anthropologist, Malinowski, has called "context of situation"). Such considerations are involved in what I mean by the "dramatistic," stressing language as an aspect of "action," that is, as "symbolic action."

The two approaches, the "scientistic" and the "dramatistic" (language as definition, and language as act), are by no means mutually exclusive. Since both approaches have their proper uses, the distinction is not being introduced invidiously. Definition itself is a symbolic act, just as my proposing of this very distinction is a symbolic act. But though at this moment of beginning, the overlap is considerable, later the two roads diverge considerably and direct our attention to quite different kinds of observation. The quickest way to indicate the differences of direction might be by this formula: The "scientistic" approach builds the edifice of language with primary stress upon a

From "Terministic Screens," in *Language as Symbolic Action*, pp. 44–55. Reprinted by permission of The University of California Press. © 1966 by The Regents of the University of California.

proposition such as "It *is,* or it *is not.*" The "dramatistic" approach puts the primary stress upon such hortatory expressions as "thou *shalt,* or thou *shalt not.*" And at the other extreme the distinction becomes quite obvious, since the scientist approach culminates in the kinds of speculation we associate with symbolic logic, while the dramatistic culminates in the kinds of speculation that find their handiest material in stories, plays, poems, the rhetoric of oratory and advertising, mythologies, theologies, and philosophies after the classic model.

The dramatistic view of language, in terms of "symbolic action," is exercised about the necessarily *suasive* nature of even the most unemotional scientific nomenclatures. And we shall proceed along those lines; thus:

Even if any given terminology is a *reflection* of reality, by its very nature as a terminology it must be a *selection* of reality; and to this extent it must function also as a *deflection* of reality.

In his seventh *Provincial Letter,* Pascal satirizes a device which the Jesuits of his day called "directing the intention." For instance, to illustrate satirically how one should "direct the intention," he used a burlesque example of this sort: Dueling was forbidden by the Church. Yet it was still a prevalent practice. Pascal satirically demonstrated how, by "directing the intention," one could both take part in a duel and not violate the Church injunctions against it. Thus, instead of intentionally going to take part in a duel, the duelists would merely go for a walk to the place where the duel was to be held. And they would carry guns merely as a precautionary means of self-protection in case they happened to meet an armed enemy. By so "directing the intention," they could have their duel without having transgressed the Church's thou-shalt-not's against dueling. For it was perfectly proper to go for a walk; and in case one encountered an enemy bent on murder, it was perfectly proper to protect oneself by shooting in self-defense.

I bring up this satirically excessive account of directing the *intention,* in the hopes that I can thereby settle for less when discussing the ways in which "terministic screens" direct the *attention.* Here the kind of deflection I have in mind concerns simply the fact that any nomenclature necessarily directs the attention into some channels rather than others. In one sense, this likelihood is painfully obvious. A textbook on physics, for instance, turns the *attention* in a different direction from a textbook on law or psychology. But some implications of this terministic incentive are not so obvious.

When I speak of "terministic screens," I have particularly in mind some photographs I once saw. They were *different* photographs of the *same* objects, the difference being that they were made with different color filters. Here something so "factual" as a photograph revealed notable distinctions in texture, and even in form, depending upon which color filter was used for the documentary description of the event being recorded.

Similarly, a man has a dream. He reports his dream to a Freudian analyst, or a Jungian, or an Adlerian, or to a practitioner of some other school. In each case, we might say, the "same" dream will be subjected to a different color filter, with corresponding differences in the nature of the event as perceived, recorded, and interpreted. (It is a commonplace that patients soon learn to have the kind of dreams best suited to the terms favored by their analysts.)

Observations Implicit in Terms

We have now moved things one step further along. Not only does the nature of our terms affect the nature of our observations, in the sense that the terms direct the *attention* to one field rather than to another. Also, *many of the "observations" are but implications of the particular terminology in terms of which the observations are made.* In brief, much that we take as observations about "reality" may be but the spinning out of possibilities implicit in our particular choice of terms.

Perhaps the simplest illustration of this point is to be got by contrasting secular and theological terminologies of motives. If you want to operate, like a theologian, with a terminology that includes "God" as its key term, the only sure way to do so is to put in the term, and that's that. The Bible solves the problem by putting "God" into the first sentence—and from this initial move, many implications "necessarily" follow. A naturalistic, Darwinian terminology flatly omits the term, with a corresponding set of implications—and that's that. I have called metaphysics "coy theology" because the metaphysician often introduces the term "God" not outright, as with the Bible, but by beginning with a term that *ambiguously* contains such implications; then he gradually makes these implications explicit. If the term is not introduced thus ambiguously, it can be introduced only by fiat, either outright at the beginning (like the Bible) or as a *non sequitur* (a break in the argument somewhere along the way). In Platonic dialogues, myth sometimes serves this purpose of a leap en route, a step prepared for by the fact that, in the Platonic dialectic, the methodic progress toward *higher levels of generalization* was in itself thought of as progress toward *the divine*.

But such a "terministic situation" is not by any means confined to matters of theology or metaphysics. As Jeremy Bentham aptly pointed out, all terms for mental states, sociopolitical relationships, and the like are necessarily "fictions," in the sense that we must express such concepts by the use of terms borrowed from the realm of the physical. Thus, what Emerson said in the accents of transcendental enthusiasm, Bentham said in the accents of "tough-mindedness." In Emerson's "tender-minded" scheme, "nature" exists to provide us with terms for the physical realm that are transferable to the moral realm, as the sight of a straight line gives us our word for "right," and of a crooked or twisted line our word for "wrong"; or as we derived our word for "spirit" from a word for "breath," or as "superciliousness" means literally a raising of the eyebrow. But Bentham would state the same relationship "tough-mindedly" by noting that our words for "right," "wrong," "spirit," etc. are "fictions" carried over from their strictly literal use in the realm of physical sensation. Bentham does not hope that such "fictions" can be avoided. He but asks that we recognize their nature as fictions. So he worked out a technique for helping to disclose the imagery in such ideas, and to discount accordingly. (See C. K. Ogden's book, *Bentham's Theory of Fictions.*)

But though this situation is by no means confined to the terminologies of theology and metaphysics, or even to such sciences as psychology (with terms for the out-going as vs. the in-turning, for dispositions, tendencies, drives, for the workings of the "it" in the Unconscious, and so on), by its very thoroughness theology does have a formula that we can adapt, for purely secular purposes of analysis. I have in mind the injunction, at once pious and methodological, "Believe, that you may understand (*crede, ut intelligas*)." In its theological application, this formula served to define the relation between faith and reason. That is, if one begins with "faith," which must be taken on authority, one can work out a rationale based on this faith. But the faith must "precede" the rationale. (We here impinge upon considerations of logical and temporal priority that were approached from another angle in the previous chapter.)

In my book, *The Rhetoric of Religion,* I have proposed that the word "logology" might be applied in a special way to this issue. By "logology," as so conceived, I would mean the systematic study of theological terms, not from the standpoint of their truth or falsity as statements about the supernatural, but purely for the light they might throw upon the *forms* of language. That is, the tactics involved in the theologian's "words about God" might be studied as "words about words" (by using as a methodological bridge the opening sentence in

the Gospel of John: "In the beginning was the Word, and the Word
was with God, and the Word was God").

"Logology" would be a purely empirical study of symbolic action.
Not being a theologian, I would have no grounds to discuss the truth
or falsity of theological doctrines as such. But I do feel entitled to
discuss them with regard to their nature merely as language. And it is
my claim that the injunction, "Believe, that you may understand," has
a fundamental application to the purely secular problem of "terministic screens."

The "logological" or "terministic" counterpart of "Believe" in the
formula would be: *Pick some particular nomenclature, some one terministic screen.* And for "That you may understand," the counterpart
would be: "*That you may proceed to track down the kinds of observation implicit in the terminology you have chosen, whether your
choice of terms was deliberate or spontaneous.*"

Examples

I can best state the case by giving some illustrations. But first let me
ask you to consider [the following] passage which presents the matter
in the most general sense:

> . . . can we bring ourselves to realize just how overwhelmingly much of
> what we mean by "reality" has been built up for us through nothing but
> our symbol systems? Take away our books, and what little do we know
> about history, biography, even something so "down to earth" as the rela-
> tive position of seas and continents? What is our "reality" for today (be-
> yond the paper-thin line of our own particular lives) but all this clutter of
> symbols about the past, combined with whatever things we know mainly
> through maps, magazines, newspapers, and the like about the present? In
> school, as they go from class to class, students turn from one idiom to
> another. The various courses in the curriculum are in effect but so many
> different terminologies. And however important to us is the tiny sliver of
> reality each of us has experienced firsthand, the whole overall "picture" is
> but a construct of our symbol systems. To meditate on this fact until one
> sees its full implications is much like peering over the edge of things into
> an ultimate abyss. And doubtless that's one reason why, though man is
> typically the symbol-using animal, he clings to a kind of naïve verbal real-
> ism that refuses to let him realize the full extent of the role played by
> symbolicity in his notions of reality.[1]

I hope the passage can serve at least somewhat to suggest how fan-
tastically much of our "Reality" could not exist for us, were it not for

1. See p. 5 [of *Language as Symbolic Action*—ED. NOTE].

our profound and inveterate involvement in symbol systems. Our presence in a room is immediate, but the room's relation to our country as a nation, and beyond that, to international relations and cosmic relations, dissolves into a web of ideas and images that reach through our senses only insofar as the symbol systems that report on them are heard or seen. To mistake this vast tangle of ideas for immediate experience is much more fallacious than to accept a dream as an immediate experience. For a dream really is an immediate experience, but the information that we receive about today's events throughout the world most decidedly is *not*.

But let us consider some examples of terministic screens, in a more specific sense. The child psychologist, John Bowlby, writes a subtle and perceptive paper on "The Nature of the Child's Ties to Its Mother." He observes what he calls "five instinctual responses" of infants, which he lists as: crying, smiling, sucking, clinging, following. Surely no one would deny that such responses are there to see. But at the same time, we might recall the observations of the behaviorist, John B. Watson. He, too, found things that were there to see. For instance, by careful scientific study, he discovered sure ways to make babies cry in fright or shriek with rage.

In contrast with Watson's terminology of observation regarding the nature of infantile reflexes, note that Bowlby adopted a much more *social* point of view. His terms were explicitly designed to study infantile responses that involved the mother in a reciprocal relationship to the child.

At the time I read Bowlby's paper, I happened to be doing a monograph on "Verbal Action in St. Augustine's *Confessions*." I was struck by the fact that Augustine's terms for the behavior of infants closely paralleled Bowlby's. Three were definitely the same: crying, smiling, sucking. Although he doesn't mention clinging as a particularly notable term with regard to infancy, as the result of Bowlby's list I noticed, as I might otherwise not have, that he frequently used the corresponding Latin term (*inhaerere*) regarding his attachment to the Lord. "Following" was not explicitly worked out, as an infantile response, though Augustine does refer to God as his leader. And I began wondering what might be done with Spinoza's *Ethics* in this connection, whether his persistent concern with what necessarily "follows" what in Nature could have been in part a metaphysician's transformation of a personal motive strong in childhood. Be that as it may, I was struck by the fact that Augustine made one strategically important addition to Bowlby's list: rest. Once you mention it, you realize that it is very definitely an instinctual response of the sort that Bowlby was concerned with, since it involves a social relation between mother and child. In Augustine's scheme, of course, it also allowed for a transformation from resting as an infant to hopes of ultimately "resting in God."

Our point is: All three terminologies (Watson's, Bowlby's, Augustine's) directed the attention differently, and thus led to a correspondingly different quality of observations. In brief, "behavior" isn't something that you need but observe; even something so "objectively there" as behavior must be observed through one or another kind of terministic screen that directs the attention in keeping with its nature.

Basically, there are two kinds of terms: terms that put things together, and terms that take things apart. Otherwise put, A can feel himself identified with B, or he can think of himself as disassociated from B. Carried into mathematics, some systems stress the principle of continuity, some the principle of discontinuity, or particles. And since all laboratory instruments of measurement and observation are devices invented by the symbol-using animal, they too necessarily give interpretations in terms of either continuity or discontinuity. Hence, physicists forever keep finding that some sub-sub-sub-sub-aspect of nature can be again subdivided; whereupon it's only a question of time until they discover that some new cut merges moments previously considered distinct—and so on. Knowing nothing much about physics except the terministic fact that any observation of a physicist must necessarily be stated within the resources and embarrassments of man-made terminologies, I would still dare risk the proposition that Socrates' basic point about dialectic will continue to prevail; namely, there is composition, and there is divison.

Often this shows up as a distinction between terministic screens positing differences of *degree* and those based on differences of *kind*. For instance, Darwin sees only a difference of degree between man and other animals. But the theologian sees a difference in kind. That is, where Darwin views man as *continuous* with other animals, the theologian would stress the principle of *discontinuity* in this regard. But the theologian's screen also posits a certain kind of *continuity* between man and God that is not ascribed to the relation between God and other animals.

The logological screen finds itself in a peculiar position here. It holds that, even on the purely secular level, Darwin overstated his case. And as a consequence, in his stress upon the principle of *continuity* between man and the other animals, he unduly slighted the evidence for *discontinuity* here. For he assumed that the principle of discontinuity between man and other animals was necessarily identical with a theological view of man.

Such need not be the case at all. Darwin says astonishingly little about man's special aptitudes as a symbol-user. His terministic screen so stressed the principle of continuity here that he could view the principle of discontinuity only as a case of human self-flattery. Yet, logology would point out: We can distinguish man from other animals without necessarily being overhaughty. For what other animals have yellow journalism, corrupt politics, pornography, stock market manipulators, plans for waging thermonuclear, chemical, and bacteriological war? I think we can consider ourselves different in kind from the other animals, without necessarily being overproud of our distinction. We don't need theology, but merely the evidence of our characteristic sociopolitical disorders, to make it apparent that man, the typically symbol-using animal, is alas! something special.

Further Examples

Where are we, then?

We *must* use terministic screens, since we can't say anything without the use of terms; whatever terms we use, they necessarily constitute a corresponding kind of screen; and any such screen necessarily directs the attention to one field rather than another. Within that field there can be different screens, each with its ways of directing the attention and shaping the range of observations implicit in the given terminology. All terminologies must implicitly or explicitly embody choices between the principle of continuity and the principle of discontinuity.

Two other variants of this point about continuity and discontinuity should be mentioned. First, note how it operates in political affairs: During a national election, the situation places great stress upon a *division* between the citizens. But often such divisiveness (or discontinuity) can be healed when the warring factions join in a common cause against an alien enemy (the division elsewhere thus serving to reestablish the principle of continuity at home). It should be apparent how either situation sets up the conditions for its particular kind of scapegoat, as a device that unifies all those who share the same enemy.

For a subtler variant (and here I am somewhat anticipating the specific subject matter of the next chapter) we might cite an observation by D. W. Harding, printed in *Metaphor and Symbol,* a collection of essays by various writers on literary and psychological symbolism. The author concedes that the Freudian terminology is highly serviceable in calling attention to ideas that are not given full conscious recognition because they are *repressed.* But he asks: Why can there not also be ideas that are unclear simply because we have not yet become familiar enough with a situation to take them adequately into account? Thus, when we see an object at a distance, we do not ordinarily "repress" the knowledge of its identity. We don't recognize it simply because we must come closer, or use an instrument, before we can see it clearly enough to know precisely what it is. Would not a terminology that features the unconscious *repression* of ideas automatically deflect our attention from symbols that are not *repressed* but merely *remote?* (At this point, of course, a Jungian terministic screen would ascribe the remoteness of many dream-symbols to their misty survival from an earlier stage in man's development—a terministic device that I have called the "temporizing of essence," since the nature of conditions *now* is stated quasi-narratively in terms of *temporal priority,* a vestigial derivation from "prehistory.")

One more point will end this part of our discussion. Recently I read a paper in which one sociologist accused other sociologists of "oversocializing" their terms for the discussion of human motives. (The article, "The Oversocialized Conception of Man in Modern Sociology," by Dennis H. Wrong, appears in the April 1961 issue of the *American Sociological Review.*)

This controversy brings us to a variant of the terministic situation I discussed in distinguishing between terms for poetics in particular and terms for language in general. But the author's thesis really has a much wider application than he claims for it. To the extent that all scientific terminologies, by their very role in specialized disciplines, are designed to focus attention upon one or another particular field of observation, would it not be technically impossible for any such specialized terminology to supply an adequate definition for the discussion of *man in general?* Each might serve to throw light upon one or another aspect of human motives. But the definition of man in general would be formally possible only to a *philosophic* terminology of motives (insofar as philosophy is the proper field for thoughts on man in general). Any definition of man in terms of specialized scientific nomenclatures would necessarily be "over-socialized," or "over-biologized," or "over-psychologized," or "over-physicized," or "over-poetized," and so on, depending upon which specialized terministic screen was being stretched to cover not just its own special field but a more comprehensive area. Or, if we try to correct the excesses of *one terminology,* by borrowing from several, what strictly *scientific* canon (in the modern sense of scientific specialization) could we adduce as sanction? Would not such an eclectic recipe itself involve a generalized philosophy of some sort?

Our Attempt to Avoid Mere Relativism

And now where are we? Must we merely resign ourselves to an endless
catalog of terministic screens, each of which can be valued for the light
it throws upon the human animal, yet none of which can be considered central? In one sense, yes. For, strictly speaking, there will be as
many different world views in human history as there are people. (*Tot
homines, tot sententiae*.) We can safely take it for granted that no one's
"personal equations" are quite identical with anyone else's. In the un-
written cosmic constitution that lies behind all man-made Constitutions, it is decreed by the nature of things that each man is "necessarily
free" to be his own tyrant, inexorably imposing upon himself the peculiar combination of insights associated with his peculiar combination of experiences.

At the other extreme, each of us shares with all other members of
our kind (the often-inhuman human species) the fatal fact that, however the situation came to be, all members of our species conceive of
reality somewhat roundabout, through various *media* of symbolism.
Any such medium will be, as you prefer, either a way of "dividing" us
from the "immediate" (thereby setting up a kind of "alienation" at
the very start of our emergence from infancy into that state of articulacy somewhat misleadingly called the "age of reason"); or it can be
viewed as a paradoxical way of "uniting" us with things on a "higher
level of awareness," or some such. (Here again, we encounter our
principles of continuity and discontinuity.)

Whether such proneness to symbolic activity be viewed as a privilege or a calamity (or as something of both), it is a distinguishing
characteristic of the human animal in general. Hence it can properly
serve as the basis of a general or philosophic definition of this animal.
From this terministic beginning, this intuitive grounding of a position,
many observations "necessarily follow." But are we not here "necessarily" caught in our own net? Must we not concede that a screen
built on this basis is just one more screen and that it can at best be
permitted to take its place along with all the others? Can we claim for
it special favors?

If I, or any one person, or even one particular philosophic school,
had invented it, such doubts would be quite justified. But if we pause
to look at it quizzically, I think we shall see that it is grounded in a
kind of "collective revelation," from away back. This "collective revelation" involves the pragmatic recognition of a distinction between
persons and things. I say "pragmatic" recognition, because often the
distinction has not been *formally* recognized. And all the more so be-

cause, if an object is closely associated with some person whom we know intimately, it can readily become infused with the identity of that person.

Reverting now to our original term, "dramatistic," I would offer this basic proposition for your consideration: Despite the evidences of primitive animism (that endows many sheer things with "souls") and the opposite modes of contemporary behaviorism (designed to study people as mere things), we do make a pragmatic distinction between the "actions" of "persons" and the sheer "motions" of "things." The slashing of the waves against the beach, or the endless cycle of births and deaths in biologic organisms would be examples of sheer motion. Yet we, the typically symbol-using animal, cannot relate to one another sheerly as things in motion. Even the behaviorist, who studies man in terms of his laboratory experiments, must treat his colleagues as *persons,* rather than purely and simply as automata responding to stimuli.

I should make it clear: I am not pronouncing on the metaphysics of this controversy. Maybe we are but things in motion. I don't have to haggle about that possibility. I need but point out that, whether or not we are just things in motion, we think of one another (and especially of those with whom we are intimate) as *persons.* And the difference between a thing and a person is that the one merely *moves* whereas the other *acts.* For the sake of the argument, I'm even willing to grant that the distinction between *things moving* and *persons acting* is but an illusion. All I would claim is that, illusion or not, the human race cannot possibly get along with itself on the basis of any other intuition. The human animal, as we know it, *emerges into personality* by first mastering whatever tribal speech happens to be its particular symbolic environment.

We could not here list even summarily the main aspects of the dramatistic screen without launching into a whole new project. For present purposes, I must only say enough to indicate my grounds for contending that a dramatistic screen does possess the philosophic character adapted to the discussion of man in general, as distinct from the kinds of insight afforded by the application of special scientific terminologies.

In behalf of my claim that the "dramatistic screen" is sanctioned by a "collective revelation" of long standing, suffice it to recall such key terms as *tao, karma, dike, energeia, hodos, actus*—all of them words for *action* (to which we might well add *Islam,* as the name for a submissive *attitude* with its obviously active possibilities). The Bible starts with God's act, by creative fiat. Contemporary sociological theories of "role-taking" fit into the same general scheme. Terms like "transactions," "exchange," "competition," "cooperation," are but more specific terms for "action." And there are countless words for specific acts: give, take, run, think, etc. The contemporary concern with "game theories" is obviously a subdivision of the same term. Add the gloomy thought that such speculative playfulness now is usually concerned with "war games." But in any case, the concept of such games must involve, in however fragmentary a fashion, the picture of persons acting under stress. And even when the "game" hypothetically reduces most of the players to terms of mere pawns, we can feel sure in advance that, if the "game" does not make proper allowance for the "human equation," the conclusions when tested will prove wrong.

But the thought should admonish us. Often it is true that people can be feasibly reduced to terms of sheer motion. About fifty years ago, I was suddenly *startled* into thinking when (encountering experience purely "symbolwise," purely via the news) I read of the first German attacks against a Belgian fortress in World War I. The point was simply this: The approach to the fortress was known to be mined. And the mines had to be exploded. So wave after wave of human flesh was sent forward, as conditioned cattle, to get blown up, until all the mines had been touched off. Then the next wave, or the next two or three waves thereafter, could take the fort. Granted, that comes pretty close to sheer motion, doubtless conceived in the best war-game tradition.

Basically, the dramatistic screen involves a methodic tracking down of the implications in the idea of symbolic action, and of man as the kind of being that is particularly distinguished by an aptitude for such action. To quote from Webster's *Third New International Dictionary,* which has officially recognized "dramatism" in my sense of the term, as treated schematically in my *Grammar of Motives,* it is "a technique of analysis of language and thought as basically modes of action rather than as means of conveying information." I would but note that such an "ism" can also function as a philosophy of human relations. The main consideration to keep in mind, for present purposes, is that two quite different but equally justifiable positions are implicit in this approach to specifically human motivation.

There is a gloomy route, of this sort: If *action* is to be our key term, then *drama;* for drama is the culminative form of action (this is a variant of the "perfection" principle discussed in [chapter two of *Language as Symbolic Action*]). But if *drama,* then *conflict.* And if *conflict,* then *victimage.* Dramatism is always on the edge of this vexing problem, that comes to a culmination in tragedy, the song of the scapegoat.

7

Motives as Action

Motives Are Shorthand Terms for Situations

What are our words for motive, then, if considered in the light of associational linkage, of stimulus and response? When it is realized that the experiences of actual life do not have the simplicity of the laboratory experiments, being rarely of the obvious dinner-bell sort but presenting very complex matters for interpretation, must we not expect to find some indication of this fact in our introspective or moralistic vocabularies of human motivation? The discovery of a law under simple conditions is not *per se* evidence that the law operates similarly under highly complex conditions. We may be justified, however, in looking for evidence of its operation in some form, as it either becomes redirected or persists vestigially.

Now, there is general agreement that, whatever the so-called phenomenon of consciousness may be, it occurs in situations marked by conflict. It thus ranges from the simple consciousness of deliberate choice, through an indecisive weighing of all the facts and consequences, to deep conscientiousness at the scrupulous fear that some important aspect of the case has been slighted, and thence to the aggravated crises of conscience. A distinguishing feature of consciousness is likewise a concern with motives and a feeling that we must consider the motives for our choices.

Would not such facts all converge to indicate that our introspective words for motives are rough, shorthand descriptions for certain typical patterns of discrepant and conflicting stimuli? If we say that we perform an act under the motivation of duty, for instance, we generally use the term to indicate a complex stimulus-situation wherein certain stimuli calling for one kind of response are linked with certain stimuli calling for another kind of response. We act out of duty as against love when we finally respond in the way which gives us less

From "Motives," in *Permanence and Change, Third Edition with a New Afterword,* pp. 29–36. Reprinted by permission of The University of California Press. © 1984 by Kenneth Burke.

immediate satisfaction (we do not throw up our job and elope) though promising more of the eventual satisfactions that may come of retaining the goodwill of irate parent or censorious neighbors. Linkages involving acquiescent response to stimuli having a pleasure-character (the thought of the elopement) are brought into conflict with linkages involving acquiescent response to stimuli having a displeasure-character ("what will people say?")—and if one finally decides to remain, on looking into his motives he will find that he has acted out of duty. In such a case, duty will be nothing other than his recognition of a particular pattern of conflict among his stimuli, a pattern recurrent frequently enough in the experiences of his group for him to have at his command a special word for it.

Or again: A man informs us that he "glanced back in suspicion." Thus, suspicion was his motivation. But suspicion is a word for designating a complex set of signs, meanings, or stimuli not wholly in consonance with one another. The concoction is somewhat as follows: danger-signs ("there is something ominous about that fellow"); reassurance-signs ("but nobody would try to rob me here"); social-signs ("I don't want to make a fool of myself if there is nothing wrong, but I could just glance back along the pavement as though I had dropped something"), etc. By his word "suspicion" he was referring to the situation itself—and he would invariably pronounce himself motivated by suspicion whenever a similar pattern of stimuli recurred. Incidentally, since we characterize a situation with reference to our general scheme of meanings, it is clear how motives, as shorthand words for situations, are assigned with reference to our orientation in general. And we may understand why *The Daily Worker* is forever outraging the bourgeoisie by attributing such awful motives to their politicians.

If our words for motive are in reality words for situation, we may even observe perhaps the "words" of motivation in a dog—for we may note in his typical postures his recognition of diverse situational patterns. There is one posture for greeting his master, another when a stranger passes along the road, another when threatened with a beating, a fourth when told to go home, a fifth when he has come upon a fresh scent, etc. He has, let us say, a vocabulary of twenty or thirty typical or recurrent situations, and we soon learn to recognize his utterance of them. A sleek young terrier in the country has a vocabulary of motives considerably different from that of a fat, coddled, overfed poodle in the city, whose only adventures are confined to candy and a constitutional on hard pavements.

This account of motives would go far to explain why so many rival theories of motivation have arisen with increasing frequency during recent centuries, to gain currency for a time among one group of specialists or one class of people. We have had people's conduct explained by an endless variety of theories: ethnological, geographical, sociological, physiological, historical, endocrinological, economic, anatomical, mystical, pathological, and so on. A particular form of art even came to flourish—the psychological or scientific novel—which devoted special attention to telling us *why* people did things, presumably because motivation had become a matter of extreme doubtfulness. Such art gave information on the subject of conduct, its style becoming less and less poetic or ingratiating, and more and more trimmed to the needs of exposition and explanation.

In great eras of drama, the audiences *know* why characters act as they do. The characters themselves may be in a quandary, but the audience has merely to see them act and hear them talk, and the motives are taken for granted. But we even become muddled as to the motives in these earlier dramas—hence our development of an art form with motivation as its specific subject-matter. This fact in itself should indicate our growing instability; for in highly stable eras, the recurrent patterns of life are highly stabilized, hence the combinations of complex stimuli become standardized, hence the matter of motives is settled. At such times of cultural integration a man may *lie* about his motives, but the suspicion that he might not know them himself is unthinkable.

By our interpretation such an attitude is justified, since his statement of his motives would simply name what particular pattern or combination of incompatible stimuli his situation appeared to contain. But in an age of marked instability, of great and shifting contrasts, typical patterns of stimuli would be less likely to run through the group as a whole, or even a large part of it. Many of its stimulus-combinations will thus be unnamed (at least as regards this deepest kind of naming: certainty as to motive and universalization of the terms for designating motive). In such vicissitudinous times as ours, however, with the advances of technology straining against the political, social, economic, æsthetic, moral orientations established at a period when the needs of society were radically different, is it not to be expected that the entire matter of motivation would again become liquid?

Our nomadism, our vast reversals from year to year in economic status, our cataclysmic shifts in the organization of the nation under war, prosperous peace, and depression, our wide diversification of occupational habits, our total blankness of expectancy as to how the world is going or where we may fit into it all five years from now, the complete disappearance of the "like father like son" attitude except perhaps in our rural districts—all such factors make for the *individualization* of one's typical, or recurrent, patterns of stimuli, as against their highly *socialized*, or *universalized* character during a period of relative stability. This state of affairs should reveal itself barometrically in the question of motives, as it does.

Indeed, it is worth noticing on this score that the attack upon introspective psychology was particularly popular in America. America is precisely the place where, on looking into one's head, one is least likely to find a vast store of regular, stabilized, recurrent experiences imbedded there, except for a few simple groups of stimuli, not highly complex at all, such as the lure of a new refrigerator, the fear of losing one's job, the distinction of smoking a certain brand of cigarette, etc. Thus, it is precisely here that the introspective search for motives might reveal something dangerously like total emptiness. Might this not be precisely the "culture" on which a behavioristic psychology could rise and take form, with its theories that education is not a drawing forth of insights from a vast store of possibilities, but a mere pumping of experiential content into an almost empty vat?

Perhaps the work most thoroughly embodying the tendency to discuss motives as situations is the *Integrative Psychology* of William Marston and his colleagues. They postulate as the fundamental drives of conduct, the nutritive, sexual, and procreative. Our social activities in all their variety are interpreted as satisfying these drives either directly or indirectly. The drives have derivative aspects: the hunger drive can be converted into commercial ambition, the sexual drive can be expressed as a concern for the welfare of society, the procreative drive can be turned into art, etc. The four motivations of "unit response" are: compliance, dominance, inducement, and submission. Compliance is the response of yielding, against our will, to a force considered superior. (The prisoner in his prison complies.) Dominance is the response of forcing things to be as we would have them. (It is seen in infancy, as the child resists the attempt to withdraw a rod from his grasp.) Inducement is accomplishment by wheedling, as in salesmanship, advertising, publicity, flattery, petition. ("The well trained child learns, during early infancy, that he must *dominate things*, and *induce human beings and animals*.") Submission is to Inducement what Compliance is to Dominance. The happy lover does not comply to dominance, but submits to inducement. The customer submits to the salesman's inducements. ("It would seem to us that all spontaneous, naïve, imitative behavior on the part of both animals and human beings is motivated by Submission. The older instinct theories usually included imitation as one of the primary instincts. Moreover it would seem that all imitative behavior must contain an element of submissive motivation even though the behavior as a whole may be controlled by dominant or compliant motives.") But of course, the opportunity for a simple "unit response" is rare in most cases of judgment. As soon as we come to complex situations, involving conflict among the drives, their derivative activities, and the four typical responses, we find that our vocabulary for motives and emotions seems to characterize stimulus-response situations as complex as those of the "moral arithmetic" which Bentham yearned to establish. The authors tentatively analyze hundreds of complex situations which popular speech names subjectively in the vocabulary of motives. The work also offers a neurological explanation of consciousness as it arises out of these conflicts in response, due to the conflicting character of stimuli.

The additional consideration which I am stressing concerns the character of the stimuli themselves. Stimuli do not possess an *absolute* meaning. Even a set of signs indicating the likelihood of death by torture has another meaning in the orientation of a comfort-loving skeptic than it would for the ascetic whose world-view promised eternal reward for martyrdom. Any given situation derives its character from the entire framework of interpretation by which we judge it. And differences in our ways of sizing up an objective situation are expressed subjectively as differences in our assignment of motive.

But the question of motive brings us to the subject of communication, since motives are distinctly linguistic products. We discern situational patterns by means of the particular vocabulary of the cultural group into which we are born. Our minds, as linguistic products, are composed of concepts (verbally molded) which select certain relationships as meaningful. Other groups may select other relationships as meaningful. These relationships are not *realities,* they are *interpretations* of reality—hence different frameworks of interpretation will lead to different conclusions as to what reality is.

Some things happen *in spite of* others, some *because of* others, and some *regardless of* others. If we knew everything, we should probably eliminate the *in spite of* and the *regardless of*—but all finite schemes of interpretation differ mainly in their ways of dividing up these three categories. The naturalist, for instance, may say that *A* was hurt in an accident *regardless of* his wickedness—the super-naturalist might say that the accident occurred *because of* *A*'s wickedness. Shifts of interpretation result from the different ways in which we group events in the *because of, in spite of,* and *regardless of* categories.

Such shifts of interpretation make for totally different pictures of reality, since they focus the attention upon different orders of relationship. We learn to single out certain relationships in accordance with the particular linguistic texture into which we are born, though we may privately manipulate this linguistic texture to formulate still other relationships. When we do so, we invent new terms, or apply our old vocabulary in new ways, attempting to socialize our position by so manipulating the linguistic equipment of our group that our particular additions or alterations can be shown to fit into the old texture. We try to point out new relationships as meaningful—we interpret situations differently; in the subjective sphere, we invent new accounts of motive. Since both the old and the new motives are linguistically constructed, and since language is a *communicative* medium, the present discussion has taken us from orientation, through motivation, to communication. And the remainder of this section will deal with communication.

III

DRAMATISTIC ANALYSIS

8

Dramatistic Method

Dramatism

Dramatism is a method of analysis and a corresponding critique of terminology designed to show that the most direct route to the study of human relations and human motives is via a methodical inquiry into cycles or clusters of terms and their functions.

The dramatistic approach is implicit in the key term "act." "Act" is thus a terministic center from which many related considerations can be shown to "radiate," as though it were a "god-term" from which a whole universe of terms is derived. The dramatistic study of language comes to a focus in a philosophy of language (and of "symbolicity" in general); the latter provides the basis for a general conception of man and of human relations. The present discussion will consider primarily the dramatistic concern with the resources, limitations, and paradoxes of terminology, particularly in connection with the imputing of motives.

The Dramatistic Approach to Action

Dramatism centers on observations of this sort: for there to be an *act*, there must be an *agent*. Similarly, there must be a *scene* in which the agent acts. To act in a scene, the agent must employ some means, or *agency*. And it can be called an act in the full sense of the term only if it involves a *purpose* (that is, if a support happens to give way and one falls, such motion on the agent's part is not an act, but an accident). These five terms (act, scene, agent, agency, purpose) have been labeled the *dramatistic pentad*; the aim of calling attention to them in this way is to show how the functions which they designate operate in the imputing of motives (*A Grammar of Motives and a Rhetoric of Motives* 1962, Introduction). The pattern is incipiently a hexad when

From "Dramatism" by Kenneth Burke. Reprinted by permission of Macmillan Publishing Co. from the *International Encyclopedia of the Social Sciences*, edited by David L. Sills, vol. 7, pp. 445–47. © 1968 by Crowell Collier and Macmillan, Inc.

viewed in connection with the different but complementary analysis of *attitude* (as an ambiguous term for *incipient* action) undertaken by George Herbert Mead (1938) and by I. A. Richards (1923).

Later we shall consider the question whether the key terms of dramatism are literal or metaphorical. In the meantime, other important things about the terms themselves should be noted.

Obviously, for instance, the concept of scene can be widened or narrowed (conceived of in terms of varying "scope" or circumference). Thus, an agent's behavior ("act") might be thought of as taking place against a polytheistic background; or the overall scene may be thought of as grounded in one god; or the circumference of the situation can be narrowed to naturalistic limits, as in Darwinism; or it can be localized in such terms as "Western civilization," "Elizabethanism," "capitalism," "D day," "10 Downing Street," "on this train ride," and so on, endlessly. Any change of the circumference in terms of which an act is viewed implies a corresponding change in one's view of the quality of the act's motivation. Such a loose yet compelling correspondence between act and scene is called a "scene-act ratio" [*A Grammar of Motives* and *A Rhetoric of Motives*, 1962, pp. 1–7].

All the terms are capable of similar relationships. A "purpose-agency ratio," for instance, would concern the logic of "means selecting," the relation of means to ends (as the Supreme Court might decide that an emergency measure is constitutional because it was taken in an emergency situation). An "agent-act ratio" would reflect the correspondence between a man's character and the character of his behavior (as, in a drama, the principles of formal consistency require that each member of the dramatis personae act in character, though such correspondences in art can have a perfection not often found in life). In actual practice, such ratios are used sometimes to explain an act and sometimes to *justify it* (*ibid.*, pp. 15–20). Such correlations are not strict, but analogical. Thus, by "scene-act ratio" is meant a proposition such as: Though agent and act are necessarily different in many of their attributes, some notable element of one is implicitly or analogously present in the other.

David Hume's *An Inquiry Concerning Human Understanding* (first published in 1748) throws a serviceable light upon the dramatistic "ratios." His treatise begins with the observation that "moral philosophy, or the science of human nature, may be treated after two different manners." One of these "considers man chiefly as born for action." The other would "consider man in the light of a reasonable rather than an active being, and endeavor to form his understanding more than cultivate his manners" ([1748] 1952, 451). Here, in essence, is the distinction between a dramatistic approach in terms of *action* and an approach in terms of *knowledge*. For, as a "reasonable being," Hume says, man "receives from science" his proper food and nourishment. But man "is a sociable, no less than a reasonable being. . . . Man is also an active being; and from that disposition, as well as from the various necessities of human life, must submit to business and occupation" (Hume 1952, 452).

Insofar as men's actions are to be interpreted in terms of the circumstances in which they are acting, their behavior would fall under the heading of a "scene-act ratio." But insofar as their acts reveal their different characters, their behavior would fall under the heading of an "agent-act ratio." For instance, in a time of great crisis, such as a shipwreck, the conduct of all persons involved in that crisis could be expected to manifest in some way the motivating influence of the crisis. Yet, within such a "scene-act ratio" there would be a range of "agent-act ratios," insofar as one man was "proved" to be cowardly, another bold, another resourceful, and so on.

Talcott Parsons, in one of his earlier works, has analytically unfolded, for sociological purposes, much the same set of terministic functions that is here being called dramatistic (owing to their nature as implied in the idea of an "act"). Thus, in dealing with "the unit of action systems," Parsons writes:

> An "act" involves logically the following: (1) It implies an agent, an "actor." (2) For purposes of definition the act must have an "end," a future state of affairs toward which the process of action is oriented. (3) It must be initiated in a "situation" of which the trends of development differ in one or more important respects from the state of affairs to which the action is oriented, the end. This situation is in turn analyzable into two elements: those over which the actor has no control, that is which he cannot alter, or prevent from being altered, in conformity with his end, and those over which he has such control. The former may be termed the "conditions" of action, the latter the "means." Finally (4) there is inherent in the conception of this unit, in its analytical uses, a certain mode of relationship between these elements. That is, in the choice of alternative means to the end, in so far as the situation allows alternatives, there is a "normative orientation" of actions. (1937, 44)

Aristotle, from whom Aquinas got his definition of God as "pure act," gives us much the same lineup when enumerating the circumstances about which we may be ignorant, with corresponding inability to act voluntarily:

[Handwritten marginalia: "Hume / action God and knowledge ↓ goes back to physical + moral / S+A ratio= circumstances / A+A ratio= character / example"]

A man may be ignorant, then, of who he is, what he is doing, what or whom he is acting on, and sometimes also what (e.g. what instrument) he is doing it with, and to what end (e.g. he may think his act will conduce to some one's safety), and how he is doing it (e.g. whether gently or violently). (*Nichomachean Ethics* 1111a5)

This pattern became fixed in the medieval questions: *quis* (agent), *quid* (act), *ubi* (scene defined as place), *quibus auxiliis* (agency), *cur* (purpose), *quo modo* (manner, "attitude"), *quando* (scene defined temporally).

9

Ways of Placement

Introduction: The Five Key Terms of Dramatism

What is involved, when we say what people are doing and why they are doing it? An answer to that question is the subject of this book. *thought* The book is concerned with the basic forms of thought which, in accordance with the nature of the world as all men necessarily experi- *+ motives* ence it, are exemplified in the attributing of motives. These forms of thought can be embodied profoundly or trivially, truthfully or falsely. They are equally present in systematically elaborated metaphysical structures, in legal judgments, in poetry and fiction, in political and scientific works, in news and in bits of gossip offered at random.

We shall use five terms as generating principle of our investigation. They are: act, scene, agent, agency, purpose. In a rounded statement about motives, you must have some word that names the *act* (names what took place, in thought or deed), and another that names the *scene* (the background of the act, the situation in which it occurred); also, you must indicate what person or kind of person (*agent*) performed the act, what means or instruments he used (*agency*), and the *disagreement* *purpose*. Men may violently disagree about the purposes behind a given act, or about the character of the person who did it, or how he did it, or in what kind of situation he acted; or they may even insist upon totally different words to name the act itself. But be that as it *But* may, any complete statement about motives will offer *some kind of* answers to these five questions: what was done (act), when or where it was done (scene), who did it (agent), how he did it (agency), and why (purpose).

If you ask why, with a whole world of terms to choose from, we select these rather than some others as basic, our book itself is offered as the answer. For, to explain our position, we shall show how it can be applied.

Act, scene, agent, agency, purpose. Although, over the centuries,

From *A Grammar of Motives*, pp. xv–xxiii, 3–9, 15–20. Reprinted by permission of The University of California Press. © 1969 by Kenneth Burke.

men have shown great enterprise and inventiveness in pondering matters of human motivation, one can simplify the subject by this pentad of key terms, which are understandable almost at a glance. They need never to be abandoned, since all statements that assign motives can be shown to arise out of them and to terminate in them. By examining them quizzically, we can range far; yet the terms are always there for us to reclaim, in their everyday simplicity, their almost miraculous easiness, thus enabling us constantly to begin afresh. When they might become difficult, when we can hardly see them, through having stared at them too intensely, we can of a sudden relax, to look at them as we always have, lightly, glancingly. And having reassured ourselves, we can start out again, once more daring to let them look strange and difficult for a time.

In an exhibit of photographic murals (*Road to Victory*) at the Museum of Modern Art, there was an aerial photograph of two launches, proceeding side by side on a tranquil sea. Their wakes crossed and recrossed each other in almost an infinity of lines. Yet despite the intricateness of this tracery, the picture gave an impression of great simplicity, because one could quickly perceive the generating principle of its design. Such, ideally, is the case with our pentad of terms, used as generating principle. It should provide us with a kind of simplicity that can be developed into considerable complexity and yet can be discovered beneath its elaborations.

We want to inquire into the purely internal relationships which the five terms bear to one another, considering their possibilities of transformation, their range of permutations and combinations—and then to see how these various resources figure in actual statements about human motives. Strictly speaking, we mean by a grammar of motives a concern with the terms alone, without reference to the ways in which their potentialities have been or can be utilized in actual statements about motives. Speaking broadly we could designate as "philosophies" any statements in which these grammatical resources are specifically utilized. Random or unsystematic statements about motives could be considered as fragments of a philosophy.

One could think of the grammatical resources as *principles* and of the various philosophies as *casuistries* which apply these principles to temporal situations. For instance, we may examine the term scene simply as a blanket term for the concept of background or setting *in general,* a name for *any* situation in which acts or agents are placed. In our usage, this concern would be "grammatical." And we move into matters of "philosophy" when we note that one thinker uses "God" as his term for the ultimate ground or scene of human action, another uses "nature," a third uses "environment," or "history," or "means of production," etc. And whereas a statement about the grammatical principles of motivation might lay claim to a universal validity, or complete certainty, the choice of any one philosophic idiom embodying these principles is much more open to question. Even before we know what act is to be discussed, we can say with confidence that a rounded discussion of its motives must contain a reference to *some kind of* background. But since each philosophic idiom will characterize this background differently, there will remain the question as to which characterization is "right" or "more nearly right."

It is even likely that, whereas one philosophic idiom offers the best calculus for one case, another case answers best to a totally different calculus. However, we should not think of "cases" in too restricted a sense. Although, from the standpoint of the grammatical principles inherent in the internal relationships prevailing among our five terms, any given philosophy is to be considered as a casuistry, even a cultural situation extending over centuries is a "case" and would probably require a much different philosophic idiom as its temporizing calculus of motives than would be required in the case of other cultural situations.

In our original plans for this project, we had no notion of writing a "grammar" at all. We began with a theory of comedy, applied to a treatise on human relations. Feeling that competitive ambition is a drastically overdeveloped motive in the modern world, we thought this motive might be transcended if men devoted themselves not so much to "excoriating" it as to "appreciating" it. Accordingly, we began taking notes on the foibles and antics of what we tended to think of as "the Human Barnyard."

We sought to formulate the basic stratagems which people employ, in endless variations, and consciously or unconsciously, for the outwitting or cajoling of one another. Since all these devices had a "you and me" quality about them, being "addressed" to some person or to some advantage, we classed them broadly under the heading of a rhetoric. There were other notes, concerned with modes of expression and appeal in the fine arts and with purely psychological or psychoanalytic matters. These we classed under the heading of symbolic.

We had made still further observations, which we at first strove uneasily to class under one or the other of these two heads, but which we were eventually able to distinguish as the makings of a grammar. For we found in the course of writing that our project needed a grounding in formal considerations logically prior to both the rhetorical and the psychological. And as we proceeded with this introduc-

tory groundwork, it kept extending its claims until it had spun itself
from an intended few hundred words into nearly 200,000, of which
the present book is revision and abridgement.

Theological, metaphysical, and juridical doctrines offer the best illustration of the concerns we place under the heading of grammar; the
forms and methods of art best illustrated the concerns of symbolic;
and the ideal material to reveal the nature of rhetoric comprises observations on parliamentary and diplomatic devices, editorial bias,
sales methods and incidents of social sparring. However, the three
fields overlap considerably. And we shall note, in passing, how the
rhetoric and the symbolic hover about the edges of our central theme,
the grammar.

A perfectionist might seek to evolve terms free of ambiguity and
inconsistency (as with the terministic ideals of symbolic logic and logical positivism). But we have a different purpose in view, one that
probably retains traces of its "comic" origin. We take it for granted
that, insofar as men cannot themselves create the universe, there must
remain something essentially enigmatic about the problem of motives,
and that this underlying enigma will manifest itself in inevitable ambiguities and inconsistencies among the terms for motives. Accordingly, what we want is *not terms that avoid ambiguity,* but *terms that
clearly reveal the strategic spots at which ambiguities necessarily arise.*
Occasionally, you will encounter a writer who seems to get great
exaltation out of proving, with an air of much relentlessness, that
some philosophic term or other has been used to cover a variety of
meanings and who would smash and abolish this idol. As a general
rule, when a term is singled out for such harsh treatment, if you look
closer you will find that it happens to be associated with some cultural
or political trend from which the writer would dissociate himself;
hence there is a certain notable ambiguity in this very charge of ambiguity, since he presumably feels purged and strengthened by bringing to bear upon this particular term a kind of attack that could, with
as much justice, be brought to bear upon any other term (or "title")
in philosophy, including of course the alternative term, or "title," that
the writer would swear by. Since no two things or acts or situations
are exactly alike, you cannot apply the same term to both of them
without thereby introducing a certain margin of ambiguity, an ambiguity as great as the difference between the two subjects that are given
the identical title. And all the more may you expect to find ambiguity
in terms so "titular" as to become the marks of a philosophic school,
or even several philosophic schools. Hence, instead of considering it
our task to "dispose of" any ambiguity by merely disclosing the fact

that it is an ambiguity, we rather consider it our task to study and clarify the *resources* of ambiguity. For in the course of this work, we shall deal with many kinds of *transformation*—and it is in the areas of ambiguity that transformations take place; in fact, without such areas, transformation would be impossible. Distinctions, we might say, arise out of a great central moltenness, where all is merged. They have been thrown from a liquid center to the surface, where they have congealed. Let one of these crusted distinctions return to its source, and in this alchemic center it may be remade, again becoming molten liquid, and may enter into new combinations, whereat it may be again thrown forth as a new crust, a different distinction. So that A may become non-A. But not merely by a leap from one state to the other. Rather, we must take A back into the ground of its existence, the logical substance that is its causal ancestor, and on to a point where it is consubstantial with non-A; then we may return, this time emerging with non-A instead.

And so with our five terms: certain formal interrelationships prevail among these terms, by reason of their role as attributes of a common ground or substance. Their participation in a common ground makes for transformability. At every point where the field covered by any one of these terms overlaps upon the field covered by any other, there is an alchemic opportunity, whereby we can put one philosophy or doctrine of motivation into the alembic, make the appropriate passes, and take out another. From the central moltenness, where all the elements are fused into one togetherness, there are thrown forth, in separate crusts, such distinctions as those between freedom and necessity, activity and passiveness, cooperation and competition, cause and effect, mechanism and teleology.

Our term, "agent," for instance, is a general heading that might, in a given case, require further subdivision, as an agent might have his act modified (hence partly motivated) by friends (co-agents) or enemies (counter-agents). Again, under "agent" one could place any personal properties that are assigned a motivational value, such as "ideas," "the will," "fear," "malice," "intuition," "the creative imagination." A portrait painter may treat the body as a property of the agent (an expression of personality), whereas materialistic medicine would treat it as "scenic," a purely "objective material"; and from another point of view it could be classed as an agency, a means by which one gets reports of the world at large. Machines are obviously instruments (that is, agencies); yet in their vast accumulation they constitute the industrial scene, with its own peculiar set of motivational properties. War may be treated as an agency, insofar as it is a means to an end; as a collective act, subdivisible into many individual acts; as a purpose, in schemes proclaiming a cult of war. For the man inducted into the army, war is a scene, a situation that motivates the nature of his training; and in mythologies war is an agent, or perhaps better a super-agent, in the figure of the war god. We may think of voting as an act, and of the voter as an agent; yet votes and voters both are hardly other than a politician's medium or agency; or from another point of view, they are a part of his scene. And insofar as a vote is cast without adequate knowledge of its consequences, one might even question whether it should be classed as an activity at all; one might rather call it passive, or perhaps sheer motion (what the behaviorists would call a response to a stimulus).

Or imagine that one were to manipulate the terms, for the imputing of motives, in such a case as this: The hero (agent) with the help of a friend (co-agent) outwits the villain (counter-agent) by using a file (agency) that enables him to break his bonds (act) in order to escape (purpose) from the room where he has been confined (scene). In selecting a casuistry here, we might locate the motive in the agent, as were we to credit his escape to some trait integral to his personality, such as "love of freedom." Or we might stress the motivational force of the scene, since nothing is surer to awaken thoughts of escape in a man than a condition of imprisonment. Or we might note the essential part played by the *co-agent,* in assisting our hero to escape—and, with such thoughts as our point of departure, we might conclude that the motivations of this act should be reduced to social origins.

Or if one were given to the brand of speculative enterprise exemplified by certain Christian heretics (for instance, those who worshipped Judas as a saint, on the grounds that his betrayal of Christ, in leading to the Crucifixion, so brought about the opportunity for mankind's redemption) one might locate the necessary motivational origin of the act in the *counter-agent.* For the hero would not have been prodded to escape if there had been no villain to imprison him. Inasmuch as the escape could be called a "good" act, we might find in such motivational reduction to the counter-agent a compensatory transformation whereby a bitter fountain may give forth sweet waters. In his *Anti-Dühring* Engels gives us a secular variant which no one could reasonably call outlandish or excessive:

> It was slavery that first made possible the division of labour between agriculture and industry on a considerable scale, and along with this, the flower of the ancient world, Hellenism. Without slavery, no Greek state, no Greek art and science; without slavery, no Roman Empire. But without Hellenism and the Roman Empire as a basis, also no modern Europe.

We should never forget that our whole economic, political and intellectual development has as its presupposition a state of things in which slavery was as necessary as it was universally recognized. In this sense we are entitled to say: Without the slavery of antiquity, no modern socialism.

Pragmatists would probably have referred the motivation back to a source in *agency*. They would have noted that our hero escaped by using an *instrument*, the file by which he severed his bonds; then in this same line of thought, they would have observed that the hand holding the file was also an instrument; and by the same token the brain that guided the hand would be an instrument, and so likewise the educational system that taught the methods and shaped the values involved in the incident.

True, if you reduce the terms to any one of them, you will find them branching out again; for no one of them is enough. Thus, Mead called his pragmatism a philosophy of the *act*. And though Dewey stresses the value of "intelligence" as an instrument (agency, embodied in "scientific method"), the other key terms in his casuistry, "experience" and "nature," would be the equivalents of act and scene respectively. We must add, however, that Dewey is given to stressing the *overlap* of these two terms, rather than the respects in which they are distinct, as he proposes to "replace the traditional separation of nature and experience with the idea of continuity." (The quotation is from *Intelligence and the Modern World*.)

As we shall see later, it is by reason of the pliancy among our terms that philosophic systems can pull one way and another. The margins of overlap provide opportunities whereby a thinker can go without a leap from any one of the terms to any of its fellows. (We have also likened the terms to the fingers, which in their extremities are distinct from one another, but merge in the palm of the hand. If you would go from one finger to another without a leap, you need but trace the tendon down into the palm of the hand, and then trace a new course along another tendon.) Hence, no great dialectical enterprise is necessary if you would merge the terms, reducing them even to as few as one; and then, treating this as the "essential" term, the "causal ancestor" of the lot, you can proceed in the reverse direction across the margins of overlap, "deducing" the other terms from it as its logical descendants.

This is the method, explicitly and in the grant style, of metaphysics which brings its doctrines to a head in some overall title, a word for being in general, or action in general, or motion in general, or development in general, or experience in general, etc., with all its other terms distributed about this titular term in positions leading up to it and away from it. There is also an implicit kind of metaphysics, that often goes by the name of No Metaphysics, and aims at reduction not to an overall title but to some presumably underlying atomic constituent. Its vulgar variant is to be found in techniques of "unmasking," which would make for progress and emancipation by applying materialistic terms to immaterial subjects (the pattern here being, "X is nothing but Y," where X designates a higher value and Y a lower one, the higher value being thereby reduced to the lower one).

The titular word for our own method is "dramatism," since it invites one to consider the matter of motives in a perspective that, being developed from the analysis of drama, treats language and thought primarily as modes of action. The method is synoptic, though not in the historical sense. A purely historical survey would require no less than a universal history of human culture; for every judgment, exhortation, or admonition, every view of natural or supernatural reality, every intention or expectation involves assumptions about motive, or cause. Our work must be synoptic in a different sense: in the sense that it offers a system of placement, and should enable us, by the systematic manipulation of the terms, to "generate," or "anticipate" the various classes of motivational theory. And a treatment in these terms, we hope to show, reduces the subject synoptically while still permitting us to appreciate its scope and complexity.

It is not our purpose to import dialectical and metaphysical concerns into a subject that might otherwise be free of them. On the contrary, we hope to make clear the ways in which dialectical and metaphysical issues *necessarily* figure in the subject of motivation. Our speculations, as we interpret them, should show that the subject of motivation is a philosophic one, not ultimately to be solved in terms of empirical science.

Container and Thing Contained

The Scene-Act Ratio

Using "scene" in the sense of setting, or background, and "act" in the sense of action, one could say that "the scene contains the act." And using "agents" in the sense of actors, or acters, one could say that "the scene contains the agents."

It is a principle of drama that the nature of acts and agents should be consistent with the nature of the scene. And whereas comic and grotesque works may deliberately set these elements at odds with one another, audiences make allowance for such liberty, which reaffirms the same principle of consistency in its very violation.

The nature of the scene may be conveyed primarily by suggestions built into the lines of the verbal action itself, as with the imagery in the dialogue of Elizabethan drama and with the descriptive passages of novels; or it may be conveyed by nonlinguistic properties, as with the materials of naturalistic stage-sets. In any case, examining first the relation between scene and act, all we need note here is the principle whereby the scene is a fit "container" for the act, expressing in fixed properties the same quality that the action expresses in terms of development.

Ibsen's *An Enemy of the People* is a good instance of the scene-act ratio, since the correlations between scene and act are readily observable, beginning with the fact that this representative middle-class drama is enacted against a typical middle-class setting. Indeed, in this work written at the very height of Ibsen's realistic period, we can see how readily realism leads into symbolism. For the succession of scenes both *realistically reflects* the course of the action and *symbolizes* it.

The first act (we are now using the word "act" in the purely technical sense, to designate the major division of a play, a sense in which we could even reverse our formula and say that "the act contains its scenes")—the first act takes place in Dr. Stockmann's sitting room, a background perfectly suited to the thoroughly bourgeois story that is to unfold from these beginnings. In the course of this act, we learn of a scene, or situation, prior to the opening of the play, but central to its motivation. Dr. Stockmann refers to an earlier period of withdrawal, spent alone in the far North. During his isolation, he had conceived of his plan for the public Baths. This plan may be considered either realistically or symbolically; it is the dramatist's device for materializing, or objectifying, a purely spiritual process, since the plot has to do with pollution and purification on a moral level, which has its scenic counterpart in the topic of the Baths.

Act II. Still in Dr. Stockmann's sitting room. Dr. Stockmann has learned that the Baths, the vessels of purification, are themselves polluted, and that prominent business and professional men would suppress this fact for financial reasons. This opposition is epitomized in the figure of Peter Stockmann, the Doctor's brother. The intimate, familial quality of the setting thus has its counterpart in the quality of the action, which involves the struggle of two social principles, the conservative and the progressive, as objectified and personalized in the struggle of the two brothers.

Act III takes place in the editorial office of the *People's Messenger*, a local newspaper in which Dr. Stockmann has hoped to publish his evidence that the water supply was contaminated. The action takes on a more forensic reference, in keeping with the nature of the place. In this Act we have the peripety of the drama, as Dr. Stockmann's expectations are reversed. For he learns that the personal and financial influence of his enemies prevents the publication of the article. This turn of the plot has its scenic replica in mimicry involving Peter Stockmann's hat and stick, properties that symbolize his identity as mayor. In false hope of victory, Dr. Stockmann had taken them up, and strutted about burlesquing his brother. But when Dr. Stockmann learns that the editor, in response to the pressure of the conservatives, will not publish the article, it is Peter Stockmann's turn to exult. This reversal of the action is materialized (made scenic) thus:

> PETER STOCKMANN: My hat and stick, if you please. (Dr. Stockmann *takes off the hat and lays it on the table with the stick. Peter Stockman takes them up.*) Your authority as mayor has come to an untimely end.

In the next Act Dr. Stockmann does contrive to lay his case before a public tribunal of a sort: a gathering of fellow-townsmen, assembled in "a big old-fashioned room," in the house of a friend. His appeal is unsuccessful; his neighbors vote overwhelmingly against him, and the scene ends in turbulence. As regards the scene-act ratio, note that the semi-public, semi-intimate setting reflects perfectly the quality of Dr. Stockmann's appeal.

In Act V, the stage directions tell us that the hero's clothes are torn, and the room is in disorder, with broken windows. You may consider these details either as properties of the scene or as a reflection of the hero's condition after his recent struggle with the forces of reaction. The scene is laid in Dr. Stockmann's *study*, a setting so symbolic of the direction taken by the plot that the play ends with Dr. Stockmann announcing his plan to enroll twelve young *disciples* and with them to found a *school* in which he will work for the *education* of society.

The whole plot is that of an internality directed outwards. We progress by stages from a scene (reported) wherein the plan of social purification was conceived in loneliness, to the scene in his study where the hero announces in the exaltation of a dramatic finale: "The strongest man in the world is he who stands most alone." The pronouncement is modified by the situation in which it is uttered: as Dr. Stockmann speaks, he is surrounded by a loyal and admiring family circle, and his educational plan calls not for complete independence, but for cooperation. He is not setting himself up as the strongest man in the world, but merely as one headed in the same direction. And, with the exception of his brother Peter, we may consider his family circle as aspects of his own identity, being under the aegis of "loneliness" since it began so and retains the quality of the ancestry.

The end of the third play in O'Neill's trilogy, *Mourning Becomes Electra*, presents a contrasting instance of the scene-act ratio:

> LAVINIA: (*turns to him sharply*) You go now and close the shutters and nail them tight.
> SETH: Ayeh.
> LAVINIA: And tell Hannah to throw out all the flowers.
> SETH: Ayeh. (*He goes past her up the steps and into the house. She ascends to the portico—and then turns and stands for a while, stiff and square-shouldered, staring into the sunlight with frozen eyes. Seth leans out of the window at the right of the door and pulls the shutters closed with a decisive bang. As if this were a word of command, Lavinia pivots sharply on her heel and marches woodenly into the house, closing the door behind her.*)
>
> CURTAIN

We end here on the motif of the shut-in personality, quite literally objectified. And the closing, novelistic stage-directions are beautifully suited to our purpose; for note how, once the shutters have been closed, thereby placing before our eyes the scenic replica of Lavinia's mental state, this scene in turn becomes the motivation of her next act. For we are told that she walks like an automaton in response to the closing of the shutter, "as if this were a word of command."

Hamlet contains a direct reference to the motivational aspect of the scene-act ratio. In an early scene, when Hamlet is about to follow the Ghost, Horatio warns:

> What if it tempt you toward the flood, my lord,
> Or to the dreadful summit of the cliff
> That beetles o'er his base into the sea,
> And there assume some other horrible form,
> Which might deprive your sovereignty of reason
> And draw you into madness? Think of it;
> The very place puts toys of desperation,
> Without more motive, into every brain
> That looks so many fathoms to the sea
> And hears it roar beneath.

In the last four lines of this speech, Horatio is saying that the sheer natural surroundings might be enough to provide a man with a motive for an act as desperate and absolute as suicide. This notion (of the natural scene as sufficient motivation for an act) was to reappear, in many transformations, during the subsequent centuries. We find a variant of it in the novels of Thomas Hardy, and in other regionalists who derive motivations for their characters from what Virgil would have called the *genius loci*. There are unmistakable vestiges of it in scientific theories (of Darwinian cast) according to which men's behavior and development are explained in terms of environment. Geopolitics is a contemporary variant.

From the motivational point of view, there is implicit in the quality of a scene the quality of the action that is to take place within it. This would be another way of saying that the act will be consistent with the scene. Thus, when the curtain rises to disclose a given stage-set, this stage-set contains, simultaneously, implicitly, all that the narrative is to draw out as a sequence, explicitly. Or, if you will, the stage-set contains the action *ambiguously* (as regards the norms of action)— and in the course of the play's development this ambiguity is converted into a corresponding *articulacy.* The proportion would be: scene is to act as implicit is to explicit. One could not deduce the details of the action from the details of the setting, but one could deduce the quality of the action from the quality of the setting. An extreme illustration would be an Expressionistic drama, having for its scenic reflex such abstract properties as lines askew, grotesque lighting, sinister color, and odd objects.

We have, of course, chosen examples particularly suited to reveal the distinction between act and scene as well as their interdependence. The matter is obscured when we are dealing with scene in the sense of the relationships prevailing among the various *dramatis personae.* For the characters, by being in interaction, could be treated as scenic conditions or "environment," of one another; and any act could be treated as part of the context that modifies (hence, to a degree motivates) the subsequent acts. The principles of dramatic consistency would lead one to expect such cases of overlap among the terms; but while being aware of them we should firmly fix in our minds such cases as afford a clear differentiation. Our terms lending themselves to both merger and division, we are here trying to divide two of them while recognizing their possibilities of merger.

The Scene-Agent Ratio

The scene-agent ratio, where the synecdochic relation is between person and place, is partly exemplified in this citation from Carlyle's *Heroes and Hero-Worship:*

> These Arabs Mohammed was born among are certainly a notable people. Their country itself is notable; the fit habitation for such a race. Savage inaccessible rock-mountains, great grim deserts, alternating with beautiful

strips of verdure; wherever water is, there is greenness, beauty; odoriferous balm-shrubs, date-trees, frankincense-trees. Consider that wide waste horizon of sand, empty, silent, like a sand-sea, dividing habitable place from habitable place. You are all alone there, left alone with the universe; by day a fierce sun blazing down on it with intolerable radiance; by night the great deep heaven with its stars. Such a country is fit for a swift-handed, deep-hearted race of men.

The correlation between the quality of the country and the quality of its inhabitants is here presented in quite secular terms. There is a sonnet by Wordsworth that is a perfect instance of the scene-agent ratio treated theologically:

It is a beauteous evening, calm and free,
The holy time is quiet as a Nun
Breathless with adoration; the broad sun
Is sinking down in its tranquillity;
The gentleness of heaven broods o'er the Sea;
Listen! the mighty Being is awake,
And doth with his eternal motion make
A sound like thunder—everlastingly.

Dear Child! Dear Girl! that walkest with me here,
If thou appear untouched by solemn thought,
Thy nature is not therefore less divine:
Thou liest in Abraham's bosom all the year;
And worship'st at the Temple's inner shrine,
God being with thee when we know it not.

By selecting a religious image in which to convey the purely naturalistic sense of hush, the octave infuses the natural scene with hints of a wider circumference, supernatural in scope. The sestet turns from scene to agent; indeed, the octave is all scene, the sestet all agent. But by the logic of the scene-agent ratio, if the scene is supernatural in quality, the agent contained by this scene will partake of the same supernatural quality. And so, spontaneously, purely by being the kind of agent that is at one with this kind of scene, the child is "divine." The contents of a divine container will synecdochically share in its divinity.

Swift's satire on philosophers and mathematicians, the Laputans in the third book of *Gulliver's Travels,* offers a good instance of the way in which the scene-agent ratio can be used for the depiction of character. To suggest that the Laputans are, we might say, "up in the air," he portrays them as living on an island that floats in space. Here the nature of the inhabitants is translated into terms of their habitation.

Variants of the scene-agent ratio abound in typical nineteenth-century thought, so strongly given to the study of motives by the dialectic pairing of people and things (man and nature, agent and scene). The ratio figures characteristically in the idealist's concern with the *Einklang zwischen Innen- und Aussenwelt.* The paintings of the pointillist Seurat carry the sense of consistency between scene and agent to such lengths that his human figures seem on the point of dissolving into their background. However, we here move beyond strictly scene-agent matters into the area better covered by our term, agency, since the extreme impression of consistency between scene and agent is here conveyed by stressing the distinctive terms of the method, or medium (that is, agency), which serves as an element common to both scene and agents.

The logic of the scene-agent ratio has often served as an embarrassment to the naturalistic novelist. He may choose to "indict" some scene (such as bad working conditions under capitalism) by showing that it has a "brutalizing" effect upon the people who are indigenous to this scene. But the scene-agent ratio, if strictly observed here, would require that the "brutalizing" situation contain "brutalized" characters as its dialectical counterpart. And thereby, in his humanitarian zeal to save mankind, the novelist portrays characters which, in being as brutal as their scene, are not worth saving. We could phrase this dilemma in another way: our novelist points up his thesis by too narrow a conception of scene as the motive-force behind his characters; and this restricting of the scene calls in turn for a corresponding restriction upon personality, or rôle.

·   ·   ·

Range of All the Ratios

Though we have inspected two ratios, the five terms would allow for ten (scene-act, scene-agent, scene-agency, scene-purpose, act-purpose, act-agent, act-agency, agent-purpose, agent-agency, and agency-purpose). The ratios are principles of determination. Elsewhere in the grammar we shall examine two of these (scene-purpose and agency-purpose) in other connections; and the rest will figure in passing. But the consideration of words for "ways" calls for special attention to the *act-agent* ratio.

Both act and agent require scenes that "contain" them. Hence the scene-act and scene-agent ratios are in the fullest sense positive (or "positional"). But the relation between act and agent is not quite the same. The agent does not "contain" the act, though its results might be said to "pre-exist virtually" within him. And the act does not "synecdochically share" in the agent, though certain ways of acting may be said to induce corresponding moods or traits of character. To this writer, at least, the act-agent ratio more strongly suggests a temporal or sequential relationship than a purely positional or geometric one. The agent is an author of his acts, which are descended from him, being good progeny if he is good, or bad progeny if he is bad, wise progeny if he is wise, silly progeny if he is silly. And, conversely, his acts can make him or remake him in accordance with their nature. They would be his product and/or he would be theirs. Similarly, when we use the scene-act and scene-agent ratios in reverse (as with the sequence from act or agent to corresponding scene) the image of derivation is stronger than the image of position.

One discerns the workings of the act-agent ratio in the statement of a former cabinet member to the effect that "you can safely lodge responsibility with the President of the United States," owing to "the tremendous sobering influence of the Presidency on any man, especially in foreign affairs." Here, the sheer nature of an office, or position, is said to produce important modifications in a man's character. Even a purely symbolic act, such as the donning of priestly vestments, is often credited with such a result. And I have elsewhere quoted a remark by a political commentator: "There seems to be something about the judicial robes that not only hypnotizes the beholder but transforms the wearer."

Ordinarily, the scene-act and scene-agent ratios can be extended to cover such cases. Thus, the office of the Presidency may be treated as a "situation" affecting the agent who occupies it. And the donning of vestments brings about a symbolic situation that can likewise be treated in terms of the scene-agent ratio. But there are cases where a finer discrimination is needed. For instance, the resistance of the Russian armies to the Nazi invasion could be explained "scenically" in terms of the Soviet political and economic structure; or one could use the act-agent ratio, attributing the power and tenacity to "Russian" traits of character. However, in deriving the act from the scene, one would have to credit socialism as a major scenic factor, whereas a derivation of the act from the agents would allow for a much more felicitous explanation from the standpoint of capitalist apologetics.

Thus, one of our leading newspapers asked itself whether Hitler failed "to evaluate a force older than communism, more instinctive than the mumbling cult of Stalin—the attachment of the peasant masses to 'Mother Russia,' the incoherent but cohesive force of Russian patriotism." And it concluded that "the Russian soldier has proved the depth of his devotion to the Russian soil." Patriotism, attachment to the "mother," devotion to the soil—these are essentially motives located in the agent, hence requiring no acknowledgment of socialist motives.

There is, of course, scenic reference in the offing; but the stress upon the term, agent, encourages one to be content with a very vague treatment of scene, with no mention of the political and economic factors that form a major aspect of national scenes. Indeed, though our concern here is with the grammar of motives, we may note a related resource of rhetoric: one may deflect attention from scenic matters by situating the motives of an act in the agent (as were one to account for wars purely on the basis of a "warlike instinct" in people): or conversely, one may deflect attention from the criticism of personal motives by deriving an act or attitude not from traits of the agent but from the nature of the situation.

The difference between the use of the scene-act and act-agent ratios can also be seen in the motivations of "democracy." Many people in Great Britain and the United States think of these nations as "vessels" of democracy. And democracy is felt to reside in us, intrinsically, because we are "a democratic people." Democratic acts are, in this mode of thought, derived from democratic agents, agents who would remain democratic in character even though conditions required the temporary curtailment or abrogation of basic democratic rights. But if one employed, instead, the scene-act ratio, one might hold that there are certain "democratic situations" and certain "situations favorable to dictatorship, or requiring dictatorship." The technological scene itself, which requires the planning of a world order, might be thought such as to favor a large measure of "dictatorship" in our political ways (at least as contrasted with the past norms of democracy). By the act-agent ratio, a "democratic people" would continue to perform "democratic acts"; and to do so they would even, if necessary, go to the extent of restoring former conditions most favorable to democracy. By the scene-act ratio, if the "situation" itself is no longer a "democratic" one, even an "essentially democratic" people will abandon democratic ways.

A picturesque effect can be got in imaginative writings by the conflicting use of the scene-act and act-agent ratios. One may place "fools" in "wise situations," so that in their acts they are "wiser than they know." Children are often "wise" in this sense. It is a principle of incongruity that Chaplin has built upon. Empson would call it an aspect of "pastoral."

Here is an interesting shift of ratios in a citation from an address by Francis Biddle when he was Attorney General:

The change of the world in terms of time and space in the past hundred years—railroad, telegraph, telephone, automobile, movie, airplane, radio—has hardly found an echo in our political growth, except in the necessary patches and arrangements which have made it so extraordinarily complex without making it more responsive to our needs.

Note first that all the changes listed here refer to *agencies* of communication (the pragmatist emphasis). Then, having in their accumulation become scenic, they are said to have had a motivating effect upon our political acts ("growth"). But though the complexity of the scene has called forth "the necessary patches and arrangements" (another expression for "acts"), we are told that there are still unsatisfied "needs." Now, "needs" are a property of agents; hence an act designed to produce a situation "more responsive to our needs" would have its most direct locus of motivation under the heading of agent, particularly if these were said to be "primal needs" rather than "new needs," since "new needs" might best be treated as "a function of the situation." I borrow the expression from a prominent educator, Eduard C. Lindeman, who shortly after the Japanese attack at Pearl Harbor complained of a tendency "to believe that morale will now become a function of the situation and that hence it is less important to plan for education."

The ratios may often be interpreted as principles of selectivity rather than as thoroughly causal relationships. That is, in any given historical situation, there are persons of many sorts, with a corresponding variety in the kinds of acts that would be most representative of them. Thus, a given political situation may be said not to change people in their essential character, but rather to favor, or bring to the fore (to "vote for"), certain kinds of agents (with their appropriate actions) rather than others. Quick shifts in political exigencies do not of a sudden make all men "fundamentally" daring, or all men "fundamentally" cautious, in keeping with the nature of the scene; but rather, one situation calls for cautious men as its appropriate "voice," another for daring men, one for traditionalists, another for innovators. And the inappropriate acts and temperaments simply do not "count for" so much as they would in situations for which they are a better fit. One set of scenic conditions will "implement" and "amplify" given ways and temperaments which, in other situations, would remain mere potentialities, unplanted seeds, "mute inglorious Miltons." Indeed, there are times when out-and-out materialistic philosophies, which are usually thought of as "tough," can be of great solace to us precisely because they encourage us to believe in the ratios as a selective principle. For we may tell ourselves that the very nature of the materials with which men deal will not permit men to fall below a certain level of sloth, error, greed, and dishonesty in their relations with one another, as the cooperative necessities of the situation implement and amplify only those traits of character and action that serve the ends of progress.

There is, of course, a circular possibility in the terms. If an agent acts in keeping with his nature as an agent (act-agent ratio), he may change the nature of the scene accordingly (scene-act ratio), and thereby establish a state of unity between himself and his world (scene-agent ratio). Or the scene may call for a certain kind of act, which makes for a corresponding kind of agent, thereby likening agent to scene. Or our act may change us and our scene, producing a mutual conformity. Such would be the Edenic paradigm, applicable if we were capable of total acts that produce total transformations. In reality, we are capable of but partial acts, acts that but partially represent us and that produce but partial transformations. Indeed, if all the ratios were adjusted to one another with perfect Edenic symmetry, they would be immutable in one unending "moment."

Theological notions of creation and re-creation bring us nearest to the concept of total acts. Among the controversies surrounding Lutheranism, for instance, there was a doctrine, put forward by the theologian Striegel, who held that Christ's work on the Cross had the effect of changing God's attitude toward mankind, and that men born after the historical Christ can take advantage of this change. Here we have something like the conversion of God himself, brought about by Christ's sacrifice (a total action, a total passion). From the godlike nature came a godlike act that acted upon God himself. And as regards mankind, it amounts to a radical change in the very structure of the Universe, since it changed God's attitude toward men, and in God's attitude toward men resides the ultimate ground of human action.

A similar pattern is implicated in the close of Aeschylus's trilogy, the *Oresteia*, where the sufferings of Orestes terminate in the changed identity of the Furies, signalized by their change of name from Erinyes to Eumenides. Under the influence of the "new gods," their nature as motives takes on a totally different accent; for whereas it was their previous concern to avenge evil, it will henceforth be their concern to reward the good. An *inner* goad has thus been cast forth, externalized; whereby, as Athena says, men may be at peace within, their "dread passion for renown" thereafter being motivated solely by "war from without."

Only the scene-act and scene-agent ratios fit with complete comfort in this chapter on the relation between container and contained. The act-agent ratio tugs at its edges; and we shall close noting concerns that move us still farther afield. In the last example, we referred to God's *attitude*. Where would attitude fall within our pattern? Often it is the *preparation* for an act, which would make it a kind of symbolic act, or incipient act. But in its character as a state of *mind* that may or may not lead to an act, it is quite clearly to be classed under the head of *agent*. We also spoke of Christ's sacrifice as "a total action, a total passion." This suggests other "grammatical" possibilities that involve a dialectic pairing of "active" and "passive." And in the reference to a *state* of mind, we casually invite a dialectic pairing of "actus" and "status."

This group of concerns will be examined in due course. Meanwhile, we should be reminded that the term *agent* embraces not only all words general or specific for person, actor, character, individual, hero, villain, father, doctor, engineer, but also any words, moral or functional, for *patient*, and words for the motivational properties or agents, such as "drives," "instincts," "states of mind." We may also have collective words for agents, such as nation, group, the Freudian "super-ego," Rouseau's "*volonté générale*," the Fichtean "generalized I."

10

Vocabularies of Motive

Scope and Reduction

The Representative Anecdote

reflections + selections
deflection
missing context?

Men seek for vocabularies that will be faithful *reflections* of reality. To this end, they must develop vocabularies that are *selections* of reality. And any selection of reality must, in certain circumstances, function as a *deflection* of reality. Insofar as the vocabulary meets the needs of reflection, we can say that it has the necessary scope. In its selectivity, it is a reduction. Its scope and reduction become a deflection when the given terminology, or calculus, is not suited to the subject matter which it is designed to calculate.

Dramatism suggests a procedure to be followed in the development of a given calculus, or terminology. It involves the search for a "representative anecdote," to be used as a form in conformity with which the vocabulary is constructed. For instance, the behaviorist uses his experiments with the conditioned reflex as the anecdote about which to form his vocabulary for the discussion of human motives; but this anecdote, though notably *informative,* is not *representative,* since one cannot find a representative case of human motivation in animals, if only because animals lack that property of linguistic rationalization which is so typical of human motives. A representative case of human motivation must have a strongly linguistic bias, whereas animal experimentation necessarily neglects this.

If the originating anecdote is not representative, a vocabulary developed in strict conformity with it will not be representative. This embarrassment is usually avoided in practice by a break in the conformity at some crucial point; this means in effect that the vocabulary ceases to have the basis which is claimed for it. The very man who, with a chemical experiment as his informing anecdote, or point of departure, might tell you that people are but chemicals, will induce

From "Scope and Reduction," in *A Grammar of Motives,* pp. 59–61, 77–85, 108–17. Reprinted by permission of The University of California Press. © 1969 by Kenneth Burke.

responses in people by talking to them, whereas he would not try to make chemicals behave by linguistic inducement. And to say that people are "chemicals that talk" is the same thing as saying that people aren't "just chemicals," since chemicals don't talk. It is to confront the paradox of substance in a terminology unsuited to the illumination of this paradox.

Conversely, the notion of chemical affinity about which Goethe organizes his novel of sorrowing love, *Die Wahlverwandtschaften*, is not really the chemicalizing of human substance, but rather the humanizing of chemical substance. For the motive is defined by the action of the characters in a way totally unrepresentative of chemicals; and the situation is not chemical, but thoroughly social. Nothing makes this more quickly apparent than the closing paragraph, where the dead lovers lie buried side by side, surely their nearest approach to a purely chemical condition. Yet the novelist refers to a "peace that hovers over them" and to "the kindred images of angels looking upon them." And what a "gracious moment" it will be, he says, when in the future (*dereinst*) the lovers awaken together.

Subsequently we shall consider at some length this question of the "representative anecdote," itself so dramatistic a conception that we might call it the dramatistic approach to dramatism: an *introduction to* dramatism that is *deduced from* dramatism, and hence gains plausibility in proportion as dramatism itself is more fully developed. For the present it is enough to observe that the issue arises as soon as one considers the relation between representation and reduction in the choice and development of a motivational calculus. A given calculus must be supple and complex enough to be representative of the subject-matter it is designed to calculate. It must have scope. Yet it must also possess simplicity, in that it is broadly a reduction of the subject-matter. And by selecting drama as our representative, or informative anecdote, we meet these requirements. For the vocabulary developed in conformity with this form can possess a systematically interrelated structure, while at the same time allowing for the discussion of human affairs and the placement of cultural expressions in such typically human terms as personality and action (two terms that might be merged in the one term, "role").

The informative anecdote, we could say, contains *in nuce* the terminological structure that is evolved in conformity with it. Such a terminology is a "conclusion" that follows from the selection of a given anecdote. Thus the anecdote is in a sense a *summation*, containing implicitly what the system that is developed from it contains explicitly. Once we have set seriously to work developing a systematic terminology out of our anecdote, another kind of summation looms up. We might call it the "paradigm" or "prototype."

In selecting drama as our anecdote, for instance, we discover that we have made a selection in the realm of *action*, as against scientific reduction to sheer *motion*. And we thereupon begin to ask ourselves: What would be "the ultimate act," or "the most complete act"? That is, what would be the "pure" act, an act so thoroughly an act that it could be considered the form or prototype of all acts? For if we could have a conception of a consummate act, any less thorough acts could be seen as departures from it, as but partial exemplifications of it. But whatever qualities it possessed clearly, by reason of its nature as an absolute summation, we could then discern dimly in all lesser acts.

What then would be the "pure act" or "pure drama" that one might use as the paradigm of action in general? Such a paradigm or prototype of action, the concept of an ultimate or consummate act, is found in the theologians' concern with the Act of Creation. It "sums up" action quite as the theory of evolution sums up motion, but with one notable difference: whereas one must believe in evolution literally, one can discuss the Act of Creation "substantially," or "in principle."

We shall, then, examine the resources and embarrassments involved in The Creation. And if this seems like a round-about approach to the subject of our chapter, let one ask himself if he could possibly get a more advantageous position from which to observe the aspects of scope and reduction than by beginning with a subject of such comprehensive scope and reducing it.

Before going further, however, we should note that still another kind of reduction (different from both informative anecdote and paradigmatic summation) arises in the dramatist perspective. This is contained in our formula: the basic unit of action in the human body in purposive motion. We have here a kind of "lowest common denominator" of action, a minimal requirement that should appear in every act, however many more and greater are the attributes of a complex act. This is the nearest approach which dramatism affords to the "building block" kind of reduction in materialistic philosophies.

. . .

Circumference

This time all we need for our text is a single word from James, his word "circumference," as when he says that, if one would avoid pantheism, "the Creator must be the all, and the act by which the creature is set over against him has its motive within the creative circumference." The word reminds us that, when "defining by location," one may place the object of one's definition in contexts of varying scope. And our remarks on the scene-act ratio, for instance, suggest that the choice of circumference for the scene in terms of which a given act is to be located will have a corresponding effect upon the interpretation of the act itself. Similarly, the logic of the scene-agent ratio will figure in our definition of the individual, insofar as principles of dramatic consistency are maintained.

That is, if we locate the human agent and his act in terms of a scene whose orbit is broad enough to include the concept of a supernatural Creator, we get a different kind of definition than if our location were confined to a narrower circumference that eliminated reference to the "supernatural" as a motivating element in the scene and did not permit the scenic scope to extend beyond the outer limits of "nature." Or we may reduce the circumference still further, as when we define motivations in terms of the temporally or geographically local scenes that become a "second nature" to us, scenes that may themselves vary in circumference from broad historical situations to the minutely particularized situations of back-stairs gossip.

Now, it seems undeniable, by the very nature of the case, that in definition, or systematic placement, one must see things "in terms of . . ." And implicit in the terms chosen, there are "circumferences" of varying scope. Motivationally, they involve such relationships as are revealed in the analysis of the scene-act and scene-agent ratios whereby the quality of the context in which a subject is placed will affect the quality of the subject placed in that context. And since one must implicitly or explicitly select a circumference (except insofar as he can seem to avoid the predicament by adopting a slung-together terminology that contains a muddle of different circumferences) we are properly admonished to be on the look-out for these terministic relationships between the circumference and the "circumfered," even on occasions that may on the surface seem to be of a purely empirical nature.

Thus, when the behaviorist experiments with animals to discover, under "controlled laboratory conditions," the springs of conduct that operate also in human beings, we consider his experiment fully as important as he does, though for a totally different reason. For we take it to indicate, with the utmost clarity possible, the terministic relationship between the circumscription and the circumscribed. For no matter how much a matter of purely empirical observation it may seem to be, it actually is a very distinct choice of circumference for the placement of human motives. By the very nature of the case it chooses to consider human motives in terms of an animal circumference, an acutely terministic matter, not a matter of merely "empirical observation." And, ironically enough, it is most likely to reveal something about human motives distinctively, only insofar as the conditions established by the laboratory place the animals in a "human" circumference. But though nothing is more distinctly "human" than a scientific laboratory in one sense (for no other species but man is known ever to have made and used one), it is the kind of "humanity" we get in mechanization (a "part of" man that became so poignantly, in industrial routines, "apart from" man). And by the logic of the scene-act ratio, the study of conduct in terms of so mechanistic a scene led to a correspondingly mechanistic interpretation of the act.

This would probably be a good place to repeat that we do not deny the importance of seeking always for "controlled" cases, as anecdotes in conformity with which to form one's terminology for the analysis of human motives. But we maintain that one can avoid the bias of his instruments (that is, the bias of terms too simplist) only if he chooses a *representative* example of an act. Animal experiments have taught us however (we should at least grant them this) that school-teachers like to send animals to school, that physical sadists who have mastered scientific method like to torture animals methodically, and that those whose ingenuity is more psychiatrically inclined like to go on giving the poor little devils mental breakdowns, ostensibly to prove over and over again that it can be done (though this has already been amply proved to everybody's satisfaction but that of the experimenters).

We cherish the behaviorist experiment precisely because it illustrates the relation between the circumference and the circumscribed in mechanistic terms; and because the sharpest instance of the way in which the altering of the scenic scope affects the interpretation of the act is to be found in the shift from teleological to mechanistic philosophies. Christian theology, in stressing the rational, personal, and purposive aspects of the Creation as the embodiment of the Creator's pervasive will, had treated such principles as *scenic*. That is, they were not merely traits of human beings, but extended to the outer circumference of the ultimate ground. Hence, by the logic of the scene-act ratio, they were taken as basic to the constitution of human motives and could be "deduced" from the nature of God as an objective, extrinsic principle defining the nature of human acts. But when the circumference was narrowed to naturalistic limits, the "Creator" was left out of account, and only the "Creation" remained (remained not as an "act," however, but as a concatenation of motions).

The narrowing of the circumference thus encouraged a shift from the stress upon "final cause" to the stress upon "efficient cause," the kind of cause that would reside not in a "prime mover," but in a "last mover" (as the lever with which a man moves a stone could be called the "last mover" of the stone). We are here in the orbit of the *vis a tergo* kind of cause, prominent in all theories of motivation that stress "instincts," "drives," or other sheerly compulsive properties. Such terminologies attain a particularly thorough form in behaviorism, with its stress upon reflex action and the conditioned reflex, and its treatment of motivation in terms of stimulus and response.

Ironically, the dramatistic logic (that is, the logic of the scene-act and scene-agent ratios) here invokes a nondramatic mode of analysis. For the naturalistic terminology, in eliminating the principles of personality and action from the ultimate ground of motives, leads consistently to ideals of definition that dissolve the personality and its actions into depersonalization and motion respectively. In naturalism there is no Creator; and nature is not an act, but simply "the given."

However, we should add several important modifications to our notions of the movement toward the dissolution of drama. In the first place, we should note that in proportion as naturalism dropped the principles of personality and action from the *scene*, humanism compensatorily stressed their presence in men as *agents*. Human personality was not "deduced"; it was simply postulated in men, as part of "the given," quite as the records of our senses are "data." This humanistic stress upon the principle of personality as peculiar to people (who are conceived as set in dialectical opposition to an "impersonal" nature) could lead to a cult of "pure" personality (particularly as an overcompensation for the increasing depersonalization brought about by industrialism and as a direct response to the vagueness of role that went with the spread of leisure and unemployment). This cult of "pure" personality could in turn attain a "counter-overcompensation" on the part of the materialists, who emphasized the importance of the scenic factor in human personality (since one is a person not "absolutely," but by reason of a *role*, and such a role involves a *situation*). But in materialism the concept of role was narrowed in scope from *acting* to *doing*, until the idea of "vocation" was no wider in scope than the idea of "job." In theories of meaning the movement probably reaches its culmination in Bridgman's "operationalism."

Note that, dialectically, the concept of the "pure" personality itself contained its dissolution as its ultimate destiny. For, by the paradox of the absolute, a "pure" person would be an "im-person." This same paradox is latent even in the theological concept of personality; for God as a super-person is also, by the same token, "impersonal." Hence the monotheistic concept of an all-inclusive God was itself an ambiguous preparation for naturalism, once the circumference was narrowed to omit "God" as a necessary term in motivational statements. And the orbit could be narrowed by reason of a readily understandable procedure in language. For if nature was deemed, as it was by many of the devout, to be a perfect exemplification of God's will, then *nature's* design would accurately represent the design of *God*. Hence, reference to God as a locus of motives would involve an unnecessary duplication of terms—since a statement of motivation in terms of natural structure alone should be sufficient.

That is, if natural structure was the visible, tangible, commensurable embodiment of God's will, one would simply be duplicating his terms if his accounts of motivation had both natural and supernatural terms. The natural terms should be enough, in accordance with the Occamite principle (the keystone of scientific terminologies) that "entities should not be multiplied beyond necessity." And this naturalistic side of the equation had the further advantage of opening the way to test by experiment, as against demonstration by purely verbal manipulation. What was a narrowing of the circumference, as considered from one point of view, was a widening, as considered from another point of view. For naturalistic experimentation was a way of giving Nature itself an articulate voice in the dialectic. When properly used, it could so put questions to Nature that Nature was able to give very definite answers. The strong dramatistic feeling behind such procedures at their inception can be glimpsed in Galileo's reference to the experiment as the "ordeal," a significance that is also in our word "trial," whose bearing upon the attenuated drama of education can be glimpsed somewhat in the expression, "trial and error," as applied to the learning of animals in a maze.

We have spoken of Spinoza's explicit equation, "God or Nature." Note that there was also an implicit equation lurking in the word "design," as when we speak of "God's design" and "Nature's design." In the first case, "design" means "intention." In the second case, it can mean simply "structure"; we could even speak of a "design produced by accident." In this pun there is, accordingly, much the same equation as that explicitly put forward by Spinoza. To make the two meanings explicitly synonymous, as they are allowed to be synonymous in the original ambiguity of the word, we might phrase the corresponding equation thus: "intention or absence of intention," where the "or" means not "the alternative to" but "the same as." Stating the matter with reference to the genitive, Nature's design as "a part of" God's design becomes available to treatment as "apart from" God's design (or otherwise put: the *synecdochically* related part of the divine whole becomes the *divisively* related part).

Such implicit or explicit equations in which distinctions are merged serve historically as bridges from one terminology to another, precisely by reason of the Occamite principle. For if the two terms, or the two aspects of the one term, are taken as synonymous, then one side of the equation can be dropped as "unnecessary." If you say that the laws of electrochemical transformation are exactly as God would have them, then it follows that their structure represents the will of God. Whereupon, you are invited to treat of motives in terms of these electrochemical transformations. For why shouldn't you, if their design is to be equated with God's design, plus the fact that their design lends itself to empirical study in the scientific laboratory? Thereupon, almost imperceptibly, the terministic logic has taken you from supernaturalism to "chemism."

Hence, in the course of time, it becomes clear that we have gone from one bank to the other, by reason of an expression that bridged the gulf between them. Often the given writer who first gave vigor to the equation did not, however, intend it as a "bridge" in this historical sense, as a way of abandoning one position and taking up its opposite. Rather he cherished it precisely because this midway quality itself was *his* position, as with that motionless crossing expressed by Wordsworth in his sonnet "Composed upon Westminster Bridge," where the significance of his vision lies in the very fact that he is placed midway between the City of the Living and the City of the Dead, as he sees London transfigured in the early dawn:

Dear God! the very houses seem asleep;
And all that mighty heart is lying still!

An equation of two terms hitherto considered unequal can, of course, lead two ways. We can make the "wider" circle of the same circumference as the "narrower" circle either by narrowing the wider, or by widening the narrower. At the close of the middle ages, such equations, or bridging terms, would generally lead from supernaturalism towards naturalism, rather than *vice versa,* precisely because their role as a point of departure came at a time when it was only the supernatural vocabulary that was sufficiently developed to be departed from.

Earlier in this book, we observed that "if all the ten ratios were adjusted to one another with perfect Edenic symmetry, they would be immutable in one unending 'moment.'" That is, the quality of scene, act, agent, agency, and purpose would be all the same, all of one piece; hence there would be no opportunity for a new "beginning" whereby the agent would undertake a different quality of act that might change the quality of himself or of his scene, etc. Thus, there could be no becoming, but only unending being; there could be no *"alloiosis,"* or qualitative change, no development, no origin and destination, no whence and whither, for all the terms would contain what all the other terms contained. We suggested an answer in the consideration that men are capable of but *partial* acts, acts that but partially represent themselves and but partially conform to their scenes. We might now expand our statement in the light of our remarks on the subject of "circumferences."

If the scene-act ratio prevails, for instance, how would it be possible for a man to perform a "good" act in a "bad" situation? Or, by reason of the scene-agent ratio, how could a man be "good" in a "bad" situation? Or, to take a specific case, here is a statement by Stark Young, made in a discussion of Clifford Odets' *Night Music:*

> Can we demand from a dramatist, in an age like ours, scattered, distracted, surging, wide, chopped-up and skimmy, that he provide his play with a background of social conceptions that are basic, sound, organized, prophetic, deep-rooted? Shall he, in sum, be asked to draw the hare of heaven from a shallow cap?

And to this, Mr. Young, in keeping with the genius of the scene-act ratio (and who should implicitly abide by it, if not a dramatic critic?) makes answer:

> The answer is no, we can scarcely demand that. In general we should remind ourselves that there is no reason to ask any theatre to surpass its epoch in solidity, depth or philosophic summation.

There are all sorts of tricks lurking in that one. When we were young, we used to ask one another whether, since we were living in a boring age, it would be possible to write works of art that were not themselves boring or that were not exclusively concerned with boring people in boring situations. Later we found that, whatever the bad character of our age might be, it was not boring. This interpretation of the scene had evidently been a function of our situation as adolescents. Indeed, we discovered that, if no better motives came along, merely the attempt to work one's way out of fear and anger was enough to stave off boredom.

There are all sorts of modifications possible when considering Mr. Young's statement. Surely the dramatic work of Shakespeare, for instance, can be said to "surpass its epoch in solidity, depth or philosophic summation," except insofar as we define the nature of the epoch itself in terms of Shakespeare. But as a matter of fact, Shakespeare has not only "surpassed his epoch" in such properties, but he has surpassed whole centuries, whole populations, whole cultures.

However, it is not our intention here to bring up the many quibbles which Mr. Young's brief statement can invite. We would say only enough to point up the fact that, when confronting such issues, one has *a great variety of circumferences* to select as characterizations of a given agent's scene. For a man is not only in the situation peculiar to his era or to his particular place in that era (even if we could agree on the traits that characterize his era). He is also in a situation extending through centuries; he is in a "generically human" situation; and he is in a "universal" situation. Who is to say, once and for all, which of these circumferences is to be selected as the motivation of his act, insofar as the act is to be defined in scenic terms?

In confronting this wide range in the choice of a circumference for the location of an act, men confront what is distinctively the human freedom and the human necessity. This necessity is a freedom insofar as the choice of circumference leads to an adequate interpretation of motives; and it is an enslavement insofar as the interpretation is inadequate. We might exploit the conveniences of "substance" by saying that, in necessarily confronting such a range of choices, men are "substantially" free.

The contracting and expanding of scene is rooted in the very nature of linguistic placement. And a selection of circumference from among this range is in itself an act, an "act of faith," with the definition or interpretation of the act taking shape accordingly. In times of adversity one can readily note the workings of the "circumferential" logic, in that men choose to define their acts in terms of much wider orbits than the orbit of the adversity itself. The "solace of religion," for instance, may have its roots not in a mere self-deception, whereby one can buoy himself up with false promises or persuade himself that the situation is not bad when it is so palpably bad; but it may stem from an accurate awareness that one can define human nature and human actions in much wider terms than the particularities of his immediate circumstances would permit; and this option is not an "illusion," but a fact, and as true a fact as any fact in his immediate circumstances.

In *The Brothers Karamazov*, Dostoevsky tells how Mitya dreams of a new life with Grushenka, who had "loved him for one hour":

> With a sinking heart he was expecting every moment Grushenka's decision, always believing that it would come suddenly, on the impulse of the moment. All of a sudden she would say to him: "Take me, I'm yours for ever," and it would all be over. He would seize her and bear her away at once to the ends of the earth. Oh, then he would bear her away at once, as far, far away as possible; to the furthest end of Russia, if not of the earth, then he would marry her, and settle down with her incognito, so that no

one would know anything about them, there, here, or anywhere else. Then, oh then, a new life would begin at once!

Of this different, reformed and "virtuous" life ("it must, it must be virtuous") he dreamed feverishly at every moment. He thirsted for that reformation and renewal. The filthy morass, in which he had sunk of his own free will, was too revolting to him, and, like very many men in such cases, he put faith above all else in change of place. If only it were not for these people, if only it were not for these circumstances, if only he could fly away from this accursed place—he would be altogether regenerated, would enter on a new path.

In brief, he trusted that a new scene would make possible a new act, by reason of the scene-act ratio, and the new act would make a new man, by reason of the act-agent ratio. And he hoped to attain this new structure of motivation by sheer locomotion. Maybe he could have—for the changes he thinks of might very well be sufficiently different in their circumstances to produce in him a correspondingly new bundle of motives. But the mystic Alyosha, we may recall, was in the same scene as his elder brother Mitya; and for him its motivations were entirely different, and precisely because for him it had a different circumference, so that all actions were interpreted in greatly different terms. His terms amounted to a migration in a subtler sense: by a "transcendence," a "higher synthesis," that in effect "negates" the terms of the scene as Mitya interpreted it. For Alyosha's terms implied a wider *circumference*.

.   .   .

Money as Substitute for God

Reverting to our hypothetical model of the universe: whatever our philosophy of God and Nature may be, there is the temporal world of a "second nature" that calls for a reduction of circumference to the limits imposed by the "materials." We might still cling to our hypothetical somewhat Berkeleyan model of the world as a structure of "ideas" joined by their common grounding in the mind of God. Yet, within this *total* ideality, we should have to distinguish between the kind of "ideas" that seem like ideas to us and the kind that seem like "objects." And to define situations in terms of such objects would be in effect a reduction to a materialist circumference, as regards "operational" matters, though we still defined the "ultimate reality" as "ideal."

There is one notable difference between the materials of nature and the materials of our "second nature." The materials of our second nature are largely man-made. These accumulations of properties and methods have culminated in the complex of technological inventions that mothered their own peculiar kinds of necessity. And though men have been undergoing fantastic hardships in order to develop and retain these "conveniences," the fact remains that their "materiality" is at the same time an "ideality," in that every invention has been the emanation of some human mind. Nature is "given," but the environments to which we adapt ourselves as to a second nature are the creations of agents. In adapting ourselves to machinery, we are adapting ourselves to an aspect of ourselves. This would be reduction to a higher or a lower circumference, as you prefer, but in either case a reduction.

Since technology, as the primary characterizing feature of our second nature today, is "substantially" human, in accordance with the paradox of substance it can become quite "inhuman." For while the accumulations of the industrial plant are "in principle" the externalization or alienation of intrinsically human virtues, there are many unintended byproducts. Many people would vote for cities—but only a few real estate men would vote *explicitly* for slums. (We are not talking of the millions who regularly vote *implicitly* for slums.) The carrying out of any human purpose can be expected to reveal the kind of alienation that accompanies any act of generating or creating, which is an embodiment from within the self, and as such is a representative part that can, by the fact of division, become an antithetical part.

For this externalization of internal aptitudes is different in its state of *being* than in its *becoming*. It is in its *becoming* that technology most fully represents the human agent, since his inventing of it is an act, and a rational act. In its state of *being* (or perhaps we might better say its state of *having become*) it can change from a *purpose* into a *problem*. And surely much of the anguish in the modern world derives from the paradoxical fact that machinery, as the embodiment of rationality in its most rational moments, has in effect translated rationality itself from the realm of ideal aims to the realm of material requirements. Few ironies are richer in complexities than the irony of man's servitude to his mechanical servants. For though it is nothing less than an act of genius to *invent* a machine, it is the nagging drudgery of mere motion to *feed* one.

Occupational *diversification* equals by definition occupational *classification,* a splitting of mankind into *classes* that are separated from one another with varying degrees of distinctness and fixity at different periods in history, and with varying degrees of felicity or infelicity in their relationships to one another. And occupational diversity signifies a corresponding motivational diversity. The reader may ask: "Do you mean that, because of occupational classification, all plumbers have a set of social values distinct from those of carpenters, clerks, farmers, teachers, etc., all of which are equally demarcated from one another?"

Perhaps in the early days of the guilds something of this sort could have been noted, though the sense of a common membership in a single Church with a single body of tradition would presumably have supplied the common ground of mediation among the diversity of group motives, with heresy, sect, and schism as evidence of a divisive motivation. But in recent history, with the great occupational fluidity that has accompanied industrial innovation, it would be absurd to look for the most significant aspect of motivation in occupational diversity *per se*. For such a great diversity and fluidity of occupational classifications made it impossible to develop such distinctness of classes as we find, for instance, in the caste system of India. In fact, the present-day jurisdictional disputes among the unions in the United States reveals that the constantly changing methods of technology are continually making new cuts on the bias across the traditional classifications, so that it would be hard for any one to say for a certainty whether a certain new material should be applied by masons, plasterers, or carpenters, and so with a great number of other new products and processes.

Confronting such a state of affairs, we should seek for the significant overall motivating factor in the nature of the medium by which this great occupational diversity and fluidity, with its almost infinite variety of motives, is "reduced" to a common rationale. And this reduction is made, of course, in terms of money. Monetary symbolism is the "simple," the "god-term," in terms of which all this great complexity attains a unity transcending distinctions of climate, class, nation, cultural traditions, etc.

But reduction to money, we have said, is reduction to a simple, thus to a purity or absolute—and we have said that things in their "pure" state are something else. Hence, in reducing the subject of motivation to a "pure" state, we must warn ourselves against the risk of falling into our own variant of "inverted perfectionism" No human being could be a "perfect" capitalist, since no human being could be motivated by the rationale of money alone.

We may note, however, that the monetary reference is the overall *public* motive for mediating among the endless diversity of occupational and private (or "preoccupational") motives. We thus encounter from another angle our notion that the monetary motive can be a "technical substitute for God," in that "God" represented the unitary substance in which all human diversity of motives was grounded. And we thus see why it was "grammatically correct" that the religious should fear the problem of money.

Usually this notion of money as the "root of all evil" is taken in a very superficial sense, to indicate the power of money as a "temptation" to dishonest dealings. On the contrary, it is more likely that the diabolic role of money as "tempter" has helped to call forth a whole new gamut of scrupulosities here; and for every ethical defeat in the way of theft or "graft," etc. there must be countless moral victories on the part of men who resisted such temptation. No, any "diabolical" effect in this sense would be a "moralizing" effect, the devil being the dialectical counterpart of God.

Money, as active temptation, could be expected to perform the dialectical role of all such counter-agents in provoking the agent to active combat, hence increasing the realm of scrupulosity (hence leading us from the simplicity of *innocence* into the complexity of *virtue*). And it could probably be said, in this respect, that pecuniary civilizations show a greater range of scruples or "tender-mindedness" (in the way of idealistic, humanitarian attitudes) than is usually the case with realistic "tough-mindedness" of more primitive cultures. Such humanitarian scruples are made possible also by reason of the fact that money, in promoting great *indirectness* or *vicariousness,* has made it possible for great numbers of people to avoid many of the harsher realities entirely. For one need simply pay to have "insensitive" things done by others instead of doing them oneself. Nor is this expedient possible only to the rich. Think how many people eat meat and how few work in slaughter-houses.

No, where religion is tested by "ethical sensitiveness" and "humanitarianism," the monetary motive has probably added to it rather than subtracted from it. Rather, money endangers religion in that money can serve as universal symbol, the unitary ground of all action. And it endangers religion not in the dramatic, agonistic way of a "tempter," but in its quiet, rational way as a *substitute* that performs its mediatory role more "efficiently," more "parsimoniously," with less "waste motion" as regards the religious or ritualistic conception of "works." And since money thus substitutes technically or scientifically for the godhead as a *public* principle, do we not see the results of this substitution in the fact that Protestantism, arising in response to the growth of occupational diversity, trade, and the necessarily increased dependence upon the use of money, stressed on the contrary the function of the godhead as a *private* principle? For where monetary symbolism does the work of religious symbolism (as a lowest common denominator for mediating among many motives could more efficiently replace a "highest common denomination") the locus of this titular role would have to be placed elsewhere than at the point of public mediation. This was found in the doctrine of communication directly with God.

The humanistic emphasis that arose with the secularization of middle-class culture was new not in the sense that humanism itself was new but in the sense that humanism began to undergo a strategic transformation. We might describe this as a change from a "consistent" humanism to a "compensatory" humanism. "Consistent" humanism had placed human personality as the lineal descendant of a "principle of personality" felt to be present in the universal ground. But with the increasingly secular emphasis, the motivations of the universal ground were viewed not in terms of a superhuman personality but in terms of naturalistic impersonality. And human personality was affirmed in dialectical opposition to the quality of the ground. For when the scene was narrowed to a secular circumference, human personality could no longer be "logically *de*duced" familially from the divine personality. But it might be vigorously affirmed simply as an "empirical fact," as part of "the given," in contrast with any new calculus in which the personality was "logically *re*duced" to atomistic, naturalistic terms of impersonality.

 At this point a calculus of "therefore" was supplanted by a calculus of "nevertheless." By a change in the tactics of grammar, men ceased to think, "God's personality, *therefore* human personality" and began to think, "nature's impersonality, *nevertheless* human personality," the first pair being related consistently, the second oppositionally. And the experience of an *impersonal* motive was empirically intensified in proportion as the rationale of the monetary motive gained greater authority and organization within the realm of men's "second nature." We may discern these transformations behind the shift from "consistent" religious humanism to the "compensatory" secular humanitarianism of science and money.

The Nature of Monetary "Reality"

Where are we now? We must consider the possible charge that in our discussion of the monetary motive we have ourselves been guilty of "inverted perfectionism." For if money is viewed as a *medium* of exchange, then we have reduced our field of discussion to terms of *agency*, from which we would in turn derive all else as though it were pervaded by the same ancestral spirit.

In the first place, as we noted previously, money is *not a mere agency*, in our civilization, but is a *rationalizing ground* of action. In contrast with the psychosis that would accompany a barter economy, for instance, our monetary economy must be accompanied by a distinctive "capitalist" psychosis. For any important motivational emphasis must have its corresponding emphasis in the thinking of those whose efforts and expectancies are formed with reference to its motivating powers, resources and risks. And we could speak of a "capitalist psychosis" not in the sense of one who thinks that by eliminating capitalism one would eliminate psychosis, but in the sense of one who thinks that, given any pronounced social structure, there will be a "psychosis" corresponding to it. That is, there will be a particular recipe of overstressings and understressings peculiar to the given institutional structure. And the tendency of the culture will be to see everything in terms of this particular recipe of emphases, as the typical apologist of ideal *laissez-faire* capitalism would think "freedom" itself lost if we lost "free market freedom," since he conceived of freedom in these terms.

In this sense, we may legitimately isolate the monetary motive as an essence and may treat many apparently disrelated manifestations as its accidents. It would not be a primary motive in the sense that it "gave rise to" ethics, philosophy, art, etc. But we could feature it in the sense that its effects could be seen as a significant influence in the ethics, philosophy, art that flourished at a time when it had to be so significantly taken into account (at a time when it rationalized the adoption of new methods, for instance, in contrast with times when the norms of tradition were taken as the major rationalizing test of "right" ways).

In its nature as a "purity" or "simplicity," however, it cannot prevail in this imperfect world. Hence we must recognize that, even in the heyday of capitalism, the monetary motive is but one member of the "power" family. And the possible transformations here are many. As early as the Calvinistic sanctioning of "usury," it was apparent that a primary aspect of our monetary economy was its stress upon *credit*—and the receiving of credit is *indebtedness*. Thus, in addition to its strongly *futuristic* nature as investment, in its connotations of *owing* it provides a technical normalization of "guilt" or "sin" by converting a religious psychology of "retribution" or "penance" into a commercialist psychology of "ambition." The fact that the symbolism of debt itself can be manipulated by the resources of accountancy adds further notable convertibilities. For instance the nature of nationalist integers, formed of abstract relations in keeping with the abstractions of money, makes it readily possible for men to carry out projects that privately enrich themselves while publicly adding to the national debt, as when a "national's" interests abroad are protected by government agencies supported by a tax upon the people as a whole. We here have simultaneously an apposition of individual and collectivity on the "spiritual" level and an opposition on the practical level. When "we" get air bases, who is this "we"?

The relations of any one individual to the public medium can be understood only by examining the "clusters" or "equations" in his particular "psychic economy." In the economy of one man, monetary power may be *compensatory* to some other kind of power (physical, sexual, moral, stylistic, intellectual, etc.). That is, he may seek by the vicarage of money to "add a cubit to his stature." But in the economy of another man, monetary power may be *consistent* with one or all of these. A sense of moral guilt, for instance, or a sense of social inferiority, may "compensatorily" incite one man to seek a fortune, while the same motives may "consistently" prevent another from demanding what his services are worth. Paradoxically, an "anti-social" attitude may sometimes reach expression through the prompt paying of debts, since by the payment one's bonds or obligations would be severed. And the shady promoter may be motivated by a genuine sense of "sociality," to which men instinctively respond in letting themselves be taken in by his "cordiality," a "sociality" and "cordiality" which are not "in principle" dishonest at all, but which he finally "reduces" to the simplified idiom by leaving debts unpaid (that is, by keeping bonds of attachment between him and his creditors).

A wider circle, culminating in thoughts of life and death, may be matched by a narrower circle, culminating in thoughts of solvency and poverty. The two may be so related that each can stand for the other. And so one can seek more and more money, as a symbolic way of attaining immortality. That is, one may thus vicariously seek "more and more life," in the attempt to attain a higher *quality* in terms of a higher *quantity*, for it is easy to think of a "more intense" life in quantitative terms. Conversely, the religious injunction to "live a dying life" can be followed, in an unconscious secular translation, by systematically keeping oneself poor (thus "going to meet" death).

Obviously we could not chart here the many private roads that lead up to, or away from, the monetary Rome. And besides, this phase of our subject more properly falls under the heading of symbolic. We might in passing, however, refer the reader to André Gide's novel, *The Counterfeiters*. Gide is very discriminating in his ironic appreciation of the ways in which the patterns of religion survive in ingenious secular distortions. He is profoundly, if perversely, a Protestant. In *The Counterfeiters*, the relationships among the important characters are symbolized in monetary terms, as with the lad of homosexual bent, who also ambiguously loves a girl and as a memento gives her a coin that is counterfeit.

We have said that the rationale of money had much to do with the innovation, specialization, diversification, partialization, and classification of economic motives. For the great changes that the rationale of technological processes and products effected in our "second nature" could not have taken place without a universal idiom to the terms of which all the diversity could be reduced. But clearly we could with as much justice state this ratio the other way round, saying that monetary symbolism could not assume so dominant a role in the rationalization of motives without technological diversity as a ground. Various kinds of occupational diversity (or classification of status) in the past have given us the lineaments of capitalism—but only when symbiotic with applied science could it produce the peculiar kind of motivation that we know as modern capitalism.

This symbiosis of money and technology has made a "double genesis" possible in the imputing of motives, as the thinker may attribute to "capitalism" the aspects of our civilization he dislikes and to "technology" the aspects in which he places his hopes, or *vice versa*. Since both money and technology are objective "powers" existing in history, we might properly expect them to manifest the ambivalence of such powers. Either, that is, should be capable of acting favorably or unfavorably, favorably if properly "discounted," unfavorably when its workings are protected from criticism, as the money motive is piously protected in some quarters by being made synonymous with the national godhead of patriotism, and as the technological motive is protected in other quarters where it is granted immunity in the name of "science" as an absolute good. Also, our very aversion to "talking about money matters" has done much to conceal our understanding of it as a motive, though it is worth noting that this aversion in itself indicates the "godhead" of money, since in formal religions men fear to behold or name lightly their God, or motivational center.

There is an ironic possibility that orthodox capitalism, fascism, and communism may all three be variants of the "monetary psychosis" insofar as all three are grounded in the occupational diversity (classification) of technology. In any case Russian communism was the most "idealistic" of the three, since technology was *willed* there in accordance with Marxist values, rather than being the material ground out of which such values arise. Voluntaristic philosophies would find nothing unusual in this sequence, but it would seem to be a paradox from the standpoint of dialectical materialism.

Though communist industrialism relies upon financial accountancy, neither communism nor fascism will accord to money the primary order of "reality" it possessed for, say, the financial priesthood of capitalism. Shortly after a disastrous hurricane had swept through several northern states, destroying houses, uprooting forests, undermining railroads, and doing much other damage, all "to the value of hundreds of millions of dollars," we recall an article on the stock market page of a New York City newspaper which remarked that, great as the "losses" had been, they were much less than the shrinkage of stock values in a recent market "recession." The whole point of this article was the author's implicit assumption that the two cases were essentially analogous. Note that in the case of the *symbolic* losses of stock market value, the aggregate material wealth of the world had not been diminished one particle. The railroad that had shrunk so in value was exactly the same railroad, with the same equipment, the same trained personnel, the same physical ability to perform useful services. But in the case of the hurricane, much real material wealth had been destroyed. Yet so "instinctively" did this writer think "in terms of" the monetary idiom of reduction, so thoroughly had it become a "second nature" with him, that he made no differentiation whatsoever between these two kinds of "losses." "Spirituality" of this particular sort is lessened under either the explicitly materialist coordinates of Marxism or the realism implicit in the national barter projects of fascism. Also, the fascists are able to have a less pious attitude toward monetary symbolism because of their cynical attitude toward the manipulation of symbols in general. And we should note how German fascism, by centering its attention about industrial empire, was fast approaching a position where it could have destroyed the empire of Britain, which was coming more and more to think of rule in the pure financial terms of The City.

IV

RHETORICAL ACTION

11

Identification

We considered, among those "uses" to which *Samson Agonistes* was put, the poet's identification with a blind giant who slew himself in slaying enemies of the Lord; and we saw identification between Puritans and Israelites, Royalists and Philistines, identification allowing for a ritualistic kind of historiography in which the poet could, by allusion to a biblical story, "substantially" foretell the triumph of his vanquished faction. Then we came upon a more complicated kind of identification: here the poet presents a motive in an essentially magnified or perfected form, in some way tragically purified or transcended; the imagery of death reduces the motive to *ultimate* terms, dramatic equivalent for an "entelechial" pattern of thought whereby a thing's nature would be classed according to the fruition, maturing, or ideal fulfillment, proper to its kind.

As seen from this point of view, then, an imagery of slaying (slaying of either the self or another) is to be considered merely as a special case of identification in general. Or otherwise put: the imagery of slaying is a special case of transformation, and transformation involves the ideas and imagery of *identification*. That is: the *killing* of something is the *changing* of it, and the statement of the thing's nature before and after the change is an *identifying* of it.

Perhaps the quickest way to make clear what we are doing here is to show what difference it makes. Noting that tragic poets identify motives in terms of killing, one might deduce that "they are essentially killers." Or one might deduce that "they are essentially identifiers." Terms for identification in general are wider in scope than terms for killing. We are proposing that our rhetoric be reduced to this term of wider scope, with the term of narrower scope being treated as a species of it. We begin with an anecdote of killing, because invective, eristic, polemic, and logomachy are so pronounced an aspect of rhetoric. But we use a dialectical device (the shift to a higher level of generalization) that enables us to transcend the narrower implications of

From *A Rhetoric of Motives*, pp. 19–29, 43–46. Reprinted by permission of The University of California Press. © 1969 by Kenneth Burke.

this imagery, even while keeping them clearly in view. We need never deny the presence of strife, enmity, faction as a characteristic motive of rhetorical expression. We need not close our eyes to their almost tyrannous ubiquity in human relations; we can be on the alert always to see how such temptations to strife are implicit in the institutions that condition human relationships; yet we can at the same time always look beyond this order, to the principle of identification in general, a terministic choice justified by the fact that the identifications in the order of love are also characteristic of rhetorical expression. We may as well be frank about it, since our frankness, if it doesn't convince, will at least serve another important purpose of this work: it will reveal a strategic resource of terminology. Being frank, then: Because of our choice, we can treat "war" as a "*special case of peace*"— not as a primary motive in itself, not as *essentially* real, but purely as a *derivative* condition, a *perversion*.

Identification and "Consubstantiality"

A is not identical with his colleague, B. But insofar as their interests are joined, A is *identified* with B. Or he may *identify himself* with B even when their interests are not joined, if he assumes that they are, or is persuaded to believe so.

Here are ambiguities of substance. In being identified with B, A is "substantially one" with a person other than himself. Yet at the same time he remains unique, an individual locus of motives. Thus he is both joined and separate, at once a distinct substance and consubstantial with another.

While consubstantial with its parents, with the "firsts" from which it is derived, the offspring is nonetheless apart from them. In this sense, there is nothing abstruse in the statement that the offspring both is and is not one with its parentage. Similarly, two persons may be identified in terms of some principle they share in common, an "identification" that does not deny their distinctness.

To identify A with B is to make A "consubstantial" with B. Accordingly, since our *Grammar of Motives* was constructed about "substance" as key term, the related rhetoric selects its nearest equivalent in the areas of persuasion and dissuasion, communication and polemic. And our third volume, *Symbolic of Motives*, should be built about *identity* as titular or ancestral term, the "first" to which all other terms could be reduced and from which they could then be derived or generated, as from a common spirit. The thing's *identity* would here be its uniqueness as an entity in itself and by itself, a demarcated unit having its own particular structure.

However, "substance" is an abstruse philosophic term, beset by a long history of quandaries and puzzlements. It names so paradoxical a function in men's systematic terminologies, that thinkers finally tried to abolish it altogether—and in recent years they have often persuaded themselves that they really did abolish it from their terminologies of motives. They abolished the *term,* but it is doubtful whether they can ever abolish the *function* of that term, or even whether they should *want* to. A doctrine of *consubstantiality,* either explicit or implicit, may be necessary to any way of life. For substance, in the old philosophies, was an *act;* and a way of life is an *acting-together;* and in acting together, men have common sensations, concepts, images, ideas, attitudes that make them *consubstantial.*

yet we are still separate

The *Grammar* dealt with the universal paradoxes of substance. It considered resources of placement and definition common to all thought. The *Symbolic* should deal with unique individuals, each its own peculiarly constructed act, or form. These unique "constitutions" being capable of treatment in isolation, the *Symbolic* should consider them primarily in their capacity as singulars, each a separate universe of discourse (though there are also respects in which they are consubstantial with others of their kind, since they can be classed with other unique individuals as joint participants in common principles, possessors of the same or similar properties).

The *Rhetoric* deals with the possibilities of classification in its *partisan* aspects; it considers the ways in which individuals are at odds with one another, or become identified with groups more or less at odds with one another.

Why "at odds," you may ask, when the titular term is "identification"? Because, to begin with "identification" is, by the same token, though roundabout, to confront the implications of *division.* And so, in the end, men are brought to that most tragically ironic of all divisions, or conflicts, wherein millions of cooperative acts go into the preparation for one single destructive act. We refer to that ultimate *disease* of cooperation: *war.* (You will understand war much better if you think of it, not simply as strife come to a head, but rather as a disease, or perversion of communion. Modern war characteristically requires a myriad of constructive acts for each destructive one; before each culminating blast there must be a vast network of interlocking operations, directed communally.)

is Burke a pacifist?

Identification is affirmed with earnestness precisely because there is

or Burke is an idealist

[margin note: role of negatives]

division. Identification is compensatory to division. If men were not apart from one another, there would be no need for the rhetorician to proclaim their unity. If men were wholly and truly of one substance, absolute communication would be of man's very essence. It would not be an ideal, as it now is, partly embodied in material conditions and partly frustrated by these same conditions; rather, it would be as natural, spontaneous, and total as with those ideal prototypes of communication, the theologian's angels, or "messengers."

[margin note: Grammar]

[margin note: Symbolic]

The *Grammar* was at peace insofar as it contemplated the paradoxes common to all men, the universal resources of verbal placement. The *Symbolic* should be at peace, in that the individual substances, or entities, or constituted acts are there considered in their uniqueness, hence outside the realm of conflict. For individual universes, as such, do not compete. Each merely *is*, being its own self-sufficient realm of discourse. And the *Symbolic* thus considers each thing as a set of interrelated terms all conspiring to round out their identity as participants in a common substance of meaning. An individual does in actuality compete with other individuals. But within the rules of symbolic, the individual is treated merely as a self-subsistent unit proclaiming its peculiar nature. It is "at peace," in that its terms *cooperate* in modifying one another. But insofar as the individual is involved in conflict with other individuals or groups, the study of this same individual would fall under the head of *Rhetoric*.

[margin note: Rhetoric]

Or considered rhetorically, the victim of a neurotic conflict is torn by parliamentary wrangling; he is heckled like Hitler within. (Hitler is said to have confronted a constant wrangle in his private deliberations, after having imposed upon his people a flat choice between conformity and silence.) Rhetorically, the neurotic's every attempt to legislate for his own conduct is disorganized by rival factions within his own dissociated self. Yet, considered symbolically, the same victim is technically "at peace," in the sense that his identity is like a unified, mutually adjusted set of terms. For even antagonistic terms, confronting each other as parry and thrust, can be said to "cooperate" in the building of an overall form.

The *Rhetoric* must lead us through the Scramble, the Wrangle of the Market Place, the flurries and flare-ups of the Human Barnyard, the Give and Take, the wavering line of pressure and counterpressure, the Logomachy, the onus of ownership, the Wars of Nerves, the War. It too has its peaceful moments: at times its endless competition can add up to the transcending of itself. In ways of its own, it can move from the factional to the universal. But its ideal culminations are more often beset by strife as the condition of their organized expression, or material embodiment. Their very universality becomes transformed into a partisan weapon. For one need not scrutinize the concept of "identification" very sharply to see, implied in it at every turn, its ironic counterpart: division. Rhetoric is concerned with the state of Babel after the Fall. Its contribution to a "sociology of knowledge" must often carry us far into the lugubrious regions of malice and the lie.

↳ mournful, dismal / gloomy

The Identifying Nature of Property

Metaphysically, a thing is identified by its *properties*. In the realm of Rhetoric, such identification is frequently by property in the most materialistic sense of the term, economic property, such property as Coleridge, in his "Religious Musings," calls a

> twy-streaming fount,
> Whence Vice and Virtue flow, honey and gall.

And later:

> From Avarice thus, from Luxury and War
> Sprang heavenly Science; and from Science, Freedom.

Coleridge, typically the literary idealist, goes one step further back, deriving "property" from the workings of "Imagination." But meditations upon the dual aspects of property as such are enough for our present purposes. In the surrounding of himself with properties that name his number or establish his identity, man is ethical. ("Avarice" is but the scenic word "property" translated into terms of an agent's attitude, or incipient act.) Man's moral growth is organized through properties, properties in goods, in services, in position or status, in citizenship, in reputation, in acquaintanceship and love. But however ethical such an array of identifications may be when considered in itself, its relation to other entities that are likewise forming their identity in terms of property can lead to turmoil and discord. Here is *par excellence* a topic to be considered in a rhetoric having "identification" as its key term. And we see why one should expect to get much insight from Marxism, as a study of capitalistic rhetoric. Veblen is also, from this point of view, to be considered a theorist of rhetoric. (And we know of no better way to quickly glimpse the range of rhetoric than to read, in succession, the articles on "Property" and "Propaganda" in *The Encyclopaedia of the Social Sciences*.)

Bentham's utilitarian analysis of language, treating of the ways in which men find "eulogistic coverings" for their "material interests," is

thus seen to be essentially rhetorical, and to bear directly upon the
motives of property as a rhetorical factor. Indeed, since it is so clearly
a matter of rhetoric to persuade a man by identifying your cause with
his interests, we note the ingredient of rhetoric in the animal experimenter's ways of conditioning, as animals that respond avidly at a
food signal suggest, underlying even human motives, the inclination,
like a house dog, to seek salvation in the Sign of the Scraped Plate.
But the lessons of this "animal rhetoric" can mislead, as we learn from
the United States' attempts to use food as an instrument of policy in
Europe after the war. These efforts met with enough ill will to suggest
that the careful "screening" of our representatives, to eliminate re-
formist tendencies as far as possible and to identify American aid only
with conservative or even reactionary interests, practically *guaranteed*
us a dismal rhetoric in our dealings with other nations. And when
Henry Wallace, during a trip abroad, began earning for our country
the genuine good will of Europe's common people and intellectual
classes, the Genius of the Screening came into its own: our free press,
as at one signal, began stoutly assuring the citizens of both the United
States and Europe that Wallace did not truly represent us. What did
represent us, presumably, was the policy of the Scraped Plate, which
our officialdom now and then bestirred themselves to present publicly
in terms of a dispirited "idealism," as heavy as a dead elephant. You
see, we were not to be identified with very resonant things; our press
assured our people that the outcome of the last election had been a
"popular mandate" to this effect. (We leave this statement unrevised.
For the conditions of Truman's reelection, after a campaign in which
he out-Wallaced Wallace, corroborated it "in principle.")

    In pure identification there would be no strife. Likewise, there
would be no strife in absolute separateness, since opponents can join
battle only through a mediatory ground that makes their communication possible, thus providing the first condition necessary for their
interchange of blows. But put identification and division ambiguously
 together, so that you cannot know for certain just where one ends and
the other begins, and you have the characteristic invitation to rhetoric.
Here is a major reason why rhetoric, according to Aristotle, "proves
opposites." When two men collaborate in an enterprise to which they
contribute different kinds of services and from which they derive different amounts and kinds of profit, who is to say, once and for all, just
where "cooperation" ends and one partner's "exploitation" of the
other begins? The wavering line between the two cannot be "scientifically" identified; rival rhetoricians can draw it at different places, and
their persuasiveness varies with the resources each has at his com-

mand. (Where public issues are concerned, such resources are not confined to the intrinsic powers of the speaker and the speech, but depend also for their effectiveness upon the purely technical means of communication, which can either aid the utterance or hamper it. For a "good" rhetoric neglected by the press obviously cannot be so "communicative" as a poor rhetoric backed nationwide by headlines. And often we must think of rhetoric not in terms of some one particular address, but as a general *body of identifications* that owe their convincingness much more to trivial repetition and dull daily reenforcement than to exceptional rhetorical skill.)

If you would praise God, and in terms that happen also to sanction one system of material property rather than another, you have forced rhetorical considerations upon us. If you would praise science, however exaltedly, when that same science is at the service of imperialist-militarist expansion, here again you bring things within the orbit of rhetoric. For just as God has been identified with a certain worldly structure of ownership, so science may be identified with the interests of certain groups or classes quite *unscientific* in their purposes. Hence, however "pure" one's motives may be actually, the impurities of identification lurking about the edges of such situations introduce a typical rhetorical wrangle of the sort that can never be settled once and for all, but belongs in the field of moral controversy where men properly seek to "prove opposites."

Thus, when his friend, Preen, wrote of a meeting where like-minded colleagues would be present and would all be proclaiming their praise of science, Prone answered: "You fail to mention another colleague who is sure to be there too, unless you take care to rule him out. I mean John Q. Militarist-Imperialist." Whereat, Preen: "This John Q. Militarist-Imperialist must be quite venerable by now. I seem to have heard of him back in Biblical times, before Roger B. Science was born. Doesn't he get in everywhere, unless he is explicitly ruled out?" He does, thanks to the ways of identification, which are in accordance with the nature of property. And the rhetorician and the moralist become one at that point where the attempt is made to reveal the undetected presence of such an identification. Thus in the United States after the second World War, the temptations of such an identification became particularly strong because so much scientific research had fallen under the direction of the military. To speak merely in praise of science, without explicitly dissociating oneself from its reactionary implications, is to identify oneself with these reactionary implications by default. Many reputable educators could thus, in this roundabout way, *function* as "conspirators." In their zeal to get federal subsidies for the science department of their college or university, they could help to shape educational policies with the ideals of war as guiding principle.

Identification and the "Autonomous"

As regards "autonomous" activities, the principle of rhetorical identification may be summed up thus: The fact that an activity is capable of reduction to intrinsic, autonomous principles does not argue that it is free from identification with other orders of motivation extrinsic to it. Such other orders are extrinsic to it, as considered from the standpoint of the specialized activity alone. But they are not extrinsic to the field of moral action as such, considered from the standpoint of human activity in general. The human agent, *qua* human agent, is not motivated solely by the principles of a specialized activity, however strongly this specialized power, in its suggestive role as imagery, may affect his character. Any specialized activity participates in a larger unit of action. "Identification" is a word for the autonomous activity's place in this wider context, a place with which the agent may be unconcerned. The shepherd, *qua* shepherd, acts for the good of the sheep, to protect them from discomfiture and harm. But he may be "identified" with a project that is raising the sheep for market.

Of course, the principles of the autonomous activity can be considered irrespective of such identifications. Indeed, two students, sitting side by side in a classroom where the principles of a specialized subject are being taught, can be expected to "identify" the subject differently, so far as its place in a total context is concerned. Many of the most important identifications for the specialty will not be established at all, until later in life, when the specialty has become integrally interwoven with the particulars of one's livelihood. The specialized activity itself becomes a different thing for one person, with whom it is a means of surrounding himself with family and amenities, than it would be for another who, unmarried, childless, loveless, might find in the specialty not so much a means of gratification as a substitute for lack of gratification.

Carried into unique cases, such concern with identifications leads to the sheer "identities" of symbolic. That is, we are in pure symbolic when we concentrate upon one particular integrated structure of motives. But we are clearly in the region of rhetoric when considering the identifications whereby a specialized activity makes one a participant in some social or economic class. "Belonging" in this sense is rhetorical. And, ironically, with much college education today in literature and the fine arts, the very stress upon the pure autonomy of such activities is a roundabout way of identification with a privileged class, as the doctrine may enroll the student stylistically under the banner of a privileged class, serving as a kind of social insignia promising preferment. (We are here obviously thinking along Veblenian lines.)

The stress upon the importance of autonomous principles does have its good aspects. In particular, as regards the teaching of literature, the insistence upon "autonomy" reflects a vigorous concern with the all-importance of the text that happens to be under scrutiny. This cult of patient textual analysis (though it has excesses of its own) is helpful as a reaction against the excesses of extreme historicism (a leftover of the nineteenth century) whereby a work became so subordinated to its background that the student's appreciation of first-rate texts was lost behind his involvement with the collateral documents of fifth-rate literary historians. Also, the stress upon the autonomy of fields is valuable methodologically; it has been justly praised because it gives clear insight into some particular set of principles; and such a way of thinking is particularly needed now, when pseudoscientific thinking has become "unprincipled" in its uncritical cult of "facts." But along with these sound reasons for a primary concern with the intrinsic, there are furtive temptations that can figure here too. For so much progressive and radical criticism in recent years has been concerned with the social implications of art, that affirmations of art's autonomy can often become, by antithesis, a roundabout way of identifying oneself with the interests of political conservatism. In accordance with the rhetorical principle of identification, whenever you find a doctrine of "nonpolitical" esthetics affirmed with fervor, look for its politics.

But the principle of autonomy does allow for historical shifts whereby the nature of an identification can change greatly. Thus in his book, *The Genesis of Plato's Thought*, David Winspear gives relevant insight into the aristocratic and conservative political trends with which Plato's philosophy was identified at the time of its inception. The Sophists, on the other hand, are shown to have been more closely allied with the rising business class, then relatively "progressive" from the Marxist point of view, though their position was fundamentally weakened by the fact that their enterprise was based on the acceptance of slavery. Yet at other periods in history the Platonist concern with an ideal state could itself be identified with wholly progressive trends.

During the second World War many good writers who had previously complained of the Marxist concern with propaganda in art, themselves wrote books in which they identified their esthetic with an

Burke w/ concerned w/ underlying identification

anti-fascist politics. At the very least such literature attributed to Hitlerite Germans and their collaborators the brutal and neurotic motives which in former years had been attributed to "Everyman." (Glenway Wescott's *Apartment in Athens,* for instance.) So the overgeneralized attempt to discredit *Marxist* rhetoric by discrediting *all* rhetoric was abandoned, at least by representative reviewers whose criticism was itself a rhetorical act designed to identify the public with anti-fascist attitudes and help sell anti-fascist books (as it later contributed to the forming of anti-Soviet attitudes and the sale of anti-Soviet books). In the light of such developments, many critics have become only too accommodating in their search for covert and overt identifications that link the "autonomous" field of the arts with political and economic orders of motivation. Head-on resistance to the questioning of "purity" in specialized activities usually comes now from another quarter: the liberal apologists of science.

. . .

Realistic Function of Rhetoric

Gaining courage as we proceed, we might even contend that we are not so much proposing to import anthropology into rhetoric as proposing that anthropologists recognize the factor of rhetoric in their own field. That is, if you look at recent studies of primitive magic from the standpoint of this discussion, you might rather want to distinguish between magic as "bad science" and magic as "primitive rhetoric." You then discover that anthropology does clearly recognize the rhetorical *function* in magic; and far from dismissing the rhetorical aspect of magic merely as bad science, anthropology recognizes in it a pragmatic device that greatly assisted the survival of cultures by promoting social cohesion. (Malinowski did much work along these lines, and the Kluckhohn essay makes similar observations about witchcraft.) But now that we have confronted the term "magic" with the term "rhetoric," we'd say that one comes closer to the true state of affairs if one treats the socializing aspects of magic as a "primitive rhetoric" than if one sees modern rhetoric simply as a "survival of primitive magic."

For rhetoric as such is not rooted in any past condition of human society. It is rooted in an essential function of language itself, a function that is wholly realistic, and is continually born anew; the use of language as a symbolic means of inducing cooperation in beings that by nature respond to symbols. Though rhetorical considerations may carry us far afield, leading us to violate the principle of autonomy separating the various disciplines, there is an intrinsically rhetorical motive, situated in the persuasive use of language. And this persuasive use of language is not derived from "bad science," or "magic." On the contrary, "magic" was a faulty derivation from it, "word magic" being an attempt to produce linguistic responses in kinds of beings not accessible to the linguistic motive. However, once you introduce this emendation, you can see beyond the accidents of language. You can recognize how much of value has been contributed to the New Rhetoric by these investigators, though their observations are made in terms that never explicitly confront the rhetorical ingredient in their field of study. We can place in terms of rhetoric all those statements by anthropologists, ethnologists, individual and social psychologists, and the like, that bear upon the *persuasive* aspects of language, the function of language as *addressed*, as direct or roundabout appeal to real or ideal audiences, without or within.

Are we but haggling over a term? In one sense, yes. We are offering a rationale intended to show how far one might systematically extend the term "rhetoric." In this respect, we are haggling over a term; for we must persist in tracking down the *function* of that term. But to note the ingredient of rhetoric lurking in such anthropologist's terms as "magic" and "witchcraft" is not to ask that the anthropologist replace his words with ours. We are certainly not haggling over terms in that sense. The term "rhetoric" is no substitute for "magic," "witchcraft," "socialization," "communication," and so on. But the term rhetoric designates a *function* which is present in the areas variously covered by those other terms. And we are asking only that this *function* be recognized for what it is: a linguistic function by nature as *realistic* as a proverb, though it may be quite far from the kind of realism found in strictly "scientific realism." For it is essentially a realism of the *act:* moral, persuasive—and acts are not "true" and "false" in the sense that the propositions of "scientific realism" are. And however "false" the "propositions" of primitive magic may be, considered from the standpoint of scientific realism, it is different with the peculiarly *rhetorical* ingredient in magic, involving ways of identification that contribute variously to social cohesion (either for the advantage of the community as a whole, or for the advantage of special groups whose interests are a burden on the community, or for the advantage of special groups whose rights and duties are indeterminately both a benefit and a tax on the community, as with some business enterprise in our society).

The "pragmatic sanction" for this function of magic lies outside the realm of strictly true-or-false propositions; it falls in an area of deliberation that itself draws upon the resources of rhetoric; it is itself a subject matter belonging to an art that can "prove opposites."

To illustrate what we mean by "proving opposites" here: we read

function of rhetoric

an article, let us say, obviously designed to dispose the reading public favorably toward the "aggressive and expanding" development of American commercial interests in Saudi Arabia. It speaks admiringly of the tremendous changes which our policies of commerce and investment will introduce into a vestigially feudal culture and of the great speed at which the rationale of finance and technology will accomplish these changes. When considering the obvious rhetorical intent of these "facts," we suddenly, in a perverse *non sequitur*, remember a passage in the Kluckhohn essay, involving what we would now venture to call "the rhetoric of witchcraft":

> In a society like the Navaho which is competitive and capitalistic, on the one hand, and still familistic on the other, any ideology which has the effect of slowing down economic mobility is decidedly adaptive. One of the most basic strains in Navaho society arises out of the incompatibility between the demands of familism and the emulation of European patterns in the accumulating of capital.

And in conclusion we are told that the "survival of the society" is assisted by "any pattern, such as witchcraft, which tends to discourage the rapid accumulation of wealth" (witchcraft, as an "ideology," contributing to this end by identifying new wealth with malign witchery). Now, when you begin talking about the optimum rate of speed at which cultural changes should take place, or the optimum proportion between tribal and individualistic motives that should prevail under a particular set of economic conditions, you are talking about something very important indeed, but you will find yourself deep in matters of rhetoric: for nothing is more rhetorical in nature than a deliberation as to what is too much or too little, too early or too late; in such controversies, rhetoricians are forever "proving opposites."

Where are we now? We have considered two main aspects of rhetoric: its use of *identification* and its nature as *addressed*. Since identification implies division, we found rhetoric involving us in matters of socialization and faction. Here was a wavering line between peace and conflict, since identification is got by property, which is ambivalently a motive of both morality and strife. And inasmuch as the ultimate of conflict is war or murder, we considered how such imagery can figure as a terminology of reidentification ("transformation" or "rebirth"). For in considering the wavering line between identification and division, we shall always be coming upon manifestations of the logomachy, avowed as in invective, unavowed as in stylistic subterfuges for presenting real divisions in terms that deny division.

We found that this wavering line between identification and division was forever bringing rhetoric against the possibility of malice and the lie; for if an identification favorable to the speaker or his cause is made to seem favorable to the audience, there enters the possibility of such "heightened consciousness" as goes with deliberate cunning. Thus, roundabout, we confronted the nature of rhetoric as *addressed* to audiences of the first, second, or third person. Socialization itself was, in the widest sense, found to be addressed. And by reason of such simultaneous identification-with and division-from as mark the choice of a scapegoat, we found that rhetoric involves us in problems related to witchcraft, magic, spellbinding, ethical promptings, and the like. And in the course of discussing these subjects, we found ourselves running into another term: persuasion. Rhetoric is the art of persuasion, or a study of the means of persuasion available for any given situation. We have thus, deviously, come to the point at which Aristotle begins his treatise on rhetoric.

So we shall change our purpose somewhat. Up to now, we have been trying to indicate what kinds of subject matter not traditionally labeled "rhetoric" should, in our opinion, also fall under this head. We would now consider varying views of rhetoric that have already prevailed; and we would try to "generate" them from the same basic terms of our discussion.

As for the relation between "identification" and "persuasion": we might well keep it in mind that a speaker persuades an audience by the use of stylistic identifications; his act of persuasion may be for the purpose of causing the audience to identify itself with the speaker's interests; and the speaker draws on identification of interests to establish rapport between himself and his audience. So, there is no chance of our keeping apart the meanings of persuasion, identification ("consubstantiality") and communication (the nature of rhetoric as "addressed"). But, in given instances, one or another of these elements may serve best for extending a line of analysis in some particular direction.

And finally: The use of symbols, by one symbol-using entity to induce action in another (persuasion properly addressed) is in essence not magical but *realistic*. However, the resources of identification whereby a sense of consubstantiality is symbolically established between beings of unequal status may extend far into the realm of the *idealistic*. And as we shall see later, when on the subject of order, out of this idealistic element there may arise a kind of magic or mystery that sets its mark upon all human relations.

12

Terms of Rhetoric

Order

Positive, Dialectical, and Ultimate Terms

First, we take it, there are the positive terms. They name par excellence the things of experience, the *hic et nunc*, and they are defined *per genus et differentiam*, as with the vocabulary of biological classification. Here are the words for what Bentham called "real entities," in contrast with the "fictitious entities" of the law. ("Tree" is a positive term, but "rights" or "obligations" are legal fictions.) In Kant's alignment, the thing named by a positive term would be a manifold of sensations unified by a concept. Thus, the "sensibility" receives a bundle of "intuitions," intimations of size, shape, texture, color, and the like; and as the "understanding" clamps a unifying term, a "concept," upon the lot, we can say, "This is a house."

The imagery of poetry is positive to the extent that it names things having a visible, tangible existence. We have already observed that there is an important difference between a house as a practically existing object and the image "house" as it appears in a poem. But we are now considering only the respect in which the poetic image, house, can also be defined *per genus et differentiam:* that is, the respect in which, when a poet uses the term, "house," we could get his meaning by consulting Webster's, where we are told that a house is "a structure intended or used as a habitation or shelter for animals of any kind; but especially, a building or edifice for the habitation of man; a dwelling place."

A positive term is most unambiguously itself when it names a visible and tangible thing which can be located in time and place. Hence, the positive ideal is a "physicalist" vocabulary that reduces reference to terms of *motion*. Since the modern mathematics of submicroscopic motion is far indeed from the visible and tangible, the sensory aspect of positive experience can become quite tenuous. But since such manifestations must, in the last analysis, reveal themselves on dials, in

From "Order," in *A Rhetoric of Motives*, pp. 183–203. Reprinted by permission of The University of California Press. © 1969 by Kenneth Burke.

I feel like Richard would like this section @ all — not like he even think "positive" as a theme — would think terms are
motion as a theme

measurements and meter readings of one sort or another, the hypothetical entities of electronics can be considered as "positive," insofar as they are capable of empirical recording. A skeptic might offer reasons to believe that such science is less positive than its apologists take it to be. Particularly one might ask himself whether the terms for *relationships* among things are as positive as are the names for the things themselves. But we need not attempt to decide that question here; we need only note that there is a basic terminology of perception grounded on sensation, memory, and "imagination" (in the general, psychological, nonpoetic meaning of the word). And whatever else it may be in its ultimate reaches, such a terminology of perception is "positive" in its everyday, empirical availability. There is nothing "transcendent" about it, for instance.

Bentham's reference to "fictitious entities" of the law indicates another order, comprising terms which we would call "dialectical." These have no such strict location as can be assigned to the objects named in words of the first order. Even insofar as the positive terminology acquires theoretical champions who proclaim the "principles of positivism," we are in the realm of the purely dialectical. "Positivism" itself is not a positive term. For though you may locate the positive referent for the expression "house," you will have a hard time trying to locate a similarly positive referent for the expression, "principles of positivism." Here are words that belong, not in the order of *motion and perception,* but rather in the order of *action and idea.* Here are words for *principles* and *essence* (as we might ask, "Just what is the *essence* of the positivist doctrine?").

Here are "titular" words. Titles like "Elizabethanism" or "capitalism" can have no positive referent, for instance. And though they sum up a vast complexity of conditions which might conceivably be reduced to a near-infinity of positive details, if you succeeded in such a description you would find that your recipe contained many ingredients not peculiar to "Elizabethanism" or "capitalism" at all. In fact, you would find that "Elizabethanism" itself looked different, if matched against, say, "medievalism," than if matched against "Victorianism." And "capitalism" would look different if compared and contrasted with "feudalism" than if dialectically paired with "socialism." Hence terms of this sort are often called "polar."

Bentham said that fictitious entities could not be adequately defined *per genus et differentiam.* He said that they required, rather, definition by *paraphrase,* hence his method of "phraseoplerosis" and "archetypation" for discovering just what people really meant when they used legal fictions. We equate his "fictitious entities" with "dialectical terms" because they refer to *ideas* rather than to *things.* Hence they are more concerned with *action* and *attitude* than with *perception* (they fall under the head of *ethics* and *form* rather than *knowledge* and *information*). You define them by asking how they *behave;* and part of an expression's behavior, as Bentham pointed out, will be revealed by the discovery of the secret modifiers implicit in the expression itself; hence Bentham's project for filling out the expression (phraseoplerosis) and discounting its images (archetypation).

If an expression were complete, such paraphrase would not be necessary. One could then derive all the modifiers explicitly by citation from the expression itself. But particularly in the strife of rhetoric, the expression is left fragmentary. If a poet says, "I love" when he really hates, he will scrupulously proceed, however enigmatically, to round out his statement with the expressions that introduce the necessary modifiers. But when Preen says to Prone, "I want to help you," his statement is incomplete, and may even require interpretation on a purely behavioristic basis. If this "help," as tested behavioristically, amounts to nothing more than what folk rhetoric calls the "run around," then the ultimate test of his meaning is extralinguistic. And much rhetorical statement requires such circumstantial interpretation.

Hypothetically, if our discrimination were keen enough, we could know by the tonalities of Preen's statement, or by the flicker of his eye, just what he meant when he said, "I want to help you." In brief, the expression itself would contain its future implications. But our discrimination is not always keen enough; and besides, the record is usually but a fragment of the expression (as the written word omits all telltale record of gesture and tonality; and not only may our "literacy" keep us from missing the omissions, it may blunt us to the appreciation of tone and gesture, so that even when we witness the full expression, we note only those aspects of it that can be written down).

In public relations, most expressions are as though wigwagged from a great distance, or as uttered behind masks, or as transmitted by hearsay. Hence, one must go to the first frank level of analysis, the extra-verbally behavioristic. Next, there are sloganlike utterances by which all men are partially fooled, the orator and his public alike. For this we have Bentham's concern with "archetypation," the images that *improperly* affect our ideas. But here we meet the need for another kind of "filling out," half behavioristic, half imaginal, an ambiguity due to the fact that so much pragmatic behavior itself has symbolic elements.

If, for instance, the church spire actually has been an image of aspirations "towards heaven," and if churchmen pay verbal tribute to the power of the supernatural, and if then on church property they erect business structures soaring far above their church, does not this combination of behavioristic and imaginal tests require us to conclude that their true expression is not in their words, but in the conditions of steel and stone which are weightily there, to dwarf you as the church spire never dwarfed you, and to put you at the bottom of a deep, windswept gulch? Regardless of what they may say in their statements telegraphed worldwide by the news agencies, without gesture, without tonality, have they not, in their mixture of behavior and image, *really* proclaimed that they live by a "post-Christian" order of motives?

If church spires mean anything, they must overtop the buildings that surround them. However, the opposition might point out: There are the catacombs of religion, too. True, there is the *underground.*

In any case, we have again come upon an area where nonverbal things, in their capacity as "meanings," also take on the nature of words, and thus require the extension of dialectic into the realm of the physical. Or, otherwise put, we come to the place where the dialectical realm of ideas is seen to permeate the positive realm of concepts. For if a church spire is a symbolic thing, then the business structure that overtowers it must participate in the same symbolic, however antithetically, as representing an alternate choice of action. Thus the ethical-dramatic-dialectical vocabulary so infuses the empirical-positive world of things that each scientific object becomes available for poetry.

But the distinction between positive and dialectical terms, with the interrelation of the two realms, can deflect attention from a third aspect of vocabulary, which might be called "ultimate." We had thought of calling it "mystical," but that designation too quickly makes readers take sides for or against us. So let us call it "ultimate," and approach this third element of vocabulary thus:

Dialectic in itself may remain on the level of parliamentary conflict, leading to compromise. It being the realm of ideas or principles, if you organize a conflict among spokesmen for competing ideas or principles, you may produce a situation wherein there is no one clear choice. Each of the spokesmen, whose ideas are an extension of special interests, must remain somewhat unconvinced by any solution which does not mean the complete triumph of his partisan interests. Yet he may have to compromise, putting through some portion of his program by making concessions to allies whom, if he could get his wishes absolutely, he would repudiate. Here are standard parliamentary tactics. "Compromise" is perhaps the neutral term, though on the edge of the dyslogistic. "Horse-trading" is clearly a dyslogistic term for the same thing. And a resoundingly dyslogistic term would be "demoralization," justifiable insofar as all "interests" can be translated into terms of "principles," and when they have thus been stylistically ennobled, any yielding on interests becomes a yielding on principles (a stylistic embarrassment upon which our State Department under General Marshall based the rigidity of its dealings with Soviet Russia).

Now, the difference between a merely "dialectical" confronting of parliamentary conflict and an "ultimate" treatment of it would reside in this: The "dialectical" order would leave the competing voices in a jangling relation with one another (a conflict solved *faute de mieux* by "horse-trading"); but the "ultimate" order would place these competing voices themselves in a *hierarchy, or sequence, or evaluative series,* so that, in some way, we went by a fixed and reasoned progression from one of these to another, the members of the entire group being arranged *developmentally* with relation to one another. The "ultimate" order of terms would thus differ essentially from the "dialectical" (as we use the term *in this particular connection*) in that there would be a "guiding idea" or "unitary principle" behind the diversity of voices. The voices would not confront one another as somewhat disrelated competitors that can work together only by the "mild demoralization" of sheer compromise; rather, they would be like successive positions or moments in a single process.

Thus, confronting the sort of "dialectical" procedure required when "interests" have been translated into a corresponding terminology of "principles," with parliamentary spokesmen aiming to further their interests somewhat by compromising with their principles—we can get a glimpse into a possible alternative, whereby a somewhat formless parliamentary wrangle can, by an "ultimate" vocabulary, be creatively endowed with design. And even though the members of the parliament, being "horse-traders" by nature, may not accept this design, it can have a contemplative effect; it can organize one's attitude towards the struggles of politics, and may suggest reasons why one kind of compromise is, in the long run, to be rated as superior to another.

Consider, for instance, how Plato treats the four kinds of "imperfect government" in *The Republic* (Book VIII and beginning of Book IX). They are presented not merely as one might draw up a list, but *developmentally*. The steps from his ideal government to "timocracy," and thence successively to "oligarchy," "democracy," and "tyranny" are interpreted as the unfolding of a single process. Here, as repeatedly in Platonic dialogues, the interrelationship among the terms for the kinds of government is "ultimate." Indeed, when Socrates celebrates dialectic as the highest kind of knowledge, rising above the separate sciences and mediating among them, he means by dialectic not merely the step from sensory terms to ideas, but also a hierarchic ordering of steps.

"Governments vary as the dispositions of men," Socrates says; and "there must be as many of one as of the other." Whereupon he seeks to define the human dispositions brought to the fore by each of the different political structures. His resulting remarks on the "timocratic man," and on the "oligarchic," "democratic," and "tyrannical man" amount to recipes for what today might be called four different "ideologies." Each of these has its own peculiar idea or summarizing term: "honor" for timocracy, "wealth" for oligarchy, "freedom" for democracy, "protection" for tyranny. And the human dispositions which he describes under these heads could be treated as four different motivational clusters which one must appeal to, when trying to win adherents in an audience typical of each such political state. "As the government, so the citizen," Plato says. Yet he is not content merely to give us four "personality types" (four corresponding types of government, each with its appropriate ideology or kind of consciousness). He is seeking to grade them with reference to their relative distance from a single norm. We are not here arguing for the justice of his grading; we are merely pointing to the principle involved. We are saying that to leave the four kinds merely confronting one another in their diversity would have been "dialectical" in the sense of the parliamentary jangle, but that this attempt to arrange them hierarchically transforms the dialectical into an "ultimate" order.

In an ultimate dialectic, the terms so lead into one another that the completion of each order leads to the next. Thus, a body of positive terms must be brought to a head in a titular term which represents the principle or idea behind the positive terminology as a whole. This summarizing term is in a different order of vocabulary. And if such titles, having been brought into dialectical commerce with one another, are given an order among themselves, there must be a principle of principles involved in such a design—and the step from principles to a principle of principles is likewise both the fulfillment of the previous order and the transcending of it.

We thought of calling the ultimate order "mystical" because the mystic invariably aims to encompass conflicting orders of motivation, not by outlawing any order, however "inferior," but by finding a place for it in a developmental series. Thus at moments when a mystic vocabulary is most accurate, we should not expect to find a flat antithesis between "body" and "spirit." Rather, we should expect "body" (in even its "lowliest" forms) to be treated as a *way into* "spirit." Since antithesis is so strong a verbal instrument in both rhetoric and dialectic, we may often find "short cuts" where the extremes of a developmental series are presented as harshly antithetical. But we should not judge by this alone. Rather, look into the writings of any mystic who has left a record of his methods, and you will find that the entry to ultimate communion is made *through* body, nature, image, systematically treated as a necessary disciplinary step. Indeed, so thoroughly is this the case, that for the most ultimate of his experiences, the mystic will again employ the terms of body, nature, image (on the assumption that, if one has gone through the proper series of steps, one knows how to discount the inadequacies of such language, while the clash of images by oxymoron comes closest to expressing the experience for someone who has not been through it).

Ultimate Elements in the Marxist Persuasion

Once you have placed your terms in a developmental series, you have an arrangement whereby each can be said to participate, within the limitations of its nature, in the ultimate perfection ("finishedness") of the series. Each stage, at its appropriate "moment," represents the movement, the ultimate direction or principle, of the entire series. In this sense, Hegel's "concrete universal" would be "mystical," in that it represents not only itself, in its nature *hic et hunc*, but the universal essence of the development in its entirety (quite as bud, preceding blossom, represents not only its own concrete bud-nature, and its nature as incipient blossom, but also the fruit, the seed, and decline, and the futurity beyond that decline). And since any moment, here and now, would thus represent a developmental principle transcending the concrete particularity of any one moment in the series, here would be a kind of mystical unity, a oneness that both is and is not, as with the paradox of substance discussed in the *Grammar*.

Marx wrote good satire on Hegel's "concrete universal." And in keeping with the same line of thought, he notes in *The German Ideology* how, by the use of an ultimate design for interpreting moments along the path of history, later history can be made to look like the goal of earlier history (as were we to say that America was discovered in order to bring about the French Revolution). Thereby, he says, "history receives its own special aims and becomes 'a person ranking with other persons' (to wit: 'self-consciousness, criticism, the Unique,' etc.), while what is designated with the words 'destiny,' 'goal,' 'germ,' or 'idea' of earlier history is nothing more than an abstraction formed from later history, from the active influence which earlier history exercises on later history."

But can a mode of thought so strongly built upon Hegelian patterns avoid the "mystical" merely by "turning Hegel upside down"? In any case, much of the *rhetorical* strength in the Marxist dialectic comes from the fact that it is "ultimate" in its order. The various classes do not confront one another merely as parliamentary voices that represent conflicting interests. They are arranged hierarchically, each with the disposition, or "consciousness," that matches its peculiar set of circumstances, while the steps from feudal to bourgeois to proletarian are grounded in the very nature of the universe.

Precisely by reason of this ultimate order, a spokesman for the proletariat can think of himself as representing not only the interests of that class alone, but the grand design of the entire historical sequence, its final outcome for all mankind. When gauging the historical situation correctly, when knowing the nature of the moment as part of a universal movement, he finds in the "revolutionary situation" precisely the double nature that permits it to be simultaneously the concrete thing it is, in its own unique combination of conditions, and a participant in the perfection of the total sequence. (To see both the "science" and the "intuition," see Lenin's letters when he had become convinced that the time was ripe in Russia.)

In general, the ultimate hierarchic order of the terminology rises materialistically from the fundamental, unknown particles of the universe, to atoms, to crystals and planetary formations, to the emergence of life, to the evolution of biological forms, to the evolution and revolution of social forms. We cite from the report of a lecture on dialectical materialism by the English physicist, J. D. Bernal, referring to this "natural hierarchy of development in the universe." But from the standpoint of rhetoric, the implanting of an ultimate hierarchy upon social forms is the important thing. Here the hierarchic ordering of the subsocial realms could be considered as an "ideological reflex" or extension of the persuasive principle experienced in the social realm. That is, rhetorically considered, the Marxist hierarchy may go not from a science of nature to a science of society, but from an ultimate dialectic of social development to a corresponding dialectic of natural development. For though there may be a "Marxist physics," Marxism is primarily a *sociology*.

In accord with such thinking as regards current positivist doctrines, one may take a stand that, while neither flatly for nor flatly against, need not be reduced merely to the lame and formless admission that "there is something to be said for both sides." Not only is the positive order of vocabulary "allowable"; we should be reluctant to leave this order. Every question should be reduced to such terms, insofar as the nature of its subject-matter permits. The positivist ideal of language is athletic and exacting. And we should object to it only when dramatic elements are present which cannot legitimately be treated in the positive order alone. The improper migration of positive terms to areas of investigation and contemplation for which they are unfit calls for a flatly antipositivist position, as regards any such cases of terministic impropriety. But from the standpoint of terminology in general, we are not thereby vowed to a doctrine of out-and-out antipositivism, since we can and should accept the positivist order of terms as the proper first stage in a hierarchy of terms.

The same admonition should be introduced with regard to our reservations on technologism, as it is manifested in the cult of manufactured commodities (the doctrine that might be summed up: "It's culture if it's something you can buy"). Man is essentially a "rational" (that is, symbol-using) animal (as stated in the opening words of St. John, "*In the beginning* was the Word," the prior in substance being here expressed as the prior in time). And when we use symbols for things, such symbols are not merely reflections of the things symbolized, or signs for them; they are to a degree a *transcending* of the things symbolized. So, to say that man is a symbol-using animal is by the same token to say that he is a "transcending animal." Thus, there is in language itself a motive force calling man to transcend the "state of nature" (that is, the order of motives that would prevail in a world without language, Logos, "reason"). And in this sense, we can recognize even the cult of commodities (which is an outgrowth of language-guided invention), as a *mode of transcendence*. So we need not be placed in the position of flatly "rejecting" it, a particularly uncomfortable position in view of the fact that the cult of commodities seems able to recruit just about as many devotees as can afford to bear witness (testifying to the sincerity of their faith by money-offerings).

An out-and-out antithetical vocabulary would require you either to live by the cult of commodities, in effect adoring them as household gods, or to reject such a cult quite as a devout believer in the One God would reject idolatry. But by using a graded vocabulary, you can instead recognize the cult of commodities as a mode of transcendence that is genuine, but inferior.

Employing the same hierarchic principle, we note that even a Hitlerite political philosophy, or any such "collusion," would require treatment, not as flatly "antisocial," but rather as a low order of sociality. Such an approach becomes particularly necessary where an in-

ferior order actually prevails, and one is so placed that a flat rejection
of the doctrine would be suicidally ineffectual, whereas a grudging
minimum acceptance of it might put one in a position to work towards its gradual improvement. But unfortunately, while this way of
reasoning is just, it readily lends itself to use unjustly.

Any improvement in social status is a kind of transcendence. And
where one is a member of an extremely underprivileged class, as with
the Negro in America, an individual attempt at the transcending of
inferior status gets increased poignancy from the fact that, atop all the
intensity of such effort in itself, there is a working at cross-purposes.
The Negro intellectual, Ralph Ellison, says that Booker T. Washington
"described the Negro community as a basket of crabs, wherein should
one attempt to climb out, the others immediately pull him back." Is
there not also an internal compulsion of the same sort, as the individual Negro visits this same judgment upon himself? For he may also
take the position of what Mead would call the "generalized other":
he may visit upon himself the antagonistic attitude of the whites; or
he may feel as "conscience" the judgment of his own class, since he
would in a sense be "disloyal" to his class, in transcending the limitations traditionally imposed upon him as a member of that class.
Striving for freedom as a human being generically, he must do so as a
Negro specifically. But to do so as a Negro is, by the same token, to
pervent oneself from doing so in the generic sense; for a Negro could
not be free generically except in a situation where the color of the skin
had no more social meaning than the color of the eyes.

Recall the lines in *The Merchant of Venice,* where Shakespeare is
considering an analogous conflict, as Shylock says:

> I am a Jew. Hath not a Jew eyes? hath not a Jew hands, organs, dimen-
> sions, senses, affections, passions? fed with the same food, hurt with the
> same weapons, subject to the same diseases, healed by the same means,
> warmed and cooled by the same winter and summer, as a Christian is? If
> you prick us, do we not bleed? if you tickle us, do we not laugh? if you
> poison us, do we not die?

Then, following this statement of his identity as a member of mankind generically, Shylock turns to the theme of his specific identity as
a Jew in Christian Venice:

> and if you wrong us, shall we not revenge? If we are like you in the rest,
> we shall resemble you in that. If a Jew wrong a Christian, what is his
> humility? Revenge. If a Christian wrong a Jew, what should his sufferance
> be by Christian example? Why, revenge. The villainy you teach me I will
> execute, and it shall go hard but I will better the instruction.

Note the paradoxical way in which the words "humility" and "sufferance" are used. Revenge as a kind of humble, Christian duty. One might call the notion Shylock's failure to understand Christian doctrine. Or, more justly, one might call it Shylock's very accurate gauging of the way in which Christians themselves characteristically distort Christian sufferance to serve the rhetoric of property. In any case, we see that Shylock would here use the advantages of vengeance itself as a kind of transcendence, a "static" way of lifting himself above his disadvantages as a Jew while in the very same act he reaffirms his status.

Such conflicts are clearly "dialectical." We are beyond the purely positive level of vocabulary; we are in the realm, not of knowledge, but of ideas and action. Hence, unless the terminology becomes ultimate, there is an unresolved, parliamentary jangle, a discordancy of conflicting voices which at best could attain an uneasy compromise, and at worst arrive at the equating of vengeance with humility (which means, in sum, accepting the judgment of the opponent, and merely turning the tables against him). Shylock's "vengeance" is but the most highly generalized statement of such a solution, which in each particular case calls for a joining in a conspiracy against the oppressor, in the hopes that eventually the roles can be reversed. In Richard Wright's *Native Son,* Bigger's criminal protest *as a Negro* is another particularization of the same response. The "humility" of such vengeance is in the acceptance of the opponent's judgment, in finally agreeing to let him set the rules, and then aiming at advantage within the restrictions he has imposed. Purely "racialist" or "nationalist" doctrines of emancipation are a more benign transformation of such "counterconspiracy" (or exclusive league of the excluded). And they may even seem like an ultimate solution, until there develop the wrangles within nationalism, and among rival nationalisms.

Clearly, the rhetorical appeal of the Marxist terminology in such situations is that it can allow for an ultimate order. You may question whether it is the "ultimate-ultimate." You may fear that, as it operates in social textures, it ceases to be the conspiracy-to-end-conspiracy that it claims to be, instead becoming but the condition of a new conspiracy. Maybe yes, maybe no. That is not for us to decide at the moment. It is enough for us to note, as students of rhetoric, that the Marxist terminology is "ultimate" enough to meet at least the primary requirements of this sort. It permits the member of a minority to place his problem in a graded series that keeps transcendence of individual status from seeming like disloyalty to one's group status, and keeps the sufferance of one's group status from assuming some form of mere "vengeance." It allows the member of an underprivileged minority, for instance, to confront the world at once specifically and generically. The Negro does not become equal to the white by a kind of intellectual "passing." He can explicitly recognize that his particular act must be adapted to the nature of his historical situation in which he happens to be placed; yet at the same time, he can view this situation universally (thereby attaining the kind of transcendence at which all men aim, and at which the Negro spiritual had aimed, though there the aim was at the spiritual transcending of a predestined material slavery, whereas the Marxist ultimates allow for a material transcending of inferior status).

True, there is much that no vocabulary can do in these matters. Where there are so many intense conflicts of an extraverbal sort, no merely verbal manipulations can remove them. But verbal manipulations may offer a more orderly approach to them, permitting them to be contemplated with less agitation. And where this is the case, verbal manipulations are the very opposite of the "evasive."

Marxism, considered as an ultimate vocabulary, also owes much of its persuasiveness to the way in which its theory of action fits its theory of order. For if any point, or "moment," in a hierarchic series can be said to represent, in its limited way, the principle or "perfection" of the ultimate design, then each tiny act shares in the absolute meaning of the total act. Thus, the "truth" is not grasped and tested by merely "perceiving" the logic of the entire series. Perception must be grounded in enactment, by participation in some local role, so that the understanding of the total order is reached through this partial involvement. There is perception from without, made possible through nonparticipation. Or there is local participation, which may become so involved in particulars that one never sees beyond them. But there is a third way, the fullest kind of understanding, wherein one gets the immediacy of participation in a local act, yet sees in and through this act an over-all design, sees and *feels* the local act itself as but the partial expression of the total development. The Marxist persuasion is in the name of this third way. Consider Lenin's *What Is to Be Done?* for instance:

We might first note in the very title a contribution to our previous concern with the relation between rhetoric and opinion. For in his *Book of Fallacies,* Bentham had distinguished between matters of fact (what was done, *quid factum*) and matters of opinion (what is to be done, *quid faciendum*). The future can only be a matter of opinion. Until it has actually come to pass, it must lie outside the orbit of empirically verifiable "scientific fact." So Lenin's question, *What Is to Be*

Done? is by such tests clearly in the realm of opinion, and to this extent in the realm of rhetoric. (It is "deliberative.")

The crucial point, as we quoted it in the *Grammar,* revolves about the distinction between trade union activity and the worker's *consciousness* of his role as member of a revolutionary proletariat. Lenin would distinguish between the "spontaneous" response to a situation and the kind of *new act* that arises under a deliberately Marxist interpretation of that situation. And we would interpret the design of Lenin's thinking in this wise: The trade unionist, as such, has no consciousness of the workers' "historical role" in the revolutionary change from capitalism to socialism. Hence, in the mere spontaneity and localism of his responses, he does not transcend the limitations of his class. He acts, and to this extent he has a profounder kind of participation than the purely outside observer. But his act is beclouded by the particulars of his situation, the day-to-day contingencies of earning a livelihood. Now add the Marxist doctrine of universal historical necessity, defining the worker's place in an *ultimate* development. The worker whose understanding becomes infused with this doctrine then sees himself not merely as an individual joining with other individuals to improve his bargaining position with his employer: he sees himself as *member of a class,* the proletariat, which is destined to play *a crucial role in the unfolding of history as a whole.* Thus, while participating with maximum activity in the particular organizational and propagandist problems that mark his local situation, he transcends the limitations of these local conditions and of his "spontaneous" nature as member of the working class. For he sees his role in terms of an *absolute,* an ultimate. In participating *locally,* he is participating in the total dialectic, communicating directly with its universal logic, or ultimate direction. Indeed, we could even say that he now sees himself in *formal* or *ritual* terms, not just as Mr. So-and-so working under such-and-such conditions, but as "*the* Proletarian," with a generic personality calling creatively to ways of action that transcend his limited nature as Mr. So-and-so, and derive their logic from motives of universal scope.

Call it fallacious if you want. That need not concern us here. We are discussing the rhetorical advantages of an ultimate vocabulary as contrasted with a vocabulary left on the level of parliamentary conflict. We are but pointing to a notable formal advantage, got by the union of drama and reason, a wholesome rhetorical procedure in itself, at a time when typical "parliamentary" works like Thurman Arnold's *The Folklore of Capitalism* would ask us rather to unite drama with unreason.

Perhaps the "ultimate" order comes most natural to narrative forms (hence its ease of adaptation to the Hegelian and Marxist "stories" of history). Usually, in narrative, it is so implicit that we may not even discern it. For instance, if the fate of our hero is developed through a succession of encounters, each of these encounters may represent a different "principle," and each of these principles or stages may so lead into the next that the culmination of one lays the ground for the next. In fact, if the work is properly constructed, it will necessarily have such a form. If one breaks down a "dramatic idea" into acts of variously related agents, the successive steps of the plot could be reduced to corresponding developments of the idea; and the agent or scene under the aegis of which a given step was enacted could be said to represent personally the motivational principle of that step. The plot is unnoticeably ultimate, as the reader need not "choose between" different phases of its unfolding, but by going through each becomes prepared for the next. Ultimate vocabularies of motivation aim at the philosophic equivalent of such narrative forms, with a series of steps that need not precede one another in time, but only "in principle," though the formal appeal in the Marxist dialectic of history seems to reside in the fact that, as with narrative, the series in time is also a series "in principle."

"Sociology of Knowledge" vs. *Platonic "Myth"*

Karl Mannheim's project for a "sociology of knowledge," as discussed in his *Ideology and Utopia,* might be described as a methodology that aims at the neutralizing and liberalizing of the Marxist rhetoric. When viewed from the standpoint of the distinction between positive, dialectical, and ultimate terminologies, it seems to go beyond the purely parliamentary kind of dialectic, yet to fall somewhat short of an ultimate order. We might improvise a term, and call it "pro-ultimate." For it would move towards a gradual increase of precision, got by an exact study of the relationship between the positive and dialectical orders.

At least, that is how we would interpret Mannheim's distinction between "relativism" and "relationism." "Relativism" would merely recognize the great variety of ideological perspectives, would describe them in their diversity, and at best would look for workable compromises among them. But "relationism" should be able to build up an exact body of knowledge about ideologies by studying the connection between these ideologies and their ground.

To this end, Mannheim generalizes the Marxist exposure of "mystification" to the point where it becomes the "unmasking" of *any* doctrinal bias. That is, a human terminology of motives is necessarily partial; accordingly, whatever its claims to universal validity, its "principles" favor the interests of some group more than others; and one may look to opposing theorists for discoveries that "unmask" the partisan limitations lurking in speciously "universal" principles.

Any such "unmasking" of an ideology's limitations is itself made from a limited point of view. But each such limited perspective can throw light upon the relation between the universal principles of an ideology and the special interests which they are consciously or unconsciously made to serve. Each point of view could thus reveal something about the relation between an ideology (we might call it a systematized verbal act) and its nonverbal conditions (the scene of that act).

One might thus use rhetorical partisanship for dialectical operations that led towards a body of exact knowledge about the relation between all ideologies and the conditions of living out of which they arise. And by this method, the specialist in such analysis should also be able to discount the partiality of his own position somewhat (a transcending of partiality to which competing specialists might contribute, by unmasking the undetected partiality of their colleagues, thereby making it possible to work steadily toward an increase in the exactitude of ways for discounting bias in views that had seemed to be universally valid). The lore gradually accumulated by such procedures would constitute a "sociology of knowledge."

Only if all the returns were in, could one lay claim to an ultimate order here. But the project for thus systematically utilizing both rhetorical and dialectical elements in the search for an ever closer approximate to absolute knowledge about the nature of "ideologies," would clearly be much nearer to an "ultimate" order than a mere relativistic study of opinions and their background would be. "Relativism" would be hardly more than the first preparation positivistic research needed to provide the material for the dialectical discipline of "relationism."

In such a project, of course, Marxism would be but one voice among many. And the edges are so knocked off the Marxist definition of ideology that Marxism too becomes analyzable as an ideology. That is, whatever its pretensions to an ultimate vocabulary, as seen from the standpoint of a "sociology of knowledge" it becomes but one step, however important, in the development from the overemphasis and underemphasis of partiality towards a perfectly balanced vocabulary which the systematic use of rhetorical and dialectical operations has wholly discounted for partisanship.

In one sense, "utopias" are but a special case of ideologies. Specifically, the utopian bias is progressive, futuristic, whereas the ideological bias is conservative or reactionary, designed to maintain a *status quo* or to reinstate an earlier social order. But Mannheim also seems to employ the term "ideology" in a more general sense, to include both kinds. This shifting of usage is made all the more necessary by the fact that changing historical conditions can change the function of a perspective, so that terms once progressive in their implications can become conservative. However, we would want to add our contention that, if you could analyze a structure of terms fully and closely enough, you should be able to discover by purely internal analysis when such a change in quality occurred, and you would not have to rely simply upon knowledge of the different uses to which the terms had been put in the two different eras.

But there may be another element hidden in the idea of utopia, as it figures in Mannheim's book. There are good reasons to believe that this "sociology of knowledge" owes some of its appeal, above the general run of sociological works, to a wholly unsociological cause. It grounds its analysis in the study of chiliastic doctrines, and for all its unwieldiness it never quite loses the resonance of this mythic anecdote. We thus have more the *feel* of an ultimate order than would be the case if the approach were strictly sociological. One can even discern here the elements, broken and reassembled, of a Platonic dialogue.

As written by Plato, the work would probably have proceeded thus: First, the setting up of several voices, each representing a different "ideology," and each aiming rhetorically to unmask the opponents; next, Socrates' dialectical attempt to build a set of generalizations that transcended the bias of the competing rhetorical partisans; next, his vision of the ideal end in such a project; and finally, his rounding out the purely intellectual abstractions by a myth, in this case the chiliastic vision. The myth would be a reduction of the "pure idea" to terms of image and fable. By the nature of the case, it would be very limited in its range and above all, if judged literally, it would be "scientifically" questionable.[1]

But insofar as the Platonic dialogue lived up to its pretensions, the bias of this concluding myth would be quite different from the bias of the rhetorical partisans with which the discussion began. For the myth should not have emerged until such rhetorical or ideological bias had

---

1. In this chapter we are adapting for our purposes the account of Platonist transcendence given in *The Myths of Plato*, by J. A. Stewart.

been dialectically transcended in terms of pure ideas. However, if you disregarded the steps by which the myth had been arrived at, you might find implicit in it much the same partiality and partisanship as was explicitly present in the opening statements of opposing "ideologies." The "myth" might then be said to represent a forward-looking partisanship, in contrast with the backward-looking partisanships of the "ideologies." And you could next scramble the elements of the dialogue, seeking to get a new dialectic by a method that transcended the partiality of both the ideologies and the myth.

There would be this difference lurking at the basis of one's dialectic: In the Platonic dialogue, the step from pure abstract ideas to imaginal myth had been simultaneously a step down and a step up. It was a step down, because it descended from the purity of abstractions to the impurity of images. It was a step up, because it here introduced a new level of motivation, motivation *beyond* the ideas, not present in the dialectical reduction to pure ideas.

However, a motivational problem arises, if you treat the mythic motive as on a par with the ideological motives. For you find that, if your method for eliminating all such bias were successful, it would deprive society of its primary motive power. For though bias is false promise, it is promise. Hence, if you eliminate bias (illusion) from men's social motives, where do you find an equally urgent social motive? Such appears to be the nostalgic problem which Mannheim, in the thoroughness of his scrambled "Platonic dialogue," finally confronts. For he explicitly asks himself where the zeal of human effort would come from, if it were not for the false promises of our utopias. And he asks this, even as he aims by scrupulous method to destroy the zeal of such false promises, or mythic utopian illusions.

His attempt is all the more justified by the fact that myths are not usually approached through the initiatory discipline of a Platonic dialogue. And insofar as they are taken literally, they do function as ideologies, hence require the kind of discounting provided by a "sociology of knowledge." But if you apply the same sociological methods to eliminate the bias from both ideologies and myth, the success of your method would necessarily transcend a sociological motivation. The mythic motive would differ from the ideological motives only insofar as it could survive the elimination of false ideological motives. But by the method of discounting prescribed for the "sociology of knowledge," it could not survive.

This is not to say that we would find fault with a method of sociological discounting as such. There is a fallacy here only if sociology is expected to provide the ultimate ground of motivation. Thus, the "pro-ultimate" nature of the sociological vocabulary should be interpreted as indigenous to the nature of sociology itself, which cannot figure ultimate motives, and but brings us to the edge of them. At that point, myth may become necessary for figuring motives not sociological at all, hence not grounded in either sociological error or sociological knowledge. And whereas such myths should always be discounted for their biased application, in a formal dialectic their nature as biased translations can be formally recognized at the start.

To review, the steps were, in sum:

1. Mutual exposure of imperfect ideas (ideas bound to the sensory image).

2. Socratic transcending of this partiality.

3. Socratic summarizing vision of the pure idea.

4. Translation of the pure idea into terms of the mythic image.

5. Whereupon enters Mannheim, who proposes to develop a "sociology of knowledge" by treating the first and last steps as though they were of the same nature. Hence, he would perfect a method for discounting the limitations of both ("unmasking" their bias).

6. But:

The step from 3 to 4 had not merely been a translation downward (an incarnation of the "pure idea" into the conditions of the mythic image). For the arrival at the level of pure ideas had been in itself but a *preparation*. It had prepared the understanding to confront a motive which, being *beyond* ideas, would not lend itself to statement in ideas. Only by going from *sensory* images to ideas, then through ideas to the end of ideas, is one free to come upon the *mythic* image. True, such an ultimate motive would not be correctly stated in terms of image. But men have only idea and image to choose from. And the *disciplined arrival at the mythic image through the dialectical transcending of sensory images and the dialectical critique of ideas*, should be a protection against a merely literal interpretation of such a mythic image (as contrasted with the purely empirical or conceptual image that forms the positive ground of dialectical operations).

But though the mythic image had thus figured a motive beyond ideas of reason, in treating the ultimate mythic image as though it were in the same order with the competing ideologies you would find no further motivational element in it than you had found in the ideologies.

Or rather, the original qualitative distinction would now look at most like a distinction between forward-looking (utopian) and backward-looking ideologies. Hence, insofar as you correct the bias of both ideology and myth (utopia), you rob yourself of a motive. But of course, if the myth had been interpreted as *figuring a motive beyond the reach of ideology,* the motive of the myth would be felt to *lie beyond the motivational order treated in the competing ideologies.* Its motive would be "ultimate," as the motives of the ideologies were not. True: the fact is that the myths in their heyday *are* taken literally, without the preparatory discipline of Socratic criticism—and to this extent they do lend themselves to admonitory analysis as ideologies. But only a "philosophy of the myth" (and the Platonist dialectic might be called that) could reveal their true nature, in figuring a motive beyond sociological knowledge, a movement from and toward a real and ultimate universal ground.

13

Rhetorical Analysis

The Rhetoric of Hitler's "Battle"

The appearance of *Mein Kampf* in unexpurgated translation has called forth far too many vandalistic comments. There are other ways of burning books than on the pyre—and the favorite method of the hasty reviewer is to deprive himself and his readers by inattention. I maintain that it is thoroughly vandalistic for the reviewer to content himself with the mere inflicting of a few symbolic wounds upon this book and its author, of an intensity varying with the resources of the reviewer and the time at his disposal. Hitler's "Battle" is exasperating, even nauseating; yet the fact remains: If the reviewer but knocks off a few adverse attitudinizings and calls it a day, with a guaranty in advance that his article will have a favorable reception among the decent members of our population, he is contributing more to our gratification than to our enlightenment.

Here is the testament of a man who swung a great people into his wake. Let us watch it carefully; and let us watch it, not merely to discover some grounds for prophesying what political move is to follow Munich, and what move to follow that move, etc.; let us try also to discover what kind of "medicine" this medicine man has concocted, that we may know, with greater accuracy, exactly what to guard against, if we are to forestall the concocting of similar medicine in America.

Already, in many quarters of our country, we are "beyond" the stage where we are being saved from Nazism by our *virtues*. And fascist integration is being staved off, rather, by the *conflicts among our vices*. Our vices cannot get together in a grand united front of prejudices; and the result of this frustration, if or until they succeed in surmounting it, speaks, as the Bible might say, "in the name of" democracy. Hitler found a panacea, a "cure for what ails you," a "snake-oil," that made such sinister unifying possible within his own nation.

From "The Rhetoric of Hitler's 'Battle,'" in *The Philosophy of Literary Form*, pp. 191–220. Reprinted by permission of The University of California Press. © 1973 by The Regents of the University of California.

211

And he was helpful enough to put his cards face up on the table, that we might examine his hands. Let us, then, for God's sake, examine them. This book is the well of Nazi magic; crude magic, but effective. A people trained in pragmatism should want to inspect this magic.

I

Every movement that would recruit its followers from among many discordant and divergent bands must have some spot toward which all roads lead. Each man may get there in his own way, but it must be the one unifying center of reference for all. Hitler considered this matter carefully, and decided that this center must be not merely a centralizing hub of *ideas*, but a mecca geographically located, toward which all eyes could turn at the appointed hours of prayer (or, in this case, the appointed hours of prayer-in-reverse, the hours of vituperation). So he selected Munich, as the *materialization* of his unifying panacea. As he puts it:

> The geo-political importance of a center of a movement cannot be overrated. Only the presence of such a center and of a place, bathed in the magic of a Mecca or a Rome, can at length give a movement that force which is rooted in the inner unity and in the recognition of a hand that represents this unity.

If a movement must have its Rome, it must also have its devil. For as Russell pointed out years ago, an important ingredient of unity in the Middle Ages (an ingredient that long did its unifying work despite the many factors driving toward disunity) was the symbol of a common enemy, the Prince of Evil himself. Men who can unite on nothing else can unite on the basis of a foe shared by all. Hitler himself states the case very succinctly:

> As a whole, and at all times, the efficiency of the truly national leader consists primarily in preventing the division of the attention of a people, and always in concentrating it on a single enemy. The more uniformly the fighting will of a people is put into action, the greater will be the magnetic force of the movement and the more powerful the impetus of the blow. It is part of the genius of a great leader to make adversaries of different fields appear as always belonging to one category only, because to weak and unstable characters the knowledge that there are various enemies will lead only too easily to incipient doubts as to their own cause.
>
> As soon as the wavering masses find themselves confronted with too many enemies, objectivity at once steps in, and the question is raised

whether actually all the others are wrong and their own nation or their own movement alone is right.

Also with this comes the first paralysis of their own strength. Therefore, a number of essentially different enemies must always be regarded as one in such a way that in the opinion of the mass of one's own adherents the war is being waged against one enemy alone. This strengthens the belief in one's own cause and increases one's bitterness against the attacker.

As everyone knows, this policy was exemplified in his selection of an "international" devil, the "international Jew" (the Prince was international, universal, "catholic"). This *materialization* of a religious pattern is, I think, one terrifically effective weapon of propaganda in a period where religion has been progressively weakened by many centuries of capitalist materialism. You need but go back to the sermonizing of centuries to be reminded that religion had a powerful enemy long before organized atheism came upon the scene. Religion is based upon the "prosperity of poverty," upon the use of ways for converting our sufferings and handicaps into a good—but capitalism is based upon the prosperity of acquisitions, the only scheme of value, in fact, by which its proliferating store of gadgets could be sold, assuming for the moment that capitalism had not got so drastically in its own way that it can't sell its gadgets even after it has trained people to feel that human dignity, the "higher standard of living," could be attained only by their vast private accumulation.

So, we have, as unifying step number one, the international devil materialized, in the visible, point-to-able form of people with a certain kind of "blood," a burlesque of contemporary neopositivism's ideal of meaning, which insists upon a *material* reference.

Once Hitler has thus essentialized his enemy, all "proof" henceforth is automatic. If you point out the enormous amount of evidence to show that the Jewish worker is at odds with the "international Jew stock exchange capitalist," Hitler replies with one hundred percent regularity: That is one more indication of the cunning with which the "Jewish plot" is being engineered. Or would you point to "Aryans" who do the same as his conspiratorial Jews? Very well; that is proof that the "Aryan" has been "seduced" by the Jew.

The sexual symbolism that runs through Hitler's book, lying in wait to draw upon the responses of contemporary sexual values, is easily characterized: Germany in dispersion is the "dehorned Siegfried." The masses are "feminine." As such, they desire to be led by a dominating male. This male, as orator, woos them—and, when he has won them, he commands them. The rival male, the villainous Jew, would on the contrary "seduce" them. If he succeeds, he poisons their blood by intermingling with them. Whereupon, by purely associative connections of ideas, we are moved into attacks upon syphilis, prostitution, incest, and other similar misfortunes, which are introduced as a kind of "musical" argument when he is on the subject of "blood-poisoning" by intermarriage or, in its "spiritual" equivalent, by the infection of "Jewish" ideas, such as democracy.[1]

The "medicinal" appeal of the Jew as scapegoat operates from another angle. The middle class contains, within the mind of each member, a duality: its members simultaneously have a cult of money and a detestation of this cult. When capitalism is going well, this conflict is left more or less in abeyance. But when capitalism is balked, it comes to the fore. Hence, there is "medicine" for the "Aryan" members of the middle class in the projective device of the scapegoat, whereby the "bad" features can be allocated to the "devil," and one can "respect himself" by a distinction between "good" capitalism and "bad" capitalism, with those of a different lodge being the vessels of the "bad" capitalism. It is doubtless the "relief" of this solution that spared Hitler the necessity of explaining just how the "Jewish plot" was to work out. Nowhere does this book, which is so full of war plans, make the slightest attempt to explain the steps whereby the triumph of "Jewish Bolshevism," which destroys *all* finance, will be the triumph of "*Jewish*" finance. Hitler well knows the point at which his "elucidations" should rely upon the lurid alone.

The question arises, in those trying to gauge Hitler: Was his selection of the Jew as his unifying devil-function, a purely calculating act? Despite the quotation I have already given, I believe that it was *not.* The vigor with which he utilized it, I think, derives from a much more complex state of affairs. It seems that, when Hitler went to Vienna, in a state close to total poverty, he genuinely suffered. He lived among the impoverished; and he describes his misery at the spectacle. He was *sensitive* to it; and his way of manifesting this sensitiveness impresses me that he is, at this point, wholly genuine, as with his wincing at the broken family relationships caused by alcoholism, which he in turn relates to impoverishment. During this time he began his attempts at political theorizing; and his disturbance was considerably increased by the skill with which Marxists tied him into knots. One passage in particular gives you reason, reading between the lines, to believe that

1. Hitler also strongly insists upon the total identification between leader and people. Thus, in wooing the people, he would in a roundabout way be wooing himself. The thought might suggest how the Führer, dominating the feminine masses by his diction, would have an incentive to remain unmarried.

the dialecticians of the class struggle, in their skill at blasting his muddled speculations, put him into a state of uncertainty that was finally "solved" by rage:

> The more I argued with them, the more I got to know their dialectics. First they counted on the ignorance of their adversary; then, when there was no way out, they themselves pretended stupidity. If all this was of no avail, they refused to understand or they changed the subject when driven into a corner; they brought up truisms, but they immediately transferred their acceptance to quite different subjects, and, if attacked again, they gave way and pretended to know nothing exactly. Wherever one attacked one of these prophets, one's hands seized slimy jelly; it slipped through one's fingers only to collect again in the next moment. If one smote one of them so thoroughly that, with the bystanders watching, he could but agree, and if one thus thought he had advanced at least one step, one was greatly astonished the following day. The Jew did not in the least remember the day before, he continued to talk in the same old strain as if nothing had happened, and if indignantly confronted, he pretended to be astonished and could not remember anything except that his assertions had already been proved true the day before.
>
> Often I was stunned.
>
> One did not know what to admire more: their glibness of tongue or their skill in lying.
>
> I gradually began to hate them.

At this point, I think, <u>he is tracing the *spontaneous* rise of his anti-Semitism.</u> He tells how, once he had discovered the "cause" of the misery about him, he could *confront it.* Where he had had to avert his eyes, he could now *positively welcome* the scene. Here his drastic structure of *acceptance* was being formed. He tells of the "internal happiness" that descended upon him.

> This was the time in which the greatest change I was ever to experience took place in me.
>
> From a feeble cosmopolite I turned into a fanatical anti-Semite,

and thence we move, by one of those associational tricks which he brings forth at all strategic moments, into a vision of the end of the world—out of which in turn he emerges with his slogan: "I am acting in the sense of the Almighty Creator: *By warding off Jews I am fighting for the Lord's work*" (italics his).

He talks of this transition as a period of "double life," a struggle of "reason" and "reality" against his "heart." [2] It was as "bitter" as it

---

2. Other aspects of the career symbolism: Hitler's book begins: "Today I consider it my good fortune that Fate designated Braunau on the Inn as the place of my birth. For

was "blissful." And finally, it was "reason" that won! Which prompts us to note that those who attack Hitlerism as a cult of the irrational should emend their statements to this extent: irrational it is, but it is carried on under the *slogan* of "Reason." Similarly, his cult of war is developed "in the name of" humility, love, and peace. Judged on a quantitative basis, Hitler's book certainly falls under the classification of hate. Its venom is everywhere, its charity is sparse. But the rationalized family tree for this hate situates it in "Aryan love." Some deep-probing German poets, whose work adumbrated the Nazi movement, did gravitate toward thinking *in the name of* war, irrationality, and hate. But Hitler was not among them. After all, when it is so easy to draw a doctrine of war out of a doctrine of peace, why should the astute politician do otherwise, particularly when Hitler has slung together his doctrines, without the slightest effort at logical symmetry? Furthermore, Church thinking always got to its wars in Hitler's "sounder" manner; and the patterns of Hitler's thought are a bastardized or caricatured version of religious thought.

I spoke of Hitler's fury at the dialectics of those who opposed him when his structure was in the stage of scaffolding. From this we may move to another tremendously important aspect of this theory: his

---

this small town is situated on the border between those two German States, the reunion of which seems, at least to us of the younger generation, a task to be furthered with every means our lives long," an indication of his "transitional" mind, what Wordsworth might have called the "borderer." He neglects to give the date of his birth, 1889, which is supplied by the editors. Again there is a certain "correctness" here, as Hitler was not "born" until many years later—but he does give the exact date of his war wounds, which were indeed formative. During his early years in Vienna and Munich, he foregoes protest, on the grounds that he is "nameless." And when his party is finally organized and effective, he stresses the fact that his "nameless" period is over (i.e., he has shaped himself an identity). When reading in an earlier passage of his book some generalizations to the effect that one should not crystallize his political views until he is thirty, I made a note: "See what Hitler does at thirty." I felt sure that, though such generalizations may be dubious as applied to people as a whole, they must, given the Hitler type of mind (with his complete identification between himself and his followers), be valid statements about himself. One *should* do what he *did*. The hunch was verified: about the age of thirty Hitler, in a group of seven, began working with the party that was to conquer Germany. I trace these steps particularly because I believe that the orator who has a strong sense of his own "rebirth" has this to draw upon when persuading his audiences that his is offering them the way to a "new life." However, I see no categorical objection to this attitude; its menace derives solely from the values in which it is exemplified. They may be wholesome or unwholesome. If they are unwholesome, but backed by conviction, the basic sincerity of the conviction acts as a sound virtue to reinforce a vice—and this combination is the most disastrous one that a people can encounter in a demagogue.

attack upon the *parliamentary.* For it is again, I submit, an important aspect of his medicine, in its function as medicine for him personally and as medicine for those who were later to identify themselves with him.

There is a "problem" in the parliament—and nowhere was this problem more acutely in evidence than in the pre-war Vienna that was to serve as Hitler's political schooling. For the parliament, at its best, is a "babel" of voices. There is the wrangle of men representing interests lying awkwardly on the bias across one another, sometimes opposing, sometimes vaguely divergent. Morton Prince's psychiatric study of "Miss Beauchamp," the case of a woman split into several subpersonalities at odds with one another, variously combining under hypnosis, and frequently in turmoil, is the allegory of a democracy fallen upon evil days. The parliament of the Habsburg Empire just prior to its collapse was an especially drastic instance of such disruption, such vocal diaspora, with movements that would reduce one to a disintegrated mass of fragments if he attempted to encompass the totality of its discordancies. So Hitler, suffering under the alienation of poverty and confusion, yearning for some integrative core, came to take this parliament as the basic symbol of all that he would move away from. He damned the tottering Habsburg Empire as a "State of Nationalities." The many conflicting voices of the spokesmen of the many political blocs arose from the fact that various separationist movements of a nationalistic sort had arisen within a Catholic imperial structure formed prior to the nationalistic emphasis and slowly breaking apart under its development. So, you had this Babel of voices; and, by the method of associative mergers, *using ideas as imagery,* it became tied up, in the Hitler rhetoric, with "Babylon," Vienna as the city of poverty, prostitution, immorality, coalitions, half-measures, incest, democracy (i.e., majority rule leading to "lack of personal responsibility"), death, internationalism, seduction, and anything else of thumbs-down sort the associative enterprise cared to add on this side of the balance.

Hitler's way of treating the parliamentary babel, I am sorry to say, was at one important point not much different from that of the customary editorial in our own newspapers. Every conflict among the parliamentary spokesmen represents a corresponding conflict among the material interests of the groups for whom they are speaking. But Hitler did not discuss the babel from this angle. He discussed it on a purely *symptomatic* basis. The strategy of our orthodox press, in thus ridiculing the cacophonous verbal output of Congress, is obvious: by thus centering attack upon the *symptoms* of business conflict, as they reveal themselves on the dial of political wrangling, and leaving the underlying cause, the business conflicts themselves, out of the case, they can gratify the very public they would otherwise alienate: namely, the businessmen who are the activating members of their reading public. Hitler, however, went them one better. For not only did he stress the purely *symptomatic* attack here. He proceeded to search for the "cause." And this "cause," of course, he derived from his medicine, his racial theory by which he could give a noneconomic interpretation of a phenomenon economically engendered.

Here again is where Hitler's corrupt use of religious patterns comes to the fore. Church thought, being primarily concerned with matters of the "personality," with problems of moral betterment, naturally, and I think rightly, stresses as a necessary feature, the act of will upon the part of the individual. Hence its resistance to a purely "environmental" account of human ills. Hence its emphasis upon the "person." Hence its proneness to seek a noneconomic explanation of economic phenomena. Hitler's proposal of a noneconomic "cause" for the disturbances thus had much to recommend it from this angle. And, as a matter of fact, it was Lueger's Christian-Social Party in Vienna that taught Hitler the tactics of tying up a program of social betterment with an anti-Semitic "unifier." The two parties that he carefully studied at that time were this Catholic faction and Schoenerer's Pan-German group. And his analysis of their attainments and shortcomings, from the standpoint of demagogic efficacy, is an extremely astute piece of work, revealing how carefully this man used the current situation in Vienna as an experimental laboratory for the maturing of his plans.

His unification device, we may summarize, had the following important features:

(1) Inborn dignity. In both religious and humanistic patterns of thought, a "natural-born" dignity of man is stressed. And this categorical dignity is considered to be an attribute of *all* men, if they will but avail themselves of it, by right thinking and right living. But Hitler gives this ennobling attitude an ominous twist by his theories of race and nation, whereby the "Aryan" is elevated above all others by the innate endowment of his blood, while other "races," in particular Jews and Negroes, are innately inferior. This sinister secularized revision of Christian theology thus puts the sense of dignity upon a fighting basis, requiring the conquest of "inferior races." After the defeat of Germany in the World War, there were especially strong emotional needs that this compensatory doctrine of an *inborn* superiority could gratify.

(2) *Projection* device. The "curative" process that comes with the ability to hand over one's ills to a scapegoat, thereby getting purification by dissociation. This was especially medicinal, since the sense of frustration leads to a self-questioning. Hence if one can hand over his infirmities to a vessel, or "cause," outside the self, one can battle an external enemy instead of battling an enemy within. And the greater one's internal inadequacies, the greater the amount of evils one can load upon the back of "the enemy." This device is furthermore given a semblance of reason because the individual properly realizes that he is not alone responsible for his condition. There *are* inimical factors in the scene itself. And he wants to have them "placed," preferably in a way that would require a minimum change in the ways of thinking to which he had been accustomed. This was especially appealing to the middle class, who were encouraged to feel that they could conduct their businesses without any basic change whatever, once the businessmen of a different "race" were eliminated.

(3) Symbolic rebirth. Another aspect of the two features already noted. The projective device of the scapegoat, coupled with the Hitlerite doctrine of inborn racial superiority, provides its followers with a "positive" view of life. They can again get the feel of *moving forward,* toward a goal (a promissory feature of which Hitler makes much). In Hitler, as the group's prophet, such rebirth involved a symbolic change of lineage. Here, above all, we see Hitler giving a malign twist to a benign aspect of Christian thought. For whereas the Pope, in the familistic pattern of thought basic to the Church, stated that the Hebrew prophets were the *spiritual ancestors* of Christianity, Hitler uses this same mode of thinking in reverse. He renounces this "ancestry" in a "materialistic" way by voting himself and the members of his lodge a different "blood stream" from that of the Jews.

(4) Commercial use. Hitler obviously here had something to sell—and it was but a question of time until he sold it (i.e., got financial backers for his movement). For it provided a *noneconomic interpretation of economic ills.* As such, it served with maximum efficiency in deflecting the attention from the economic factors involved in modern conflict; hence by attacking "Jew finance" instead of *finance,* it could stimulate an enthusiastic movement that left "Aryan" finance in control.

Never once, throughout his book, does Hitler deviate from the above formula. Invariably, he ends his diatribes against contemporary economic ills by a shift into an insistence that we must get to the "true" cause, which is centered in "race." The "Aryan" is "constructive"; the Jew is "destructive"; and the "Aryan," to continue his *con-*

struction, must *destroy* the Jewish *destruction*. The Aryan, as the vessel of *love*, must *hate* the Jewish *hate*.

Perhaps the most enterprising use of his method is in his chapter, "The Causes of the Collapse," where he refuses to consider Germany's plight as in any basic way connected with the consequences of war. Economic factors, he insists, are "only of second or even third importance," but "political, ethical-moral, as well as factors of blood and race, are of the first importance." His rhetorical steps are especially interesting here, in that he begins by seeming to flout the national susceptibilities: "The military defeat of the German people is not an undeserved catastrophe, but rather a deserved punishment by eternal retribution." He then proceeds to present the military collapse as but a "consequence of moral poisoning, visible to all, the consequence of a decrease in the instinct of self-preservation . . . which had already begun to undermine the foundations of the people and the Reich many years before." This moral decay derived from "a sin against the blood and the degradation of the race," so its innerness was an outerness after all: the Jew, who thereupon gets saddled with a vast amalgamation of evils, among them being capitalism, democracy, pacifism, journalism, poor housing, modernism, big cities, loss of religion, half measures, ill health, and weakness of the monarch.

II

Hitler had here another important psychological ingredient to play upon. If a state is in economic collapse (and his theories, tentatively taking shape in the pre-war Vienna, were but developed with greater efficiency in post-war Munich), you cannot possibly derive dignity from economic stability. Dignity must come first—and if you possess it, and implement it, from it may follow its economic counterpart. There is much justice to this line of reasoning, so far as it goes. A people in collapse, suffering under economic frustration and the defeat of nationalistic aspirations, with the very midrib of their integrative efforts (the army) in a state of dispersion, have little other than some "spiritual" basis to which they could refer their nationalistic dignity. Hence, the categorical dignity of superior race was a perfect recipe for the situation. It was "spiritual" insofar as it was "above" crude economic "interests," but it was "materialized" at the psychologically "right" spot in that "the enemy" was something you could *see*.

Furthermore, you had the desire for unity, such as a discussion of class conflict, on the basis of conflicting interests, could not satisfy. The yearning for unity is so great that people are always willing to meet you halfway if you will give it to them by fiat, by flat statement, regardless of the facts. Hence, Hitler consistently refused to consider internal political conflict on the basis of conflicting interests. Here again, he could draw upon a religious pattern, by insisting upon a *personal* statement of the relation between classes, the relation between leaders and followers, each group in its way fulfilling the same commonalty of interests, as the soldiers and captains of an army share a common interest in victory. People so dislike the idea of internal division that, where there is a real internal division, their dislike can easily be turned against the man or group who would so much as *name* it, let alone proposing to act upon it. Their natural and justified resentment against internal division itself is turned against the diagnostician who states it as a *fact*. This diagnostician, it is felt, is the *cause* of the disunity he named.

Cutting in from another angle, therefore, we note how two sets of equations were built up, with Hitler combining or coalescing *ideas* the way a poet combines or coalesces *images*. On the one side were the ideas, or images, of disunity, centering in the parliamentary wrangle of the Habsburg "State of Nationalities." This was offered as the antithesis of German nationality, which was presented in the curative imagery of unity, focused upon the glories of the Prussian Reich, with its mecca now moved to "folkish" Vienna. For though Hitler at first attacked the many "folkish" movements, with their hankerings after a kind of Wagnerian mythology of Germanic origins, he subsequently took "folkish" as a basic word by which to conjure. It was, after all, another noneconomic basis of reference. At first we find him objecting to "those who drift about with the word 'folkish' on their caps" and asserting that "such a Babel of opinions cannot serve as the basis of a political fighting movement." But later he seems to have realized, as he well should, that its vagueness was a major point in its favor. So it was incorporated in the grand coalition of his ideational imagery, or imagistic ideation; and Chapter XI ends with the vision of "a State which represents not a mechanism of economic considerations and interests, alien to the people, but a folkish organism."

So, as against the disunity equations, already listed briefly in our discussion of his attacks upon the parliamentary, we get a contrary purifying set; the wrangle of the parliamentary is to be stilled by the giving of *one* voice to the whole people, this to be the "inner voice" of Hitler, made uniform throughout the German boundaries, as leader and people were completely identified with each other. In sum: Hitler's inner voice, equals leader-people identification, equals unity, equals Reich, equals the mecca of Munich, equals plow, equals sword, equals work, equals war, equals army as midrib, equals responsibility (the personal responsibility of the absolute ruler), equals sacrifice, equals the theory of "German democracy" (the free popular choice of the leader, who then accepts the responsibility, and demands absolute obedience in exchange for his sacrifice), equals love (with the masses as feminine), equals idealism, equals obedience to nature, equals race, nation.[3]

And, of course, the two keystones of these opposite equations were Aryan "heroism" and "sacrifice" vs. Jewish "cunning" and "arrogance." Here again we get an astounding caricature of religious thought. For Hitler presents the concept of "Aryan" superiority, of all ways, in terms of "Aryan humility." This "humility" is extracted by a very delicate process that requires, I am afraid, considerable "good will" on the part of the reader who would follow it:

The Church, we may recall, had proclaimed an integral relationship between Divine Law and Natural Law. Natural Law was the expression of the Will of God. Thus, in the middle age, it was a result of natural law, working through tradition, that some people were serfs and other people nobles. And every good member of the Church was "obedient" to this law. Everybody resigned himself to it. Hence, the serf resigned himself to his poverty, and the noble resigned himself to his riches. The monarch resigned himself to his position as representative of the people. And at times the Churchmen resigned themselves to the need of trying to represent the people instead. And the pattern was made symmetrical by the consideration that each traditional "right" had its corresponding "obligations." Similarly, the Aryan doctrine is a doctrine of resignation, hence of humility. It is in accordance with the laws of nature that the "Aryan blood" is superior to all other

---

3. One could carry out the equations further, on both the disunity and unity side. In the aesthetic field, for instance, we have expressionism on the thumbs-down side, as against aesthetic hygiene on the thumbs-up side. This again is a particularly ironic moment in Hitler's strategy. For the expressionist movement was unquestionably a symptom of unhealthiness. It reflected the increasing alienation that went with the movement towards world war and the disorganization after the world war. It was "lost," vague in identity, a drastically accurate reflection of the response to material confusion, a pathetic attempt by sincere artists to make their wretchedness bearable at least to the extent that comes of giving it expression. And it attained its height during the period of wild inflation, when the capitalist world, which bases its morality of work and savings upon the soundness of its money structure, had this last prop of stability removed. The anguish, in short, reflected precisely the kind of disruption that made people *ripe* for a Hitler. It was the antecedent in a phrase of which Hitlerism was the consequent. But by thundering against this *symptom* he could gain persuasiveness, though attacking the very *foreshadowings of himself*.

bloods. Also, the "law of the survival of the fittest" is God's law, working through natural law. Hence, if the Aryan blood has been vested with the awful responsibility of its inborn superiority, the bearers of this "culture-creating" blood must resign themselves to struggle in behalf of its triumph. Otherwise, the laws of God have been disobeyed, with human decadence as a result. We must fight, he says, in order to "deserve to be alive." The Aryan "obeys" nature. It is only "Jewish arrogance" that thinks of "conquering" nature by democratic ideals of equality.

This picture has some nice distinctions worth following. The major virtue of the Aryan race was its instinct for self-preservation (in obedience to natural law). But the major vice of the Jew was his instinct for self-preservation; for, if he did not have this instinct to a maximum degree, he would not be the "perfect" enemy—that is, he wouldn't be strong enough to account for the ubiquitousness and omnipotence of his conspiracy in destroying the world to become its master.

How, then, are we to distinguish between the benign instinct of self-preservation at the roots of Aryanism and the malign instinct of self-preservation at the roots of Semitism? We shall distinguish thus: The Aryan self-preservation is based upon *sacrifice*, the sacrifice of the individual to the group, hence, militarism, army discipline, and one big company union. But Jewish self-preservation is based upon individualism, which attains its cunning ends by the exploitation of peace. How, then, can such arrant individualists concoct the worldwide plot? By the help of their "herd instinct." By their sheer "herd instinct" individualists can band together for a common end. They have no real solidarity, but unite opportunistically to seduce the Aryan. Still, that brings up another technical problem. For we have been hearing much about the importance of the *person*. We have been told how, by the "law of the survival of the fittest," there is a sifting of people on the basis of their individual capacities. We even have a special chapter of pure Aryanism: "The Strong Man is Mightiest Alone." Hence, another distinction is necessary: The Jew represents individualism; the Aryan represents "super-individualism."

I had thought, when coming upon the "Strong Man is Mightiest Alone" chapter, that I was going to find Hitler at his weakest. Instead, I found him at his strongest. (I am not referring to *quality*, but to *demagogic effectiveness*.) For the chapter is not at all, as you might infer from the title, done in a "rise of Adolph Hitler" manner. Instead, it deals with the Nazis' gradual absorption of the many disrelated "folkish" groups. And it is managed throughout by means of a spontaneous identification between leader and people. Hence, the Strong

Man's "aloneness" is presented as a *public* attribute, in terms of tactics for the struggle against the *Party's* dismemberment under the pressure of rival saviors. There is no explicit talk of Hitler at all. And it is simply *taken for granted* that *his* leadership is the norm and all other leaderships the abnorm. There is no "philosophy of the superman," in Nietzschean cast. Instead, Hitler's blandishments so integrate leader and people, commingling them so inextricably, that the politician does not even present himself as candidate. Somehow, the battle is over already, the decision has been made. "German democracy" has chosen. And the deployments of politics are, you might say, the chartings of Hitler's private mind translated into the vocabulary of nationalistic events. He says *what he thought* in terms of *what parties did*.

Here, I think, we see the distinguishing quality of Hitler's method as an instrument of persuasion, with reference to the question whether Hitler is sincere or deliberate, whether his vision of the omnipotent conspirator has the drastic honesty of paranoia or the sheer shrewdness of a demagogue trained in *Realpolitik* of the Machiavellian sort.[4] Must we choose? Or may we not, rather, replace the "either—or" with a "both—and"? Have we not by now offered grounds enough for our contention that Hitler's sinister powers of persuasion derive from the fact that he spontaneously evolved his "cure-all" in response to inner necessities?

III

So much, then, was "spontaneous." It was further channelized into the anti-Semitic pattern by the incentives he derived from the Catholic Christian-Social Party in Vienna itself. Add, now, the step into *criti-*

---

4. I should not want to use the word "Machiavellian," however, without offering a kind of apology to Machiavelli. It seems to me that Machiavelli's *Prince* has more to be said in extenuation than is usually said of it. Machiavelli's strategy, as I see it, was something like this: He accepted the values of the Renaissance rule as a *fact*. That is: whether you like these values or not, they were there and operating, and it was useless to try persuading the ambitious ruler to adopt other values, such as those of the Church. These men believed in the cult of material power, and they had the power to implement their beliefs. With so much as "the given," could anything in the way of benefits for the people be salvaged? Machiavelli evolved a typical "Machiavellian" argument in favor of popular benefits, on the basis of the prince's own scheme of values. That is: the ruler, to attain the maximum strength, requires the backing of the populace. That this backing be as effective as possible, the populace should be made as strong as possible. And that the populace be as strong as possible, they should be well treated. Their gratitude would further repay itself in the form of increased loyalty.

It was Machiavelli's hope that, for this roundabout project, he would be rewarded with a well-paying office in the prince's administrative bureaucracy.

cism. Not criticism in the "parliamentary" sense of doubt, of hearkening to the opposition and attempting to mature a policy in the light of counterpolicies; but the "unified" kind of criticism that simply seeks for conscious ways of making one's position more "efficient," more thoroughly itself. This is the kind of criticism at which Hitler was an adept. As a result, he could *spontaneously* turn to a scapegoat mechanism, and he could, by conscious planning, perfect the symmetry of the solution towards which he had spontaneously turned.

This is the meaning of Hitler's diatribes against "objectivity." "Objectivity" is interference-criticism. What Hitler wanted was the kind of criticism that would be a pure and simple coefficient of power, enabling him to go most effectively in the direction he had chosen. And the "inner voice" of which he speaks would henceforth dictate to him the greatest amount of realism, as regards the tactics of efficiency. For instance, having decided that the masses required certainty, and simple certainty, quite as he did himself, he later worked out a 25-point program as the platform of his National Socialist German Workers Party. And he resolutely refused to change one single item in this program, even for purposes of "improvement." He felt that the *fixity* of the platform was more important for propagandistic purposes than any revision of his slogans could be, even though the revisions in themselves had much to be said in their favor. The astounding thing is that, although such an attitude gave good cause to doubt the Hitlerite promises, he could explicitly explain his tactics in his book and still employ them without loss of effectiveness.[5]

Hitler also tells of his technique in speaking, once the Nazi party had become effectively organized, and had its army of guards, or bouncers, to maltreat hecklers and throw them from the hall. He would, he recounts, fill his speech with *provocative* remarks, whereat his bouncers would promptly swoop down in flying formation, with swinging fists, upon anyone whom these provocative remarks provoked to answer. The efficiency of Hitlerism is the efficiency of the one voice, implemented throughout a total organization. The trinity of

5. On this point Hitler reasons as follows: "Here, too, one can learn from the Catholic Church. Although its structure of doctrines in many instances collides, quite unnecessarily, with exact science and research, yet it is unwilling to sacrifice even one little syllable of its dogmas. It has rightly recognized that its resistibility does not lie in a more or less great adjustment to the scientific results of the moment, which in reality are always changing, but rather in a strict adherence to dogmas, once laid down, which alone give the entire structure the character of creed. Today, therefore, the Catholic Church stands firmer than ever. One can prophesy that in the same measure in which the appearances flee, the Church itself, as the resting pole in the flight of appearances, will gain more and more blind adherence."

government which he finally offers is: *popularity* of the leader, *force* to back the popularity, and popularity and force maintained together long enough to become backed by a *tradition.* Is such thinking spontaneous or deliberate—or is it not rather both?[6]

Freud has given us a succinct paragraph that bears upon the spontaneous aspect of Hitler's persecution mania. (A persecution mania, I should add, different from the pure product in that it was constructed of *public* materials; all the ingredients Hitler stirred into his brew were already rife, with spokesmen and bands of followers, before Hitler "took them over." Both the pre-war and post-war periods were dotted with saviors, of nationalistic and "folkish" cast. This proliferation was analogous to the swarm of barter schemes and currency-tinkering that burst loose upon the United States after the crash of 1929. Also, the commercial availability of Hitler's politics was, in a low sense of the term, a *public* qualification, removing it from the realm of "pure" paranoia, where the sufferer develops a wholly *private* structure of interpretations.)

I cite from *Totem and Taboo:*

> Another trait in the attitude of primitive races towards their rulers recalls a mechanism which is universally present in mental disturbances, and is openly revealed in the so-called delusions of persecution. Here the importance of a particular person is extraordinarily heightened and his omnipotence is raised to the improbable in order to make it easier to attribute to him responsibility for everything painful which happens to the patient. Savages really do not act differently towards their rulers when they ascribe to them power over rain and shine, wind and weather, and then dethrone them or kill them because nature has disappointed their expectation of a good hunt or a ripe harvest. The prototype which the paranoiac reconstructs in his persecution mania is found in the relation of the child to its

6. Hitler also paid great attention to the conditions under which political oratory is most effective. He sums up thus:

"All these cases involve encroachments upon man's freedom of will. This applies, of course, most of all to meetings to which people with a contrary orientation of will are coming, and who now have to be won for new intentions. It seems that in the morning and even during the day men's will power revolts with highest energy against an attempt at being forced under another's will and another's opinion. In the evening, however, they succumb more easily to the dominating force of a stronger will. For truly every such meeting presents a wrestling match between two opposed forces. The superior oratorical talent of a domineering apostolic nature will now succeed more easily in winning for the new will people who themselves have in turn experienced a weakening of their force of resistance in the most natural way, than people who still have full command of the energies of their minds and their will power.

"The same purpose serves also the artificially created and yet mysterious dusk of the Catholic churches, the burning candles, incense, censers, etc."

father. Such omnipotence is regularly attributed to the father in the imagination of the son, and distrust of the father has been shown to be intimately connected with the heightened esteem for him. When a paranoiac names a person of his acquaintance as his "persecutor," he thereby elevates him to the paternal succession and brings him under conditions which enable him to make him responsible for all the misfortune which he experiences.

I have already proposed my modifications on this account when discussing the symbolic change of lineage connected with Hitler's project of a "new way of life." Hitler is symbolically changing from the "spiritual ancestry" of the Hebrew prophets to the "superior" ancestry of "Aryanism," and has given his story a kind of bastardized modernization, along the lines of naturalistic, materialistic "science," by his fiction of the special "blood-stream." He is voting himself a new identity (something contrary to the wrangles of the Habsburg Babylon, a soothing national unity); whereupon the vessels of the old identity become a "bad" father, i.e., the persecutor. It is not hard to see how, as his enmity becomes implemented by the backing of an organization, the rôle of "persecutor" is transformed into the rôle of persecuted, as he sets out with his like-minded band to "destroy the destroyer."

Were Hitler simply a poet, he might have written a work with an anti-Semitic turn and let it go at that. But Hitler, who began as a student of painting, and later shifted to architecture, himself treats his political activities as an extension of his artistic ambitions. He remained, in his own eyes, an "architect," building a "folkish" state that was to match, in political materials, the "folkish" architecture of Munich.

We might consider the matter this way (still trying, that is, to make precise the relationship between the drastically sincere and the deliberately scheming): Do we not know of many authors who seem, as they turn from the rôle of citizen to the rôle of spokesman, to leave one room and enter another? Or who has not, on occasion, talked with a man in private conversation and then been almost startled at the transformation this man undergoes when addressing a public audience? And I know persons today who shift between the writing of items in the class of academic, philosophic speculation to items of political pamphleteering and whose entire style and method changes with this change of rôle. In their academic manner, they are cautious, painstaking, eager to present all significant aspects of the case they are considering; but when they turn to political pamphleteering, they hammer forth with vituperation, they systematically misrepresent the position of their opponent, they go into a kind of political trance, in which, during its throes, they throb like a locomotive; and behold, a moment later, the mediumistic state is abandoned, and they are the most moderate of men.

Now, one will find few pages in Hitler that one could call "moderate." But there are many pages in which he gauges resistances and opportunities with the "rationality" of a skilled advertising man planning a new sales campaign. Politics, he says, must be sold like soap— and soap is not sold in a trance. But he did have the experience of his trance, in the "exaltation" of his anti-Semitism. And later, as he became a successful orator (he insists that revolutions are made solely by the power of the spoken word), he had this "poetic" rôle to draw upon, plus the great relief it provided as a way of slipping from the burden of logical analysis into the pure "spirituality" of vituperative prophecy. What more natural, therefore, than that a man so insistent upon unification would integrate this mood with less ecstatic moments, particularly when he had found the followers and the backers that put a price, both spiritual and material, upon such unification?

Once this happy "unity" is under way, one has a "logic" for the development of a method. One knows when to "spiritualize" a material issue and when to "materialize" a spiritual one. Thus, when it is a matter of materialistic interests that cause a conflict between employer and employee, Hitler here disdainfully shifts to a high moral plane. He is "above" such low concerns. Everything becomes a matter of "sacrifices" and "personality." It becomes crass to treat employers and employees as different *classes* with a corresponding difference in the classification of their interests. Instead, relations between employer and employee must be on the "personal" basis of leader and follower, and "whatever may have a divisive effect in national life should be given a unifying effect through the army." When talking of national rivalries, however, he makes a very shrewd materialistic gauging of Britain and France with relation to Germany. France, he says, desires the "Balkanization of Germany" (i.e., its breakup into separationist movements—the "disunity" theme again) in order to maintain commercial hegemony on the continent. But Britain desires the "Balkanization of *Europe*," hence would favor a fairly strong and unified Germany, to use as a counterweight against French hegemony. *German* nationality, however, is unified by the *spiritual* quality of Aryanism (that would produce the national organization via the Party) while this in turn is *materialized* in the myth of the blood-stream.

What are we to learn from Hitler's book? For one thing, I believe that he has shown, to a very disturbing degree, the power of endless repetition. Every circular advertising a Nazi meeting had, at the bottom, two slogans: "Jews not admitted" and "War victims free." And the substance of Nazi propaganda was built about these two "complementary" themes. He describes the power of spectacle; insists that mass meetings are the fundamental way of giving the individual the sense of being protectively surrounded by a movement, the sense of "community." He also drops one wise hint that I wish the American authorities would take in treating Nazi gatherings. He says that the presence of a special Nazi guard, in Nazi uniforms, was of great importance in building up, among the followers, a tendency to place the center of authority in the Nazi party. I believe that we should take him at his word here, but use the advice in reverse, by insisting that, where Nazi meetings are to be permitted, they be policed by the authorities alone, and that uniformed Nazi guards to enforce the law be prohibited.

And is it possible that an equally important feature of appeal was not so much in the repetitiousness per se, but in the fact that, by means of it, Hitler provided a "world view" for people who had previously seen the world but piecemeal? Did not much of his lure derive, once more, from the *bad* filling of a *good* need? Are not those who insist upon a purely *planless* working of the market asking people to accept far too slovenly a scheme of human purpose, a slovenly scheme that can be accepted so long as it operates with a fair degree of satisfaction, but becomes abhorrent to the victims of its disarray? Are they not then psychologically ready for a rationale, *any* rationale, if it but offer them some specious "universal" explanation? Hence, I doubt whether the appeal was in the sloganizing element alone (particularly as even slogans can only be hammered home, in speech after speech, and two or three hours at a stretch, by endless variations on the themes). And Hitler himself somewhat justifies my interpretation by laying so much stress upon the *half-measures* of the middle-class politicians and the contrasting *certainty* of his own methods. He was not offering people a *rival* world view; rather, he was offering a world view to people who had no other to pit against it.

As for the basic Nazi trick: the "curative" unification by a fictitious devil-function, gradually made convincing by the sloganizing repetitiousness of standard advertising technique—the opposition must be as unwearying in the attack upon it. It may well be that people, in their human frailty, require an enemy as well as a goal. Very well: Hitlerism itself has provided us with such an enemy—and the clear example of its operation is guaranty that we have, in him and all he stands for, no purely fictitious "devil-function" made to look like a

world menace by rhetorical blandishments, but a reality whose ominousness is clarified by the record of its conduct to date. In selecting
his brand of doctrine as our "scapegoat," and in tracking down its
equivalents in America, we shall be at the very center of accuracy. The
Nazis themselves have made the task of clarification easier. Add to
them Japan and Italy, and you have *case histories* of fascism for those
who might find it more difficult to approach an understanding of its
imperialistic drives by a vigorously economic explanation.

But above all, I believe, we must make it apparent that Hitler appeals by relying upon a bastardization of fundamentally religious patterns of thought. In this, if properly presented, there is no slight to
religion. There is nothing in religion proper that requires a fascist
state. There is much in religion, when misused, that does lead to a
fascist state. There is a Latin proverb, *Corruptio optimi pessima,* "the
corruption of the best is the worst." And it is the corruptors of religion
who are a major menace to the world today, in giving the profound
patterns of religious thought a crude and sinister distortion.

Our job, then, our anti-Hitler battle, is to find all available ways of
making the Hitlerite distortions of religion apparent, in order that
politicians of his kind in America be unable to perform a similar swin-
dle. The desire for unity is genuine and admirable. The desire for national unity, in the present state of the world, is genuine and admirable. But this unity, if attained on a deceptive basis, by emotional
trickeries that shift our criticism from the accurate locus of our
trouble, is no unity at all. For, even if we are among those who happen
to be "Aryans," we solve no problems even for ourselves by such so-
lutions, since the factors pressing toward calamity remain. Thus, in
Germany, after all the upheaval, we see nothing beyond a drive for
ever more and more upheaval, precisely because the "new way of life"
was no new way, but the dismally oldest way of sheer deception—
hence, after all the "change," the factors driving toward unrest are left
intact and even strengthened. True, the Germans had the resentment
of a lost war to increase their susceptibility to Hitler's rhetoric. But in
a wider sense, it has repeatedly been observed, the whole world lost
the War—and the accumulating ills of the capitalist order were but
accelerated in their movements toward confusion. Hence, here too
there are the resentments that go with frustration of men's ability to
work and earn. At that point a certain kind of industrial or financial
monopolist may, annoyed by the contrary voices of our parliament,
wish for the momentary peace of one voice, amplified by social organizations, with all the others not merely quieted, but given the quietus.
So he might, under Nazi promptings, be tempted to back a group of

gangsters who, on becoming the political rulers of the state, would protect him against the necessary demands of the workers. His gangsters, then, would be his insurance against his workers. But who would be his insurance against his gangsters?

V

DIALECTICAL METHOD

14

The Paradox of Substance

Antinomies of Definition

Paradox of Substance

There is a set of words comprising what we might call the Stance family, for they all derive from a concept of place, or placement. In the Indo-Germanic languages the root for this family is *stā*, to stand (Sanscrit, *sthā*). And out of it there has developed this essential family, comprising such members as: consist, constancy, constitution, contrast, destiny, ecstasy, existence, hypostatize, obstacle, stage, state, status, statute, stead, subsist, and system. In German, an important member of the Stance family is *stellen*, to place, a root that figures in *Vorstellung*, a philosopher's and psychologist's word for representation, conception, idea, image.

Surely, one could build a whole philosophic universe by tracking down the ramifications of this one root. It would be "implemented" too, for it would have stables, staffs, staves, stalls, stamens, stamina, stanchions, stanzas, steeds, stools, and studs. It would be a quite regional world, in which our Southern Agrarians might take their stand.

Unquestionably, the most prominent philosophic member of this family is "substance." Or at least it used to be, before John Locke greatly impaired its prestige, so that many thinkers today explicitly banish the term from their vocabularies. But there is cause to believe that, in banishing the *term*, far from banishing its *functions* one merely conceals them. Hence, from the dramatistic point of view, we are admonished to dwell upon the word, considering its embarrassments and its potentialities of transformation, so that we may detect its covert influence even in cases where it is overtly absent. Its relation to our five terms will become apparent as we proceed.

First we should note that there is, etymologically, a pun lurking behind the Latin roots. The word is often used to designate what some thing or agent intrinsically *is*, as *per* these meanings in Webster's: "the

From *A Grammar of Motives*, pp. 21–33. Reprinted by permission of The University of California Press. ©1969 by Kenneth Burke.

most important element in any existence; the characteristic and essential components of anything; the main part; essential import; purport." Yet etymologically "substance"is a scenic word. Literally, a person's or a thing's sub-stance would be something that stands beneath or supports the person or thing.

Let us cite a relevant passage in *An Essay Concerning Human Understanding* (Chapter XXIII, "Of Our Complex Ideas of Substances"):

1. *Ideas of particular substances, how made.* The mind being, as I have declared, furnished with a great number of the simple ideas conveyed in by the senses, as they are found in exterior things, or by reflection on its own operations, takes notice, also, that a certain number of these simple ideas go constantly together; which being presumed to belong to one thing, and words being suited to common apprehensions, and made use of for quick despatch, are called, so united in one subject, by one name; which, by inadvertency, we are apt afterward to talk of and consider as one simple idea, which indeed is a complication of many ideas together; because, as I have said, not imagining how these simple ideas can subsist by themselves, we accustom ourselves to suppose some *substratum* wherein they do subsist, and from which they do result; which therefore we call *substance*.

2. *Our obscure idea of substance in general.*—So that if anyone will examine himself concerning his notion of pure substance in general, he will find he has no other idea of it at all, but only a supposition of he knows not what support of such qualities which are capable of producing simple ideas in us; which qualities are commonly called accidents. If anyone should be asked, what is the subject wherein color or weight inheres, he would have nothing to say but, the solid extended parts. And if he were demanded, what is it that solidity and extension inhere in, he would not be in a much better case than the Indian before mentioned, who, saying that the world was supported by a great elephant, was asked, what the elephant rested on; to which his answer was, a great tortoise; but being again pressed to know what gave support to the broad-backed tortoise, replied—something, he knew not what. And thus here, as in all other cases where we use words without having clear and distinct ideas, we talk like children: who, being questioned what such a thing is which they know not, readily give this satisfactory answer, that it is *something;* which in truth signifies no more, when so used, either by children or men, but that they know not what; and that the thing they pretend to know and talk of, is what they have no distinct idea of at all, and so are perfectly ignorant of it, and in the dark. The idea, then, we have, to which we give the *general* name substance, being nothing but the supposed, but unknown support of those qualities we find existing, which we imagine cannot subsist *sine re substante,* "without something to support them," we call that support *substantia;* which according to the true import of the word, is, in plain English, standing under, or upholding.

The same structure is present in the corresponding Greek word, *hypostasis*, literally, a standing under: hence anything set under, such as stand, base, bottom, prop, support, stay; hence metaphorically, that which lies at the bottom of a thing, as the groundwork, subject-matter, argument of a narrative, speech, poem; a starting point, a beginning. And then come the metaphysical meanings (we are consulting Liddell and Scott): subsistence, reality, real being (as applied to mere appearance), nature, essence. In ecclesiastical Greek, the word corresponds to the Latin *Persona*, a Person of the Trinity (which leads us back into the old argument between the homoousians and the homoiousians, as to whether the three persons were of the same or similar substance). Medically, the word can designate a suppression, as of humours that ought to come to the surface; also matter deposited in the urine; and of liquids generally, the sediment, lees, dregs, grounds. When we are examining, from the standpoint of symbolic, metaphysical tracts that would deal with "fundamentals" and get to the "bottom" of things, this last set of meanings can admonish us to be on the look-out for what Freud might call "cloacal" motives, furtively interwoven with speculations that may on the surface seem wholly abstract. An "acceptance" of the universe on this plane may also be a roundabout way of "making peace with the faeces."

But returning to the pun as it figures in the citation from Locke, we might point up the pattern as sharply as possible by observing that the word "substance," used to designate what a thing *is,* derives from a word designating something that a thing *is not.* That is, though used to designate something *within* the thing, *intrinsic* to it, the word etymologically refers to something *outside* the thing, *extrinsic* to it. Or otherwise put: the word in its etymological origins would refer to an attribute of the thing's *context,* since that which supports or underlies a thing would be a part of the thing's context. And a thing's context, being outside or beyond the thing, would be something that the thing is *not.*

Contextual Definition

Here obviously is a strategic moment, an alchemic moment, wherein momentous miracles of transformation can take place. For here the intrinsic and the extrinsic can change places. To tell what a thing is, you place it in terms of something else. This idea of locating, or placing, is implicit in our very word for definition itself: to *define,* or *determine* a thing, is to mark its boundaries, hence to use terms that possess, implicitly at least, contextual reference. We here take the pun seriously because we believe it to reveal an *inevitable* paradox of definition, an antinomy that must endow the concept of substance with unresolvable ambiguity, and that will be discovered lurking beneath any vocabulary designed to treat of motivation by the deliberate outlawing of the *word* for substance.

Nor is the perplexity confined to abstruse metaphysical theorizing. Note the Tory usage, for instance, in the expression, "a man of substance," or a man of "standing." Note how readily we shunt here between an intrinsic and an extrinsic reference. For those who admire someone as a man of substance, or standing, have in mind not only his personal traits of character, but also the resources that spring from his environmental connections, the external powers that his position, income, status put at his command, the outside factors that, in backing or supporting him, enable him to make his personal characteristics count. (Another meaning for the Greek *hypostasis,* incidentally, was steadfastness, endurance, firmness.) And when our Southern Agrarians issue a volume entitled *I'll Take My Stand* (their "stand in Dixie"), their claims as to what they *are* get definition in terms of scene, environment, situation, context, ground. Indeed, in the title we can also see another important ambiguity of motive emerging. When taking their stand *in* Dixie, they are also taking their stand *for* Dixie. Their stand *in* Dixie would be a "conditioning" kind of cause; but a corresponding stand *for* Dixie would be a teleological or purposive kind of cause.

In Spinoza we confront the full intensity of the contextual paradox. Indeed, from our point of view, we might translate both his concept of "God" and his concept of "nature" as "the total, or ultimate scene," since he pantheistically held that God and nature are identical. In the Judaic and Christian theologies, since nature was said to have its ultimate ground in God as a person, God was a context for nature, as nature-and-God was the context for man. But Spinoza, in equating God and nature, gave us a concept of nature that could have no scene beyond it. For nature was *everything*—and beyond *everything,* considered as a totality, there could be nothing to serve as its context.

Hence, starting from the Aristotelian notion that a substance, or being, is to be considered "in itself" (*kath auto,* which Spinoza rendered *id quod per se concipitur*), Spinoza went on to observe that nothing less than the *totality of all that exists* can meet this requirement. In Aristotle, each stone, or tree, or man, or animal, could be a substance, capable of being considered "in itself." But Spinoza held that no single thing could be considered "by itself." A distinction between "in itself" and "by itself" might be made here, but the Spinozistic calculus is designed rather to work in the area where the two meanings overlap. Thinking contextually, Spinoza held that each single object in the universe is "defined" (determined, limited, bounded) by the other things that surround it. And in calling upon men to see things "in terms of eternity" (*sub specie aeternitatis*) Spinoza meant precisely that we should consider each thing in terms of its total context, the universal scene as a whole. Only when considering the universe as a whole, and its parts in terms of the whole, would we be making an "intrinsic" statement about substance, since there was but one substance, the universal totality.

And thoroughly in keeping with his contextual strategy of definition, Spinoza explicitly held that all definition is "negation," which is another way of saying that, to define a thing in terms of its context, we must define it in terms of what it is not. And with scholastic succinctness, he formulated the paradox of contextual definition in four words: "all determination is negation; *omnis determinatio est negatio.*" Since determined things are "positive," we might point up the paradox as harshly as possible by translating it, "Every positive is negative."

When we refer to "everything," our reference is indefinite, infinite, undetermined, indeterminate. Hence, to treat of things in terms of "everything" is to treat of them in terms of the infinite. Indeed, since "everything" is the "absolute" (that is, unloosed, absolved, "freed," for I think it is good to remind ourselves of the dramatic meanings lurking behind that strategic metaphysical term) we have here a variant of the so-called "negative theology," which conceived of God as the absence of all qualities; and to see things as contextually "determined" by the "absolute" is thus to see them simultaneously in terms of "necessity" and "freedom." For Spinoza, says Windelband, "the deity is all and thus—nothing." But we should also remember that the deity is equated with nature. Hence, though Spinoza's pantheism was an important step towards naturalism, in itself it had strongly mystical ingredients.

Contextual definition might also be called "positional," or "geometric," or "definition by location." The embarrassments are often revealed with particular clarity when a thinker has moved to a high level of generalization, as when motivational matters are discussed in terms of "heredity and environment," or "man and nature," or "mind and matter," or "mechanism and teleology," where each of the paired terms is the other's "context" in the universe of discourse. To define or locate "man" in terms of "nature," for instance, is to "dissolve" man "into" nature. Hence, the more thorough one is in carrying out his enterprise, the more surely he opens himself to the charge of failing

to discuss man "in himself." Historicists who deal with art in terms of
its background are continually suffering from the paradox of contextual definition, as their opponents accuse them of slighting the work
of art in its esthetic aspects; and on the other hand, critics who would
center their attention upon the work "in itself" must wince when it is
made apparent that their inquiries, in ignoring contextual reference,
frustrate our desire to see the products of artistic action treated in
terms of the scene-act, scene-agent, and agent-act ratios.

Familial Definition

However, there is another strategy of definition, usually interwoven
with the contextual sort, yet susceptible of separate observation. This
is the "tribal" or "familial" sort, the definition of a substance in terms
of ancestral cause. Under the head of "tribal" definition would fall
any variant of the idea of biological descent, with the substance of the
offspring being derived from the substance of the parents or family.

The Christian notion that the most important fact about mankind
and the world is their derivation from God is an instance of "ancestral" definition on the grand scale. We find bastardized variants in
political doctrines of race supremacy, such as the Nazi "blood" philosophy. The Latin word *natura*, like its Greek equivalent *physis*, has
a root signifying to become, to grow, to be born. And the Aristotelian
genus is originally not a logical, but a biological, concept. We can
discern the tribal pattern behind the notion, so characteristic of Greek
nationalism, that like causes like or that like recognizes like, as with
Democritus' theory of perception. Similarly, there was an *ancestral*
notion behind the Platonic theory of forms; in fact, it was this tribal
ingredient that recommended it so strongly to the ages of Western
feudalism. Each thing in this world had, as it were, an eponym in
heaven, a perfect form from which it was derived—and it shared this
derivation with all the other members of its class, or genus. And I
think we might most quickly understand the mediaeval speculations
as to whether universals were "before the thing, in the thing, or after
the thing" if we first tried a dramatist translation of the three formulae
respectively thus: "Does the tribe give birth to its members (universal
ante rem), or does the tribe exist in its members (universal *in re*), or is
the tribe merely a name for the sum of its members (universal *post
rem*)?"

To say yes to the first would make you an extreme mediaeval real-
ist. A realism of this sort was well attuned to feudal collectivism. To
say yes to the third would make you a thorough-going nominalist,
who treated general terms as mere *flatus vocis*, conventions of speech,

and thus moved toward the disintegration of tribal thinking. To say yes to the second would make you an Aristotelian. The motives would be situated in the individual, yet they would be motives common to the species, or tribe, of which it was a member. That is, an individual stone would have motives proper to stones as a class, an individual man motives proper to men as a class, etc. This doctrine came to a head in the Aristotelian concept of the "entelechy," which we might call the individual's potentialities for becoming a fully representative member of its class. However, we need not here give more than a cursory glance at any particular use of the ancestral method. It is sufficient if we can indicate its range.

All told, perhaps the quickest and surest way to find oneself at the centre of the subject would be to ponder the four words, "general," "generic," "genetic," "genitive." Though they are all from the same root, only the third *unambiguously* reveals ancestral connotations. Next removed is "genitive," which refers to either source or possession. But to say that nature is "a part of" God or that man is "a part of" nature would be to use a genitive construction in which one could clearly discern ancestral reference. When we come to "generic," the tribal connotations are beginning more noticeably to face, as purely biological concepts can be replaced by logical notions of classification. And with "general" this extinction of the familial can be complete. A "family of right-angled triangles in general," for instance, would just about have lost the notion of generation, although we can still, with a little effort, look upon them as a family in the sense that a common set of principles is required for the generating of them.

Similarly, the members of a class derive their *generic* nature from the "idea" of the class in which they are placed. If I make up a classification, for instance, such as "bald-headed carpenters under forty," I shall have "generated" a corresponding class of "objects." These objects (the people who fit the requirements of the class) will be "imperfect copies" of my "idea" or "pure form," since they will all possess other attributes that lie outside the strict definition of the class. This would be the strictly methodological equivalent for Plato's doctrine of archetypes. Thinking in familial terms, Plato looked upon the objects of this world as imperfect replicas of their pure "forms" or "ideas" in heaven.

In sum, contextual definition stresses *placement*, ancestral definition stresses derivation. But in any sustained discussion of motives, the two become interwoven, as with theologies which treat God both as "causal ancestor" of mankind and as the ultimate ground or context of mankind.

And if we were to extend the Stance family by including different roots similar in meaning, we would promptly move into a set of live and dead metaphors ("abstractions") where our five terms, our ratios, and our strategies of definition could be seen emerging in all sorts of places.

For instance, the key philosophic term, sub-ject (in Latin, thrown under) is the companion to the Greek *hypokeimenon* (underlying), a word that can refer to the subject of a sentence, or to the "sub-strate" of the world (the essential constitution of things, hence indeterminately a kind of basis or a kind of causal ancestor). The word can also refer to what is assumed as a ground of argument, in which capacity it serves as a passive for *hypotithemi* (to place or put under, as a base or foundation, to assume as a principle, take for granted, suppose, from the root of which we get such words as theme, thesis, antithesis, synthesis, while a similar development in Latin, from *pono*, to place, gives us position, proposition, opposition, composition, positive, and that neat now-you-see-me-and-now-you-don't metaphysical nuance, "posit," whereby the metaphysician is enabled to discuss the "positing" of principles without being too clear as to what kind of base they are being *placed* upon).

The mention of "substrates" brings us close to a third aspect of definition, the kind we get in projects that discuss the world in terms of the "building blocks" of which it is thought to be composed, as were one to define a kind of house in terms of the materials and operations needed for its construction, or to define an action by reducing it to terms of its necessary motions. But from the dramatistic point of view, we can best observe this strategy later, when we consider the subject of "circumference" (in the sense that the location, or definition, of an act with reference to "the Mississippi valley" as its motivating scene could be said to involve a narrower circumference than its definition in terms of "the United States"). And we shall here pause to survey characteristic forms which the grammar of substance may embody in particular calculi:

Survey of Terms for Substance

Geometric substance. An object placed in its setting, existing both in itself and as part of its background. Participation in a context. Embodied most completely in Spinoza's cult of "Euclidean" relations, logically ("necessarily") derivable from one another. These relations exist all at once, implicitly, though they may manifest themselves, or be made manifest, in various *sequences*. (As soon as certain antecedent steps are taken in the demonstration, certain consequent steps are "inevitable.") The plastic connotations can lead readily into strictly materialistic notions of determinism, as with the novelist, Theodore Dreiser, who professes to view all ultimate motives in terms of "chemism."

Familial substance. In its purity, this concept stresses common ancestry in the strictly biological sense, as literal descent from maternal or paternal sources. But the concept of family is usually "spiritualized," so that it includes merely social groups, comprising persons of the same nationality or beliefs. Most often, in such cases, there is the notion of some founder shared in common, or some covenant or constitution or historical act from which the consubstantiality of the group is derived. Doctrines of creation extend the concept of familial descent to cover the relationship between the craftsman and his product ("the potter and the pot," as with the agent-act ratio).

This in turn moves us closer to purely logical derivations, of actualities from potentialities, of the explicit from the implicit, of conclusions from principles (that is, "firsts"). Plotinus' characterization of God as *to proton* would be a case in point, or Bonaventura's notion of the world's development from *rationes seminales,* an expression clearly combining the ideas of logical and biological descent. The stress upon the informative nature of beginnings can in turn lead us to treat christenings, inaugurations, and the like in aspects of familial substance. There is the girl of high spirits, for instance, who says of herself that she was born during a hurricane, as though the quality of her temper in later life were derived from the quality of the scene prevailing at her birth.

Biologists, in their concern with vital reproduction, necessarily give prominence to concepts of familial substance, in terms for genus and species, cellular structure, and the like. Often they study the responses of organisms at various levels of development, in the expectation that laws of behavior discovered at one level will apply to levels far higher in the scale of complexity. They expect differences, of course, but they also expect the processes at both the higher and lower levels to be "substantially" the same. Thus in an article of biological vulgarization published in one of the "cultural" magazines, a writer observed that, though we may lose confidence in the brotherhood of man, we can still be sure of our consubstantiality in a more inclusive concept of family: "protoplasm" (incidentally, another "first").

Since the taking of nourishment involves a *transubstantiation* of external elements into elements within, we might treat nutritive substance as a combination of the contextual and familial sufficiently notable to deserve a separate designation. Just as the organism dies when deprived of all food, so it will die in part when certain strategic ingredients are absent from its food. Thus, though one might not want to contend that a sufficiency of iodine will make men wise, we can say that a deficiency of iodine will greatly prod them to be stupid. And manganese has been called the chemical of "mother love" because, without manganese, hens won't set. (Similarly, the pituitary has been called the "mother love" gland, since a deficiency of the pituitary hormone in the female is accompanied by "lack of devotion to its offspring.") Modern chemistry prompts us to stress the scenic aspect of the nutritional motive, as the chemist would seek to reduce the efficient principle in both manganese and the pituitary hormone to a common basis. Even a stock to which a scion has been grafted may be considered, from this point of view, as a part of the scion's environment, hence an environmental control upon food supply. For any motivational special factor which is theoretically assigned to the organism (in the sense that a horse and a tiger, a dandelion and a daisy, exemplify in their behavior and development different loci of motion), can be theoretically dissolved into the environmental. If you put a hungry horse and a hungry tiger in a cage together, for instance, you would thereby get not one environment but two, since the tiger would be so drastically momentous an aspect of the horse's environment, and the horse would be a nutrient aspect of the tiger's environment. And any change of nutritive elements such as accompanies glandular transplantations or the injection of hormones is analyzable as a "new physical situation." Dr. Andras Angyal observed in his *Foundations for a Science of Personality,* "A *morphological* distinction between organism and environment is impossible." He also reminds us, "The blood has been called 'internal environment' by Claude Bernard." Accordingly, he employs the concept of a "biosphere" in which "subject (organism)" and "object (environment)" are merged as a single process.

The title of Robert M. Coates's fantasy, *Eater of Darkness,* could be translated: "The agent whose substance is one with the substance of darkness" (though we should next have to make an inquiry into the author's use of "darkness" to discover the special attributes of the term in his particular thesaurus). Totemic rites and the sacrament of the Eucharist are instances where the nutritive emphasis becomes submerged in the notion of familial consubstantiality. "Tell me what you eat, and I'll tell you what you are."

Directional substance. Doubtless biologically derived from the experience of free motion, since man is an organism that lives by locomotion. Frequently, with metaphors of "the way," the directional stresses the sense of motivation from within. Often strongly futuristic, purposive, its slogan might be: Not "Who are you?" or "Where are you from?" but "Where are you going?" Thought in terms of directional substance gained many fresh motives since the Renaissance, and the greater mobility that went with the development from status to contract, alienation of property, the growth of the monetary rationale, and revolutionary innovations in the means of transportation and communication. The directional is also susceptible of conversion from "free" motion into the "determined." Thus, one may "freely" answer a call, yet the call may be so imperious that one could not ignore it without disaster. And statistical treatment of supposedly "free" choices may disclose a uniform response prevailing among the lot.

The directional has encouraged much sociological speculation in terms of "tendencies" or "trends." With such terms, the substantial paradox is not far in the offing. If a man did *not* make a certain decision, for instance, we might nonetheless choose to say that he had a "tendency toward" the decision. Indeed, any tendency *to* do something is, by the same token, a tendency *not* to do it.

The directional is embedded in the very word, "motivation." And we may note four related nuances, or perhaps puns, with corresponding philosophies. Doctrines that reduce mental states to materialistic terms treat *motion* as motive. When an individual's acts are referred to some larger curve, we get *movement* as motive. For instance, individual immigrants came to America as part of a general movement westward. "Movement" in such cases can be either purposive or necessitarian, since one's place in a "movement" is like one's enlistment in a "cause" (and Latin *causa* is defined as: *that by, on account of, or through which anything takes place* or *is done; a cause, reason, motive, inducement*). Terminologies that situate the driving force of human action in human passion treat *emotion* as motive. (In his *Principles of Literary Criticism*, I. A. Richards offers a good pun for reducing *emotion* in turn to *motion*, when he proposes that we speak not of the *emotions* aroused in us by art but of the *commotions*.) And one can mystically select the *moment* as motive. Such "moments" are directional in that, being led up to and away from, they summarize the foregoing and seminally contain the subsequent. But in themselves they "just are," being an "eternal present" that has wound up the past and has the future wound up.

All metaphors or generalizations, such as *homo homini lupus*, or "life a pilgrimage," or "the economic man," that treat one order of motivation in terms of a higher order or lower order, are examples of substantiation; and they reveal the paradox of substance in that the given subject both is and is not the same as the character with which and by which it is identified. Such statements about motivating essence, often made in passing and sometimes serving as the midrib of a work, are the stock in trade of imaginative literature. As such, they can be most fully studied under the heading of symbolic. And much that we have written in *Permanence and Change, Attitudes Toward History,* and *The Philosophy of Literary Form* could be read as an elaboration of this paragraph. The name of any well-developed character in a fiction is the term for a peculiar complexity of motives.

15

Irony and Dialectic

Four Master Tropes

I refer to metaphor, metonymy, synecdoche, and irony. And my primary concern with them here will be not with their purely figurative usage, but with their rôle in the discovery and description of "the truth." It is an evanescent moment that we shall deal with—for not only does the dividing line between the figurative and literal usages shift, but also the four tropes shade into one another. Give a man but one of them, tell him to exploit its possibilities, and if he is thorough in doing so, he will come upon the other three.

The "literal" or "realistic" applications of the four tropes usually go by a different set of names. Thus:

For *metaphor* we could substitute *perspective;*
For *metonymy* we could substitute *reduction;*
For *synecdoche* we could substitute *representation;*
For *irony* we could substitute *dialectic.*[1]

We must subsequently try to make it clear in what respects we think these substitutions are justifiable. It should, however, be apparent at a glance that, regardless of whether our proposed substitutions are justifiable, considered in themselves they do shade into another, as we have said that the four tropes do. A dialectic, for instance, aims to give us a representation by the use of mutually related or interacting perspectives—and this resultant perspective of perspectives will necessarily be a reduction in the sense that a chart drawn to scale is a reduction of the area charted.

Metaphor is a device for seeing something *in terms of* something else. It brings out the thisness of a that, or the thatness of a this. If we employ the word "character" as a general term for whatever can be thought of as distinct (any thing, pattern, situation, structure, nature, person, object, act, rôle, process, event, etc.) then we could say that

From *A Grammar of Motives,* pp. 503–17. Reprinted by permission of The University of California Press. © 1969 by Kenneth Burke.

1. "Dialectic" is here used in the restricted sense. In a broader sense, all the transformations considered in this essay are dialectical.

metaphor tells us something about one character as considered from the point of view of another character. And to consider A from the point of view of B is, of course, to use B as a *perspective* upon A.

It is customary to think that objective reality is dissolved by such relativity of terms as we get through the shifting of perspectives (the perception of one character in terms of many diverse characters). But on the contrary, it is by the approach through a variety of perspectives that we establish a character's reality. If we are in doubt as to what an object is, for instance, we deliberately try to consider it in as many different terms as its nature permits: lifting, smelling, tasting, tapping, holding in different lights, subjecting to different pressures, dividing, matching, contrasting, etc.

Indeed, in keeping with the older theory of realism (what we might call "poetic realism," in contrast with modern "scientific realism") we could say that characters possess *degrees of being* in proportion to the variety of perspectives from which they can with justice be perceived. Thus we could say that plants have "more being" than minerals, animals have more being than plants, and men have more being than animals, because each higher order admits and requires a new dimension of terms not literally relevant to the lower orders.

By deliberate coaching and criticism of the perspective process, characters can be considered tentatively, in terms of other characters, for experimental or heuristic purposes. Examples may be offered at random: for instance, human motivation may, with varying degrees of relevance and reward, be considered in terms of conditioned reflexes, or chemicals, or the class struggles, or the love of God, or neurosis, or pilgrimage, or power, or movements of the planets, or geography, or sun spots, etc. Various kinds of scientific specialists now carry out the implications of one or another of such perspectives with much more perseverance than that with which a seventeenth-century poet might in one poem pursue the exploitation of a "conceit."

In *Permanence and Change* I have developed at some length the relationship between metaphor and perspective. I there dealt with such perspectives as an "incongruity," because the seeing of something in terms of something else involves the "carrying-over" of a term from one realm into another, a process that necessarily involves varying degrees of incongruity in that the two realms are never identical. But besides the mere desire not to restate this earlier material, there is another reason why we can hurry on to our next pair (metonymy and reduction). For since the four pairs overlap upon one another, we shall be carrying the first pair with us as we proceed.

II

Science, concerned with processes and "processing," is not properly concerned with substance (that is, it is not concerned with "being," as "poetic realism" is). Hence, it need not be concerned with motivation. All it need know is correlation. The limits of science, *qua* science, do not go beyond the statement that, when certain conditions are met, certain new conditions may be expected to follow. It is true that, in the history of the actual development of science, the discovery of such correlations has been regularly guided by philosophies of causation ("substantial" philosophies that were subsequently "discredited" or were so radically redefined as to become in effect totally different philosophies). And it is equally true that the discovery of correlations has been guided by ideational forms developed through theology and governmental law. Such "impurities" will always be detectable *behind* science as the act of given scientists; but science *qua* science is abstracted from them.

Be the world "mind," or "matter," or "both," or "several," you will follow the same procedure in striking a match. It is in this sense that science, *qua* science, is concerned with operations rather than with substances, even though the many inventions to do with the chemistry of a match can be traced back to a source in very explicit beliefs about substances and motivations of nature—and even of the supernatural.

However, as soon as you move into the social realm, involving the relation of man to man, mere *correlation* is not enough. Human relationships must be *substantial*, related by the copulative, the "is" of "being." In contrast with "scientific realism," "poetic realism" is centered in this emphasis. It seeks (except insofar as it is affected by the norms of "scientific realism") to place the motives of action, as with the relation between the seminal (potential) and the growing (actualized). Again and again, there have been attempts to give us a "science of human relations" after the analogy of the natural sciences. But there is a strategic or crucial respect in which this is impossible; namely: there can be no "science" of substance, except insofar as one is willing to call philosophy, metaphysics, or theology "sciences" (and they are not sciences in the sense of the positive scientific departments).

Hence, any attempt to deal with human relationships after the analogy of naturalistic correlations becomes necessarily the *reduction* of some higher or more complex realm of being to the terms of a lower or less complex realm of being. And, recalling that we propose to treat *metonymy* and *reduction* as substitutes for each other, one may realize why we thought it necessary thus to introduce the subject of metonymy.

The basic "strategy" in metonymy is this: to convey some incorporeal or intangible state in terms of the corporeal or tangible. E.g., to speak of "the heart" rather than "the emotions." If you trail language back far enough, of course, you will find that all our terms for "spiritual" states were metonymic in origin. We think of "the emotions," for instance, as applying solely to the realm of consciousness, yet obviously the word is rooted in the most "materialistic" term of all, "motion" (a key strategy in Western materialism has been the reduction of "consciousness" to "motion"). In his *Principles of Literary Criticism*, Richards is being quite "metonymic" in proposing that we speak not of the "emotions" aroused in the reader by the work of art, but the "commotions."

Language develops by metaphorical extension, in borrowing words from the realm of the corporeal, visible, tangible and applying them by analogy to the realm of the incorporeal, invisible, intangible; then in the course of time, the original corporeal reference is forgotten, and only the incorporeal, metaphorical extension survives (often because the very conditions of living that reminded one of the corporeal reference have so altered that the cross reference no longer exists with near the same degree of apparentness in the "objective situation" itself); and finally, poets regain the original relation, in reverse, by a "metaphorical extension" back from the intangible into a tangible equivalent (the first "carrying-over" from the material to the spiritual being compensated by a second "carrying-over" from the spiritual back into the material); and this "archaicizing" device we call "metonymy."

"Metonymy" is a device of "poetic realism"—but its partner, "reduction," is a device of "scientific realism." Here "poetry" and "behaviorism" meet. For the poet spontaneously knows that "beauty *is* as beauty *does*" (that the "state" must be "embodied" in an actualization). He knows that human relations require actions, which are *dramatizations,* and that the essential medium of drama is the posturing, tonalizing body placed in a material scene. He knows that "shame," for instance, is not merely a "state," but a movement of the eye, a color of the cheek, a certain quality of voice and set of the muscles; he knows this as "behavioristically" as the formal scientific behaviorist who would "reduce" the state itself to these corresponding bodily equivalents.

He also knows, however, that these bodily equivalents are but part of the *idiom of expression* involved in the act. They are "figures." They are hardly other than "symbolizations." Hence, for all his "archaicizing" usage here, he is not offering his metonymy as a *substantial* reduction. For in "poetic realism," states of mind as the motives of action are not reducible to materialistic terms. Thus, though there is a sense in which both the poetic behaviorist and the scientific behaviorist are exemplifying the strategy of metonymy (as the poet translates the spiritual into an idiom of material equivalents, and may even select for attention the same bodily responses that the scientist may later seek to measure), the first is using metonymy as a *terminological* reduction whereas the scientific behaviorist offers his reduction as a "real" reduction. (However, he does not do this *qua* scientist, but only by reason of the materialist metaphysics, with its assumptions about substance and motive, that is implicit in his system.)

III

Now, note that a reduction is a *representation*. If I reduce the contours of the United States, for instance, to the terms of a relief map, I have within these limits "represented" the United States. As a mental state is the "representation" of certain material conditions, so we could—reversing the process—say that the material conditions are "representative" of the mental state. That is, if there is some kind of correspondence between what we call the act of perception and what we call the thing perceived, then either of these equivalents can be taken as "representative" of the other. Thus, as reduction (metonymy) overlaps upon metaphor (perspective) so likewise it overlaps upon synecdoche (representation).

For this purpose we consider synecdoche in the usual range of dictionary sense, with such meanings as: part for the whole, whole for the part, container for the contained, sign for the thing signified, material for the thing made (which brings us nearer to metonymy), cause for effect, effect for cause, genus for species, species for genus, etc. All such conversions imply an integral relationship, a relationship of convertibility, between the two terms.

The "noblest synecdoche," the perfect paradigm or prototype for all lesser usages, is found in metaphysical doctrines proclaiming the identity of "microcosm" and "macrocosm." In such doctrines, where the individual is treated as a replica of the universe, and vice versa, we have the ideal synecdoche, since microcosm is related to macrocosm as part to whole, and either the whole can represent the part or the part can represent the whole. (For "represent" here we could substitute "be identified with.") One could thus look through the remotest astronomical distances to the "truth within," or could look within to learn the "truth in all the universe without." Leibniz's monadology is a good instance of the synecdochic on this grand scale. (And "representation" is his word for his synecdochic relationship.)

A similar synecdochic form is present in all theories of political representation, where some part of the social body (either traditionally established, or elected, or coming into authority by revolution) is held to be "representative" of the society as a whole. The pattern is essential to Rousseau's theory of the *volonté générale*, for instance. And though there are many disagreements within a society as to what part should represent the whole and how this representation should be accomplished, in a complex civilization any act of representation automatically implies a synecdochic relationship (insofar as the act is, or is held to be, "truly representative").

Sensory representation is, of course, synecdochic in that the senses abstract certain qualities from some bundle of electrochemical activities we call, say, a tree, and these qualities (such as size, shape, color, texture, weight, etc.) can be said "truly to represent" a tree. Similarly, artistic representation is synecdochic, in that certain relations within the medium "stand for" corresponding relations outside it. There is also a sense in which the well-formed work of art is internally synecdochic, as the beginning of a drama contains its close or the close sums up the beginning, the parts all thus being consubstantially related. Indeed, one may think what he will of microcosm-macrocosm relationships as they are applied to "society" or "the universe," the fact remains that, as regards such a "universe" as we get in a well-organized work of art, at every point the paradoxes of the synecdochic present themselves to the critic for analysis. Similarly, the realm of psychology (and particularly the psychology of art) requires the use of the synecdochic reversals. Indeed, I would want deliberately to "coach" the concept of the synecdochic by extending it to cover such relations (and their reversals) as: before for after, implicit for explicit, temporal sequence for logical sequence, name for narrative, disease for cure, hero for villain, active for passive. At the opening of *The Ancient Mariner,* for instance, the Albatross is a *gerundive:* its nature when introduced is that of something *to be* murdered, and it implicitly contains the future that is to become explicit. In *Moby Dick,* Ahab as pursuer is pursued; his action is a passion.

Metonymy may be treated as a special application of synecdoche. If, for instance, after the analogy of a correlation between "mind and body" or "consciousness and matter (or motion)" we selected quality

and quantity as a "synecdochically related pair," then we might propose to treat as synecdoche the substitution of either quantity for
quality or quality for quantity (since either side could be considered
as the sign, or symptom, of the other). But only *one* of these, the
substitution of quantity for quality, would be a metonymy. We might
say that representation (synecdoche) stresses a *relationship* or *connectedness* between two sides of an equation, a connectedness that,
like a road, extends in either direction, from quantity to quality or
from quality to quantity; but reduction follows along this road in only
one direction, from quality to quantity.[2]

[margin handwritten notes: diff b/twn Syn. + metony]

   Now "poetic realism," in contrast with "scientific realism," cannot
confine itself to representation in this metonymic, one-direction sense.
True, every art, in its nature as a medium, reduces a state of consciousness to a "corresponding" sensory body (so material that it can be
reproduced, bought and sold). But the aim of such *embodiment* is to
produce in the observer a corresponding state of *consciousness* (that
is, the artist proceeds from "mind" to "body" that his representative
reduction may induce the audience to proceed from "body" to
"mind"). But there is an important difference between representing
the quality of an experience thus and reducing the quality to a quantity. One might even "represent" the human body in the latter, reductive sense, by reducing it to ashes and offering a formula for the resultant chemicals. Otto Neurath's "isotypes" (see his *Modern Man in
the Making,* or our review of it, "Quantity and Quality," in the ap-
pendix of *The Philosophy of Literary Form*) are representations in the
latter, reductive sense, in contrast with the kind of representation we
get in realistic portrait-painting.

   Our point in going over this old ground is to use it as a way of
revealing a tactical error in the attempt to treat of *social* motivations.
We refer to the widespread belief that the mathematico-quantitative
ideal of the physical sciences can and should serve as the ideal of
the "social sciences," a belief that has led, for instance, to the almost
fabulous amassing of statistical surveys in the name of "sociology."
Or, if one insisted upon the right to build "sciences" after this
model (since no one could deny that statistics are often revealing) our

---

2. Unfortunately, we must modify this remark somewhat. Reduction, *as per scientific
realism,* would be confined to but one direction. Reduction, that is, as the word is now
generally used. But originally, "reduction" was used in ways that make it closer rather
to the margin of its overlap upon "perspective," as anything considered in terms of
anything else could be said to be "reduced"—or "brought back" ("referred")—to it, so
that the consideration of art in terms of morality, politics, or religion could have been
called "the reduction" of art to morality, or politics, or religion.

claim would be that science in this restricted sense (that explains higher orders by reduction to lower orders, organic complexities by reduction to atomistic simplicities, being by reduction to motion, or quality by reduction to number, etc.) could not *take the place* of metaphysics or religion, but would have to return to the role of "handmaiden."

Let us get at the point thus: *A terminology of conceptual analysis, if it is not to lead to misrepresentation, must be constructed in conformity with a representative anecdote—whereas anecdotes "scientifically" selected for reductive purposes are not representative.* E.g., think of the scientist who, in seeking an entrance into the analysis of human motivations, selects as his "informative anecdote" for this purpose some laboratory experiment having to do with the responses of animals. Obviously, such an anecdote has its peculiarly simplificatory ("reductive") character, or genius—and the scientist who develops his analytic terminology about this anecdote as his informative case must be expected to have, as a result, a terminology whose character or genius is restricted by the character or genius of the model for the description of which it is formed. He next proceeds to transfer (to "metaphor") this terminology to the interpretation of a different order of cases, turning for instance from animals to infants and from infants to the acts of fully developed adults. And when he has made these steps, applying his terminology to a kind of anecdote so different from the kind about which it was formed, this misapplication of his terminology would not give him a representative interpretation at all, but a mere "debunking." Only insofar as the analyst had not lived up to his claims, only insofar as his terminology for the analysis of a higher order of cases was *not* restricted to the limits proper to the analysis of a lower order of cases, could he hope to discuss the higher order of cases in an adequate set of terms. Otherwise, the genius of his restricted terminology must "drag the interpretation down to their level."

This observation goes for any terminological approach to the analysis of human acts or relationships that is shaped in conformity with an unrepresentative case (or that selects as the "way in" to one's subject an "informative anecdote" belonging in some other order than the case to be considered). For instance, insofar as Alfred Korzybski really does form his terminology for the analysis of meaning in conformity with that contraption of string, plugs, and tin he calls the "Structural Differential," his analysis of meaning is "predestined" to misrepresentation, since the genius of the contraption itself is not a representative example of meaning. It is a "reduction" of meaning, a reduction in the restricted sense of the term, as Thurman Arnold's reduction of social relations into terms of the psychiatric metaphor is reductive.

What then, it may be asked, would be a "representative anecdote?" But that takes us into the fourth pair: irony and dialectic.

IV

A treatment of the irony-dialectic pair will be much easier to follow if we first delay long enough to consider the equatability of "dialectic" with "dramatic."

A human rôle (such as we get in drama) may be summed up in certain slogans, or formulae, or epigrams, or "ideas" that characterize the agent's situation or strategy. The rôle involves properties both intrinsic to the agent and developed with relation to the scene and to other agents. And the "summings-up" ("ideas") similarly possess properties derived both from the agent and from the various factors with which the agent is in relationship. Where the ideas are in action, we have drama; where the agents are in ideation, we have dialectic.

Obviously, there are elements of "dramatic personality" in dialectic ideation, and elements of dialectic in the mutual influence of dramatic agents in contributing to one another's ideational development. You might state all this another way by saying that you cannot have ideas without persons or persons without ideas. Thus, one might speak of "Socratic irony" as "dramatic," and of "dramatic irony" as "Socratic."

Relativism is got by the fragmentation of either drama or dialectic. That is, if you isolate any one agent in a drama, or any one advocate in a dialogue, and see the whole in terms of his position alone, you have the purely relativistic. And in relativism there is no irony. (Indeed, as Cleanth Brooks might say, it is the very absence of irony in relativism that makes it so susceptible to irony. For relativism sees everything in but one set of terms—and since there are endless other terms in which things could be seen, the irony of the monologue that makes everything in its image would be in this ratio: the greater the *absolutism* of the statements, the greater the *subjectivity* and *relativity* in the position of the agent making the statements.)

Irony arises when one tries, by the interaction of terms upon one another, to produce a *development* which uses all the terms. Hence, from the standpoint of this total form (this "perspective of perspectives"), none of the participating "sub-perspectives" can be treated as either precisely right or precisely wrong. They are all voices, or personalities, or positions, integrally affecting one another. When the dialectic is properly formed, they are the number of characters needed to produce the total development. Hence, reverting to our suggestion that we might extend the synecdochic pattern to include such reversible pairs as disease-cure, hero-villain, active-passive, we should "ironically" note the function of the disease in "perfecting" the cure, or the function of the cure in "perpetuating" the influences of the disease. Or we should note that only through an internal and external experiencing of folly could we possess (in our intelligence or imagination) sufficient "characters" for some measure of development beyond folly.

People usually confuse the dialectic with the relativistic. Noting that the dialectic (or dramatic) explicitly attempts to establish a distinct set of characters, all of which protest variously at odds or on the bias with one another, they think no further. It is certainly relativistic, for instance, to state that any term (as per metaphor-perspective) can be seen from the point of view of any other term. But insofar as terms are thus encouraged to participate in an orderly parliamentary development, the dialectic of this participation produces (in the observer who considers the whole from the standpoint of the participation of all the terms rather than from the standpoint of any one participant) a "resultant certainty" of a different quality, necessarily ironic, since it requires that all the sub-certainties be considered as neither true nor false, but *contributory* (as were we to think of the resultant certainty or "perspective of perspectives" as a noun, and to think of all the contributory voices as necessary modifiers of that noun).

To be sure, relativism is the constant *temptation* of either dialectic or drama (consider how often, for instance, Shakespeare is called a relativist). And historians for the most part *are relativistic*. But where one considers different historical characters from the standpoint of a total development, one could encourage each character to comment upon the others without thereby sacrificing a perspective upon the lot. This could be got particularly, I think, if historical characters themselves (i.e., periods or cultures treated as "individual persons") were considered never to begin or end, but rather to change in intensity or poignancy. History, in this sense, would be a dialectic of characters in which, for instance, we should never expect to see "feudalism" overthrown by "capitalism" and "capitalism" succeeded by some manner of national or international or non-national or neo-national or postnational socialism—but rather should note elements of all such positions (or "voices") existing always, but attaining greater clarity of expression or imperiousness of proportion of one period than another.

Irony is never Pharisaic, but there is a Pharisaic temptation in irony. To illustrate the point, I should like to cite a passage from a poet and critic who knows a good deal about irony, and who is discussing a poet who knows a good deal about irony—but in this particular instance, I submit, he is wrong. I refer to a passage in which Allen Tate characterizes the seduction scene in *The Waste Land* as "ironic" and the poet's attitude as that of "humility." (I agree that "humility" is the proper partner of irony—but I question whether the passage is ironic enough to embody humility.)

Mr. Tate characterizes irony as "that arrangement of experience, either premeditated by art or accidentally appearing in the affairs of men, which permits to the spectator an insight superior to that of the actor." And he continues:

> The seduction scene is the picture of modern and dominating man. The arrogance and pride of conquest of the "small house agent's clerk" are the badge of science, bumptious practicality, overweening secular faith. The very success of this conquest witnesses its aimless character; it succeeds as a wheel succeeds in turning; he can only conquer again.
>
> His own failure to understand his position is irony, and the poet's insight into it is humility. But for the grace of God, says the poet in effect, there go I. There is essentially the poetic attitude, an attitude that Eliot has been approaching with increasing purity.

We need not try to decide whether or not the poet was justified in feeling "superior" to the clerk. But we may ask how one could *possibly* exemplify an attitude of "humility" by feeling "superior"? There is, to be sure, a brand of irony, called "romantic irony," that might fit in with such a pattern—the kind of irony that did, as a matter of fact, arise as an aesthetic opposition to cultural philistinism, and in which the artist considered himself *outside of* and *superior to* the rôle he was rejecting. And though not "essentially *the* poetic attitude," it is essentially *a* poetic attitude, an attitude exemplified by much romantic art (a sort of pamphleteering, or external, attitude toward "the enemy").

True irony, however, irony that really does justify the attribute of "humility," is not "superior" to the enemy. (I might even here rephrase my discussion of Eliot in *Attitudes Toward History* by saying that Eliot's problem in religion has resided precisely in his attempt to convert romantic irony into classic irony, really to replace a state of "superiority" by a state of "humility"—and *Murder in the Cathedral* is a ritual aimed at precisely such purification of motives.) True irony, humble irony, is based upon a sense of fundamental kinship with the enemy, as one *needs* him, is *indebted* to him, is not merely outside him as an observer but contains him *within,* being consubstantial with him. This is the irony of Flaubert, when he recognizes that Madame Bovary is himself. One sees it in Thomas Mann—and in what he once called, when applying the term to another, "Judas psychology." And there was, if not the humility of strength, at least a humility of gentle surrender, in Anatole France.

In *The Waste Land,* the poet is not saying "there but for the grace of God go I." On the contrary, he is, if not thanking God, at least congratulating himself, that he is not like other men, such other men as this petty clerk. If this was "humility," then the Pharisee is Humble Citizen No. 1. With Newton, on the other hand, there was no "superiority" in his exclamation as he observed the criminal. He did not mean that that man was a criminal but he, Newton, thank God, was not; he meant that *he too was a criminal, but that the other man was going to prison for him.* Here was true irony-and-humility, since Newton was simultaneously both outside the criminal and within him.

"Superiority" in the dialectic can arise only in the sense that one may feel the need of *more characters* than the particular foolish characters under consideration. But in one sense he can *never* be superior, for he must realize that he also *needs this particular foolish character as one of the necessary modifiers.* Dialectic irony (or humility) here, we might even say, provides us with a kind of "technical equivalent for the doctrine of original sin." Folly and villainy are integral motives, necessary to wisdom or virtue.[3]

A third temptation of irony is its tendency toward the simplification of literalness. That is: although *all* the characters in a dramatic or dialectic development are necessary qualifiers of the definition, there is usually some one character that enjoys the rôle of *primus inter pares.* For whereas any of the characters may be viewed in terms of any other, this one character may be taken as the summarizing vessel,

---

3. I would consider Falstaff a gloriously ironic conception because we are so at one with him in his vices, while he himself embodies his vices in a mode of identification or brotherhood that is all but religious. Falstaff would not simply rob a man, from without. He *identifies himself* with the victim of a theft; he *represents* the victim. He would not crudely steal a purse; rather, he *joins forces* with the owner of the purse—and it is only when the harsh realities of this imperfect world have imposed a brutally divisive clarity upon the situation, that Falstaff is left holding the purse. He produces a new quality, a state of synthesis or merger—and it so happens that, when this synthesis is finally dissociated again into its analytic components (the crudities of the realm of practical property relationships having reduced this state of qualitative merger to a state of quantitative division), the issue as so simplified sums up to the fact that the purse has changed hands. *He* converts "thine" into "ours"—and it is "circumstances over which he has no control" that go to convert this "ours" into a "mine." A mere thief would have

or synecdochic representative, of the development as a whole. This is the rôle of Socrates in the Platonic dialogue, for instance—and we could similarly call the proletariat the Socrates of the Marxist Symposium of History, as they are not merely equal participants along with the other characters, but also represent the *end* or *logic* of the development as a whole.

This "most representative" character thus has a dual function: one we might call "adjectival" and the other "substantial." The character is "adjectival," as embodying one of the qualifications necessary to the total definition, but is "substantial" as embodying the conclusions of the development as a whole. Irony is sacrificed to "the simplification of literalness" when this duality of rôle is neglected (as it may be neglected by either the reader, the writer, or both). In Marxism as a literally libertarian philosophy, for instance, slavery is "bad," and is so treated in the rhetoric of proletarian emancipation (e.g., "wage slavery"). Yet from the standpoint of the development as a whole, slavery must be treated ironically, as with Engels's formula: "Without the slavery of antiquity, no modern socialism." Utilization of the vanquished by enslavement, he notes, was a great cultural advance over the wasteful practice of slaying the vanquished.

V

Irony, as approached through either drama or dialectic, moves us into the area of "law" and "justice" (the "necessity" or "inevitability" of the *lex talionis*) that involves matters of form in art (as form affects anticipation and fulfillment) and matters of prophecy and prediction in history. There is a level of generalization at which predictions about "inevitable" developments in history are quite justified. We may state

---

directly converted "thine" into "mine." It is the addition of these intermediate steps that makes the vital difference between a mere thief and Falstaff; for it is precisely these intermediate steps that mark him with a conviviality, a sociality, essentially religious— and in this *sympathetic* distortion of religious values resides the irony of his conception.

We might bring out the point sharply by contrasting Falstaff with Tartuffe. Tartuffe, like Falstaff, exploits the coöperative values for competitive ends. He too would convert "thine" into "mine" by putting it through the social alembic of "ours." But the conception of Tartuffe is not ironic, since he is pure hypocrite. He uses the religious values simply as a swindler. Tartuffe's piety, which he uses to gain the confidence of his victims, is a mere deception. Whereas Tartuffe is all competition and merely *simulates* the sentiments of cooperation, Falstaff is genuinely cooperative, sympathetic, a synecdochic part of his victim—but along with such rich gifts of identification, what is to prevent a purse from changing hands?

with confidence, for instance, that what arose in time must fall in time (hence, that any given structure of society must "inevitably" perish). We may make such prophecy more precise, with the help of irony, in saying that the developments that led to the rise will, by the further course of their development, "inevitably" lead to the fall (true irony always, we hold, thus involving an "internal fatality," a principle operating from within, though its logic may also be grounded in the nature of the extrinsic scene, whose properties contribute to the same development).

The point at which different casuistries appear (for fitting these "general laws of inevitability" to the unique cases of history) is the point where one tries to decide exactly what new characters, born of a given prior character, will be the "inevitable" vessels of the prior character's deposition. As an overall ironic formula here, and one that has the quality of "inevitability," we could lay it down that "what goes forth as A returns as non-A." This is the basic pattern that places the essence of drama and dialectic in the irony of the "peripety," the strategic moment of reversal.

16

Perspective by Incongruity:
Comic Correctives

This notion of *ambivalence* gets us to our main thesis with regard to propagandistic (didactic) strategy. We hold that it must be employed as an essentially *comic* notion, containing two-way attributes lacking in polemical, one-way approaches to social necessity. It is neither wholly euphemistic, nor wholly debunking—hence it provides the *charitable* attitude toward people that is required for purposes of persuasion and co-operation, but at the same time maintains our shrewdness concerning the simplicities of "cashing in." The mystifications of the priestly euphemisms, presenting the most materialistic of acts in transcendentally "eulogistic coverings," provided us with instruments too blunt for discerning the play of economic factors. The debunking vocabulary (that really flowered with its great founder, Bentham, who developed not merely a *method* of debunking but a *methodology* of debunking, while a group of mere epigones have been cashing in on his genius for a century, bureaucratizing his imaginative inventions in various kinds of "muckraking" enterprises) can disclose material interests with great precision. *Too* great precision, in fact. For though the doctrine of *Zweck im Recht* is a veritable Occam's razor for the simplification of human motives, teaching us the role that *special material interests* play in the "impartial" manipulations of the law, showing us that law can be privately owned like any other property, it can be too thorough; in lowering human dignity so greatly, it lowers us all.

A comic frame of motives avoids these difficulties, showing us how an act can "dialectically" contain both transcendental and material ingredients, both imagination and bureaucratic embodiment, both "service" and "spoils." Or, viewing the matter in terms of ecological balance, one might say of the comic frame: It also makes us sensitive to the point at which one of these ingredients becomes hypertrophied,

From "Comic Correctives," in *Attitudes Toward History, Revised Edition*, pp. 166–75. Reprinted by permission of The University of California Press. © 1984 by Kenneth Burke.

abnormal growth

with the corresponding atrophy of the other. A well-balanced ecology requires the symbiosis of the two.[1]

The comic frame of reference also opens up a whole new field for social criticism, since the overly *materialistic* coordinates of the polemical-debunking frame have unintentionally blinded us to the full operation of "alienating" processes. Historians become indignant, for

1. The incentives to take fascism as a way out of the bourgeois-commercialist confusions, and the anti-heroic difficulties that go with the *delegated* authority of parliamentary procedure, may be revealed in the attitude which even men as complex as Goethe had toward Napoleon. In Napoleon they saw the unifier of Europe, by conquests of the *pax Romana* sort whereby, once an area was subdued, it was admitted to the advantages of the imperial communicative network. Napoleon was to be the new Augustus, by establishing a complete "political monopoly" that would force into line the clashing minor monopolies. And though an "upstart," he was not a "delegated authority." He was the "man of destiny," hence his rule would be sanctioned by the same divinely fatalistic arrangements that sanctioned the "rights" of hereditary kings. Not human voting (which leads to polemical debunking) but the balloting of the heavens, would establish his appointment to the role of leader. With so many instrumentalities now on the side of privilege, we hold, a comic frame must detect the lure of such incentives, must make people conscious of their operation, if they are not to be victimized by such magic. It is because people must respect themselves, that the cult of Kings is always in the offing. Democracy can be maintained only by *complete sophistication,* once we near the "Malthusian limits" of its opportunities. The sense of frustration that accompanies the narrowing of these opportunities leads to a naive sense of guilt, for which a *Führer,* made "heroic" by the tremendous resources of modern propagandist organization, is the simplest remedy.

The anti-Semitic element that arises in Christian nations at such a critical juncture, might be explainable as follows: Historians have long noted the correlation between economic frustration and actual or symbolic pogroms. Jews are hated most actively in periods of depression. The steps are these: Economic depression means psychologically a sense of frustration. The sense of frustration means psychologically a sense of persecution. The sense of persecution incites, compensatorily, a sense of personal worth, or goodness, and one feels that this goodness is being misused. One then "magnifies" this sense of wronged goodness by identification with a hero. And who, with those having received any Christian training in childhood, is the ultimate symbol of persecuted goodness? "Christ." And who persecuted Christ? The Jews. Hence, compensatorily admiring oneself as much as possible, in the magnified version of a hero (the hero of one's first and deepest childhood impressions) the naive Christian arrives almost "syllogistically" at anti-Semitism as the "symbolic solution" of his economically caused frustrations.

True, this process may not be undergone by all men who show obedience to its results. It may fully apply only to the pivotal, the "leaders" and "prophets," the "conscientious"; and many may accept their judgments mainly by inertia, as social conveniences rather than as intensely felt assertions. They may merely "climb on the bandwagon," with material and mental rewards in keeping.

Perhaps we may clarify the significance we attach to the "comic" frame by stating our belief that the comic frame is best suited for making disclosures of this sort, which are necessary to counteract the dangers of "mystification," so momentous in their tendency to shunt criticism into the wrong channels.

instance, when reviewing the ways in which private individuals were able, in nineteenth-century America, to appropriate "legally" large areas of the public domain. (The most astounding instance being the subsidizing of the railroads, where the government *gave* private promoters the land on which to build the road, and then—with this same land as collateral for a loan—advanced the promoters, from the public treasury, the money with which to build the road.) But "public property" extends into much subtler areas than this. A social organization is also public property, and can be privately appropriated.

For instance, our network of roadways increases the hazards of travel. There thus arise both the obligation and the opportunity to insure those exposed to these hazards. This *increased insurability* is a *public liability*. But *private* insurance companies are organized to exploit it as a *private asset*. Thereby they privately appropriate a portion of the "public domain" quite as effectively as those nineteenth-century promoters who, by manipulating the center of coordination in Washington, got personal possession of public resources, in lands, timber, and mineral wealth. By this grip, they can exact a private toll for the performing of a public service. And as their interests become organized, they can fight any attempts of the government to provide such services less expensively (as they could be provided less expensively, were the private toll eliminated). And in their charges for insurance they can include the amounts required for lobbying and goodwill advertising, to keep this exploitation of a public domain in private hands. The comic analysis of exploitation prompts us to be on the lookout also for those subtler ways in which the private appropriation of the public domain continues. It admonishes us that social exigencies and "goodwill" are as *real* a vein to be tapped as any oil deposit in Teapot Dome. (Addendum, 1955: Radio and television channels, and the private use of nuclear resources developed by the government, would also be obvious examples.)

The Church thought of man as a prospective citizen of heaven. In time, the critical inaccuracy that such transcendental emphasis brought to the gauging of material relationships became bureaucratically exploited to its limits. Out of this overemphasis, a purely antithetical overemphasis developed. Against man as a citizen of heaven, thinkers opposed man in nature; and with the progress of efficiency in reasoning, we got simply to *man in the jungle*. A comic synthesis of these antithetical emphases would "transcend" them by stressing *man in society*. As such, it would come close to restoring the emphasis of Aristotle, with his view of man as a "political animal."

In the motives we assign to the actions of ourselves and our neigh-

bors, there is implicit a program of socialization. In deciding *why*
people do as they do, we get the cues that place us with relation to
them. Hence, a vocabulary of motives is important for the forming of
both private and public relationships. A comic frame of motives, as
here conceived, would not only avoid the sentimental denial of materialistic factors in human acts. It would also avoid the cynical brutality
that comes when such sensitivity is outraged, as it must be outraged
by the acts of others or by the needs that practical exigencies place
upon us.

And one is exposed indeed to the possibilities of being cheated
shamelessly in this world, if he does not accumulate at least a minimum of spiritual resources that no man can take from him. The comic
frame, as a *method of study* (man as eternal journeyman) is a better
personal possession, in this respect, than the somewhat empty accumulation of facts such as people greedily cultivate when attempting to
qualify in "Ask Me Another" questionnaires, where they are invited
to admire themselves for knowing the middle name of Robert Louis
Stevenson's favorite nephew (if he had one). Mastery of this sort
(where, if "Knowledge is power," people "get power" vicariously by
gaining possession of its "insignia," accumulated facts) may somewhat patch up a wounded psyche; but a more adventurous equipment
is required, if one is to have a private possession marked by mature
social efficacy.

The comic frame, in making a man the student of himself, makes it
possible for him to "transcend" occasions when he has been tricked
or cheated, since he can readily put such discouragements in his "assets" column, under the head of "experience." Thus we "win" by subtly changing the rules of the game—and by a mere trick of bookkeeping, like the accountants for big utility corporations, we make
"assets" out of "liabilities." And can we, in our humbleness, do better
than apply in our own way the wise devices of these leviathans,
thereby "democratizing" a salvation device as we encourage it to filter
from the top down?

In sum, the comic frame should enable people *to be observers of
themselves, while acting.* Its ultimate would not be *passiveness*, but
maximum consciousness. One would "transcend" himself by noting
his own foibles. He would provide a rationale for locating the irrational and the nonrational.[2]

2. "The irrational and the nonrational." Many of our rationalists have made things
more difficult and forbidding by confining us to a choice between two only, the "rational" and the "irrational." But if a tree puts out leaves in the spring and drops them

The materials for such a frame by no means require a new start. They are all about us. (We should question the proposal drastically, were it otherwise, for a man is necessarily talking error unless his words can claim membership in a collective body of thought.) The comic frame is present in the best of psychoanalytic criticism. It is highly present in anthropological catalogs like that of Frazer's *Golden Bough* which, by showing us the rites of magical purification in primitive peoples, gives us the necessary cues for the detection of similar processes in even the most practical and nonpriestly of contemporary acts. It is to be found, amply, in the great formulators of "economic psychoanalysis," writers like Machiavelli, Hobbes, Voltaire, Bentham, Marx, Veblen. Yet, while never permitting itself to overlook the admonitions of even the most caustic social criticism, it does not *waste* the world's rich store of error, as those parochial-minded persons waste it who dismiss all thought before a certain date as "ignorance" and "superstition." Instead, it cherishes the lore of so-called "error" as a *genuine aspect of the truth, with emphases valuable for the correcting of present emphases.*

Often, we can reapply, for incorporation in the "comic" frame, a formula originally made in the euphemistic or debunking modes of emphasis, by merely changing our *attitude* toward the formula. We "discount" it for comic purposes, subtly translating it, as Marx translated Hegel, "taking over" a mystificatory methodology for clarificatory ends. This strategy even opens us to the resources of "popular" philosophy, as embodied not only in proverbs and old saws, but also in the working vocabulary of everyday relationships. Thus we can incorporate the remarkable terms of politics and business, two terminologies which quickly chart and simplify constantly recurring relationships of our society. The vocabulary of crime is equally valuable, in such ingenious shortcuts as "ganging up on" and "putting on the spot."

You have heard tributes to "folk art." You should also give thought to "folk criticism." We are not here proposing to cultivate such terms "esthetically," for their purely "picturesque" value. We are consider-

---

in the autumn, its act is neither rational nor irrational, but nonrational. And so it is with many human processes, even mental ones, like the "identification" that the non-heroic reader makes with the hero of the book he is reading. To call such processes "irrational" is to desire their complete elimination. But we question whether social integration can be accomplished without them. If we consider them simply as "nonrational," we are not induced to seek elaborate techniques for their excision—instead we merely, as rational men, "watch" them, to guard ourselves against cases where they work badly. Where they work well, we can salute them, even coach them.

ing them as a collective philosophy of motivation, arising to name the relationships, or social situations, which people have found so pivotal and so constantly recurring as to need names for them. The metaphorical migration of a term from some restricted field of action into the naming of acts in other fields is a kind of "perspective by incongruity" that we merely propose to make more "efficient" by proposing a *methodology* for encouraging still further metaphorical migrations. And this efficiency, while open to distrust, is to be tested in turn by tests of "ecological balance," as we extend the orthodox range of a term by the perspective of a totality.

The comic frame of acceptance but carries to completion the translative act. It considers human life as a project in "composition," where the poet works with the materials of social relationships. Composition, translation, also "revision," hence offering maximum opportunity for the resources of *criticism*.

The comic frame might give a man an attitude that increased his spiritual wealth, by making even bad books and trivial remarks legitimate objects of study. It might mitigate somewhat the difficulties in engineering a shift to new symbols of authority, as required by the new social relationships that the revolutions of historic environment have made necessary. It might provide important cues for the composition of one's life, which demands accommodation to the structure of others' lives.[3]

It could not, however, remove the ravages of boredom and inanition that go with the "alienations" of contemporary society. The necessities of earning a living may induce men actually to compete "of their own free will" to get the most incredible kinds of jobs, jobs that make them rot in the dark while the sun is shining, or warp their

---

3. Tactics of the intellectuals: Intellectuals as "advance guard." Nor is there anything particularly noble or distinguished about that—since it is, by the very nature of the case, *easier* for the intellectuals to advocate ideals on paper, in the "perfect world" of blueprints, than it is for those completely implicated in the "imperfect world" of the practical. Intellectuals must bargain for a lot, in order that there still be something left after the inevitable discounting that occurs when a society attempts to carry out their policies. "Oriental bargaining." The seller asks ten, the buyer offers two—they finally agree on five. Had the seller asked five, they would have agreed on three.

However, the intellectuals must advocate their extreme policy in such a way that they do not organize a counter-extreme. The seller must not ask so much that the buyer simply will not bargain.

The comic frame, we submit, offers the best cues for the embodiment of this policy. For one thing, it warns against too great reliance upon the conveniences of moral indignation. Nothing organizes a counter-morality more efficiently than do the intellectuals who promiscuously "move in on" the resources of secular prayer open to the morally indignant.

bodies and their minds by overlong sedentary regimentation and grotesque devotion to all the unadventurous tasks of filing and recording that our enormous superstructure, for manipulating the mere abstract symbols of exchange, has built up. The need of wages may induce men "voluntarily" to scramble for such "opportunities," even plotting to elbow themselves into offices which, in earlier economies, would not have been performed at all except by slaves and criminals under compulsion. For alienations of this sort (the stifling of adventure that, as a by-product, has come with the accumulations of the venturesome) the comic frame could not, and should not, offer recompense. Its value should only reside in helping to produce a state of affairs whereby these rigors may abate.

17

The Transformation of Terms

Dialectic Substance

From the standpoint of our present study, all the foregoing types could be considered as special cases of a more inclusive category: dialectic substance. Dialectically considered (that is, "dramatistically" considered) men are not only *in nature*. The cultural accretions made possible by the language motive become a "second nature" with them. Here again we confront the ambiguities of substance, since symbolic communication is not a merely external instrument, but also intrinsic to men as agents. Its motivational properties characterize both "the human situation" and what men are "in themselves."

Whereas there is an implicit irony in the other notions of substance, with the dialectic substance the irony is explicit. For it derives its character from the systematic contemplation of the antinomies attendant upon the fact that we necessarily define a thing in terms of something else. "Dialectic substance" would thus be the overall category of dramatism, which treats of human motives in the terms of verbal action. By this statement we most decidedly do not mean that human motives are confined to the realm of verbal action. We mean rather that the dramatistic analysis of motives has its *point of departure* in the subject of verbal action (in thought, speech, and document).

A poem, by shifting the imagery of its metaphors, permits us to contemplate the subject from the standpoint of various objects. This effect is dialectical in the sense that we see something in terms of some other. In a more restricted sense, however, the dialectical considers things in terms not of *some* other, but of *the* other. The sharpest instance of this is an *agon* wherein the protagonist is motivated by the nature of the antagonist, as with the situating of socialist motives in resistance to capitalism, or the unifying effect of the Allied Nations' joint opposition to Hitler. There is a grim pleasantry that runs, "Of course we're Christians—but what are we being Christians *against*?"

From *A Grammar of Motives*, pp. 33–38. Reprinted by permission of The University of California Press. © 1969 by Kenneth Burke.

In earlier days, when the devil enjoyed great personal prominence, he could perform this noteworthy role of agonistic unification which, in our era of humanistic progress, we generally assign exclusively to human vessels.

The ambiguity of external and internal motivation has recently plagued some enemies of fascism who saw that an effective war against the fascist nations would require many "fascist" measures on the part of the anti-fascists. As the Irish poet, George Russell, once stated the form of their predicament: "We become the image of the thing we hate." And the great dialectician, Coleridge, has observed that *rivales* are the opposite banks of the *same* stream. And it was dialectically, or dramatically, necessary that the *devil* should be an *angel;* for were he of any less noble substance, the Christian *agonia* would to that degree have fallen short of thoroughness in imagining a common ground on which the two great conflicting motives, good and evil, can join battle.

The most thoroughgoing dialectical opposition, however, centers in that key pair, Being and Not-Being. For the contextual approach to substance, by inducing men to postulate a ground or context in which everything that is, is placed, led thinkers "by dialectical necessity" to affirm that the only ground of "Being" is "Not-Being" (for "Being" is so comprehensive a category that its dialectical opposite, "Not-Being," is the only term that would be left to designate its ground). The Neo-Platonist, Plotinus, carried such thinking to its ultimate limits, in the direction of that "negative theology" whereby the divine substance, as the ground of all that we experience in the material world, could be designated only by the absence of any attributes such as we in our material existence can conceive of. He would evolve a dialectical process that, beginning with material things, in the end had completely transcended its beginnings, thus arriving at a totally immaterial vision of God as an abstract Oneness. Accordingly, in his belief that material existence is estrangement from God, he is said to have been unwilling to name either his parents or his birthplace (the abstract concept of dialectical substance here leading him to proclaim his identity by a *negative* reference to the familial and the geometric).

The process of transcendence may, of course, be reversed. Then the ultimate abstract Oneness is taken as a source, a "first"; and the steps leading up to it are interpreted as stages emanating from it. Or terms that are contextual to each other (such as Being and Not-Being, Action and Rest, Mechanism and Purpose, the One and the Many) can be treated as familially related (as were Being to be derived from Not-Being, Action from Rest, Mechanism from Purpose, the Many from the One). Or, in general, actualities may be derived from potentialities that are in a different realm than the actualities. The most obvious instance of such a derivation would be a naturalistic assertion that the "conscious" is derived from a "pre-Conscious," or that the state of life is derived from a condition of "pre-life." However, many less apparent variants are possible. The human person, for instance, may be derived from God as a "super-person." Or human purpose may be derived from All Purpose, or Cosmic Purpose, or Universal Purpose, or Absolute Purpose, or Pure Purpose, or Inner Purpose, etc. And instead of a "pre-conscious" as the source or latent form of consciousness, we may have a subconscious or unconscious or "collective unconscious," etc.

The Paradox of Purity

Such pairs are in contrasted orders, with one a transcendence of the other, the one latent or covert, the other patent or overt. And the ambiguities of substance here take a form that we would call the "paradox of purity," or "paradox of the absolute." We confront this paradox when deriving the nature of the human person from God as "super-person," as "pure," or "absolute" person, since God as a super-person would be impersonal—and the impersonal would be synonymous with the *negation* of personality. Hence, Pure Personality would be the same as No Personality: and the derivation of the personal principle from God as pure person would amount to its derivation from an impersonal principle. Similarly, a point that Hegel made much of, Pure Being would be the same as Not-Being; and in Aristotle, God can be defined either as "Pure Act" or as complete repose, a rest that is "eternal, unchangeable, immovable." And Leibniz was able to propose something pretty much like unconscious ideas in his doctrine of the "virtual innateness of ideas." (We might point up the oxymoron here by translating "unconscious ideas" as "unaware awarenesses.")

The painter Kandinsky illustrates our subject when, on the subject of Schönberg's esthetic, he says that, to the uninitiate, the "inner beauty" of music must seem like ugliness. And when discussing Julien Gracq's *Chateau d'Argol*, Parker Tyler comes upon the paradox of the absolute thus:

> In the eighth chapter of the book, Albert and Heide, the woman, follow a road which is said to "symbolize *pure direction*. But looking back, they realize that behind them the avenue seems to peter out and to be blocked by thicket and underbrush. It is a blind alley . . ." Like passage through water, passage through his Hegelian reality is pure direction, meaning that,

wherever you turn in it, the way must be created, because behind you, the way has *ceased to be.*

The citation is from the surrealist magazine, *View,* in another copy of which Harold Rosenberg, writing on "the art of escape," says that "in democratic society, this art tends, like all the other arts, to become *Pure.*" And if the fugitive "can combine within himself perfectly all the elements of the art, he will be able to free himself perpetually." The thought suggests the element of "pure escape" that lies at the roots of liberalism. And it suggests the paradox of "pure escape." For in freeing oneself *perpetually,* one would in a sense remain perpetually a prisoner, since one would never have definitively escaped.

With regard to symbolic, one may expect to encounter the paradox of purity whenever he finds what we have called elsewhere the "withinness of withinness," or the "atop the atop," as when Melville writes in *Moby Dick:* "It was a negro church; and the preacher's text was about the blackness of darkness," or as with the pattern in "The Garden," by Andrew Marvell, when the poet speaks of the mind as

> ... that ocean where each kind
> Does streight its own resemblance find;
>
> Annihilating all that's made
> To a green thought in a green shade.

And in another issue of *View,* when Parker Tyler is reviewing a manual of judo as though this kind of combat were simply a kind of dance, a "pure" art done for love of the figures involved, not for the utilitarian purpose of victory over an adversary, he states his position in a similar "atop the atop" kind of image. For he sums up his thesis in an image by observing that the high-speed camera has shown us how "a drop of milk falling into a mass of milk creates at the moment a perfectly symmetrical crown, with several points suspended in the air like jewels." His article concludes:

> In the largest sense, Mars is an enemy of Apollo. It is only on the esthetic grounds of fantasy that they may meet and fraternize with each other. So, beyond our capacity to discipline our thoughts in relation to "realities," the instinct of free movement typified by Isadora's dance asserts itself, and we may imagine as eternal, if we like, a drop of American blood being poured into its own mass, and erecting over that precious surface a fragile crown of rubies.

In theological and metaphysical works, we can recognize the paradox of the absolute readily enough. Often, in fact, it is explicitly discussed. But in historicist writings it more easily goes unnoticed. Yet the paradox may be implicit in any term for a *collective* motivation, such a concept of class, nation, the "general will," and the like. Technically, it becomes a "pure" motive when matched against some individual locus of motivation. And it may thus be the *negation* of an individual motive. Yet despite this position as dialectical antithesis of the individual motive, the collective motive may be treated as the source or principle from which the individual motive is familially or "substantially" derived in a "like begets like" manner. That is, to derive the individual motive from the collective motive would be like deriving the personal principle familially from the super-personal principle, whereas contextually the "super-personal" principle would be the *other* of the personal.

What we are here considering formally, as a paradox of substance, can be illustrated quickly enough by example. A soldier may be *nationally* motivated to kill the enemies of his country, whereas *individually* he is motivated by a horror of killing his own enemies. Or conversely, as a patriot he may act by the motive of sacrifice in behalf of his country, but as an individual he may want to profit. Or a man's business code may differ so greatly from his private code that we can even think of him as a "split personality" (that is, a man of "two substances," or "divided substance"). Or one will find a resistance to people in particular "balanced by" a humanitarian sympathy for mankind in general.

Such histories can be imagined in an endless variety of details. What we are suggesting here is that they all embody a *grammatical form* in accordance with which we should not expect a dualism of motives to be automatically dissolved, as with those apologists of science who believe that in a scientific world ethics become unnecessary. However, to consider these possibilities further, we should move into the areas of symbolic, involving modes of transubstantiation, rituals of rebirth, whereby the individual identifies himself in terms of the collective motive (an identification by which he both is and is not one with that with which and by which he is identified). At present it is enough to note in a general way how the paradox of the absolute figures grammatically in the dialectic, making for a transcending of one term by its other, and for the reversed ambiguous derivation of the term from its other as ancestral principle.

18

Transcendence

"Heads I Win, Tails You Lose"

A device whereby, if things turn out one way, your system accounts
for them—and if they turn out the opposite way, your system also
accounts for them. When we first came upon this formula, we thought
we had found a way of discrediting an argument. If a philosopher
outlined a system, and we were able to locate its variant of the "heads
I win, tails you lose" device, we thought that we had exposed a fatal
fallacy. But as we grew older, we began to ask ourselves whether there
is any other possible way of thinking. And we now absolutely doubt
that there is. Hence, we should propose to control the matter not by
elimination, but by channelization. That is, we merely ask that the
thinker _co-operate with us_ in the attempt to track down his variant of *huh*
the "heads I win, tails you lose" strategy. It will necessarily be implicit
in his work. And we merely ask him, as a philosopher whose proper
game is Cards-face-up-on-the-table, to help us find it, that we may
thereby be assisted in "discounting" it properly.

The whole matter is related to the scholastic distinction between
"essence" and "existence." A thing has many aspects, good, bad, indifferent. You "transcend" this confusion when, by secular prayer,
you "vote" that _one_ of these aspects is the _essence_ of the lot. For
instance, you may vote that the essence of man is "the way in which
he is like a god"; or you may vote that his essence is "the way in which
he is like an animal." When you have, by an "act of will" (a "moral"
choice) completed your balloting, the attributes that do not confirm
your choice of "essence" are labeled "accidents."

Thus, in our discussion of principles and policies: the constant
principle is the "essence" of motivation, and the shifting policies,
often directly contrary to one another, are the "accidental" variants.
If you decree by secular prayer that man is "essentially" a warrior (as
did Nietzsche) you may then proceed, by casuistic stretching, to dis-

From *Attitudes Toward History, Revised Edition*, pp. 260–63, 336–38. Reprinted by
permission of The University of California Press. © 1984 by Kenneth Burke.

cern the warlike ingredient present even in love. If on the contrary you legislated to the effect that man is essentially a communicant, you could discern the co-operative ingredient present "essentially" even in war. Capitalism is "essentially" competitive (on this point, both opponents and proponents agree). But despite this essence, we note the presence of many noncompetitive ingredients (there are many examples of true "partnership" in the competitive struggle).

"Heads I win, tails you lose" is a technical equivalent of the formula named moralistically "opportunism." Thus you get the "opportunism" of Whitman who, by his doctrine of "unseen existences," could welcome an event in spirit ("in principle") where the same event, in its raw existential attributes, might have wounded him. That is, the "essence" of a real estate boom was in its "unseen existence"; and this unseen existence was not speculation for profit, but the zeal and zest of collectively building up a continent; when beholding men *building capitalism,* he could "transcendentally" welcome their existential act by a vote that they were *building socialism,* as, to an extent, they actually were. (Addendum, 1955: In either case, they would be *building sociality.*)

"Perspective by incongruity" is a "heads I win, tails you lose" device—and we hereby lay our cards on the table by saying so. For example, take the excellent "planned incongruity" in Palme-Dutt's intellectual pun (his definition of fascism as "the organization of decay"). By the pliancy of this term, you can't lose.[1] You name the militaristic ingredients of the Nazis by italicizing one of the words: the organization of *decay.* You name the co-operative ingredients by italicizing the other: the *organization* of decay. Decay is the "essential," organization the "accidental."

We select this formula for exposure because we ourselves would wholeheartedly vote for it. Philosophers, in helping us to play Cards-face-up-on-the-table, should look for two other manifestations of the "heads I win, tails you lose" formula in their work. They should seek to discover the "master metaphor" they are employing as the cue for the organizing of their work. Thus: "man is herein to be considered a god, an ape, a machine," etc.—and I shall tell you what can be said of him by the use of this metaphor. Or, further, I shall try to help you in discovering just where I mix my metaphors and subtly shift from

---

1. When the banished Duke in *As You Like It* says his speech about the theme, "Sweet are the uses of adversity," he is carrying out a "perspective by incongruity" for "heads I win, tails you lose" purposes. While banished, he seeks the "rewards" of banishment—and when his ducal properties are restored to him at the end of the play, he is ready to resume the rewards of dukedom.

one to another. I started by saying that I would consider man as a machine, for instance, but at this strategic point you will note that I "opportunistically shift and begin discussing him as a hero (that is, a god)."

One must say why he feels called upon to choose the metaphor he does choose. We choose the "man as communicant" metaphor, for instance, because we feel that it brings out the emphases needed for handling present necessities. We modify it with the dead, mixed metaphor "bureaucratization of the imaginative" because we think that people thereby are kept from being too sensitively exposed to disillusionment as they are affronted by the "let down" that necessarily occurs when a tender imaginative-utopian possibility is implemented by being given its practical embodiment in "this imperfect world."

. . .

Transcendence

When approached from a certain point of view, A and B are "opposites." We mean by "transcendence" the adoption of another point of view from which they cease to be opposites. This is, at present, the nearest approach we can make to the process by verbal means. As a matter of fact, such verbalizations completely slight an all-important qualitative ingredient (what even the articulate French might be willing to call a *je ne sais quoi*) that makes all the difference between a true transcendence and the empty acquisition of the verbal paraphernalia.

Thus, an act might be debunkingly motivated, in efficient popular shorthand, as "sour grapes." The comic frame (halfway between the extremes of "hagiography" and "iconoclasm") should say "sour grapes plus." But one might be an unregenerate debunker, yet "take up the slack" verbally by *saying* "sour grapes plus," while his attitude was still chemically pure "sour grapes." Such simple "secular prayer" might *eventually* "redeem" him, preparing the way for "transcendence" to the comic frame. But the verbalization would not *per se* signalize the change in quality.

Primitive peoples recognize the process of transcendence in their initiation rites whereby, at different periods in the life of the individual, he is symbolically endowed with a new identity, as he enters some new corporate grouping within the tribe. The church tries to coach a similar process by its rites of communion. One discerns it behind even the crudest of hazing ceremonies, that seek to impress, by picturesqueness, terror, or wound, the sense of a new identification (a new way of defining the individual's identity with relation to a corporate identity). Purely secular, scientific investigators like Jean Piaget are concerned with it in their studies of the ways whereby the child changes from "autistic" to "socialized" thinking (or, as we might say, attempts to integrate the forensic with the pre-forensic).

Our terms "transcendence downward" and "transcendence upward" are also at best bungling approximates. If one says that a human act is done "for the greater glory of God," his euphemism is the simplest possible example of "transcendence upward." (Heretics may drive the "logic" to its extreme conclusion by deducing the theory that such "spirituality" requires as its corollary the deliberate degradation of the flesh.) "Debunking," the doctrine that a human act "is done purely for gravy," is the simplest example of "transcendence downwards." (Such naive materialism is the heretical over-doing of "dialectical materialism.")

One may "transcendentally" organize his interpretation of human motives by the following broad emphases: a human act is done for God, for an ideal (humanity, culture, justice, truth), for a corporate grouping (political or otherwise), for oneself. Historical-collectivistic emphases generally play about an intermingling of *ideal* and *corporate grouping*.

VI

SYMBOLS AND THE SOCIAL ORDER

19

Order and Hierarchy

Dramatistic Analyses of Order

Following a lead from Bergson (1907, especially chapter 4), dramatism is devoted to a stress upon the all-importance of the negative as
a specifically linguistic invention. But whereas Bergson's fertile chapter on "the idea of nothing" centers in the propositional negative ("It
is not"), the dramatistic emphasis focuses attention upon the "moralistic" or "hortatory" negative ("Thou shalt not"). Burke has applied
this principle of negativity to a cycle of terms implicit in the idea of
"order," in keeping with the fact that "order," being a polar term,
implies a corresponding idea of "disorder," while these terms in turn
involve ideas of "obedience" or "disobedience" to the "authority"
implicit in "order" (with further terministic radiations, such as the
attitude of "humility" that leads to the act of obedience or the attitude
of "pride" that leads to the act of disobedience, these in turn involving
ideas of guidance or temptation, reward or punishment, and so on).

On the side of order, or control, there are the variants of faith and
reason (faith to the extent that one accepts a given command, pro-
scription, or statement as authoritative; reason to the extent that one's
acceptance is contingent upon such proofs as are established by a
methodic weighting of doubts and rebuttals). On the side of disorder
there are the temptations of the senses and the imagination. The senses
can function as temptations to the extent that the prescribed order
does not wholly gratify our impulses (whether they are natural or a
by-product of the very order that requires their control). Similarly, the
imagination falls on the side of disorder insofar as it encourages interests inimical to the given order, though it is serviceable to order if used
as a deterrent by picturing the risks of disorder—or, in other words,
if it is kept "under the control of reason."

Midway between the two slopes of order and disorder (technically

From "Dramatism" by Kenneth Burke. Reprinted by permission of Macmillan Publishing Co. from the *International Encyclopedia of the Social Sciences,* edited by David L.
Sills, vol. 7, pp. 450–51. © 1968 by Crowell Collier and Macmillan, Inc.

the realm where one can say yes or no to a thou-shalt-not) there is an area of indeterminacy often called the will. Ontologically, action is treated as a function of the will. But logologically the situation is reversed: the idea of the will is viewed as derivable from the idea of an act.

From ideas of the will there follow in turn ideas of grace, or an intrinsic ability to make proper choices (though such an aptitude can be impaired by various factors), and sacrifice (insofar as any choices involve the "mortification" of some desires). The dramatistic perspective thus rounds out the pattern in accordance with the notion that insofar as a given order involves sacrifices of some sort, the sacrificial principle is intrinsic to the nature of order. Hence, since substitution is a prime resource available to symbol systems, the sacrificial principle comes to ultimate fulfillment in vicarious sacrifice, which is variously rationalized, and can be viewed accordingly as a way to some kind of ultimate rewards.

By tracing and analyzing such terms, a dramatistic analysis shows how the negativistic principle of guilt implicit in the nature of order combines with the principles of thoroughness (or "perfection") and substitution that are characteristic of symbol systems in such a way that the sacrificial principle of victimage (the "scapegoat") is intrinsic to human congregation. The intricate line of exposition might be summed up thus: If order, then guilt; if guilt, then need for redemption; but any such "payment" is victimage. Or: If action, then drama; if drama, then conflict; if conflict, then victimage.

Adapting theology ("words about God") to secular, empirical purposes ("words about words"), dramatistic analysis stresses the perennial vitality of the scapegoat principle, explaining why it fits so disastrously well into the "logologic" of man's symbolic resources. It aims to show why, just as the two primary and sometimes conflicting functions of religion (solace and control) worked together in the doctrines of Christianity, we should expect to find their analogues in any society. Dramatism, as so conceived, asks not how the sacrificial motives revealed in the institutions of magic and religion might be eliminated in a scientific culture, but what new forms they take (A Grammar of Motives and A Rhetoric of Motives 1962, 406–8).

This view of vicarious victimage extends the range of those manifestations far beyond the areas ordinarily so labeled. Besides extreme instances like Hitlerite genocide, or the symbolic "cleansings" sought in wars, uprisings, and heated political campaigns, victimage would include psychogenic illness, social exclusiveness (the malaise of the "hierarchal psychosis"), "beatnik" art, rabid partisanship in sports, the excessive pollution of air and streams, the "bulldozer mentality" that rips into natural conditions without qualms, the many enterprises that keep men busy destroying in the name of progress or profit the ecological balance on which, in the last analysis, our eventual well-being depends, and so on.

The strongly terministic, or logological, emphasis of dramatism would view the scapegoat principle not primarily as a survival from earlier eras, but as a device natural to language here and now. Aristotle, in the third book of his *Rhetoric* (chapter 10), particularly stresses the stylistic importance of antithesis as a means of persuasion (as when a policy is recommended in terms of what it is *against*). In this spirit dramatism would look upon the scapegoat (or the principle of vicarious victimage) as but a special case of antithesis, combined with another major resource of symbol systems, namely, substitution.

In the polemics of politics, the use of the scapegoat to establish identification in terms of an enemy shared in common is also said to have the notable rhetorical advantage that the candidate who presents himself as a spokesman for "us" can prod his audience to consider local ills primarily in terms of alien figures viewed as the outstanding causes of those ills. In accord with this emphasis, when analyzing the rhetorical tactics of *Mein Kampf*, Burke (see pp. 219) lays particular stress upon Hitler's use of such deflections to provide a "noneconomic interpretation of economic ills."

While recognizing the amenities of property and holding that "mine-ownness" or "our-ownness" in some form or other is an inevitable aspect of human congregation, dramatistic analysis also contends that property in any form sets the conditions for conflict (and hence culminates in some sort of victimage). It is pointed out that the recent great advances in the development of technological power require a corresponding extension in the realm of negativity (the "thou-shalt-nots" of control). Thus, the strikingly "positive" nature of such resources (as described in terms of "sheer motion") is viewed dramatistically as deceptive; for they may seem too simply like "promises," whereas in being *powers* they are *properties,* and all properties are *problems,* since powers are bones of contention ("Motion, Action, Words," *Teachers' College Record* [1960] 62: 244–49).

A dramatistic view of human motives thus culminates in the ironic admonition that perversions of the sacrificial principle (purgation by scapegoat, congregation by segregation) are the constant temptation of human societies, whose orders are built by a kind of animal exceptionally adept in the ways of symbolic action (*The Philosophy of Literary Form,* [1941] 1957, 87–113).

20

Terms for Order

Introduction: On *Theology* and *Logology*

If we defined "theology" as "words about God," then by "logology" we should mean "words about words." Whereupon, thoughts on the necessarily verbal nature of religious doctrines suggest a further possibility: that there might be fruitful analogies between the two realms. Thus statements that great theologians have made about the nature of "God" might be adapted *mutatis mutandis* for use as purely secular observations on the nature of *words*.

Insofar as man is the "typically symbol-using animal," it should not be surprising that men's thoughts on the nature of the divine embody the principles of verbalization. And insofar as "God" is a *formal* principle, any thorough statements about "God" should be expected to reveal the formality underlying their genius as statements. The Biblical avowal that *man* is made in *God's image* has made us wary of the reversed anthropomorphic tendency to conceive of *God* in *man's image*. But the present inquiry stands midway between those two positions, contending merely that, insofar as religious doctrine is verbal, it will necessarily exemplify its nature as verbalization; and insofar as religious doctrine is thorough, its ways of exemplifying verbal principles should be correspondingly thorough.

Hence, it should be possible to analyze remarks about the "nature of 'God,'" like remarks about the "nature of 'Reason,'" in their sheer formality as observations about the nature of language. And such a correspondence between the theological and "logological" realms should be there, whether or not "God" actually *exists*. For regardless of whether the entity named "God" exists outside his nature sheerly as key term in a system of terms, words "about him" must reveal their nature as words.

It is not within the competence of our project to decide the question either theistically or atheistically, or even agnostically. This investiga-

From *The Rhetoric of Religion*, pp. 1–3, 183–96. Reprinted by permission of The University of California Press. ©1970 by Kenneth Burke.

tion does not require us to make any decisions about the validity of theology *qua* theology. Our purpose is simply to ask how theological principles can be shown to have usable secular analogues that throw light upon the nature of language.

St. Augustine, having arrived at his Trinitarian idea of God, saw manifestations of this supernatural principle in all sorts of sheerly natural phenomena. Every triad, however secular, was for him another sign of the Trinity. For our purposes, we can be content with the analogy alone. We need not decide either with or against Augustine. For our purposes, it doesn't matter whether the supernatural Trinity is or is not made manifest in everything that Roget would list under such a variety of terms as: triad, triplet, trefoil, triangle, trident, tierce, terza, trio, trey, trinomial, triumvirate, etc., etc. We need but note that all members of the lot are analogically classifiable together by reason of their three-ness. However, as we shall try to show when we come to our study of Augustine, regardless of whether or not there is a Holy Trinity such as he postulates, the trinitarian pattern in his idea of God must be considered as a radical aspect of his psychology, though we conceived of that psychology in a purely secular sense.

As for a unitary concept of God, its linguistic analogue is to be found in the nature of any name or title, which sums up a manifold of particulars under a single head (as with the title of a book, or the name of some person or political movement). Any such summarizing word is functionally a "god-term." What, then, might be the relation between such a term and the countless details classifiable under its "unifying" head? Is there not a sense in which the summarizing term, the overall name or title, could be said to "transcend" the many details subsumed under that head, somewhat as "spirit" is said to "transcend matter"? The question indicates the ways in which the study of theology might be applied "logologically."

· · ·

Tautological Cycle of Terms for "Order"

> When reading this section, and later references to the same subject, the reader might find it helpful to consult the accompanying chart—Cycle of Terms Implicit in the Idea of "Order"—outlining the "Terministic Conditions for 'Original Sin' and 'Redemption' (intrinsic to the Idea of 'Order')."

First, consider the strategic ambiguity whereby the term "Order" may apply both to the realm of nature in general and to the special realm of human sociopolitical organizations (an ambiguity whereby, so far as sheerly empirical things are concerned, a natural order could be thought to go on existing even if all human beings, with their various sociopolitical orders, were obliterated). This is a kind of logical pun whereby our ideas of the natural order can become secretly infused by our ideas of the sociopolitical order.

One might ask: Is not the opposite possibility just as likely? Might not the terms for the sociopolitical order become infused by the genius of the terms for the natural order? They do, every time we metaphorically extend the literal meaning of a natural image to the realm of the sociopolitical. It is the point that Bentham made much of, in his Theory of Fictions, his systematic procedure ("archetypation") for locating the natural images that may lurk undetected in our ideas, and so may mislead us into attempting to deal too strictly in terms of the irrelevant image. For instance, if Churchillian rhetoric gets us to thinking of international relations in such terms as "iron curtains" and "power vacuums," then we must guard lest we respond to the terms too literally—otherwise we shall not conceive of the political situation accurately enough. The nations of the Near East are no "vacuum." Theologians have made similar observations about the use of natural images to express the idea of godhead.

But it is much more important, for our present purposes, to spot the movement in the other direction. We need to stress how a vision of the natural order can become infused with the genius of the verbal and sociopolitical orders.

Thus, from the purely logological point of view, we note how, inasmuch as the account of the Creation in Genesis involves on each "day" a kind of enactment done through the medium of God's "Word," the sheerly "natural" order contains a verbal element or principle that, from the purely empirical point of view, could belong only in the sociopolitical order. Empirically, the natural order of sheerly astrophysical motion depends upon no verbal principle for its existence. But theologically, it does depend upon a verbal principle. And even though one might say that God's creative fiats and his words to Adam and Eve are to be conceived as but *analogous* to ordinary human verbal communication, our point remains the same. For, from the empirical point of view, there would not even be an *analogy* between natural origins and responses to the power of words. The world of natural, nonverbal motions must be empirically the kind of world that could continue with its motions even if it contained no species, such as man, capable of verbal action; and it must be described without any reference to a creation by verbal fiat, whether or not there had been such.

By a dramatistic ambiguity, standard usage bridges this distinction

Cycle of Terms Implicit in the Idea of "Order"
God as Author and Authority

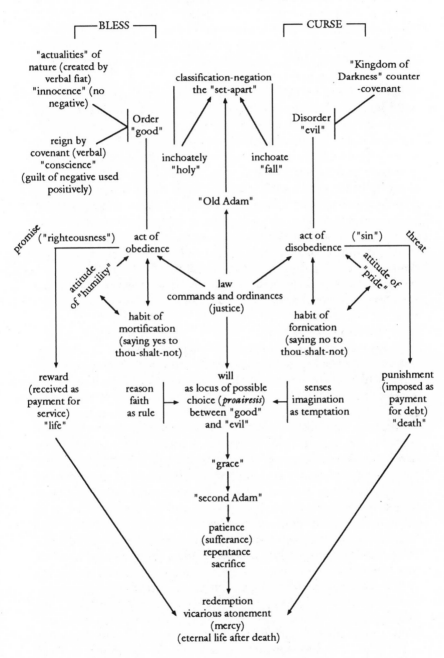

between the realms of verbal action and nonverbal motion when it speaks of sheerly natural objects or processes as "actualities." Here even in a purely secular usage we can discern a trace of the theological view that sees nature as the sign of God's action—and thus by another route we see the theological way of merging the principle of the natural order with the principle of verbal contract or covenant intrinsic to legal enactment in the sociopolitical order.

But to proceed with the "tautologies":

If, by "order," we have in mind the idea of a command, then obviously the corresponding word for the proper response would be "obey." Or, there would be the alternative, "disobey." Thus we have the proportion: order is to disorder as obedience is to disobedience. However, there is a logological sense in which the things of nature could be called "innocent." They cannot disobey commands, since they cannot understand commands. They do not have a "sense of right and wrong," or, more generically, a "sense of yes and no." They simply do as they do—and that's that. Such would be the *non posse peccare* of natural things, or even of humans insofar as their "natural" state was not bound by moralistic negatives. All was permissive in Eden but the eating of the one forbidden fruit, the single negative that set the conditions for the Fall (since, St. Paul pointed out, only the law can make sin, as Bentham was later to point out that only the law can make crime). The biblical myth pictures natural things as coming into being through the agency of God's Word; but they can merely do as they were designed to do, whereas with God's permission though not without his resentment, the seed of Adam can do even what it has been explicitly told not to do. The word-using animal not only understands a thou-shalt-not; it can carry the principle of the negative a step further, and answer the thou-shalt-not with a disobedient No. Logologically, the distinction between natural innocence and fallen man hinges about this problem of language and the negative. Eliminate language from nature, and there can be no moral disobedience. In this sense, moral disobedience is "doctrinal." Like faith, it is grounded in language.

"Things" can but *move* or *be moved.* "Persons" by definition can "act." In being endowed with words (symbols) by which they can frame responses to questions and commands, by the same token they have "responsibility."

Looking into the *act* of disobedience, we come upon the need for some such term as "pride," to name the corresponding *attitude* that precedes the act. And some such term as "humility" names the idea of the attitude that leads into the act of obedience.

But implicit in the distinction between obedience and disobedience there is the idea of some dividing line, some "watershed" that is itself midway between the two slopes. Often a word used for naming this ambiguous moment is "will," or more fully, "free will," which is thought of as a faculty that makes possible the choice between the yea-saying of humble obedience or the nay-saying of prideful disobedience (the choice between *serviam* and *non serviam*).

Ontologically, and theologically, we say that this locus of freedom makes possible the kind of personal choice we have in mind when we speak of "action." But note that, logologically, the statement should be made the other way round. That is, whereas ontologically or theologically we say that by being endowed with free will man is able to act morally, the corresponding logological statement would be: Implicit in the idea of an act is the idea of free will. (Another version of the formula would be: Implicit in the idea of an act is the idea of freedom).

The ontological and theological statements may or may not be true. The logological statement would be "true logologically" even if it were not true ontologically. That is, even if we hypothetically suppose, with strict behaviorists, cyberneticists and the like, that there is no such thing as "free will," that all "action" is reducible to terms of mechanical "motion," it would still remain true that implicit in the idea of action there is the idea of freedom. If one cannot make a choice, one is not acting, one is but being moved, like a billiard ball tapped with a cue and behaving mechanically in conformity with the resistances it encounters. But even if men are doing nothing more than that, the *word* "act" *implies* that they are doing more—and we are now concerned solely with the implications of terms.

As regards the dramatistic tautology in general, an act is done by an agent in a scene. But such an act is usually preceded by a corresponding attitude, or "incipient act" (as when an act of friendliness grows out of a friendly attitude on the part of the agent). The scene is motivational locus of the act insofar as the act represents a scene-act ratio (as, for instance, when an "emergency situation" is said to justify an "emergency measure"). But insofar as the act derives from an attitude of the agent, the agent-act ratio can be narrowed to an attitude-act ratio, as when a friendly agent does a friendly act. The term "will" is apparently designed to assign a "place" to the choice between different possibilities of attitude-act development. Here a verb is thought of as a noun; the idea of "the will" as willing is conceived after the analogy of rain raining, though we do not speak of fear as fearing. But the idea of such a locus for "the will" brings up a further problem: What in turn influences "the will"?

On the disorder side, this role is assigned to the imagination, insofar as the imagination's close connection with sensory images is thought both to make it highly responsive to the sensory appetites and to make sensory appetites more enticing. In brief, the combination of imagination and the senses, by affecting the will from the side of disorder, is said to predispose toward temptation, *except* insofar as imagination in turn is corrected from the side of order by the controls of reason and faith (which can also be thought of as having a controlling effect upon each other). Another refinement here is the notion that, once imagination is on the side of reason, it can contribute to order, rather than to disorder, by making reasonable things seem sensible, and thus inducing the wills of persons weak in reason to nonetheless freely choose, as it were reasonably, and thus to act on the side of order, eschewing temptation.

The idea of reason, in such a system, is obviously permeated with ideas of dominion, owing to its identification with ideas of control, and as indicated in the formula, "the Rule of Reason." So it brings us clearly back to the principle of sovereignty underlying the general idea of Order by Covenant. The relation between reason and faith becomes ambiguous because of the possible shift between the natural order and the sociopolitical order as grounds of reason. For if the sociopolitical order is conceived in "ultimate" terms (as it is in the idea of a Covenant derived from God), then faith must be a higher kind of control than reason, insofar as reason is identified with "Natural Law" and with purely wordly rules of governance. (Incidentally, we might note the strongly verbal element in both, as indicated by the close relation between rational and logical, and by St. Paul's statement that the doctrines of the faith are learned "by hearing." However, there is said to be a further stage of supernatural awareness, called by St. Anselm *contemplatio* and by Spinoza *scientia intuitiva,* which would, by definition, transcend the verbal.)

There is also an act-agent ratio, as with the Aristotelian notion of *hexis, habitus,* the notion that a person may develop a virtuous disposition by the practices of virtue, or a vicious disposition by repeated indulgence in vice. And this brings us to the subtlest term of all, as regards the set of major dramatistic terms clustering about the idea of order, namely:

Mortification.

Of all theology-tinged terms that need logological reclamation and refurbishment, this is perhaps the most crucial. Here the motives of sacrifice and dominion come to a head in everyday living. The possibility is that most ailments now said to be of "psychogenic" origin are but secularized variants of what might be called "mortification in spite of itself." That is, if we are right in assuming that governance makes "naturally" for victimage, either of others (homicidally) or of ourselves (suicidally), then we may expect to encounter many situations in which a man, by attitudes of self-repression, often causes or aggravates his own bodily and mental ills.

The derived meaning (humiliation, vexation, chagrin) would figure here. But mainly we have in mind the Grand Meaning, "subjection of the passions and appetites, by penance, abstinence or painful severities inflicted on the body," mortification as a kind of governance, an extreme form of "self-control," the deliberate, disciplinary "slaying" of any motive that, for "doctrinal" reasons, one thinks of as unruly. In an emphatic way, mortification is the exercising of oneself in "virtue"; it is a systematic way of saying no to disorder, or obediently saying yes to order. Its opposite is license, *luxuria*, "fornication," saying yes to disorder, or disobediently saying no to order.

The principle of mortification is particularly crucial to conditions of empire, which act simultaneously to awaken all sorts of odd and exacting appetites, while at the same time imposing equally odd and exacting obstacles to their fulfillment. For "mortification" does not occur when one is merely "frustrated" by some external interference. It must come from within. The mortified must, with one aspect of himself, be saying no to another aspect of himself—hence the urgent incentive to be "purified" by "projecting" his conflict upon a scapegoat, by "passing the buck," by seeking a sacrificial vessel upon which he can vent, as from without, a turmoil that is actually within. "Psychogenic illness" would occur in cases where one is scrupulous enough to deny oneself such easy outgoing relief, and instead, in all sorts of roundabout ways, scrupulously circles back upon himself, unintentionally making his own constitution the victim of his hierarchically goaded entanglements. At least, that's the idea.

To complete the pattern: On the side of order, where the natural actualities created by verbal fiat are completed in sovereignty and subjection by covenant, with obedience goes promise of reward (as payment for service), while on the other side goes disobedience, with threat of punishment as enforced payment for disservice.

Then comes the Grand Rounding Out, where the principle of reward as payment (from the order side) merges with the principle of punishment as payment (from the disorder side), to promise redemption by vicarious atonement. Sovereignty and subjection (the two poles of governance) are brought together in the same figure (Christ as King and Christ as Servant respectively)—and the contradiction between these principles is logically resolved by a narrative device, the notion of two advents whereby Christ could appear once as servant and the second time as king. Here is the idea of a "perfect" victim to cancel (or "cover") what was in effect the "perfect" sin (its technical perfection residing in the fact that it was the first transgression of the first man against the first and foremost authority).

However, the symmetry of the design does not resolve the problem of the "watershed moment," the puzzle of the relation between "determinism" and "free will." The search for a cause is itself the search for a scapegoat, as Adam blames Eve, Eve blames the serpent, the serpent could have blamed Lucifer, and Lucifer could have blamed the temptations implicit in the idea of order (the inchoate "fall" that, as we saw in the quotation from Coleridge, is intrinsic to the "creation of the nonabsolute"). Adam himself has a hint of the Luciferian rejoinder when he says to the Lord God that he received the fruit from "the woman whom thou gavest to be with me." Also, from the purely imagistic point of view, there is a sense in which the Lord God has caused Adam to be tempted by an aspect of himself, in accordance with the original obstetrical paradox whereby woman was born of man.

Here would be a purely "grammatical" way of stating the case: If order, implying the possibility of disorder, implies a possible *act* of disobedience, then there must be an agent so endowed, or so minded, that such an act is possible to him—and the *motives* for such an act must eventually somehow be referred to the *scene* out of which he arose, and which thus somehow contains the principles that in their way make a "bad" act possible.

Arrived at this point, we might shift the problem of the "watershed moment" to another plane, by recalling that the same conditions of divisiveness also make for the inchoately "holy," inasmuch as the Hebrew word for "holy," *qodesh*, means literally the "separate," the "set apart," as does the word *qadesh*, which means "Sodomite." This verbal tangle has often been commented on, and applies also to the New Testament word, *hagios*, which means both "holy" and "accursed," like its Latin counterpart, *sacer*. Here, we might say, is a purely terministic equivalent of the problem of choice, or motivational slope. The question of de-terminism narrows down to a kind of term that within itself contains two slopes (two different judgments or "crises").

As regards the matter of terms, we could move into the area of personality proper by equating human personality with the ability to use symbol-systems (centering in the feeling for the negative, since "reason," in its role as the "sense of right and wrong," is but a special case of the "sense of yes and no"). Thus, more broadly, we could say that the conception of the creative verbal fiat in Genesis is essentially the *personal principle*. But insofar as personal character is defined by choice (cf. Aristotle on *proairesis*[1]), the question then becomes one of deciding how far back the grounds of choice must be traced (atop the primary logological fact that the *perfection* of choice comes to a head in the formal distinction between yes and no). Insofar as Genesis would depict us as arising from a scene that is the act of a super-person, and insofar as redemption is thought to be got by voluntary enlistment on the side of order, conceived sacrificially, then the ultimate formula becomes that of Jeremiah 31:18: "Turn thou me, and I shall be turned" (*converte me, et convertar*). Here the indeterminate watershed of "free" choice is reducible to a question of this sort: Though all men are given enough "grace" to be saved, how can anyone be saved but by being given enough grace to be sure of using it? Yet how could he have as much saving grace as that, without in effect being *compelled* to be saved (in which case he would not, in the last analysis, have "free will")?

Fortunately, it is not our duty, as logologers, to attempt solving this ultimate theological riddle, entangled in ideas of providence, predestination, and the possibilities of an elect, chosen from among the depraved, all of whom deserve eternal damnation, but some of whom are saved by God in his mysterious mercy, and may attest to their future glory by becoming a kind of materially prosperous elite here and now (or at least by being able to answer without question).

Fortunately, as logologers, we need but consider the ways in which such ideas are interwoven with the conditions of dominion, as they prevail among human symbol-using animals. As seen in this light, the thought of all such issues leads us to revision of our initial dialectical pattern. That is, the order-disorder pair is not enough. And what we need now is another kind of antithesis, setting order against counter-order.

Methodologically, we might say that we have now come upon the penalties resulting from our earlier decision to approach this problem in terms of "order" rather than in terms of "covenant." For the idea of a "counter-covenant" would have been somewhat different from the idea of such a mere disintegration as is usually suggested by the term "disorder."

In sum, there is a notable qualitative difference between the idea of a mere "fall" from a position in which one still believes but to which one is at times unequal, and the idea of a deliberate turn to an alter-

1. *Poetics*, VI, 24.

native allegiance. It would be a difference between being "weak in virtue" and being "strong in sin."

But perhaps we should try to sum up the line of reasoning we have been pursuing in these last paragraphs. We have been considering the problem of a possible ultimate ground for "temptation." Logologically, "temptation" is but a tautological aspect of the idea of "order." It is grounded in the idea of a verbal command, which by its very nature contains possibilities of both obedience and disobedience. We don't "command" the nonverbalizing things of nature. To the best of our ability, we simply set up conditions which we think likely to bring about the kind of situation we desire. We reserve our commands (or requests!) for language-using entities that can, to varying degrees, resist. And the command is backed, explicitly or implicitly, by promises or threats. However:

Ontologically, or theologically, such a purely "tautological" point of view would not be enough. And we confront such problems as St. Augustine was concerned with, in his battles with the Manichaeans. We may, like the Manichaeans, conceive of an ultimate Tempter, existing in his own right, and with powers rivaling those of God. Or we may derive everything from a God who is by definition merciful, and good, the author of a wholly good creation, yet who not only lets man sin, but permits the existence and incessant schemings of a supernatural tempter endowed with diabolical ingenuity and persuasiveness. Hence arises the "problem of evil" (as with Augustine's urgent question, "*Unde malum?*"). We have considered in the previous talk how Augustine proposed to solve the problem theologically by his notion of evil as a "deficient cause," a kind of "eclipse."

But logologically, the question takes on a different form. Logologically, moral "evil" is a species of *negative,* a purely linguistic (or "rational") principle. And insofar as natural calamities are viewed in terms of moral retribution, we should say that the positive events of nature are being seen through the eyes of moral negativity (another instance of ways whereby the genius of the verbal and sociopolitical orders can come to permeate our ideas of the natural order). All told, "evil" is implicit in the idea of "order" because "order" is a polar, or dialectical term, implying an idea of "disorder."

But there can be two kinds of "disorder": (1) a tendency toward failure to obey completely always; (2) disobedience due to an out-and-out enrollment in the ranks of a rival force. We might call this a distinction between mere disorder and deliberate allegiance to a counterorder. (There is an analogous situation in contemporary politics, since a person's disagreements with those in authority may be interpreted either as temperamental deviation from the prevailing orthodoxy or as sinister, secret adherence to an organized enemy alien power.)

Theologically, perhaps the analogous distinction would be between the kind of "temptation" that is intrinsic to the possibility of choice and the kind that attains its ideal perfection in the notion of a Faustian pact with the Devil—the difference between ordinary "backsliding" and "heresy" or "black magic." In Joyce's *Portrait*, it would correspond to the distinction between Stephen's sexual fall despite himself in the second section, and his deliberate choice of a "proud" aesthetic calling, as "priest of the imagination," in section four. Problems of "predestination" lie in the offing, inasmuch as different people are differently tempted or differently enlightened, and such differences are not of their own choosing but arise in connection with the accidents of each man's unique, particular destiny. (In the *Confessions*, for instance, we see St. Augustine interpreting as God's will many decisions which he had made for quite different personal reasons. And no man could sell his soul to the Devil, if God—who was necessarily present at the signing of the contract—but chose that moment to flood the victim's imagination with the full realization of his danger.)

At this point, we should look at Hobbes's *Leviathan*, since it illustrates so well the idea of disorder in this more aggressive sense, of a covenant matched by a "counter-covenant." And in the course of doing so, it well illustrates the role of the sacrificial principle which we believe to be "logologically inseparable" from the idea of dominion.

21

Sin and Redemption

Aspects of the Scapegoat in Reidentification

Since the symbolic transformation involves a sloughing off, you may expect to find some variant of killing in the work. (I treat indictment, vituperation, vindictiveness against a "villain," etc., as attenuated aspects of this same function.) So we get to the "scapegoat," the "representative" or "vessel" of certain unwanted evils, the sacrificial animal upon whose back the burden of these evils is ritualistically loaded. He becomes "charismatic" (if we may incongruously extend this word beyond the purely "benign" category into the "malign" category). We are now brought into the area of tragedy, the "goat-song"—and may profitably recall that, whereas in primitive societies, the purifying function could be ritualistically delegated to an animal, as societies grew in social complexity and sophistication, the tendency was to endow the sacrificial animal with social coordinates, so that the goat became replaced by the "sacrificial King."

This vessel, delegated to the rôle of sacrifice, must obviously be "worthy" of sacrifice. A few basic strategies for making him so may be listed:

(1) He may be made worthy legalistically (i.e., by making him an offender against legal or moral justice, so that he "deserves" what he gets).

(2) We may make him worthy by leading toward sacrifice fatalistically (as when we so point the arrows of the plot that the audience comes to think of him as a marked man, and so prepares itself to relinquish him). Portents, auguries, meteorological omens, and prophecies have regularly been thus used for functional purposes—while the transition into the sacrifice may often employ an intermingling of this second kind of worthiness with the first, as when the Greek dramatists reinforced the fatalistic operations with a personal flaw, *hubris*, punishable pride, the pride that goes before a fall.

From *The Philosophy of Literary Form*, pp. 39–51. Reprinted by permission of The University of California Press. © 1973 by The Regents of the University of California.

(3) We may make him worthy by a subtle kind of poetic justice, in making the sacrificial vessel "too good for this world," hence of the *highest* value, hence the *most perfect* sacrifice (as with the Christ theme, and its secular variants, such as little Hanno Buddenbrooks, whose exceptional sensitivity to music made him worthy to be sacrificed to music).

Incidentally, when thinking of the sacrificial vessel from this point of view, we get a much more charitable explanation of the Oedipus complex than is usually given in psychoanalytic doctrine. That is, we should not have to consider the child's dream of a parent's death as symbolizing simply the child's desire for the parent's removal, as a rival for affection. In many cases, at least, such a dream might well symbolize some *fear of personal disaster* on the child's part, while the child in its dream places the burden of this fear upon the protective parent, whose shoulders are more able to bear it (the parent having already become identified with such a protective rôle). Rivalries might also enter, to reinforce such a solution with "legalistic" or "rationalized" ingredients, without thereby being the sole ingredient in the recipe of motivation.

We should also note that a change of identity, *to be complete from the familistic point of view,* would require nothing less drastic than the *obliteration of one's whole past lineage.* A total rebirth would require a change of *substance;* and in the overlapping realm of familistic and causal ancestry ("like father like son" and the "genetic fallacy" of evaluating a thing in terms of its causal descent) a thorough job of symbolic rebirth would require the revision of one's ancestral past itself—quite as mystics hold that in becoming wholly transformed one not only can alter the course of the future but can even remake the past (the crudest act of this sort being such revision of the past as we get in official Nazi historiography). Hence, from this point of view, we might interpret symbolic parricide as simply an extension of symbolic suicide, a more thoroughgoing way of obliterating the substance of one's old identity—while, as we have said before, this symbolic suicide itself would be but *one* step in a process which was not completed until the substance of the abandoned identity had been replaced by the new substance of a new identity. Hitler's voting himself a "blood stream" distinct from that of the Hebrew patriarchs is a symbolic transubstantiation of this sort—while an attentuated social variant or reidentification is to be seen in the legal adoption of a new family name, or in pseudonyms, *noms de plume,* secret lodge names, etc.

Applying such a calculus to the interpretation of symbolic incest in much modern literature, we should have cause to admonish against a view of it as simply the symbolization of incestuous desire. Sometimes it may well be just that. But until such an interpretation is forced upon us by many other aspects of the plot's imagery, we might do well to watch for a totally different possibility: that symbolic incest is often but a roundabout mode of self-engrossment, a narcissistic independence, quite likely at the decadent end of individualism, where the poet is but expressing in sexual imagery a pattern of thought that we might call simply "communion with the self," and is giving this state of mind concrete material body in the imagery of sexual cohabitation with someone "of the same substance" as the self.

Such an explanation seems particularly applicable to the plays of O'Neill prior to his return to the collective frame of the Catholic Church. In the earlier plays, as a *renegade* Catholic, he symbolized tangential states of mind, homeless individualists who had broken "free," and in the immaturity of their freedom were usually infused with satanism (the character that prays to the Dynamo in *Dynamo*, for instance, is but making obeisance to the Catholic Devil, thus materialistically refurbished). In *Macro Millions* there is a homecoming, but it is cynical and brutal; no adequate home. In *Mourning Becomes Electra* we see most clearly the ways in which symbolic incest merges into self-engrossment, with Lavinia at the end throwing out the flowers and closing the shutters, the thorough dramatization of a turning inwards. In *The Hairy Ape* we see this narcissistic quality, without the roundabout complications of symbolic incest, as the lonely, quarrelsome individual, Yank, on confronting the Hairy Ape (his *alter ego* who is but a drastically efficient reflection of himself), proclaims their identity of substance ("Ain't we both members of de same club—de Hairy Apes?"), gives the Ape the "secret grip" ("Come on, Brother. . . . Shake—de secret grip of our order")—whereupon the Ape embraces him ("Hey, I didn't say kiss me")—and in this embrace Yank dies. (We might here introduce, as relevant gloss on this death, a sentence from "Three Revolutions in Poetry," by Cleanth Brooks, Jr., *The Southern Review*, Autumn, 1935: "He [F. C. Prescott] shows that the verb 'to die' was used in the seventeenth century with the meaning 'to experience the consummation of the sexual act.'" The structure of the plot in *The Hairy Ape* gives cause to believe that O'Neill is drawing upon a similar ambiguity, though doubtless without any intention of borrowing from a seventeenth-century usage, or probably without even knowledge of it, but arriving at it by the same associated processes, linking bodily and mental events, through which the pun originally arose.)

The incest motif also appears in Joyce's recent work, *Finnegans*

Wake. And here also I should want to interpret it not on its face value but as a narcissistic pattern dramatized in the idiom of sexual imagery. And I should be led here to place this interpretation upon the imagery because of its bearing upon the whole nature of Joyce's aesthetic. Language, of all things, is most public, most collective, in its substance. Yet Joyce has methodically set about to produce a private language, a language that is, as far as possible, the sheer replica of inturning engrossments. His medium is of the identical substance with himself—and with this medium he communes, devoting his life to the study of its internalities. Hence, the whole quality of his efforts would admonish us to look for such union of same substance with same substance as would be perfectly conveyed in the imagery of incest. Joyce seems to have taken the last step into chemical perfection, by symbolizing a homosexual incest, the identity of substance thus gaining its ultimate symmetry.[1]

Applying in another way this same general strategy of motivation (i.e., interpreting the malign as an inferior idiom of the benign, rather than interpreting the benign as the malign deceptively refurbished): we might note that the elements which the scapegoat process draws upon seem to be variants of a response essentially *charitable*. I have in mind the sense of *familistic consubstantiality* by which parents take personal gratification in noting the delight of their child, when the child has been given some plaything or is engrossed in some event. The child is at once *outside* them and *of* them, so that their pleasure by identification could not properly be called either wholly self-regarding or wholly extra-regarding. Their act is as much a *giving* as an *appropriation*. It is a giving *from* them, whatever may be its satisfactions *to* them.

1. This theory might throw some light upon exogamy among primitive tribes, a practice accompanied by concepts of incest that seem to our culture arbitrary. The savage considers incestuous any cohabitation with anyone who shares his totem, though there is no blood relationship involved. It is almost as though we were to call it incest if a man and woman of the same church, lodge, or political party cohabited. Now, in primitive tribes the individual very closely identifies himself with all members of the clan having the same totem. The whole clan is "consubstantial." Hence, he could "avoid himself" only by copulation with the partaker of a different totemic substance. Sexual union with a member of his own totem would be a "cohabitation or communion with the self." However, this theory is not offered as an alternative to economic explanations of exogamy, but as a theory of the psychological processes that go with the economic ones. So also with the period of servitude that accompanied marriage into another clan. Such marriage would require a change of identity, hence the elements of regression and guilt that go with symbolic rebirth. And the period of servitude, explainable economically as a form of purchase, would function psychologically as a symbolic redemption of guilt.

Similarly, the delegation of one's burden to the sacrificial vessel of the scapegoat is a giving, a socialization, albeit the socialization of a loss, a transference of something, deeply within, devoutly a part of one's own self—and perhaps in its relation to consubstantiality it draws more from the attitude of child to parent than from the attitude of parent to child. It delegates the personal burden to an external bearer, yet the receiver of this burden possesses consubstantiality with the giver, a pontification that is contrived (where the scapegoat is the "bad" father) by objectively attributing one's own vices or temptations to the delegated vessel.

An *explicit ritual* of such transference may, paradoxically, often be the best way of protecting the individual from the deceptions of this pseudoscientific objectivity. For in explicit ritual, the vessel is *formally appointed;* but in its concealed pseudoscientific variants, where one's vices are simply "projected" upon the scapegoat, and taken literally to be an objective, absolute, nonfunctional, intrinsic attribute of the scapegoat (a "scientific fact" about the scapegoat's "true nature"), there is less incentive to *discounting.* A ritualistic scapegoat is felt both *to have* and *not to have* the character formally delegated to it—but a pseudoscientific scapegoat, endowed by "projection" without an explicit avowal of the process, is felt purely and simply *to have* the assigned character. We may discount the ritualistic scapegoat by knowing that there is an element of mummery in the process of transference; but pseudoscientific projection suggests no discount: the scapegoat is taken to possess intrinsically the qualities we assign to it.

The Sacrifice and the Kill

We should also note an important ambiguity in the scapegoat as a "suppurating" device (that brings the evil "to a head"). I refer to an ambiguity of sacrifice and kill. In the sacrifice there is a kill; in the kill there is a sacrifice. But one or the other of this pair may be stressed as the "essence" of the two. Hemingway, for instance, stresses the *kill* in the purifying rôle played by the sacrificial animal, as against the stress upon the *sacrifice* in the story of Christ. In both Hemingway and Malraux we get the kill as the act from which the purified vision follows. (We may perceive the distinction by contrasting the assassination in the opening pages of "Man's Fate" with the slaying of the uncle in *Hamlet,* where the play deals with a *long and cautious preparation for the kill,* with insight dramatically deduced from the *initiation* rather than from the *act.* Perhaps *Macbeth* is closer to the contemporary emphasis, as *Hamlet* was closer to the modalities of liberalism; indeed, we might call Hamlet the "perfect liberal Christ" whose agony inaugurated the liberal era.)

In the pattern of the Crucifixion itself, we find Christ surrounded by two criminals. Should we treat this merely as an instance of what Trotsky would call an "amalgam" (i.e., a stratagem for visually and dramatically saying, in effect, "The so-called King of the Jews is to be put in the same class with men obviously and unequivocally criminal")? Or should we not, even if we hypothetically granted that this was the motivation on the part of the local authorities who were behind the crucifixion, attribute its duration throughout nearly two thousand years of tradition to a much more deep-lying appeal? To me, the design suggests a featuring of good, with the threat of evil about the edges (a dramatically or dialectically contrasting frame that "points up" the goodness by "polarity"). But in our contemporary modes, we often find the design retained with the positions reversed: in the "criminal Christs" of gangster stories and "hard-boiled" fiction, it is the evil that is featured, with promise of good as the frame. These various forms of disreputable character "die that we may live." And the Hemingway emphasis upon the kill implicit in the sacrifice seems to be a variant of this reversed design. The sacrificial bulls and wild game die in behalf of the slayer (dying that he may "live more intensely").[2]

2. In *Attitudes Toward History* (Vol. II, footnote, pp. 13–15) I propose a distinction between "factional" and "universal" tragedy that has bearing upon the scapegoat device as employed in a *politicalized* setting. In comparing and contrasting Mann's early "universal" tragedy, *Death in Venice*, with his later factional tragedy, "Mario and the Magician" (where the guilt is not that of "Everyman," but is dissociatively relegated to the fascist enemy), I tried to show that the later work is the earlier one rewritten. In Aeschylus we seem to find this order of development reversed. It is in an earlier play, his *Persae*, that we find "factional" tragedy (the crime of *hubris* being attributed to Xerxes, the royal representative of the political enemy). Later, the crime is removed from a politicalized to a universalized setting, becoming the temptation of Everyman.

A critic has recently used a similar mode of analysis in a polemic article on Hemingway, noting that the Hemingway of the hunt and the bull-fight mode shared sympathetically in the misfortunes of the sacrificed, whereas in his later political mode the fascist enemy takes over the rôle of quarry, and the poet confronts them from without, wholly antagonistically. By this approach, the political opposition becomes interpreted as a mere "rationalization" of cruelty, a façade of social purpose concealing in more "justified" guise the same sadistic impulses.

The whole problem of the scapegoat, I submit, is still not charted thoroughly enough to be exploited thus simply for polemic or vindictive ends. At least, not until the critic has explicitly stated and explicitly disposed of an alternative account, that might run thus: The poet, in enlisting his services in the cause of the Loyalists in Spain, had perfectly rational grounds for his choice; but in the course of elaborating a poetic act that symbolized this enlistment, he necessarily drew on methods he had developed in the

We are now in the thick of the problem of criminality in general, as it applies to the devices of tragedy and purification. A tragedy is not profound unless the poet *imagines* the crime—and in thus imagining it, he symbolically commits it. Similarly, insofar as the audience participates in the imaginings, it also participates in the offense. So we get Mann's "sympathy with the abyss," Gide's suggestion that in "thou shalt not" there is implicit "what would happen if . . . ," Hopkins' "tykishness," or Goethe's statement that the poet contains the capacity for all crime. We also discern the same concern behind Coleridge's distinction between "innocence" and "virtue," with the latter and more mature of these two states being possible only by reason of temptation.

However, though we may say that the tragic dramatist, to write an ideal tragedy, must meet the crime halfway (or that no work on the Crucifixion is complete unless the poet and the audience vicariously assist in the crucifying), this is far from vowing us to a simple psychoanalytic interpretation to the effect that the poet merely "sublimates" his criminality by aesthetic subterfuge. I have seen consternation on people's faces, for instance, when I have suggested that Mann contains within his work all the errors to which the Nazis are prone. The remark is but preparation for a very important revision, namely: *He contains them, but encompasses them within a wider frame—and as so encompassed, they act entirely differently than they would if "efficiently" isolated in their "purity."* They are but part of a wider configuration, and their function in this wider configuration is not at all the same function as they would have, if not thus harnessed.[3]

---

past. The selection of the fascist as enemy scapegoat would, by this interpretation, be not "rationalized" (in the psychoanalytic sense of the term), but *rational*. That is, the fascist was, in the most objective sense of the term, an enemy.

The matter is further complicated, in the religious sphere, by the fact that, whereas on its face, the emphasis upon the sacrifice is much superior to the emphasis upon the kill, in the dialectic of concrete historical situations important matters of *insignia* figure. Both history and anthropology supply us with plenty of instances in which a priesthood has exploited the sounder method for malign purposes (in consciously or unconsciously so interweaving it with essentially unrelated structures of ownership and special privilege that in actual practice its function becomes the very reverse of a religious one). The result is alienation and anguish that may lead, by the simplifications of dialectical pressure, to the adoption of a counter-method (saying in effect, in the words with which Virginia Woolf ended an early story: "You go this way; alas! I go that"). When the Devil quotes scripture, poets try to avoid the ambiguity by a Black Mass (B having replaced A, they would make amends by having A replace B).

3. There is, however, a pattern in Mann's work that must increasingly give him trouble, if he continues with the Joseph story. I refer to the nature of his irony, which is

Obviously, vicarious crime requires vicarious modes of expiation. William Troy has called attention to the fact that, in the case of Lawrence, the score is settled by the poet's offering of himself as the victim, as sacrificial king-god (which is more commendable as efficiency than as modesty). I have heard a writer of fiction state a somewhat similar aesthetic position; it is her task, she told me, to undergo great discomfort in the pains of composition, that readers may in their reading be comforted.

Another variant is seen in the many strategies of satanism, the "Byronic" line that we see emerging in Milton, and that is handed down through Coleridge, Poe, Baudelaire, Rimbaud, and Gide (with novelists like Stendhal and Dostoevsky also to be included). Its purest form is perhaps revealed in the old heresy of the Iscariotae, who maintained that Judas, rather than Christ, should be our primary object of worship; for if the human race was given the possibility of redemption by the sacrifice of Christ, it was Judas' act of betrayal that brought about this sacrifice—and Christ is now with the Father, whereas Judas, for his rôle in the redemption of man, damned himself to rot in eternal hell. Gide's ingeniously perverted scrupulosity has perhaps given us

---

most clearly revealed in his early story, "Tonio Kröger." Here the form is constructed about a flat antithesis between "bourgeois" and "Bohemian," with Tonio Kröger's sympathies directly contrary to his position. When he is among the burghers, he thinks yearningly of Bohemia; when he is among the Bohemians, his nostalgic vote is for the burghers.

Applying this ironic ambiguity to Mann's present situation, we are led to suspect a predicament of this sort: That Mann would be more likely to continue his Joseph story from an anti-Nazi point of view if he had remained in Germany than in his present situation as exile. For insofar as the Tonio Kröger pattern of irony is characteristic of his method, his situation as an exile would dispose him towards a greater measure of interpretation from the Nazi point of view; i.e., with an *anti-Semitic* emphasis.

Whatever may be Mann's method as an imaginative writer, however, we know that, as a citizen, a critic, a writer of hortatory political pamphlets, he is wholly the liberal in his attitude towards anti-Semitism. Hence, he would seem to have a choice between leaving the Joseph story unfinished or radically altering his characteristic mode of irony this late in life (for it is unthinkable that he would consent to go on with the story in terms of a Nazi perspective). Incidentally, since I first thought of this problem in strategy, I have been told that Mann has written a piece to "Bruder Hitler" (which would be translatable, in our present coordination, as "consubstantial Hitler"). I have not seen the piece, and the rumor may be inaccurate, but the rumor goes that it is written in a mood of amicable cajolery. If this is the case, it would seem to be an attempt, on Mann's part, to retain his earlier pattern while modifying it for the exigencies of his present situation. Another response may be noted in his turn to *The Beloved Returns,* a theme politically ambiguous, in that Goethe's love affair can be shared by Nazis and anti-Nazis alike.

some of the most interesting variations on this theme, culminating in his great sympathy with the *fils naturel* as the ideal type (the man of guilt-laden substance, like Lafcadio, whose father is vague, but whose mother was on surprisingly intimate terms with a surprisingly large number of "uncles"—precisely the familistic rôle that the Elizabethans, with their strong sense of feudalistic identity, would select for their "villains").

Perhaps the most normal mode of expiation is that of socialization (the "socialization of losses"). So the church founded the notion of brotherhood on the concept of original sin, the preoccupational basis of a guild of the guilty (such expressions as "misery loves company," "all in the same boat," "all doing the same" will suggest the motivating basis here). And the patriot may slay for his country, his act being exonerated by the justice of serving his group. I do not see how we could categorically accept or reject the strategy of expiation by the socialization of losses. In different concrete social textures, there are different modes of such socialization, with varying degrees of accuracy and scope. The gangster who slays an informer to protect his gang (i.e., out of *loyalty*) enacts this strategy just as truly as would the revolutionary emancipator, like Washington or Lenin. Thus, the strategy could not be categorically approved or condemned, but would require a place in a ladder or *hierarchy* of such strategies.[4]

4. In Schumann, we see a variant of the socializing strategy, in his fiction of a Bund, the *Davidsbündler,* in league with him against the Philistines. Here he socialized his sense of persecution by the notion of an imaginary union against a common enemy. Subsequently, in nervous exhaustion, he fell under the obsession of one relentlessly persistent note that pursued him like a gadfly, never ceasing its drastic oneness. (As the sacred syllable AUM was felt, by the mystic, to sum up all existence in a benign oneness, so we got here a reversed malign counterpart, concentrating all evil into a single vessel of sound.) In anguish, he turned to self-destruction, his own disintegration being the only "solution" for such perfect integration on the part of "the enemy."

Mystic theories of immediate communion between the Self as microcosm and the Universe as macrocosm (between the Self as a Universe *in parvo* and the Universe as the Self writ large) may lead to another variant of malignity in the socializing strategy. Where this communion is *direct* (i.e., felt to be without the intervention of institutions or other persons) we may get, through merger of subject and object, a merging of the two "secrets," the secret of the unutterable Self and the Enigma of the Universe. Here the vessel of the private secret has intercourse with the vessel of the universal secret. Hence, the Universe being conceived after the analogy of the private Self, and the private secret being guilt-laden, the Universe itself may become guilt-laden.

22

Ideology and Myth

As a first rough approximate, we might use this proportion: "Ideology is to myth as rhetoric is to poetry." The formula is valid at least to the extent that ideology points more in the direction of rhetoric, myth more in the direction of poetry. But rhetoric itself, to heighten its effectiveness, often adapts the resources of poetry; and there are in myth many kinds of inducement typical of poetry.

Ideology, like rhetoric, gravitates to the side of ideas (the term originally referred to systems of ideas considered *in themselves* without reference to external factors); and myth, like poetry, gravitates to the side of image. But perhaps Nazi pageantry had something to do with the fact that we so often class political ideas under the heading of "myth," since the Nazi showmen were so skilled in using imagery and ritual to reenforce the appeal of their political ideology. But we can see the overlap between idea and image quickly enough, if we think, for instance, of the invitation to treat of international affairs in terms of life-lines, soft underbellies, iron curtains, and power vacuums. Are such expressions "ideas" or "images," rhetoric or poetry? Are they ideological or mythic?

An ideology, in the sense with which we are concerned, is, according to the Larousse, "the system of ideas that constitute a political or social doctrine and inspire the acts of a government or party." In the news recently, I have seen such applications as these: "It is dangerous to unify under any ideology a belligerent people like the Germans." . . . The C.I.O. was said to be embarrassed by "the ideological division of the liberal forces of the country." . . . Starvation "renders a people an uneasy prey to any ideology, however evil, which bears with it life-sustaining food." . . . The so-called Greek Communists "have little ideological knowledge of what communism is." . . . Most crime and neurosis "comes not from the inheritance of instincts, but from the transmission of false rationalizations and ideologies." . . . "Life-negating ideologies . . . are the basis of dictatorships." And Freud

From "Ideology and Myth," *Accent Magazine* 7 (Summer 1947): 195–205. Reprinted by permission of Charles Shattuck for *Accent Magazine*.

should be rebuked when he began "to create justifications for an ascetic ideology."

Also, I heard a poignant reference to the word over the radio when a returned reporter was telling of his travels through the small European countries invaded by Germany. Among the natives whom he asked about their attitude toward the United States, he repeatedly heard the charge that "we refuse to treat them as people with problems" and "too often miss the people for the ideology."

This last item is particularly poignant because, as regards our international dealings, the nearest approach to "reality" available for most of us is through the radio and press. Thus we almost necessarily use "ideological" terms when thinking of other nations and of our policies regarding them.

But none of these examples clearly reveals the most important feature of an "ideology," as viewed from what people now generally call the "semantic" point of view. So let us take a closer look, this time as a statement by Thomas Hamilton, chief United Nations reporter for the *New York Times:*

> "I think that the American people will do themselves and the world a disservice if they allow their dealings with Russia to be controlled by ideological considerations, if they put it on the basis that we're a democracy and Russia totalitarian," he said.
>
> "Ideologies are brought in afterwards to support views taken because of national interests," he added.

Mr. Hamilton is here admonishing us along Benthamite lines. He is telling us to view "ideals" in terms of the "material interests" behind them. Such idealizations Bentham called "eulogistic coverings," or "fig leaves of the mind."

But note how, even while admonishing us correctly in one respect, Mr. Hamilton's proposal that we look for the "national interests" hidden behind the ideological facade may mislead us in another respect. For it automatically, spontaneously, invites us to think of "national interests" as the ultimate term of analysis here. We are left to assume that, once we locate the "national interests" behind a particular ideological pretension, we have got to the basic truth of the matter.

But if we more closely scrutinize the term "national" itself, we find it splitting. It can be an adjective applying to all the nation collectively. Or it can refer to some particular citizen, or corporate enterprise, operating abroad.

Obviously, there may be many situations in which these two kinds of interest might be identical. But there are other situations in which they are drastically at odds. The special protection of a *national's* interests might run counter to the *nation's* interests. To avoid argument over facts, I'll illustrate the point by a purely hypothetical case. A *nation* occupies another nation's territory at the cost, say of *five* billion dollars. This period of occupation enables a certain small group of its *nationals* to make a profit of *one* billion dollars. All other things being equal, here would be a loss to the nation as a whole which was a gain to the special body of nationals profiting by this loss. Here would be a case where the concept of "national interest" must, for accuracy, be split into two concepts. And a usage which failed to make this distinction on occasions that required it might be called "ideological."

We can think of cases where the "ideological" confusion would be quite unconscious and unintentional, obscuring a distinction which neither the speaker nor his audience was aware of. Or we can think of cases where it was deliberately used by the speaker, as a way of inducing us to identify some national's interests with the nation's interests though he himself knew they were at odds.

A similar ideological ambiguity, though not lending itself quite so neatly to analysis, is in the identifying of religion with one particular property structure, or political or economic system. In a report of the Conference on the Church and Economic Life, convened by the Federal Council of Churches of Christ in America *New York Times,* February 21, 1947), we read:

> Property represents a trusteeship under God, and it should be held subject to the needs of the community. Under Christian perspectives no single current system of ownership universally meets this test. In fields where the present forms of ownership are difficult to regulate for the common welfare, consideration should be given to further experimentation in the forms of private, cooperative, and public ownership.

And again:

> The Christian Church must never assume that the practical meaning of its basic teachings can be crystallized once for all. The Church cannot provide blue-prints; it can give perspective. Christianity is not to be identified with any particular economic system. It is profoundly dedicated to economic justice and order but not to any one form of achieving these.

And again:

> Profits are characteristic of a money economy and are thoroughly defensible, subject to proper methods of accumulating and distributing them. The profit motive is a further question, concerned more directly with the motives and aspirations of men. Christians must be actuated more largely by a service motive than by a profit motive.

You will note that there is no ideological confusion at all in these statements. The dissociation of ideas is explicit. Yet we have often encountered cases where the devout are encouraged or allowed to believe that some one economic system is flatly related to another as the godly is to the godless. Or there might be an "ideological" deception lurking in a case where a churchgoer's main interest was in the profit motive, yet he verbalized it in terms of a "service motive."

Karl Mannheim's *Ideology and Utopia* is exhaustively concerned with such ambiguities. He sees them lurking in terminologies that would stabilize the *status quo,* thereby giving special comfort to the ruling groups that profited most by these conditions. And he attributes the same one-sidedness to terminologies that would prod men to action by their promissory, futuristic nature. He calls the first kind "ideologies," the second "utopias"; but the distinction is hard to maintain: a "utopia" that comes to prevail, by the same token becomes an "ideology."

Mannheim's notion is that, in the clash of the various ideologies and utopias, their advocates can unmask one another's strategic ambiguities—and from this conflict as a whole there can emerge, as with the development toward truth got by the competing kinds of opinion in a Platonic dialogue, a body of true distinctions and analytic methods which he would call a "sociology of knowledge." But we can easily think of that too being called an "ideology," particularly by someone who wanted, for his basic terminology of human motives, such a resonantly imaginative and poetic synthesis as we find rather in religious or cosmic myths.

The author sees his doctrine through to the point where he asks whether its very success might defeat it. For with the general clarification that would derive from "the unmasking of ideologies," and with the "complete disappearance of the utopian element from society as a whole," where would the goad to action come from? The "complete elimination of reality-transcending elements from our world would lead to a 'matter-of-factness' which ultimately would mean the decay of the human will."

Mannheim has here come upon an ultimate question that tugs at the edges of his method. By playing ideologies against one another, he has built up a science that transcends their factionalism. Yet his motives were derived from this same factionalism. Hence, as soon as he thinks of faction as transcended, he can find no further source of motives.

Here obviously is the place for "myth" to enter. For there are two ways of transcending political faction. There is the way of Mannheim's "sociology of knowledge," which would still think in political and social terms, using them in ways that were developed from the mutual "unmaskings" of the rival advocates. Or there could be another way: by using terms that were not strictly social or political at all, but moved to another plane. This would be the step from "ideology" to "myth."

A handy book to consider at this stage is J. A. Stewart's *Myths of Plato,* treating of myth in terms of the traditional battle between faith and reason. It is particularly good for our purposes because the Platonic dialogue is often composed of two elements, the Myth and the "argumentative conversation" which we might consider as an "ideology," at least in its original sense (of ideas being considered systematically in themselves). Also there is the strongly ideological nature of the political idea in works like *The Republic.*

The Platonic myth, Stewart reminds us, is not merely illustrative. It does not arrest the movement of the dialogue, but sustains it "at a crisis, on another plane." It has the effect of "revelation." And it takes us from the order of reason to the order of imagination.

Stewart sees the highest purpose of poetry in the communication of "transcendental feeling," and we might define this technically, as the sense of oneness with the universe in which the individual's being is grounded. We derive faith from this vital force, which needs no "argument" or "reason" to account for living. The mere "vegetative" desire to live is itself an implicit judgment that life is worth living; and since the "Good" is, in the rational vocabulary, the common word for all objects of desire, the unitary vision of "The Good" is thus the replica, in ideal terms, of this underlying "vegetative" certainty. Here, then, is the "mythic" ground of reason, itself beyond reason.

Maybe yes, maybe no. We are here considering the matter dialectically, or lexicologically, rather than as a matter of belief. We are merely trying to indicate the point at which the "ideological" gives way before the "mythic." And here is where *ideological* purpose should move on to, or back to, a grounding in *mythic* purpose. Another way of saying it is that political or social motives cannot be ultimate, since they must in turn be grounded in motives outside or beyond the political or social, as these words are used in the restricted sense.

Before allowing ourselves to become too exalted about the mythic "transcendental feeling," however, we should remember that all such transcending of local political ideologies can itself be interpreted as an ideology. Though I would certainly not subscribe to everything in David Winspear's work on *The Genesis of Plato's Thought*, it does make some very just and suggestive remarks about Plato's aristocratic politics, conservatively opposed to the rising class of business men. Even a concern with something so broadly universal as "myth" may be a special cultural manifestation of certain economic classes; hence in certain important respects it may reflect their particular kind of class consciousness and class unconsciousness—and these ethical and esthetic elements, as seen from without, from another perspective, may themselves be "unmasked" as "ideological."

By moving from sociology to philosophy, we were able to get from ideology to myth. But I'd like to view the subject from two other points of view, the anthropological and the literary.

Yet, on the anthropology I must cheat a bit. So if you have not already read the book I would cite as my text, you should look it up for yourself: Bronislaw Malinowski's *Myth and Primitive Psychology*. Besides being an authoritative book, it is a very human one, as is always the case with Malinowski's writings. But I am twisting its contents to one special purpose.

Suppose that you wanted to write a treatise sanctioning, in philosophic language, a particular political and economic order. You might write about the "substance" or "essence" of the ethical. Or you might write on "the principles of ownership and inheritance." Or on something like "the logical and philosophic sanction for the maintaining of the status quo."

But suppose that you had no such words as "substance," "essence," "principle," "logical," as used in our traditional philosophic idiom. Yet at the same time you did feel the need to justify the social practices and relations of your society, including of course whatever elements of a class structure may have taken form in your tribe. Is there any spontaneous vocabulary that might substitute for the missing terms?

There is indeed; and in primitive "myth" we see it everywhere. "Principles" means "firsts." The corresponding word in Greek is the word from which we derive "archetype," "archeology," "archaic," and the like. Hence, if you want to deal with *logical* principles, or "firsts," and don't have such a language, you get the equivalent by talking of *mythical* firsts. To derive a culture from a certain mythic ancestry, or ideal mythic type, is a way of stating that culture's essence in narrative terms.

In proportion as historicist thinking came into fashion in the West, similarly writers replaced philosophic terms by historicist terms, expressing the "logically prior" or the "essential" in terms of the "temporally prior." Thus, whenever they wanted to say that man is "essentially competitive" or "essentially good," they said that the "first men" were constantly at war or that men were "originally" good but were later corrupted by society. They postulated such "firsts" in some hypothetical past time, their thinking in this regard often being much more mythical than they suspected, and no more based on actual scientific knowledge about the past than was the "mythical" doctrine of "original" sin (which, translated philosophically, would mean "essential" sin, that is, some ineradicable difference between individual and group which the individual, eager to socialize himself, might experience as a sense of guilt).

Beautifully fitted to our purpose is Malinowski's description of an origin myth. It tells of the tribe's descent from a mythic race of beings that lived underground, and that had led an existence similar in all respects to their present life on earth. Underground men were organized in villages, clans, districts; they had distinctions of rank, they knew privileges and had claims, they owned property and were versed in magic lore. Endowed with all this, they emerged, establishing by this very act certain rights in land and citizenship, in economic prerogatives and magical pursuit. They brought with them all their culture to continue it upon this earth.

Thinking of these underground progenitors, from whom the present structure of the society was mythically derived, would it be too patly punning if we said that the myth expressed in terms of mythic narrative, what the philosophic idiom might express if it spoke of the "philosophic grounds" for the sanctioning of a social and economic situation?

There are further symmetries here, linking birth, dream (unconscious) and death with the mythic vocabulary of essence, since this same nether world from which the tribe mythically derived is also the place to which the departed spirits go. But it is enough for our purpose if we have managed to suggest how the "mythic" past is a narrative terminology of essence. And one can even discern the same ingredient in the myths of Plato, with his notion that the pure forms or archetypes of all temporal things pre-exist in Heaven, and that the particular objects of this world exist only by participating in the absolute changeless being or essence of these perfect "ancestral" ideas.

One could certainly look for the ingredient of "ideology" in such myths of origin as this Trobriand one, which so definitely sanctions the nature of things as they are. But to get an "ideology" in the fullest sense of the term, I should think that we needed a highly developed money economy, with its extreme division of labor and a maximum of abstract relationships for which the ideologist seeks to compensate by all the deliberate subterfuges for persuading people to "identify themselves" with the factions, doctrines, or policies he represents.

But before going on to our final step, we should make one point clear: there are two quite different ways of aligning the political (or ideological) with the nonpolitical (or mythic). We may, as with those who tend towards the esthetic myth, treat them simply as *mutually exclusive,* so that we could turn *to* the poetic myth only by turning *from* the political ideology. (Perhaps Mark Schorer's recent book on William Blake, showing the strong political implications and applications of his "visions," will weaken the position of this school somewhat, since Blake has usually been one of their major "mythic" ancestors.) Or we may treat the mythic as the nonpolitical ground of the political, not as antithetical to it, but as the "prepolitical" source out of which it is to be derived.

Such would, it seems to me, be the requirement for the "ideal myth" of today: a vision that transcended the political, yet that had political attitudes interwoven with it. At least, we can examine that possibility by turning to a past work that is in many respects most startlingly contemporary: Virgil's *Aeneid.*

There are many important correspondences between Virgil's situation and the situation today. In the first place, there was the very pronounced *archeological* or *museum* approach to culture that characterizes our own times. One sees it exemplified thoroughly in Joyce's elaboration of the Homeric myths. And though Virgil, in his cult of nature, broke away from the influence of the Alexandrian school, where the adapting of myths to purely literary purposes had been carried to excess, he diverged mainly in using seriously what others had used trivially. (See *Virgil,* by T. R. Glover, for a quite thorough discussion of the poet, his works, and his times.)

Virgil used the myth, we might say, as a sympathetic nonbeliever. And because so much of his mythology bears upon sleep, vision, prophecy, gods, and the afterlife, we might properly think of it as a terminology for "unconscious" motives, or at least for a level of motivation that sometimes conforms with the conscious wishes of the characters, and sometimes runs counter to them.

The use of the gods at all, by one who did not believe in their literal existence, might be treated as mere flattery, by a poet who wanted court patronage. But there are obviously more serious motives at work here. Could we put it thus: the poet is writing of Roman power. It would be esthetically fitting that he place the subject in a context of other terms for power. Imperial power, in this poetic sense, would "go

with" heroic power, divine power, the power of destiny, etc. Such surrounding of a theme with kindred images would be the only way in
which one could develop it stylistically, and contextually. There need
be no question of the "literal" here. The poet is giving us a cluster of
similar terms, joining empire, emperor, and the imperial destiny—
whereupon we find his epic saying mythically that the emperor is divine "in principle." Or, the figure of the emperor belongs with the
gods, in a Roman thesaurus of terms for superior power. Mythically,
this kinship of terms would be translated into the form of narrative
that gave the emperor divine forbears. On the sophisticated level, such
mergers could be interpreted purely in accordance with their political,
moral, and esthetic "propriety." But Virgil would probably not object
if the literal-minded interpreted such mythic lineage as "fact."

As regards ideology and myth, the figure of the Roman emperor
unites them. Here is the myth of the bringer of peace (to say as much
is to understand why the Christians treated Virgil as *anima naturaliter
Christiana*). Caesar Augustus is thus cast in the mythic role of a re-
deemer, a role that gains further in dignity by being put in the same
context with Aeneas, whose heroic piety and gravity thus serve as the
"principle" of Augustus. Augustus' role is seen in terms of Aeneas'
perfect, or archetypal, role. Poetically, mythically, Augustus is Aeneas.
(Ironically, it was a much later emperor, Marcus Aurelius, who as an
actual person came closest to the Virgilian hero imaged in Aeneas; but
by that time the Roman peace had begun noticeably to weaken.) In
the *Aeneid*, this *mythic* form, of the bringing of peace, was given its
ideological anchorage in the vision of Rome as the particular worldly
state which brought this condition about. And the real emperor, made
mythically resonant, was thus the bridge that brought both a myth
and an ideology together.

In this sense, the *Aeneid* might be considered poignantly relevant
to our own yearnings for a condition of world peace, yearnings that
have attained a loose ideological expression in the United Nations,
but still lack any appropriate grounding in myth.

But the greatest difference of all is this: the Roman peace was a
peace of pacification, a peace after victory. To those who submitted, it
was tolerant, joining their gods to the Roman pantheon, and demanding only that they accept inclusion into the Roman political economy.
In this the Roman peace was strikingly different from the Nazi theory
of racial domination, which would have made a peace of pacification
impossible for many peoples, who simply could not submit, since they
were marked for a systematic destruction or great weakening in accordance with the Nazi theories of genocide.

But even with the Nazi methods eliminated (though we must not be too sure that they are), how could we enjoy the Roman peace, the peace of pacification? Does not the nature of our modern weapons inexorably demand that, if we are going to have peace at all, it must be a peace without pacification, that is, a peace without war, a peace *before* war?

The new myth, to be the ideal myth, must give us that new vision, and not merely in its purity, as with the Christian vision of peace on earth, but in its ideological implications as well. And maybe it must do this very very soon. Or must the myth wait for quiet times, as Virgil's myth celebrated the *end* of the wars? And if it must, what will there be for the new myth to celebrate, if the magic number three is to have its sway, if there is to be a third world war?

Appendix

I should like to add a quotation which may help greatly to indicate why I think that the *Aeneid* is so fitting a prototype for the ideal myth of today. It is from J. W. Mackail's *The Meaning of Virgil for Our World of Today*. It gives a handy recipe of twelve motivational ingredients in Virgil's epic:

1. The work must be a national poem in the full sense, embodying the pageant of Roman history, the portraiture of Roman virtue, the mission and the supremacy of Rome;

2. It must establish and vindicate the vital interconnection of Rome with Italy, and register the birth, which was only then taking effect, of a nation;

3. It must link up Rome and the new nation to the Greek civilization, as that had manifested itself in mythology and history, in art and letters, in the Hellenization which had spread into the Western portion of the Mediterranean world;

4. It must emphasize the Roman State and the Italian people as not derivative from Greece, but of distinct and actually hostile origin, and absorbing and superseding Greek supremacy, and treat the conquest of the Greek world by Rome as the entrance on a predestined inheritance;

5. It must bring well into the foreground of the picture the historic conflict between Rome and Carthage, which was the greatest event in Roman history, which determined its subsequent course, and which fixed the limit to the sphere of the Asiatic races;

6. It must celebrate the feats of heroes, great deeds in battle and council and government, such as had lent immortal greatness to the *Iliad* and *Odyssey*.

7. It must find expression for the romantic spirit, in its two principal fields of love and adventure;

8. It must possess direct vital human interest, and create men and women drawn to the heroic scale and on the heroic plane, and yet embodying the qualities and passions and emotions of actual life;

9. It must connect its figures with larger and more august issues; with the laws of nature and the decrees of fate, the workings of a mysterious Providence, and the sense of human destinies as at once moulding, and interpreted by, the human soul;

10. It must exalt the new regime, and give shape and colour to its ideals of peace and justice, development and reconstruction, ordered liberty, beneficent rule;

11. It must draw the lineaments of an ideal ruler, *pater patriae,* who should hold sovereignty as the chief servant of the commonwealth; and show him as gravely conscious of his mission, rising towards its high demands, subordinating to it all thoughts of ease or luxury, all allurements of pleasure and temptations of the senses;

12. It must lift itself into a yet higher sphere, so as to touch the deepest springs of religion and philosophy, opening windows into the invisible world and kindling a pilot-light for the future.

We do not mean to imply that the corresponding myth for today should reproduce this same pattern without important modifications. For if the conditions of modern war make a "peace of pacification" impossible, bringing too much destruction for any mere cessation of actual fighting to be a true peace, then the very basis of Virgil's myth must be altered. The exaltation of a national destiny, conceived in terms of national victory and domination, must be ruled out. And once you change this aspect of your "ideal myth," you are likely to find that related changes are necessary throughout.

The ironic likelihood is that, if we fought another great war to "save" capitalism, capitalism would be done for, regardless of who "won" the war. So much of the world's productive resources would be in ruins, so much of its population sickly and reduced by atomic, chemical, and bacteriological poisons (which would also destroy much animal life, and make much of the soil infertile for years), that there would be no area capable of supporting capitalism as we know it. We boast of capitalism's "higher standard of living." But if you read the expression the other way round, you quickly see its obverse implications: that capitalism, whatever high rewards it may bring, must by the same token be a very *costly* economy. And could any large area of the world support so expensive a way of life, or support it alone, when the rest of the world was differently organized (if it was organized at all!)? We are all the more admonished to believe that war would be the end of our present economic ways, as we watch Britain turning step by step toward socialism. This course is being taken grudgingly, more from necessity than from conviction. And it is not due to "Russian ideology" or "Communist infiltration" from the other side of the "power vacuum." It is due to the fact that Britain can no longer *afford* her capitalist empire.

How, then, might a "neo-Virgilian" epic look? We asked ourselves that, and here offer twelve clauses for a hypothetical myth of today. These clauses are intended to match the Mackail recipe point by point:

1. The work must transcend nationalism. But it must survey the pageant of nationalism's emergence, the quality of its exaltation, even while considering it inadequate as an over-all political motive. The "mission" and "supremacy" of national strength could be fulfilled only in the attempt to go beyond it, not by mere decay (the usual way in which it is "transcended") but by a positive new step.

2. It must establish and vindicate the cult of the *region* (the piety of loyalty to a particular location), presenting it in ways that do not at all require the domination over other regions, but recognizing each as having its own peculiar motives, differentiating it from the totality of world-motives, but not setting it against such world-motives.

3. It must establish the vital interconnection between the modern world and as much of the past (not only Greek, but universal) as can be imaginatively encompassed.

4. It must consider the modern world, not as "superior" to other ages, but in terms of first and last things, motives which confront all ages, though in ways varying with the conditions of time and place.

5. It must be intensely concerned with the momentous conflicts that center in technology and property, and that now threaten to pit the United States against the Soviet Union somewhat as Rome and Carthage were once opposed.

6. It must celebrate the feats of heroes, great deeds in battle and council and government, such as had lent immortal greatness to the *Iliad* and *Odyssey*. But above the sincere praise of great deeds, should hover the thought of human folly, the concern ever with the ironic possibility that much courage, power, ambition have been misdirected: not the "explaining" of this so much as the constant meditating upon it.

7. It must give expression of love and adventure, though as modified by the perspectives of modern psychology.

8. "It must possess direct vital human interest," but its aim to "create men and women drawn to the heroic scale and on the heroic plane" should be confined within the limits of ironic sophistication. (The "heroic" would be conceived along the lines of mythic identity

treated by Thomas Mann in the Joseph story, conceiving of role in terms of its ritual completion, with its formal perfection being seen as its essence. Here would be the archetypal figure, situated in the mythic past, as "temporal" way of stating the "essential" aspect of the role, the aspect which is concealed behind the accidents and particulars of the role as enacted in one specific set of circumstances. Cf. also the kind of thinking preserved in the Aristotelian concept of the entelechy, a being's "perfection" residing in its fulfilling the highest potentialities of its kind.)

9. "It must connect its figures with larger and more august issues," with the laws of nature—pondering always on the direction of human destiny as regards life in general and the individual in particular.

10. It must look, as toward a Messiah, toward a new regime which it could exalt, giving "shape and colour to its ideals of peace and justice, development and reconstruction, ordered liberty, beneficent rule." But never forgetting that this cannot be the peace of pacification, the Roman peace.

11. It should draw the lineaments of an ideal citizen (at once ruler and ruled). He would be gravely conscious of his mission (even to being conscious of the possible self-congratulatory deceptions in such a posture). He would be in favor of "rising toward its high demands, subordinating to it all thoughts of ease or luxury, all allurements of pleasure and temptations of the senses," except insofar as moderate relaxations and concessions to one's own weaknesses help to prevent militant austerities and to make one less uncharitable.

12. It must think of human motives in the most incisive and comprehensive terms, as regards both conscious and unconscious orders of experience.

References in Burke Readings

Angyal, Andras. 1941. *Foundations for a Science of Personality.* New York: The Commonwealth Fund; London: H. Milford, Oxford University Press.

Aristotle. c 1968. *Poetics.* A translation and commentary for students of literature. Translation by Leon Golden; commentary by O. B. Hardison. Englewood Cliffs, NJ: Prentice-Hall.

St. Augustine. *Confessions.*

Bergson, Henri. [1907] 1944. *Creative Evolution.* New York: Modern Library.

Blackmur, R. P. 1939. "Mature Intelligence of an Artist." *The Kenyon Review* 1, no. 1 (Winter).

Brooks, Cleanth, Jr. 1935. "Three Revolutions in Poetry." *The Southern Review* (Autumn).

Carlyle, Thomas. 1900? *Heroes and Hero Worship.* Philadelphia: H. Altemus.

Chase, Stuart. 1938. *The Tyranny of Words.* New York: Harcourt, Brace and Company.

Coates, Robert M. 1926. *Eater of Darkness.* Paris: Contact Editions.

Dewey, John. 1939. *Intelligence and the Modern World.* Edited and with an Introduction by Joseph Ratner. New York: Modern Library.

Dostoevski, Fyodor. 1929. *The Brothers Karamazov.* Translated by Constance Carnett. New York: The Modern Library.

Engels, Friedrich. 1962. *Anti-Duhring: Herr Eugen Duhring's Revolution in Science.* Moscow: Foreign Languages Publishing House.

"Fichte, Johan Gottlieb." In *Encyclopedia Britannica,* 1922, 11th ed., pp. 313–17. New York: Encyclopedia Britannica.

Freud, Sigmund. 1922. *Beyond the Pleasure Principle.* London, Vienna: The International Psycho-analytical Press.

_____. 1950. *Totem and Taboo: Some Points of Agreement Between the Mental Lives of Savages and Neurotics.* Authorized translation by James Strachey. London: Routledge & Paul.

Glover, T. R. 1912. *Virgil.* 2d ed. New York: The Macmillan Company.

Hitler, Adolf. 1933. *My Battle.* Abridged and translated by E. T. S. Dugdale. New York: Houghton Mifflin Company.

Hume, David. 1952. "An Inquiry Concerning Human Understanding." In *Great Books of the Western World,* vol. 35: *Locke, Berkeley, Hume,* 451–509. Chicago: Benton.

Ibsen, Henrik. 1960. *An Enemy of the People.* Translated by Inger Lignell; dialogue and adaptations by Henry S. Taylor. London: Ginn.

Kluckhohn, Clyde. 1944. *Navaho Witchcraft.* Boston: Beacon Press.

318   *References in Burke Readings*

Liddel, Henry George, and Robert Scott. 1854. *A Hand-book of the En-grafted Words of the English Language, Embracing the Choice Gothic, Celtic, French, Latin, and Greek Words, on the Basis of the Hand-book of the Anglo-Saxon Rootwords.* New York, London: D. Appleton and Company.

Locke, John. 1947. *An Essay Concerning Human Understanding.* Abridged and edited by Raymond Wilburn. London: Dent; New York, Dutton.

Mackail, J. W. 1922. *Virgil and His Meaning to the World To-day.* Boston: Marshall Jones Company.

Marston, William, C. Daly King, and Elizabeth H. Marston. 1931. *Integrative Psychology: A Study of Unit Response.* London: Paul, Trench, Trubner, & Co.

Marvell, Andrew. 1970. *The Garden.* Edited by Thomas O. Calhoun and John M. Potter. Columbus, OH: Merrill.

Mead, George Herbert. 1938. *The Philosophy of the Act.* Chicago: University of Chicago Press.

———. 1934. *Mind, Self, and Society.* Chicago: University of Chicago Press.

Melville, Herman. 1937. *Moby Dick.* Deluxe edition. Garden City, NY: Garden City Publishing Company, Inc.

Neurath, Otto. 1939. *Modern Man in the Making.* New York & London: A. A. Knopf.

Odets, Clifford. 1940. *Night Music: A Comedy in Twelve Scenes.* New York: Random House.

Ogden, C. K. 1932. *Bentham's Theory of Fictions.* London: Kegan Paul, Trench, Trubner & Co.

O'Neill, Eugene. 1922. *The Hairy Ape, Anna Christie, The First Man.* New York: Boni and Liveright.

———. 1932. *Mourning Becomes Electra: A Trilogy.* London: J. Cape.

Parsons, Talcott. 1937. *The Structure of Social Action: A Study in Social Theory with Special Reference to a Group of Recent European Writers.* New York: McGraw-Hill.

Plato. 1943. *The Republic.* An English translation by Paul Shorey. Cambridge, MA: Harvard University Press; London: W. Heinemann Ltd.

"Propaganda" and "Property." In *Encyclopedia of the Social Sciences* 1962, 521–39. New York: Macmillan Company.

Ransom, John Crowe. 1930. *God without Thunder: An Unorthodox Defense of Orthodoxy.* New York: Harcourt, Brace and Co.

Richards, Ivor Armstrong. [1923] 1961. *Principles of Literary Criticism.* New York: Harcourt, Brace.

Shakespeare, William. 189-? *Merchant of Venice.* New York: Knickerbocker Leather and Novelty Co.

Stewart, J. A. 1905. *The Myths of Plato.* Translated with introductory and other observations by J. A. Stewart. London, New York: Macmillan.

Von Hagen, Victor Wolfgang. 1957. *Realm of the Incas.* New York: New American Library.

Weinberg, Julius Rudolph. 1960. *An Examination of Logical Positivism.* Peterson, NJ: Littlefield, Adams.

Wrong, Dennis H. 1961. "The Oversocialized Conception of Man in Modern Sociology." *American Sociological Review* 26: 183–93.

Bibliography: Kenneth Burke

Kenneth Burke has been an exceptionally prolific writer since 1920 and much of his writing has been in the form of essays originally published in journals and literary magazines. While much has been collected in individual volumes, much remains in journals. Burke has also occasioned a great deal of written comment and analysis. A complete bibliography of his work and of work about him, as of 1982, is readily available in the second edition of William Rueckert's *Kenneth Burke and the Drama of Human Relations*, published in 1982 by the University of California Press. Here I list only his books, books of his articles edited by others, and several major books and articles about him, including recent articles by sociologists.

Burke published and republished major volumes at different times, often adding another introduction or a long afterword. The University of California editions of previous works often contain such afterwords and are so noted below.

Books by Kenneth Burke

1. *The White Oxen and Other Stories*. New York: Albert and Charles Boni, 1924.
2. *Counter-Statement*. New York: Harcourt, Brace and Co., 1931; second edition, Los Altos, CA: Hermes Publications, 1953; Phoenix edition, Chicago: University of Chicago Press, 1954; third edition, Berkeley and Los Angeles: University of California Press, 1968.
3. *Towards a Better Life, Being a Series of Epistles or Declamations*. New York: Harcourt, Brace and Co., 1932; second edition, Berkeley and Los Angeles: University of California Press, 1966.
4. *Permanence and Change: An Anatomy of Purpose*. New York: New Republic, Inc., 1935; second revised edition, Los Altos, CA: Hermes Publications, 1954; third edition, with Introduction by Hugh D. Duncan, Indianapolis, IN: Bobbs-Merrill Co., Inc., 1965; fourth edition, with afterword by Kenneth Burke, Berkeley and Los Angeles: University of California Press, 1984.
5. *Attitudes Toward History*. Two volumes. New York: New Republic, Inc., 1937; second edition revised, Los Altos, CA: Hermes Publications, 1959; Beacon Paperback edition, Boston: Beacon Press, 1961; third edition with a new afterword by Kenneth Burke, Berkeley and Los Angeles: University of California Press, 1984.
6. *The Philosophy of Literary Form: Studies in Symbolic Action*. Baton

Rouge, LA: Louisiana State University Press, 1941; Vintage edition, New York: Vintage Books, 1957; third edition, Berkeley and Los Angeles: University of California Press, 1973.

7. *A Grammar of Motives.* New York: Prentice-Hall, Inc., 1945; reissue, New York: George Braziller, Inc., 1955; second edition, Berkeley and Los Angeles: University of California Press, 1974. One volume edition of *A Grammar of Motives* and *A Rhetoric of Motives*, Meddian Edition, 1962. Cleveland and New York: The World Publishing Co.

8. *A Rhetoric of Motives.* New York: Prentice-Hall, Inc., 1950; reissue, New York: George Braziller, Inc., 1955; second edition, Berkeley and Los Angeles: University of California Press, 1969.

9. *The Rhetoric of Religion: Studies in Logology.* Boston: Beacon Press, 1961; second edition, Berkeley and Los Angeles: University of California Press, 1970.

10. *Language as Symbolic Action: Essays on Life, Literature, and Method.* Berkeley and Los Angeles: University of California Press, 1966.

11. *Collected Poems, 1915–1967.* Berkeley and Los Angeles: University of California Press, 1968.

12. *The Complete White Oxen: Collected Short Fiction of Kenneth Burke.* Berkeley and Los Angeles: University of California Press, 1968.

13. *Dramatism and Development.* Worcester, MA: Clark University Press, 1972.

Selected Works about Kenneth Burke

Booth, Wayne. *Critical Understanding: The Powers and Limits of Pluralism.* Chicago: University of Chicago Press, 1979.

Duncan, Hugh Dalziel. *Language and Literature in Society.* Chicago: University of Chicago Press, 1953.

_____. *Communication and Social Order.* New York: Oxford University Press, 1962.

_____. *Symbols and Social Theory.* New York: Oxford University Press, 1969.

Gusfield, Joseph R. "The Bridge Over Separated Lands: Kenneth Burke's Significance for the Study of Social Action." In *The Legacy of Kenneth Burke,* edited by Trevor Melia and Herbert W. Simons. Madison: University of Wisconsin Press, 1988.

Lentricchia, Frank. *Criticism and Social Change.* Chicago: University of Chicago Press, 1983.

Melia, Trevor, and Herbert Simons, eds. *The Legacy of Kenneth Burke.* Madison: University of Wisconsin Press, 1989.

Overington, Michael. "Kenneth Burke and the Method of Dramatism." *Theory and Society* 4 (1977): 131–56.

_____. "Kenneth Burke as Social Theorist." *Sociological Inquiry* 47 (1977): 137–41.

Rueckert, William H. *Kenneth Burke and the Drama of Human Relations.* Berkeley and Los Angeles: University of California Press, 1982.

————, ed. *Critical Responses to Kenneth Burke, 1924–1966.* Minneapolis: University of Minnesota Press, 1969.

White, Hayden and Margaret Brose, eds. *Representing Kenneth Burke.* Baltimore: Johns Hopkins University Press, 1982.

Index

Abbreviation, 61
Absolute, paradox of, 270–72
Acceptance frames, 13–14, 33
Act, 15, 135–36, 139–40. *See also* Action; Agent-act ratio; Attitude-act ratio
Act-agent ratio. *See* Agent-act ratio
Action: and dialectic, 194; and drama, 280; dramatistic approach to, 135–38; and motion, 9, 23, 53–55, 124–25, 160, 284–87. *See also* Act; Symbolic action
Adam and Eve, 284, 286, 290
Adams, Robert M., 1
Adjustments of the organism, 108–9
Aeneas, 311
Aeneid (Virgil), 310–14
Aeschylus, 96–100, 156, 299n
Agency, 15, 135–36, 139–45, 152, 165
Agent, 15, 135–36, 139–45, 157, 165, 255. *See also* Agent-act ratio; Scene-agent ratio
Agent-act ratio, 136–37, 152–54, 243, 288
Alcoholics Anonymous, 28
Ambiguity: in grammar of motives, 142–43, 150; ideological, 305–6; of substance, 180–82, 238
American Language, The (Mencken), 82
Angyal, Andras, 244
Anselm, St., 288
Anthropology, 31, 188–89, 308–9
Anti-Dühring (Engels), 144–45
Anti-Semitism. *See* Jews
Antithesis, 73, 281. *See also* Dialectic
Aquinas, Thomas, 14, 137
Archetypation, 193–94, 284
Ariès, Phillipe, 39–40
Aristophanes, 78
Aristotle, 7, 56, 62, 263, 288, 291; on antithesis, 73, 281; and drama, 99; on entelechy, 71, 241, 315; on God, 270; on knowledge and action, 137–38; on rhetoric, 184, 191; on substance, 238, 240, 241
Arnold, Matthew, 18

Arnold, Thurman, 39, 204, 254–55
Art, 3–4, 23, 41, 44, 90; appeal of symbols in, 112; and contextual definition, 240; paradox of absolute in, 270–71; selectivity of, 113; as symbolic, 142; synecdoche in, 252, 253; and universal experiences, 107. *See also* Literature; Poetry
As You Like It (Shakespeare), 274n
Attitude(s): and acts, 157; and dialectic, 194; dramatistic study of, 135–36; in poetic meaning, 90–94; symbolic act as dancing of, 31, 79–81; as universal experiences, 107
Attitude-act ratio, 287
Attitudes Toward History (Burke), 3, 25, 26, 27; on acceptance frames, 13, 33; on dialectic, 25–27; on scapegoating, 299n
Augustine, St., 119–20, 283, 292, 293
Augustus, Caesar, 311
Austen, Jane, 108
Austin, J. L., 31
Authority, 32–34. *See also* Order, social
Autonomy, 186–88

Bateson, Gregory, 14
Baudelaire, Charles-Pierre, 301
Baumann, Sigmund, 41
Bees, sign systems of, 68
Beethoven, Ludwig van, 99–100
Behaviorism, 9–10, 79, 144, 287; in America, 129; circumference of, 161–63; poetic and scientific, 250–51; as representative anecdote, 158; and semantic ideal, 92; terministic screens of, 119–20, 124
Being and Non-Being, 269. *See also* Substance
Beloved Returns, The (Mann), 301n
Bendix, Reinhard, 25
Bentham, Jeremy, 130, 261, 265, 286; on mental state terms, 117; his theory of fictions, 183–84, 192–94, 203, 284, 304

323